Treasury of the Eye of True Teaching

Treasury of the Eye of True Teaching

Classic Stories, Discourses, and Poems of the Chan Tradition

Dahui

Translated by Thomas Cleary

SHAMBHALA

Shambhala Publications, Inc.
2129 13th Street
Boulder, Colorado 80302
www.shambhala.com

Cover art: Bamboo after Wen Tong, Ke Jiusi, 1343, Ex coll. C. C. Wang Family,
Gift of Oscar L. Tang Family, 2006
Cover design: Katrina Noble
Interior design: Greta D. Sibley

9 8 7 6 5 4 3 2 1

First Edition
Printed in the United States of America

Shambhala Publications makes every effort to print on acid-free, recycled paper.
Shambhala Publications is distributed worldwide by Penguin Random House, Inc.,
and its subsidiaries.

LIBRARY OF CONGRESS CATALOGING-IN-PUBLICATION DATA

Names: Zonggao, 1089–1163, author. | Cleary, Thomas F., 1949–2021, translator.
Title: Treasury of the eye of true teaching: classic stories, dialogues, and poems of the
Chan tradition / translated by Thomas Cleary.
Other titles: Zheng fa yan zang. English
Description: Boulder: Shambhala, 2022.
Identifiers: LCCN 2021049473 | ISBN 9781645470786 (trade paperback)
Subjects: LCSH: Zen Buddhism—Early works to 1800.
Classification: LCC BQ9366 .z6613 2022 | DDC 294.3/927—dc23/eng/20211203
LC record available at https://lccn.loc.gov/2021049473

Contents

Translator's Introduction

Treasury of the Eye of True Teaching is a classic text of Chan Buddhism, a massive compilation of speeches, stories, dialogues, poems, and commentaries extracted from Chan lore, representing teaching material used by the famous master Dahui (1089–1163).

Dahui was widely regarded as a major figure in the revitalization of Chan Buddhism in China during the Southern Song dynasty. After traveling around studying with a number of Chan masters, Dahui became a disciple and successor of Yuanwu, the author of the commentaries in the celebrated *Blue Cliff Record*. Dahui served as an attendant, assembly leader, secretary, and assistant teacher to Yuanwu, who impressed upon him the importance of using sayings and stories in the process of Chan meditation. Dahui became very famous, accorded imperial honors and installed as teaching master in a major monastery, where he attracted a following of more than seventeen hundred people. The record of his teachings was included in the Buddhist canon by imperial order a decade after his death.

Dahui was known for his challenging methodology and vigorous efforts to eliminate attachment to conventional cliché and religious ego. *Treasury of the Eye of True Teaching* alternates explicit expositions of principle and practice with inductive evocations of particular states and perspectives for contemplation and self-examination, as well as opaque anecdotes intended to arouse a type of inner tension traditionally used to stop wandering thought and break through ingrained mental habits in order to enable awakening of direct perception.

Dahui himself was described in these terms to a later master by a cabinet minister who knew him: "In the old days Dahui revived the way of Linji in the autumn of its withering and decline; but by nature he esteemed humility and emptiness. He never flaunted or advertised his insight and reason, and never in his life did he run to people of authority and power, and did not grab profit and support."* Something of his endeavor to revitalize Chan studies, and the backstory to his commentaries in the *Treasury of the Eye of True Teaching*, can be glimpsed in this notice:

The Way that is specially transmitted outside of doctrine is utterly simple and quintessential. From the beginning there is no other discussion; our predecessors carried it out without doubt and kept it without deviation.

During the Tianxi era of the Song dynasty (1012–1022), the Chan master Xuedou, using his talents of eloquence and erudition, with beautiful ideas in kaleidoscopic display, seeking freshness and polishing skill, followed the example of Fenyang in making verses on ancient stories, to catch and control the students of the time. The manner of Chan went through a change from this point on.

Then during the Xuanho era (1119–1125) Yuanwu also set forth his own ideas on the stories and verses from Xuedou, and from then on the collection was known as *The Blue Cliff Record*. At that time the perfectly complete masters of the age, like Wayfarer Ning, Huanglong Sixin, Lingyuan, and Fojian, could not contra-

---

* Thomas Cleary, *Zen Lessons: The Art of Leadership* (Boston: Shambhala Publications, 2004).

dict what he said, so new students of later generations prized his words and would recite them by day and memorize them by night, calling this the highest study. None realized this was wrong, and unfortunately students' meditational skills deteriorated.

In the beginning of the Shaoxing era (1131–1163), Yuanwu's enlightened successor Miaoxi [Dahui] went into eastern China and saw that the Chan students there were recalcitrant, pursuing the study of this book to such an extent that their involvement became an evil. So he broke up the woodblocks of *The Blue Cliff Record* and analyzed its explanations, thus to get rid of illusions and rescue those who were floundering, stripping away excess and setting aside exaggeration, demolishing the false and revealing the true, dealing with the text in a special way. Students gradually began to realize their error, and did not idolize it anymore.

So if not for Dahui's high illumination and far sight, riding on the power of the vow of compassion to save an age of dereliction from its ills, the Chan communities would be in peril.*

The title of this, *Treasury of the Eye of True Teaching,* is taken from a famous founding story of Chan in which the Buddha silently holds up a flower before a vast assembly. No one understands except the Buddha's disciple Kasyapa the Elder, who breaks out in a smile. Buddha then says, "I have the treasury of the eye of true teaching, the ineffable mind of nirvana, the most subtle of teachings on the formlessness of the form of reality. It is not defined in words, but is specially transmitted outside of doctrine."

This story raises the question of why Chan has accumulated an immense body of writings if words cannot convey its essence. The traditional answer is that it is precisely because enlightenment cannot be encapsulated in a particular formula that the teachers have resorted to such a variety of expedients over the ages, tailoring their presentations

---

*Thomas Cleary, *Zen Lessons: The Art of Leadership* (Boston: Shambhala Publications, 2004).

to the needs and capacities of learners. As it is said in a Chan proverb, "Officially, not even a needle can get through; privately, even a horse and cart can pass." Similarly, it is said that "the noumenal ground of reality does not admit so much as a particle, but in the context of myriad methods nothing is excluded." This principle is particularly emphasized in the *Lankavatara Sutra*, traditionally considered the primary scriptural source-book of early Chan:

> This scripture has multiple meanings to guide recipients of all dispositions, not disputation that is actually contradictory.
>
> The teachings indicated in all the scriptures are appeasements for subjective imaginations of ignorant people, not disputation intended to establish ultimate knowledge as it is in reality. Therefore one should follow meaning, not adherence to the expression of teachings.
>
> The word of the Buddha has no statement.
>
> Ultimate truth is not a statement, nor is ultimate truth what is expressed by a statement.
>
> The leading principle of the goal is distinguished by firsthand experience, beyond speech, imagination, and words, reaching the realm where there is no impulse, the inherent characteristic of arrival at the stage of firsthand realization, excluding all the destructive forces of speculation and dogmatism.
>
> The leading principle of instruction is discerning accommodation to people's conditions.
>
> The teachings are not literal, and yet Buddhas do not present them for no reason. They present them in consideration of mental construction. Without material to use, instruction in all the teachings would disappear. . . . The great bodhisattvas should be free of obsession with the articulation of the recital of teaching. The recital of teaching has different meanings on account of the engagement of people's mentalities.
>
> Just as if someone points out something to someone with a finger, and the latter looks only at the fingertip, in the same way

ignorant ordinary people, as if of infantile disposition, will go to
their death adhering to the fingertip of meaning as articulated,
and will not arrive at the ultimate meaning beyond the fingertip
of expression. . . . Just as the ignorant one fixated on the pointing
fingertip does not apprehend the moon, so does one attached to
the letter not know my truth.

As a physician prescribes the type of treatment according to
the illness, and there is no division in the science but treatment
is distinguished by the type of illness, so do I teach the family of
beings according to the afflictions with which they are troubled,
after having ascertained the powers of beings' capacities.*

These caveats are considered critical to a pragmatic approach to Chan
records and writings; and the explanation of the original impetus and
functional intent leading to the compilation of Dahui's *Treasury of the Eye
of True Teaching* noted above reflects this fundamental concern. In the
words of the great master Nagarjuna, considered one of the eminent Indian ancestors of Chan, summarizing the practical premise of the provisional nature of Buddhist teachings in his masterwork on the middle way,
"Without resort to conventional usage, ultimate truth cannot be pointed
out; without arriving at ultimate truth, nirvana cannot be attained."

*Translated from the original Sanskrit by Thomas Cleary.

Treasury of the Eye of True Teaching

[1]

Master Langya asked Master Ju, "Where have you just come from?"

Master Ju said, "From the riverlands."

"Did you come by boat or by land?"

"By boat."

"Where's the boat?"

"Underfoot."

"How do you utter an expression of not being on the road?"

Ju rustled his seat cloth and said, "Incompetent elders are extremely commonplace." Then he walked out.

Langya asked an attendant, "Who was that?"

"Master Ju."

Langya then went down to the transients' hall and asked, "Aren't you senior Ju?"

Ju shouted and asked, "When did you go to Fenyang, Elder?"

Langya said he went there at such and such a time. Ju remarked, "I had already heard of you when I was still in the riverland; but it turns out that your perception is only like this—how could you be famous throughout the land?"

Langya then bowed and said, "Thanks."

Dahui commented,

The guest is the guest from start to finish, the host is the host from start to finish. These two great masters took turns as host and guest in this impromptu encounter, directly bringing to light the heart and marrow of Linji. If you have not thoroughly realized the grip of transcendence and are not equipped with true perception beyond ordinary sense, you will inevitably construe this in terms of winning and losing.

Some say Ju responded truthfully to each question all along, but at the end he shouldn't have made a Buddhist rationale, and this was his "incompetence."

Some say Langya became doubtful and uncertain at heart when he was called an incompetent by Master Ju, so he immediately lay down his weapons, took off his armor, and actually importuned Master Ju to stay so he could question him about this matter, in what they call sitting inquiry.

When one dog barks at nothing, a thousand monkeys bite in actuality. Because religious leaders do not have clear insight, they originate sectarian doctrines, confusing and misleading people of later times. What they don't realize is that the two great masters' stimulus and response were like the sun and moon shining in the sky.

Where dragons and elephants tread is not for lame donkeys and blind men—how could a frog in a well or a chicken in a pot know the vastness of the universe?

I once cited this story in an interview and asked the student, "Do you agree with what Langya said?"

"No," he replied.

"Why don't you agree?"

"One shouldn't make a Buddhist rationale."

I then cited the story of Yunmen asking Dongshan, "Where have you come from?" Dongshan said, "Chadu." Yunmen asked, "Where did you spend the summer?" Dongshan said, "At Baoci in Hunan." Yunmen asked, "When did you leave there?" Dongshan said, "August 25th." Yunmen said, "I forgive you a beating of three score strokes."

Do you agree with what Yunmen said, I asked the student.

"Yes," the student replied.

"Why do you agree?"

"Yunmen had no 'Buddhist' rationale."

I said, "The questions of the teachers were the same, and the answers of the students were the same—so why do you agree with one and not the other?"

The student stood there thinking. I drove him out with a caning. I then called the student to come back for a minute; when he turned his head, I said, "If you interpret it as a caning, you drag me down and you're blind yourself." The student thereupon bowed and said, "Today I've finally realized that the encounter of Langya and Master Ju cannot be fathomed by ordinary feelings."

I said, "Look at this blind guy summing up arbitrarily," and again I drove him off with blows and shouts.

While I was in exile in Hengyang, I closed my door and retired, taking no interest in external affairs. From time to time patchrobed mendicants would ask for help, so I couldn't but answer them. The Chan men Zhongmi and Huiran took notes, which over time accumulated into a huge volume. They brought it to me and asked for a title, wishing to reveal it to later generations so that the treasury of the eye of true teaching of the Buddhas and Chan masters does not perish. So I entitled it *Treasury of the Eye of True Teaching*, and made the story of Langya the first chapter.

Thus there is no order of precedence in the adepts featured herein, nor division of sect; I have only taken their realizations of the handle of transcendence as capable of dissolving sticking points for people and untying bonds, just so they may have accurate perception.

TRANSLATOR'S NOTE

Dahui was defrocked and exiled from 1141 to 1155 through the machinations of a political opponent of one of Dahui's lay successors. He was in Hengyang during the first ten years of this period.

[2]

Chan Master Yantou instructed an assembly,

For the universal principle, the subject of the source, you need to distinguish expressions. If you do not distinguish expressions, then it is impossible to understand sayings.

What are expressions?

When you don't think of anything at all, this is called expression of the absolute. It is also called dwelling at the peak, or attaining stabilization, or clarity, or wakefulness, or directness, or the time before Buddha is born, or becoming grounded. It is also called the time of being as is, or *such* a time.

When being as such, you equally break through all affirmation and negation: as soon as it is as such, then it is not so, immediately changing, round and round. If you do not see through "This," as soon as someone sticks you in the eye you'll stare one-eyed, like a slaughtered sheep that hasn't yet died.

The ancients said that it is not good to sink into oblivion; you must be fluid to attain realization. You switch immediately on contact; as soon as it is so, then it's not so—affirmation and negation both shaved away, you naturally turn freely. What is before your eyes is naturally unveiled; sated and snoring, you don't know to reject, you don't know to bite.

Haven't you read the saying that detachment from things is superior, while pursuing things is inferior? The moment you arouse the slightest sentiment, you've already fallen on the ground.

If you are a boar-biting hound, eyes blazing red, if someone asks you what Chan is you tell him to shut his shit-hole—that's having a lot of spunk—and then you will know who is deep and who is shallow, with firm certainty.

You get to know this cat face; then you don't need to deliberately quantify it, you don't need to measure it.

There's a kind of person who doesn't know how to turn when he bumps into something, just keeping at it like someone with diarrhea running to the toilet. As for people like this, there would be no crime in beating ten thousand of them to death.

Someone who is genuine will rise to a stimulus immediately, biting people right away, like a prickly porcupine. If you preen yourself while undisturbed, but then you holler in a rage when someone provokes you, how can you approach?

If you have not yet attained such freedom, you are said to be practicing on the basis of a formula. Whatever exists must be equally refuted; then not a single thing remains, and you will know for sure—of what use are all the verbal formulas you have learned hitherto, crammed into your chest?

Haven't you read the saying, "Set aside views, set aside formulas—don't let anything outside in, don't let anything inside out"? Cut off both, and you will be spontaneously illumined, not being a partner to anything at all. This is absorption in noncontention.

If you want to attain understanding easily, just clarify the fundamental. When you couldn't leave it even if you wanted to, then you should turn around and bite through in one snap; afterward, don't pursue that which goes and stays—far or near, just go and be naturally unveiled.

Don't keep on thinking about it dully; as soon as you esteem something, it becomes a nest. This is what the ancients called clothing sticking to the body, an affliction most difficult to cure.

When I was traveling in the past, I called on the adepts in one or two places. They just taught sustained concentration day and night, sitting until you get calluses on your behind. Mouths drooling, from the outset they go to the pitch-black darkness inside the belly of the primordial Buddha and say, "I am sitting in meditation to preserve it." At such a time, there is still craving there.

Haven't you read the saying that Shakyamuni Buddha was so because he depended on nothing and craved nothing? An ancient said, "Put poison in milk, and even ghee can kill."

This is not something you can learn, not something you can abandon or retain. It is not in your physical matter; don't mistakenly accept the channels of sense, for they will cheat you on the last day of your life, when they will be in a state of punitive agitation, of no use at all.

Don't be contrived; just take care of your dressing, eating, and natural functions, and pass the time according to conditions, without disrupting social order.

Those who falsely claim to be people of the Path have one garment, which they don't dare put out to bleach in the sun, for fear they'll lose the reputation of "wayfarer." Their minds are unbalanced this way because they are hoping for praise from others.

Also, you shouldn't trust the elders in chains who beat with stumps, coming out with a stream of crap to fool people, making a special hell to put you in.

If you truly know the ancient way, that is very good. Have you not read the saying, "Being is nonbeing, nonbeing is being"? When you live this out, you will know the deep and the shallow. This is the ancient standard.

There is a type of fellow who speaks forth arbitrarily. What is there to record as a memorial? This type is only concerned with calling this the Chan way, only concerned with calling this the Word, but they are so weak they are ineffective. They may gather an audience of ten thousand, but what is the use?

Someone with sinews and bones does not need to make journeys to many places, but you have to have eyes before you can avoid being deceived by anyone. Have you not read the saying, "If you conceive interpretations of the teachings, you still fall into the realm of bedevilment"?

When expounding the teaching, it is imperative that everything flow from your own heart, expressed as a sign for others. Is there anyone like that now?

First of all, you need to discern left and right expressions; this is the point of emergence. Discern what leaves, discern what stays—these are expressions of both sides, also called right and left expressions, or affirmative and negative expressions. As soon as they occur, immediately bite through, and you will naturally be unaffected.

Do you understand when you are spoken to this way? Don't spend the days fussing and bothering; there's no end to that.

If you want to be able to understand easily, just know before sound and form; then you won't be confused by myriad objects, naturally unveiled, naturally unaffected. Spend your life before sound and form, and you will be free. You will be like a mass of fire, which burns anything that touches it—then what more concern will you have?

Haven't you read this saying? "It's not that objects don't encroach, but simply that I pay no mind."

[3]

Master Zhenjing said to an assembly,

It's hard to find people for Buddhism.

Some do not believe in the actuality of the Buddha in themselves, and merely rely on fixed formal doctrines and practices recognized by counterfeit wisdom imitating a bit of the shadows and echoes of the ancients.

When they act, they turn from awareness to matter, sticking to it, unable to get free.

If students come to them, they are like seals stamping clay, turning out a succession of imprints, not only fooling themselves but misleading others as well.

In this school there is no Buddhism to give people, just a sword that cuts down all comers, one by one, causing their lives to cease existing and their senses to disappear.

Then I meet them where their parents have not yet given birth to them. If I see them trying to approach, then I cut them down.

So even though the adamantine sword is sharp, it does not cut anyone who is blameless.

Is there anyone who is blameless? You deserve a beating!

[4]

Master Foyan said to an assembly,

A thousand talks and myriad explanations are not as good as seeing once in person. It is clear of itself, even without explanation. The allegory of the king's precious sword, the allegory of the blind men groping the elephant, in Chan studies the phenomenon of awakening on being beckoned from across the river, the matter of the crags deep in the mountains where there are no people—these are all to be seen in person; they are not in verbal explanation.

TRANSLATOR'S NOTE

The allegories of the king's precious sword and the blind men groping the elephant come from the *Mahaparinirvana Scripture*. They both refer to the observation that subjective descriptions are not objective realities.

[5]

Master Yunmen held up a fly whisk and said, "If you find an entry here, you get rid of hokum. When Zen is preached in Japan, someone in the Thirty-Third Heaven comes out and calls, 'Hum, hum! The stable boy is wearing stocks, giving evidence of his crime!'"

Dahui commented, "This old fellow is able to adapt to a quandary. Plowing a government field under an assumed name, he pays no more sprout tax."

[6]

Master Shiyan Guizong said to an assembly,

The ancient worthies since time immemorial were not without intellectual understanding, but those high-minded people were not the same as mediocrities. Nowadays people are unable to fulfill themselves and stand on their own; they pass the time in vain.

Don't misuse your mind. No one can substitute for you, and there is nowhere to apply your mind; don't seek from others. Up till now you have just been understanding based on others; you get stuck on every saying. The reason your light does not penetrate through to freedom is that there are things in front of your eyes.

A monk asked, "What is the mystic message?"

The master said, "No one can understand."

The monk asked, "What about those who turn to it?"

The master said, "If you turn to it, that is turning away from it."

The monk asked, "What about one who does not turn to it?"

The master said, "Who seeks the mystic message?" He added, "Go away—there's nowhere for you to apply your mind."

The monk asked, "Are there no expedient methods to enable a student to gain access?"

The master said, "The power of Guanyin's wondrous wisdom can save the world from suffering."

The monk asked, "What is the power of Guanyin's wondrous wisdom?"

The master tapped the lid of a cauldron three times and said, "Do you hear?"

The monk said, "I hear."

The master said, "Why don't I hear?"

The monk had no reply. Guizong drove him out with a cane.

[7]

When Master Luoshan first became the resident master of a monastery, he went up in the hall to give a speech. As soon as he had gathered up his robe and was about to sit, he said, "Fare well," and immediately got down from the high seat.

After a while he came back and said, "Anyone who doesn't know, come forward."

When a monk came forward, as soon as he bowed Luoshan said, "Misery yet!"

When the monk rose from his bows, he said, "I ask the teacher . . ."
Luoshan thereupon shouted him out.

A monk asked, "What is the special word?"

Luoshan said, "What are you saying?"

After a long while Luoshan said, "If you are a superior individual, you will understand everything the moment your foot crosses the threshold. If you make a presentation on meeting, you are still a dullard babbling; this is worthless.

"Understand? It is not Chan, not Tao, not Buddha, not Dharma. What is it? The precious sword with the spiritual point is always openly present: it can kill, and it can also give life. If you can wield it, then you may wield it; but if you are going to take the field you have to be capable enough to manage it.

"Individual potentials complement each other, individual phenomena are rootless: they are guest and host to one another. Being as how this is so, studiously avoid fixed assumptions.

"If you cry like a fox, I roar like a lion; if I cry like a fox, then you roar like a lion. If you roar like a lion, I too roar like a lion. Set out and taken up according to the time, meaning and expression are mastered.

"Thus it is said, 'In meaning is expression, in expression is meaning; but expression is not kept in meaning, and meaning is not kept in expression.' If meaning and expression are not equivalent, how do you understand?

"The meaning can shave the expression, the expression can shave the meaning; the interaction of meaning and expression is awesome. If you don't understand meaning *and* expression, if you don't penetrate fact *and* theory, then you are just an iron hammerhead with no hole, what the ancients called a common vulgar cleric. Such people are as common as rice and flax, bamboo and reeds—what use are they?

"In this school you have to be an individual, with eyes alert, turning freely at a touch. How could this be sought in your terms of purity and pollution? How can 'ordinary' or 'holy' explain it?

"A meeting of such people, superior individuals, is like a spark struck from flint, fast as the wind, swift eloquence like thunder. If attention is focused immediately, one or a half a person will be moved by their words, more than millions. If you lower your head and 'study Chan,' you can never get it.

"It is said, '"Thus" is easy, "not thus" is hard,' yet it is also said, '"Thus" is hard, "not thus" is easy.' How about it? You must pay close attention.

"To go traveling you must be perceptive: don't let anyone trap you by teaching you simply to blank out or to focus on details all the time. What a pain! Once you're locked in stocks, even though innocent, when will you ever get out?

"This is like a gourd floating on water—can anyone keep it down? It is ever-present, flowing ceaselessly, independent and free—there has never been any doctrine that could encompass it, never any doctrine that could be its equivalent. It immediately appears on stimulus, turns freely on contact, encompassing sound and form. In extension it flows everywhere, without inhibition, always manifest before the eyes.

"How could this be a state of immobility? Go out, and nothing is not it; go in, and everything returns to the source. Prior to voicing, utterly transcendent, how could it fall into being or nonbeing?

"So it is said that the unique expression prior to voicing cannot be communicated but by sages; if you haven't ever approached it, it's like being a universe away.

"Everyone knows the unique expression prior to voicing; how do you understand this? Ordinarily it is said, 'Before voicing is a road that lets you understand clearly; if you don't come forth after expression, you're still missing a half. If there is anything, however slight, that you fail to penetrate, it is like being blocked off by an iron wall.' How do you ask questions and give answers in an extraordinary meeting?

"Generally speaking, in order to expound the teaching it is necessary to understand the present, killing and giving life with meaningful expressions of life and death. The sword that kills, the sword that gives life—these were the thrusts of the devices of high antiquity and are also essential for the present time; you have to overcome bedevilment and break obsessions.

"To directly reveal truth, you have to know it is in yourself; the aim goes through the target. The great function lacks nothing; when complete pervasion is actualized, bewilderment cannot affect you. If you have not yet attained this, how should you manifest it in every aspect of conduct?

"Do you see its face? Here it is ordinarily said, 'One thought in the senses is ever uninterrupted.' But can you be like this or not?

"If you do not yet understand, then for now you must stand on your own, unveiled, not being neighbor to myriad things, so nothing at all can cover it. This is why an ancient said, 'There are no things present; concepts are present. This is not present phenomena, not within reach of the senses.'

"Most important is to get fundamental insight to appear, so the scenery of the fundamental ground is always revealed, unconcealed. When you are independent and free, and can go out and in unhindered, only then may you differ from the times; even dragons and spirits find no path to strew flowers on, outsiders secretly spying cannot see any tracks.

"This is not obliteration of form and substance; you have to penetrate the heights and the depths before you attain it. Don't just throw around a few sayings about the relative and the absolute, interjecting remarks wherever you go, pointing to the east delineating the west, citing ancients and quoting contemporaries. When it comes to people like this, what crime would it be to beat ten thousand of them to death? Tomorrow is the next day that they will entrap people's sons and daughters. Someday they'll make you ghost-bone behinds.

"The depths of Chan take the measure of your heart. It's easy to be satisfied with plain food; chew it well, and you'll hardly feel hungry. Variance from the fundamental derives from your own error; you'll labor all your life in vain. If you are gutless yet proud, whose fault is that?

"When you imbibe the words of others, distinguish what is so from what is not. If you only stick to your own strength, you'll never be right.

"Stay well. Goodbye."

[8]

Master Langya Jiao went up in the hall. A monk came forward and drew a circle. Langya held up his staff. The monk hesitated; Langya then hit him and said, "Speak!"

The monk said, "I won't speak."

"Why not?"

The monk said, "The Buddhas of past, present, and future are not beyond *here*."

Langya hit him again, and in the course of time drove him out. Then he said, "In the teachings it says that it's an offense even to point at a monk with your hand. Today I'm going to hell like an arrow shot."

[9]

By the side of Xuefeng mountain, a monk built a hut and lived there for many years, never shaving his head. He made himself a wooden dipper and used to go to a stream to scoop water to drink.

One day a monk asked him, "What is the meaning of the Chan founder's coming from the West?"

The hermit replied, "The stream is deep; the handle of the dipper is long."

The monk went back and reported this to Xuefeng. Xuefeng said, "How very unusual! Even so, I'll have to test him myself."

One day Xuefeng went with an attendant, bringing along a razor, to go visit the hermit.

As soon as they saw the hermit, Xuefeng said, "If you can speak appropriately, I won't shave your head."

The hermit immediately got some water and washed his head; Xuefeng then shaved it for him.

[10]

Master Yunju Jian was asked by a monk, "When encountering a ferocious tiger on the road, what then?"

"A thousand people, ten thousand people, do not encounter it; only you encounter it."

"What about when living alone on a solitary peak?"

"Closing down the seven-room communal hall, not providing lodging, who makes you live alone on a solitary peak?"

[11]

Master Huaitang said to an assembly,

When you know illusion, you become detached from it without employing expedients. When you detach from illusion, you wake up, without any gradual steps.

The thousand gates and myriad doors of old Shakyamuni Buddha open up all at once, at a single knock; spiritually sharp folks get right up and act on it as soon as they hear it brought up.

If you still hesitate, you are heading west while I am going east.

[12]

A monk asked Zhaozhou, "I have just entered the community—please instruct me."

Zhaozhou said, "Have you eaten breakfast yet?"

"Yes, I have."

Zhaozhou said, "Then wash your bowl."

The monk was greatly enlightened at this.

Yunmen said, "Tell me, was there an instruction or not? If you say there was, then what did Zhaozhou tell him? If you say there wasn't, then why did the monk become enlightened?"

Yunfeng Yue said, "Yunmen doesn't know good and bad; such talk is like drawing legs on a snake. I disagree. This monk being enlightened in this way goes to hell like an arrow shot!"

Dahui commented, "Old Yunmen is like a titan king shoving off the great citadel of all existence and the oceans of afflictions. Ha! Why talk in your sleep?

"As for Yunfeng, though he skillfully reaches back and takes out a golden arrow, turns around and draws a horn bow, nevertheless he misses Yunmen."

[13]

Master Huanglong Nan said to an assembly,

Master Dazhu said, "Purity of conduct, speech, and mind is called Buddha appearing in the world. Impurity of conduct, speech, and mind is called Buddha becoming extinct." A good message—the ancient's temporary expedient opens up an entryway for you.

Once you have found an entryway, you then must find a way of exit. When you climb a mountain, you should reach the peak; when you dive into an ocean, you should reach the bottom.

If you climb a mountain but don't reach the peak, you won't know how immense the universe is. If you dive into an ocean but don't reach the bottom you won't know how deep the abyss is.

Once you know immensity and depth, you kick over the four oceans with one kick, slap down the polar mountain with one slap, then go back home with your hands free, unrecognized by anyone: sparrows twitter, crows caw, among the cedar trees.

[14]

A monk asked Baofu, "What motto did Xuefeng have in everyday life that enabled him to be trackless?"

Baofu said, "It cannot be that I am unable to be Xuefeng's disciple."

[15]

Master Zhenjing said to an assembly,

Sansheng asked Xuefeng, "What does the golden fish that's passed through the net take for food?"

Xuefeng said, "I'll tell you when you get out of the net."

Sansheng said, "You're the teacher of fifteen hundred people, yet you don't even know a saying!"

How sharp! How lively! Just like a sparrow hawk! Don't be startled!

I am otherwise. "What does the gold fish that's passed through the net take for food?" "I'll tell you when you get out of the net." When he said, "You're teacher of fifteen hundred people, yet you don't know a saying," I'd just haul out my staff and drive him off the premises.

Again, very lively, like a tiger—don't get shook up! But tell me, Chan worthies, how does my liveliness compare to Sansheng's liveliness? Isn't there a lively person here? Come forth and let's see.

Ha! Even if you grabbed him by the hand, you couldn't hold him back.

[16]

Layman Pang said, "Just aspire to empty all that is; don't solidify what is not."

[17]

Master Wujiu, seeing two elders arriving, immediately asked, "Where have you two Chan uncles just come from?"

One monk said, "From Jiangxi."

Wujiu immediately hit him.

The monk said, "Long have I heard the master had this key."

Wujiu said, "Since you don't understand, let the second one come forward."

That monk tried to say something. Wujiu hit him too and said, "There's no different dirt in the same pit."

[18]

One day when Zhaozhou was in the latrine, he saw Wenyuan go by. He called to him, "Wenyuan!" When Wenyuan responded, Zhaozhou said, "I can't explain Buddhism to you in the latrine."

[19]

Master Ciming said to an assembly,

The true nature of ignorance is the nature of Buddhahood; the illusory empty body is itself embodiment of reality. If you can actually believe in this, you will undeniably save effort.

You could say when Sudhana entered Maitreya's tower [in the final book of the *Flower Ornament Scripture*] infinite teachings were thoroughly comprehended, and he attained total nonobstruction and realized that things are not born.

This is called acceptance of phenomena having no origination. Infinite realms, self and other, are undivided on a hairtip; the ten times, past and present, are never apart from the immediate moment of thought.

Now I ask you people, what is the immediate moment of thought?

The essence of your ignorance is actually the nature of subtle luminosity of your basic awareness: because you do not understand the root source of birth and death, you cling to the false as true; according to the influence of falsehood, it makes you fall into repetitious routines and experience all sorts of misery.

If you can turn awareness around to illumine within, you will spontaneously realize the original true nature is unborn and undying.

That is why it is said that the true nature of ignorance is actually the nature of Buddhahood, and the illusory empty body is actually an embodiment of reality.

The unclean physical body has no ultimate reality at all: it is like a dream, like an illusion, like a shadow, like an echo. Flowing in waves of birth and death for countless eons, restlessly compelled by craving, emerging here, submerging there, piles of bones big as mountains have piled up, oceans of pap have been consumed.

Why? Because of lack of insight, inability to understand that form, feeling, perception, habits, and consciousness are fundamentally empty, without any substantial reality. We take on birth in pursuit of falsehood, entrapped by greed, unable to get free.

This is why Buddha said, "Of the causes of all miseries, greed is the root. If we eliminate greed, we won't be dependent on anything."

If you can realize that the illusory body is not absolute but conditional, originally null, then views will not arise—it has no self, no person, no being, no liver of life. All things are thus, so it is said that the illusory empty body is none other than an embodiment of reality.

When you have awakened to the body of reality, there is not a single thing, only the Great Way of ethereal profundity, the true source with no fixation, listening to the teaching and expounding the teaching. That is why it is said that the intrinsic nature that is the fundamental source is the Buddha of natural reality.

Master Ciming also said,

The floating clouds of form, sensation, perception, habits, and consciousness go and come for naught; the bubbles of greed, hatred, and folly appear and disappear in vain. If you realize this, you cross over all miseries; boundless emotionally afflicted intellectual interpretations are all purified. This is the pure reality body.

If you reach this state, then you can emerge in one place and disappear in another, discard one embodiment and take on another. Free at will in all ways in hell or heaven, this world or another, floating and sinking, shedding light in response to people, setting down teachings according to potentials. This is called the hundred thousand million projection bodies.

A speech like this could be called talking about a dream where there is no dream, mixing with mud and water, scattering crap and piss, not knowing good and bad.

Ha, ha, ha! If you turn to the Chan school, even ten myriad eight thousand is still not enough to dream of sensing the smell of Chan sweat.

Even so, we shouldn't be one-sided in this matter. We just use temporary terms to guide people. Ha!

[20]

Master Baoning Yong said to an assembly,

> Every night I sleep embracing Buddha,
> Every morning we rise together again.
> Rising and sitting, always in company,
> Speaking and silent, living in the same abode,
> We're never apart in the slightest,
> Just like body and shadow.
> If you want to know where Buddha's gone,
> The very sound of these words is it.

This verse by Mahasattva Fu has been known to everyone past and present; many have gotten a glimpse thereby, but not a few have misunderstood.

Master Xuansha said, "Even Mahasattva Fu only recognized luminous awareness."

Master Dongshan Cong said, "Tell me, has a Chan monk ever slept in the daytime?"

These are sayings by two venerable adepts; who says there are no wizards in the world? You'd better believe there's a separate sky inside the pot.

I too have a verse:

> When I want to sleep, I sleep;
> When I want to rise, I rise.
> With water I wash my face,
> So my skin glows;

Sipping tea, I moisten my beak.
Red dust rises in the immense ocean,
Billowing waves rise on level ground.
Ha, ha! Ah, ha, ha!
La li li la li.

A monk asked, "What is the realm of Baoning?"

Baoning said, "The master of the mountain ultimately stands out."

"What is the person in the realm?"

"He hasn't half his nostrils."

"What is the manner of the house of Baoning?"

"Hard biscuits and cooked dumplings."

"Suppose a guest comes—what do you serve?"

"Simple food is quite filling—chew thoroughly, and you'll hardly hunger."

[21]

Venerable Yanyang asked Zhaozhou, "When not a single thing is brought, then what?"

Zhaozhou said, "Put it down."

Yanyang asked, "If not a single thing is brought, what is to be put down?"

Zhaozhou said, "If you can't put it down, then carry it out."

Master Huanglong Nan versified this:

Not a single thing brought forth,
Both shoulders cannot bear it.
Had he realized his error at the words,
In his heart would be limitless joy.
Once poisonous viciousness is forgotten within,
Snakes and tigers become friends.
For how many hundreds of years
The clear breeze has not ceased.

[22]

Master Fahua Ju said to an assembly,

> Shakyamuni didn't appear in the world,
> Bodhidharma didn't come from the West.
> Buddhism is everywhere under the sun;
> To speak of the mystery, the mouth won't open.

Dahui commented, "The thief has a cowardly heart."

[23]

Master Dinghui Xin asked a monk, "How do the adepts of the South evaluate National Teacher Zhong's saying about inanimate objects expounding the Dharma?"

The monk said, "Everyone says it refers to the interchange of functions of the six senses."

Xin said, "In the Teachings it says 'There are no eyes, ears, nose, tongue, body, mind'—what is there to interchange functions?"

The monk tried to think of something to say; Xin hit him right across the back.

Dharma master Sheng said, "Knock on space, and it makes a sound; knock on wood and there's no sound."

Yunmen knocked at the air with his staff and said, "Aye yay yay." He also knocked on a board and said, "Does it make a sound?"

A monk said, "It makes a sound."

Yunmen said, "You worldling!" He knocked the board again and said, "What do you call 'sound'?"

[24]

Master Xuansha asked a monk, "Where did you come from?"

The monk said, "From Ruiyuan."

Xuansha asked, "What sayings does Ruiyuan have?"

The monk said, "He calls, 'Master!' all the time, then answers himself, 'Yes?' 'Be alert, and don't let anyone fool you anymore.'"

Xuansha said, "First-class play with the spirit, but still only amounts to a little bit."

[25]

Master Huanglong Xin said to an assembly,

When a purifying crystal is dropped into turbid water, the water cannot but clear. When remembrance of Buddha is cast into the confused mind, the confused mind cannot but become Buddha. Buddha being unconfused, turbid water clears of itself. Once the turbid water has cleared, where is the merit attributed?

[After a long silence he said,] How many times has the black wind overturned the ocean—yet I've never heard of a fishing boat capsizing.

[26]

Master Jianfu Gu said to an assembly,

Once Master Baizhang Heng went up in the hall, then as soon as the assembly had gathered he said, "Have tea," and immediately exited. Another time when he went up in the hall, as soon as the crowd gathered he said, "Fare well," and immediately got off the chair. Another time when he went up in the hall, as soon as the assembly gathered he said, "Rest," and immediately got off the chair.

He used the story of these times over and over again, but the community couldn't fathom it. Eventually he himself composed a verse on these three scenarios:

> Baizhang has three secrets:
> Have tea, fare well, rest.
> Even if you get them immediately,
> I dare say you aren't done yet.

Now then, when Master Baizhang Heng composed this verse, tell me, how was his insight? Can you tell attainment from failure? Do you want to understand?

Based on those three times he went up in the hall, he seems like a good man. When he composed this verse later, he seemed like he'd carved a couple of lines of characters on his face. If you are an expert, an adept, you will know as soon as it's brought up; younger students, beginners, will find it hard to discern.

I will annotate it for you, starting from the beginning.

Baizhang has three secrets—The thief has been exposed.

Have tea. Fare well. Rest.—The loot is brought out.

Even if you get them immediately, I dare say you're not done—It's like he's clutching the loot while passing judgment on the affair.

Even so, benevolent ones, only if you have the eye to distinguish realities can you realize enlightenment; if you cannot distinguish the false from the true, you may be said to be presuming upon Buddha-nature. You need to ask further of the wise and the good. Beware of living in vain and dying a waste.

[27]

Master Guizong Bao's eulogy of Bodhidharma, the founder of Chan, along with preface:

It is futile to try to describe the real likeness of the master. It cannot be assigned to the realm of desire, form, or formlessness. If you want to place it somewhere, obviously you are greatly mistaken. It is useless effort to point it out; where can you grasp? Want to know the master's real likeness? The universe and space.

> The master's features are sought by the world:
> The master's brows are cloud fronts on opposite sides,
> The master's eyes are lightning flashing.
> The master's nose is the soaring polar mountain,
> The master's mouth has no teeth—

Whose is the fault?
He's going to cross the desert—
Why doesn't he realize his own error?
There are great men here and there—
To whom to transmit the Teaching?
He went on dwelling at Shaolin;
Repentant, he returned West.
When you meet a Chan monk,
Best give him a sound beating.
And yet, even so, if you don't understand,
You cannot be a stickler.

Seeing this eulogy, Master Langya Jiao wrote a verse:

The master's eyes are deep,
The master's nose is big.
The master's ears are open,
The master's tongue is quick.
The master's body is black,
The master's heart is respectful.
With one shoe in hand,
He went back across the desert;
His stone monument at Mount Bear Ear
Is still there now.
I'll just use this verse to test
All the Chan monks in the land.

Dahui commented, "'Respectful'—this word should not be shifted. If you're shifty, disaster strikes."

[28]

Master Zhenjing instructed an assembly,

Sansheng said, "When I meet people, I go out, but going out does not help people."

Xinghua said, "When I meet people, I do not go out; not going out is helping people."

See how these two old awls have filched a bit of Linji's livelihood; each one draws his own boundaries and stakes out his territory, with the mettle to soar into space, causing clear-eyed Channists simply to want to laugh.

Let the Chan masters say what is laughable. Do you get the point? If you do, you may tumble and fall over. If not, then for now chew on it in the complications of Sansheng and Xinghua.

[29]

When Master Zhaozhou went to Yunju, Yunju said, "You are so old, why don't you look for a place to stay?"

Zhaozhou said, "What would my dwelling place be?"

Yunju said, "There is the foundation of an ancient temple in front of this mountain."

Zhaozhou said, "You should live there yourself."

Next Zhaozhou went to Zhuyu. He also said, "You're so old, why don't you look for a place to stay?"

Zhaozhou said, "Where is my dwelling place?"

Zhuyu said, "So old and you don't even know where to stay?"

Zhaozhou said, "I've been taming horses for thirty years, but today I've been kicked by an ass."

[30]

Dongshan said, "You must realize there is something beyond Buddha."

A monk asked, "What is beyond Buddha?"

Dongshan said, "Not Buddha."

Yunmen said, "It cannot be named or described; that is why he said 'not.'"

[31]

A monk asked Master Ciming, "What is Buddha?"

He said, "Water emerging from a high source."

"How is it when traveling but not meeting anyone?"

"The fishing line presses the water."

[32]

Master Baoning Yong addressed an assembly,

I have hands and feet, but no back or front—even people with clear eyes can't see me. The sky revolves to the left; the earth rotates to the right. [Slapping his knee.] A gust of west wind comes, two or three leaves fall.

A monk asked, "What is the great meaning of Buddhism?"

The master said, "There's no cool spot in a cauldron of boiling water."

[33]

Master Dagui Zhenru cited a story about how Xuefeng once told Xuansha, "There's an Elder Nanji who can answer any question." One day Nanji came to Xuefeng, and Xuefeng had him call on Xuansha.

Xuansha asked him, "An ancient said, 'Only I can know this thing'—what about you?"

Nanji replied, "You should realize there's one who doesn't seek knowledge."

Xuansha said, "Why has the old fellow on the mountain taken so much trouble?"

Dagui said, "When I cite this, I can't budge this saying of Xuansha's. Why? It's like beating a poison drum—far or near, all who hear it perish."

[34]

Guishan asked Yangshan, "Where are you coming from?"

Yangshan said, "From the fields."

Guishan asked, "How many people are there in the fields?"

Yangshan stuck his hoe in the ground and stood there with his hands folded.

Guishan said, "Today on South Mountain there are many people cutting thatch."

Yangshan then left, dragging his hoe.

Xuedou said, "Everywhere everyone says the story of sticking the hoe in the ground is special, but that is like pursuing falsehood and chasing evil. In my view, when Yangshan was asked a question by Guishan, he only managed to bind himself with straw rope, altogether fatally."

Dahui remarked, "The benevolent seeing it call it benevolence, the wise seeing it call it wisdom. Ordinary people use it everyday without realizing it. The path of cultured people is brilliant!"

[35]

Master Huanglong Nan addressed an assembly,

A monk asked Jianfeng, "For the Blessed Ones of the ten directions there is one road, nirvana; where does the road begin?"

Jianfeng drew a line with his staff and said, "It's here."

The monk asked Yunmen for further instruction. Yunmen held up a fan and said, "This fan leaps up to the Thirty-Third Heaven and hits the emperor of gods in the nose; when the carp of the eastern sea is hit once with a cane, it rains buckets. Understand? Understand?"

Jianfeng pointed out the road for one occasion, indirectly helping beginners. Yunmen went all the way through the transformations, to cause later people not to weary.

You should fathom the intentions of the two elders without pursuing their words. When you grasp the intent, you return to the right road home. If you pursue words, you wander on misleading paths, further and further astray.

[36]

Dayu took leave of Guizong one day. Guizong asked him, "Where are you going?" Dayu said, "To study the five-flavor Chan all over." Guizong said, "They have five-flavor Chan all over; here I only have one-flavor Chan."

Dayu then asked, "What is your one-flavor Chan?"

Guizong smacked him right away. All at once Dayu was greatly enlightened. He said, "Ha, I understand."

Guizong said, "Speak, speak!"

As Dayu was about to open his mouth, Guizong hit him again and chased him out.

When Guanxi first called on Linji, as soon as he entered the door Linji grabbed him by the chest and held him. Guanxi immediately said, "I get it, I get it." Linji then pushed him away.

[37]

Master Zhenjing said to an assembly,

Buddhism does not go along with human sentiments. Elders everywhere talk big, all saying, "I know how to meditate; I know the Way!" But tell me, do they understand or not? For no reason they sit in pits of crap fooling spirits and ghosts. When people are like this, what crime is there in killing them by the thousands and feeding them to the dogs?

There is also a kind of Chan follower who is charmed by those foxes, even with eyes open, not even realizing it themselves. They wouldn't object even if they poured piss over their heads.

You are all individuals; why should you accept this kind of treatment? How should you be yourself?

[38]

A monk asked Master Muzhou, "What are words of exposition?"

Muzhou said, "Assessing capabilities to fill offices."

"What are words of nonexposition?"

Muzhou said, "Lo, the imperial cook!"

[39]

Xuefeng went to Touzi. Touzi pointed to a rock in front of his cottage and said to Xuefeng, "All the Buddhas of past, present, and future are here."

Xuefeng said, "What a dull ignoramus."

Touzi and Xuefeng traveled to Longmin. There were two roads; Xuefeng asked, "Which one is the road to Longmin?"

Touzi pointed to it with his staff.

Xuefeng said, "To the east or to the west?"

Touzi said, "What a dull ignoramus."

Xuefeng asked, "When finished at one stroke, how is that?"

Touzi said, "This is not a naturally swift person."

Xuefeng said, "How about when not even a stroke is employed?"

Touzi said, "What a dull ignoramus."

Xuefeng also asked, "Does anyone ever visit here?"

Touzi tossed a hoe in front of him.

Xuefeng said, "Then I'll dig right here."

Touzi said, "What a dull ignoramus."

[40]

Master Langya Jiao instructed an assembly,

When host and guest interact, they settle the universe; when assessment and choice are examined together, who dares look up? The sage Shakyamuni manifested extinction under twin trees; the great teacher Bodhidharma really returned to Bear Ears Mountain. Are there any

Channists with eyes in my school, any genuine followers of the Way? If not, medicine is given according to the illness; diagnosis is made for a specific time.

A monk asked, "There's Deshan's staff and Linji's shout—I ask the teacher for a separate path apart from these two routes."

Langya said, "A ten-ton catapult is not shot at a mouse."

The monk thereupon shouted.

Langya said, "An adept monk."

The monk hesitated, trying to think of something to say. Langya then hit him.

[41]

Master Daning Guan instructed an assembly,

There is nothing to Buddhism; it's just that people stray from the source on their own. When Chan masters or Buddhas emerge, everyone is squared away; thus there are teachings circulating everywhere, methods broadcast to the four quarters; all of them give up the inferior for the superior, investigating the fundamental essence. Once the fundamental essence is realized, everything is understood; taking up whatever comes to mind, you can put it to use in a thousand ways.

But tell me, does this talk accord with the concern of the Chan school? [Silence.]

No use crying till blood flows.

Better pass the rest of spring in silence.

[42]

Li Bo, the district inspector of Jiang province, asked Guizong, "I don't doubt the statement in the Teaching that a mountain contains a mustard seed, but isn't it false to say a mustard seed contains a mountain?"

Guizong said, "People say you've read ten thousand books—is that true?"

Li said, "Yes."

Guizong said, "From head to foot you're about as big as a coconut—where do you put ten thousand books?"

Li just hung his head.

Another day Li asked, "What does the Teaching of the canon illumine?"

Guizong held up his fist and said, "Understand?"

Li said, "No."

Guizong said, "You poor scholar, you've read ten thousand books for naught—you can't even recognize a fist!"

[43]

A monk asked Master Qingping, "What is the Great Vehicle?"

"A well rope."

"What is the Small Vehicle?"

"A coin string."

"What is contamination?"

"A bamboo skimmer."

"What is noncontamination?"

"A wooden ladle."

Master Fayun Yuantong said, "Great Vehicle, Small Vehicle—well rope, cash string. Contamination, noncontamination—bamboo skimmer, wooden ladle."

[44]

Master Fashang Yu said, "I want someone who doesn't 'understand Chan' to be the national teacher."

Dahui said, "Tell me, is this an expression of ghee or an expression of poison?"

Ghee, clarified butter, as a potential within milk, is used as a symbol of the Buddha-nature inherent in all beings.

[45]

Master Zhenjing instructed an assembly,

"Heaven, earth, and I have the same root, myriad things and I are one body." Toe and heel, three horizontal and four vertical; fire erupts on the northern continent, singeing the eyebrows of the emperor of gods. The dragon king of the eastern sea, unable to bear the pain, emits a blast of thunder draining ponds and overturning mountains, clouds darkening the endless sky. The crossroads empty, a bearded man awakens in the midst of intoxication. Waking up, he claps.

Ha, ha, ha! Recently there are few thieves in the city. [Holding up his staff:] Thief, thief!

[46]

Xuansha took some medicine mistakenly and developed an inflammation all over his body. A monk asked, "What is the indestructible reality body?"

Xuansha said, "Dripping with pus."

Master Huai composed a verse on this:

> Drip, drip—the whole body is inflamed and suppurating.
> He shows his family style on the fishing boat;
> People of the time only look at the line,
> They don't see the reed flowers white against the smart-
>   weed's red.

Master Duan said, "Once someone asked me, 'What is the pure body of reality?' I simply replied, 'The smell of shit stinks up the air.' I also said,

'A child born by transformation on a lotus leaf.' Now tell me, is this the same or different from the ancients?

"I too have a verse."

> The smell of shit stinking up the air is also coincidence;
> How dare I announce for you what is in the nose?
> If there is an opening through the sky,
> You may travel freely without wearing anything.

[47]

Sushan instructed an assembly,

Before the Xiantong era, I understood the matter of the reality body. After the Xiantong era I understood the matter beyond the reality body.

Yunmen asked him, "I hear you understood the matter of the reality body before the Xiantong era, and understood the matter beyond the reality body after the Xiantong era. Is that so?"

Sushan said, "Yes."

Yunmen said, "What is the matter of the reality body?"

Sushan said, "A deadwood stake."

Yunmen said, "What is the matter beyond the reality body?"

Sushan said, "Not a deadwood stake."

Yunmen said, "Will you permit a student to explain the principle?"

Sushan said, "You may explain."

Yunmen said, "Doesn't 'a deadwood stake' illustrate the matter of the reality body, and doesn't 'not a deadwood stake' illustrate the matter beyond the reality body?"

Sushan said, "Right."

Yunmen said, "The reality body includes everything, doesn't it?"

Sushan said, "Reverend, don't understand at the water jug."

Yunmen thereupon bowed.

Dahui remarked, "Yunmen's bow was not good-hearted."

[48]

Master Wuzu Yan instructed an assembly,

The founding teacher said, "I originally came to this land to transmit means of rescuing the deluded. One flower will bloom in five petals; the resulting fruit will ripen naturally." This great teacher Bodhidharma went where his feet took him and said what came out of his mouth; descendants of later generations mostly made theories and arguments. Do you want to know where the flower blooms and the fruit forms? The pears of Zheng province, the dates of Qing province; in all things, nothing surpasses a good provenance.

A monk asked, "What is Buddha?"

"Nutrition enters via the mouth."

"Are the meaning of Chan and the meaning of the Teachings the same or different?"

"When people are poor, their knowledge is short; when horses are thin, their hair is long."

[49]

Master Ciming's song on the ox-herding boy:

> The ox-herding boy is lively indeed;
> Barefoot, wearing a straw cloak, he grasps both horns.
> Snoozing on an ox's back, he sings to the sky.
> People ask how it is; the ox isn't thirsty yet.
> Turning his face, he gazes at the expanse of level fields.
> Letting it go in the four directions, he stops impeding it;
> Unfettered on eight sides, it roams at will.
> If he wants to rein it, all it takes is a tug at the rope;
> The calf is docile; stroking it, he grabs its horns.
> Its strength is not yet full—it can hardly lift him up;
> For now he lets it free on a flat hillock.
> Thinking to climb to a high peak, its four hooves run free.

Now that the sun is high, he stops the grazing
And grips the nose ring;
Young and old, he leads them together
Into the corral to sleep in the mud.
Watching them lie down east and west,
He laughs, ha, ha—isn't it fine!
Then he takes out a sideways flute
And plays it along with the wind,
Shaking up the five lakes, mountains, seas, and islands.
Riding backward on an ox, he doffs his coat.
Those who know don't look for him on the road.
If you ask where the herding boy lives,
The whip points east and west; nothing of value at all.

[50]

As Master Guizong was weeding, a lecturing monk came to call on him. Suddenly a snake slithered by; Guizong killed it with his hoe.

The monk said, "Long have I heard of Guizong, but after all you're a roughneck monk."

Holding the hoe, Guizong glared back at the monk and said, "Are you rough or am I rough?"

Later Xuefeng asked Deshan, "What was the ancient's meaning when he killed the snake?"

Deshan immediately struck him; Xuefeng walked away. Deshan called to him, and Xuefeng turned his head. Deshan said, "Later he was enlightened; only then did he realize the old guy's thoroughgoing kindness."

[51]

Master Langya Jiao instructed an assembly,

Expressions of existence and expressions of nonexistence are like vines on a tree. When the tree falls, the vines wither; that's just the time to get a beating. You tell me—where is the fault?

[Silence.]
If you don't have an artist's skill, don't claim you can do the coloring.

[52]

Master Huanglong Nan instructed an assembly,
South of the river, the springs are cold and the autumns are warm. In recent days each drop of water is a drop of ice.
A monk asked, "How is it when each drop of water becomes a drop of ice?"
"This is not yet the business of a Chan monk."
"What is the business of a Chan monk?"
"A drop of water, a drop of ice."

[53]

Nanquan, Luzu, Shanshan, and Guizong all left Mazu's place, each planning to live in a hermitage. As they were parting on the road, Nanquan stuck his staff in the ground and said, "If you can say it, you're obstructed by this; if you can't say it, you're obstructed by this."
Guizong pulled out the staff, hit Nanquan with it once, and said, "It's just this—what obstruction or nonobstruction are you talking about?"
Luzu said, "This line will circulate widely throughout the world."

[54]

Once Master Dongshan Cong was carrying a load of firewood up the mountain by himself when he encountered a monk on the way. The monk asked, "There's firewood on the mountain—why carry it up?"
Cong put the load of firewood down on the ground and said, "Understand?"
The monk said, "No."
Cong said, "I want to burn it."

[55]

A monk asked Venerable Yanyang, "What is Buddha?"

He replied, "A clod of earth."

"What is Dharma?"

"The earth moving."

"What is Sangha?"

"Eating gruel, eating rice."

"What is the water of revival?"

"In the river right in front of you."

[56]

As Baizhang Heng stood in attendance on Fayan, he asked for help with the story of the Hindu asking Buddha, "I do not ask about the spoken, I do not ask about the unspoken." Before he could even finish the citation, Fayan said, "Wait, wait! You're about to understand at the Buddha's silence!"

At this Heng was greatly enlightened.

[57]

Master Yangqi held a memorial feast on the anniversary of Ciming's death. When the assembly had gathered, he went up to the statue of Ciming, clenched both fists and put them to his head, then drew a line with his seat cloth; he described a circle, then lit incense, stepped back three paces, and curtsied.

The senior monk said, "Don't act weird."

Yangqi said, "What about you?"

The senior monk said, "Master, stop acting weird."

Yangqi said, "A baby rabbit sucks ox teat."

The second-to-senior monk approached, drew a circle, then lit incense, and also retreated three steps and curtsied. Yangqi drew near,

making a gesture of listening. The second monk tried to think of something to say. Yangqi slapped him and said, "You ignoramus, you're acting
crazily too!"

Dahui remarked, "Old Yangqi! It was as if he had sunk a whole boat of flax,
then came sweeping the inside of the bailing bucket."

[58]

When Linji left Huangbo, Huangbo asked, "Where are you going?"
  Linji said, "If not south of the river, then north of the river."
  Huangbo tried to hit him, but Linji caught and held his staff, then
gave him a slap. Huangbo laughed and called an attendant: "Bring my late
teacher's meditation brace and whisk."
  Linji called to the attendant: "Bring fire."
  Huangbo said, "Just take them and go—later on you'll cut off the
tongues of everyone on earth."

[59]

When Xiangyan first opened a hall, Guishan had someone deliver a staff
and a letter for him. Receiving them, Xiangyan said, "Alas, alas!" The
monk asked him why he said this. Xiangyan said, "Just because of carrying out the order of spring in wintertime."

[60]

Master Huanglong Nan instructed an assembly,
  Green vines, clinging, climb right to the top of the cold pines; white
clouds, pale and quiet, appear and disappear in the sky. Myriad things are
originally peaceful; it's just that people disturb themselves. What are you
disturbed about? Tsk!

[61]

Master Tianyi Huai instructed an assembly,

"Green vines, clinging, climb right to the top of the cold pines; white clouds, pale and quiet, appear and disappear in the sky." How can this compare to clouding up over the southern mountains and raining over the northern mountains? If you can understand, sweet melon is sweet to the stem; if you don't understand, bitter gourd is bitter to the root.

[62]

Master Ciming gave a lecture to an assembly; hitting the rope seat once with his staff, he said,

Everyone, do you understand? Have you not read the saying "Forgetting objects of knowledge at one stroke, you do not need training or discipline anymore. Everywhere those who arrive on the Way all say this is the highest potential." This realization of Xiangyan is already realization of the Chan of those who arrive at being as is, but he still hasn't dreamed of the Chan of the master teachers.

Now tell me, what is the strength of the Chan of the master teachers? If you take a rule from words, you will deceive and cheat people of later times. Even if you attain realization at a blow of the staff, you are turning against the sages of yore: "Myriad things are originally peaceful—it's just that people disturb themselves."

For this reason, when I lived at Fuyan I just saw the scenery of Fuyan, rising at leisure and going to sleep early, clouds sometimes rising on the blue ranges, moonlight descending into the cold pools. At the sound of voices, birds fly, crying; the flowers before the stand of wisdom are fragrant. By the peak of the mountain, holding a skinny cane, I sit on a boulder, talking at times to monks from all over about the mysterious and subtle, ashes on my head and dirt on my face.

When I lived at Xinghua, I just saw the family style of Xinghua, greeting those who came and seeing off those who left. The monastery was next to a city, filled with carriages and horses, fishermen singing on the rivers, monkeys howling in the foothills; from time to time music and song could be heard. Again I discussed the Chan way with high-minded people from everywhere within the four seas, forgetful of the passing years.

Now tell me, between living deep in the mountains and living in the city, is one better than the other? Try to say.

[Silence.]

This place is the Merciful One: there is no gateway, and no seeker.

[63]

Master Jianfeng Gu instructed an assembly,

Even the gaze of the Buddhas of all times cannot reach it; even the Chan masters all over the land get tongue-tied. Those who know it exists should keep it up on their own. As for those who don't yet know it exists, if you don't quit now, when will you ever?

[64]

Jianfeng Gu also instructed an assembly,

The sword has already fallen overboard—it's useless to mark the boat. Take care.

[65]

Master Baoning Yong said,

One is one, two is two, three is three, four is four; the numerals are quite clear, higher and lower according to position. When remaining in place, what concern is there?

[Drawing a "one" with his staff:] Everyone has all at once disarrayed the system of time.

[66]

Master Xuansha said,

Is there any Buddhism deep in the mountains, on precipitous cliffs, where human footsteps have never reached in a million years?

If you say there is, what are you calling Buddhism? If you say there isn't, then there is somewhere Buddhism doesn't reach.

[67]

Master Xuansha also instructed an assembly,

The old masters everywhere all speak of dealing with people to help the living. Suppose three kinds of handicapped people come to you—how will you treat them? Those who suffer from blindness will not see if you hold up a mallet; those who suffer from deafness will not hear anything spoken; and those who suffer from muteness will not be able to speak even if you try to get them to say something. So how could you treat these people? If you can't deal with these people, then Buddhism is ineffective.

[68]

A monk asked Yunmen for help on Xuansha's story of the three handicapped people. Yunmen said, "Bow!" The monk bowed. Then Yunmen poked at him with his cane; the monk pulled back. Yunmen said, "You're not blind!" Then he told the monk to come closer. When the monk approached, Yunmen said, "You're not deaf!" Then he stood up his cane and said, "Understand?" The monk said, "No." Yunmen said, "You're not mute!" At this the monk had an insight.

Master Fenyang Zhao versified this:

> Temporarily creating blindness, deafness, muteness, palsy,
> He wants to show our school and test for mastery.

Diamond cuts steel, which breaks like clay;
As soon as the golden fish gone through stirs, he misses Xuansha.

Master Foyan versified,

Xuansha's three kinds of invalid—
The principle's not in raising your voice.
Drawing on old Xiangyan,
He's hung him up in a tree.

[69]

Master Daning Kuan instructed an assembly,

The secret of Shaolin is the manner of the ancient Buddhas, functioning adaptively according to potential, folding and unfolding freely, like a fist making a flat hand, opening and closing at appropriate times, like water producing bubbles, which rise and vanish inconstantly. Action and stillness both reveal it, speech and silence show it all. Myriad functions are natural, not wearing out mental energy.

When you get here, this is called releasing the boat along with the current; this person can go! But tell me, when there's a counter wind and the oars are raised, who is the expert?

[Silence.]

To sport in the tide, you must be one who can sport in the tide.

[70]

A monk asked Master Dasui, "What is the concern of Dasui?"

He replied, "East, west, south, north."

Dahui remarked, "Tell me, did he answer this monk's question or not?"

[71]

National Teacher Zhong asked the imperial attendant Zilin, "Where do you come from?"

He replied, "From Chengnan."

The national teacher then asked a page boy, "What color is the grass in Chengnan?"

The boy said, "Yellow."

The national teacher said, "Even this boy could be awarded a purple robe and talk of mysticism to the emperor too!"

[72]

The day Master Letan Ying opened a hall, a monk bowed, rose, let a corner of his vestment hang down, and said, "How is it when you take off your armor?"

He said, "Happily the beacon fires are extinguished, bow and spear are hung on the wall."

The monk then readjusted his vestment and said, "How about when you rearm?"

He said, "Until you've gotten to the banks of Raven River, I know you won't stop."

The monk thereupon shouted.

Ying said, "Startled me to death!"

The monk clapped.

Ying said, "And this is finding life in the midst of death."

The monk bowed.

Ying said, "I thought you had the ability to capture one state and destroy another; after all you're just a crook selling bootleg salt."

The monk asked, "What is Buddha?"

Ying said, "The eyebrows divided, the eyes like comets."

The monk asked, "What is the meaning of the Chan founder's coming from the West?"

Ying said, "Each stroke of the cane leaves a welt."

The monk said, "Let the entire assembly witness my apology."

Ying laughed.

The monk bowed, rose, and drew a circle with his left hand. Ying stuck his whisk through it and moved it to the right. Then the monk drew a circle with his right hand. Ying stuck his whisk through it and moved it to the left. Then the monk drew a circle with both hands and held it up to present it. Ying drew a line with his whisk and said, "These thirty years I've never yet met a descendant of the Gui-Yang sect; now instead I've encountered a fellow walking on tiles of unfired clay. Is there anyone else with any questions?" [A long silence.] "There is no one."

Finally he said, "Questions are endless, and answers are never finished. Questioning and answering back and forth gets further and further from the Way. Why? This matter is such that even if you get it on impact, you are no great man for that; even if you get it at a shout, that still doesn't make you an adept. So how then could you take rules from words, running around seeking in sayings, so that your speech may be clever and new, and your wits may be swift? Those with views and interpretations like this are all burying the essence of Chan, besmirching the worthies of yore; when have they ever dreamed of seeing our Chan way?

"When our Buddha, the one who arrived at thusness, was about to pass away into ultimate extinction, he said, 'I have the treasury of perception of truth, the subtle mind of nirvana, which I entrust to Kasyapa.' Kasyapa entrusted it to Ananda, and then Shanavasa, Upagupta, and other great masters succeeded one another. When it reached Bodhidharma, he came from the West [to China], pointing directly to the human mind to reveal its nature and make it enlightened, without establishing writings or sayings.

"Is this not the ancient sages' path of expedient method? It's just that when the individual concerned does not have faith, then he subjectively mistakes his reflection for his head and runs off following paths of insanity, which cause him to wander destitute in life and death.

"Chan worthies, if you can turn the light around for a moment and reverse your attention, critically examining your own standpoint, it may be said the gate will open wide, story upon story of the tower will appear manifest throughout the ten directions, and the oceanic congregations will become equally visible. Then the ordinary and the holy, the wise and the foolish, the mountains, rivers, and earth, will all be stamped with the seal of the oceanic reflection state of concentration, with no leakage whatsoever.

"When I preach like this, a real Chan monk hearing it would, I dare say, cover his ears and leave, laughing off that talk. But tell me, how do you utter an expression appropriate to real Chan monks?"

[A long silence.]

"On the horizon, snow buries a thousand feet; how many pines are broken by the ice on the arches?"

[73]

Heshan instructed an assembly,

Cultivating learning is called "hearing," transcending learning is called "proximity." Beyond these two is called real transcendence.

A monk asked, "What is real transcendence?"

Heshan said, "Knowing how to beat the drum."

"What is real truth?"

Heshan said, "Knowing how to beat the drum."

"Mind itself is Buddha—I don't question this. What is neither mind nor Buddha?"

Heshan said, "Knowing how to beat the drum."

"When people who have gone beyond come, how do you deal with them?"

Heshan said, "Knowing how to beat the drum."

[74]

Layman Pang asked Grand Master Ma, "Who is it that is not a companion of myriad things?"

Ma said, "When you drink up the water of West River in one sip, then I'll tell you."

A monk asked, "What is Buddha?"

Grand Master Ma said, "Mind itself is Buddha."

[75]

Master Dagui Zhenru addressed a crowd,

A la la! What cogitation is this? "The moment the Oven Breaker's staff strikes, one knows one's turned away from self." [Striking the incense stand with his staff.] Fallen, fallen!

A monk asked, "What is the meaning of Zhaozhou's 'cypress tree in the yard'?"

Zhenru said, "At night the weather's severe; the lone traveler's the first to feel cold."

The monk said, "What about the statement that he never said this?"

Zhenru said, "Only the traveler knows his pains."

The monk said, "Ten years walking in the red dust, today the body's revealed alone."

Zhenru said, "Frost on top of snow."

TRANSLATOR'S NOTE

The story of the Oven Breaker is found in *The Blue Cliff Record*; see chapter 297 below. The story of the cypress tree in the yard is found in the *Book of Serenity*.

[76]

Master Tianyi Huai addressed an assembly,

The universe is not absolute; what is wrong with distinctions? The sixth grand master of Chan said, "When leaves fall, they return to the root; when we came we had no mouth." If you understand this talk, you will enter directly into the room of Vimalakirti, abide in the glow of golden light, and see the four kinds of sages and six kinds of ordinary beings in the worlds of the ten directions, as if you were looking at a fruit in the palm of your hand.

You will also see a species of being who sleeps through the long night of birth and death, oblivious, aslumber, unaware, unknowing. Wouldn't it be a joy to make the cry of the golden rooster announcing the dawn, to wake them up? If you can do this, then you can use this profound mind to serve infinite lands. This is called requiting your debt to Buddha.

Even so, an ancient said, "Those who smile at me are many, those who laugh at me are few."

TRANSLATOR'S NOTE

"The room of Vimalakirti" refers to the main setting of the popular scripture *Vimalakirti's Advice* and represents the emptiness of absolute reality in conditional phenomena.

[77]

Master Fahua Ju said to an assembly,

Participatory study requires you to have the eye to distinguish things; you can't fudge it. If you attain precision and clarity of accurate perception, there is no inhibition at all.

Haven't you read the saying of the ancient? "Every statement must contain three mysteries; each mystery must contain three essentials." What was the ancient's meaning in speaking thus? "The king goose that can pick milk from water is not in the same class as the ducks."

A monk asked, "I don't ask about 'not a fleck of cloud for myriad miles'—what about the matter of the 'single frosty blade'?"

The master said, "Who dares set it in motion?"

The monk bowed.

The master said, "A small kindness prevents a great kindness," and hit him.

The monk asked, "How is it when at the place knowledge doesn't reach?"

The master said, "The triple gate has never opened."

The monk said, "Who is a knower?"

The master said, "The mouth is like the nose."

TRANSLATOR'S NOTE

"The mouth is like the nose" means "silent." For the three mysteries and three essentials, see notes to chapter 216.

[78]

Master Longji said to an assembly,

Complete ordinariness is not known to ordinary people; complete sagehood is not understood by sages. If sages understood, they would be ordinary people; if ordinary people knew, they would be sages.

This saying has one principle and two meanings: if people can discern them, undeniably they have some penetration of Buddhism. If you can't discern, don't say you don't wonder.

Dahui remarked, "It is easier to turn stones into gold and jewels than to get people to set aside affirmation and negation."

Longji also said,

Affirming the pillars, you don't see the pillars; negating the pillars, you don't see the pillars. After detachment from affirmation and negation, understand in the midst of affirmation and negation.

Dahui remarked, "Tsk! He's starting all over again!"

[79]

Master Lingyuan said to an assembly,

The Buddhas of all times do not know existence; a debt is not repaid twice. Cats and cows know existence; effort's expended wastefully. When you clarify the great function and awaken the great potential, your trail is inconceivable; go back unknown to anyone. Bursting open the blue sky, a thousand feet of pine; cutting through the red dust, a valley stream of water.

[80]

Master Dongshan Chu said to an assembly,

On the northern faces of the mountains of Chu, along the southern reaches of the Han River, they beat the drum of the teaching, assemble Chan groups, bring up the way of the school, and explain the intent of the founders.

If you take up "raising the eyebrows and glaring," holding up a fist or raising a finger, coughing or clearing the throat, or sayings like "a dish-cloth in the refectory," "what are you saying?" "understand?" "a mendicant's worn-out sandals" "blind fellow!" "ignoramus!" "playing with the psyche," "all is thus," "all is not so," and consider this to be bringing up the perennial concern, all of it is demonic activity, slandering the Great Vehicle, exterminating the Chan folk—it is totally irrelevant to you.

But tell me, what principle does a Chan practitioner rely on? Come forth and speak in front of the gathering.

Around a broken-legged kettle, if each puts forth a single hand in hopes of keeping the vehicle of the source going, this too represents a spiritual community. Is there anyone?

If not, I will unstintingly go on hinting.

The hint is right before your eyes—myriad forms, the universe, the earth, the hundreds and thousands of Buddhas, the sun, moon, stars, and planets, the hells, the three mires, arousal of mind and stirring of thoughts, the experiences of everyday life—these are all your self; why not focus here to seek? All at once you will manage to see independently and clearly, without going journeying for naught, attaining the state of peace on your own.

These words of mine are making medicine for a dead horse—if a clear-eyed Chan practitioner should stuff a straw sandal in my mouth, could I blame him?

Blaming is not blaming—you tell me why. Take it in your grip; find it out under your feet. The slightest deviation will break you in half; better not be coarse-minded.

A monk asked, "Looking for pearls in red water still refers to worldly valuables; what is sung out in concert with the clouds is certainly not talk beyond convention. What do you use to direct people today?"

[The master said,] "Hearing the ghost-propitiation drum at night, listening to the mooring songs in the morning."

"How is it when words transcend images and speech is uttered beyond the blue sky?"

"There's rhyme in the voice of the travelers on the shore; the fishermen in the boats harmonize unevenly."

"What about the matter of recondite mystery?"

"The hook is long, the line is short."

"I hear the master bringing out the meaning in the pond—what about the business of penetrating directly through the blue sky?"

"A *jia-si* year begins with *bing*."

"What is the business of today?"

"Very nice snow."

"What is Buddha?"

"Three pounds of flax."

"What is the mind of extinct Buddhas?"

"A nest knows the wind, a cave knows the rain."

"How was Niutou before meeting the fourth grand master?"

"A rough-hewn staff."

"How about after meeting?"

"The cloth shirt of the Dou's eighth son."

"I don't ask about Buddhism; what is the perennial concern?"

"Seeing someone play a wooden flute with your eyes."

TRANSLATOR'S NOTE

Jia-si and *bing* are terms used in the traditional calendry system. The reference here is to what is referred to in Chan as "ordinary reality," in this dialogue implying return to the world after transcendence.

[81]

Master Dasui said to an assembly,

The virtuous ones of antiquity all sought reality, not deceiving themselves. How could they be compared to flighty moths casting themselves into flames, injuring and destroying themselves? They clearly understood life and death, so repetitive cycles couldn't hold them back.

That is why "cognition cannot conceive it, knowledge cannot know it." Haven't you heard how Shakyamuni Buddha closed the door, and the enlightened layman Vimalakirti kept silent? The saint Subhuti explained without speaking, the gods Indra and Brahma heard without listening. This matter is very difficult, very difficult!

A monk asked, "On meeting an ancient Buddha on the road, then what?"

"Suppose you encounter a donkey, a camel, an elephant, or a horse—what do you call it?"

"Myriad things come from mind—where does mind come from?"

"A stone ox gallops along the river, sparks in the water burn the sky."

"What is the mark of a great man?"

"He doesn't stick a sign on his belly."

[82]

Master Ciming asked a monk, "Where have you just come from?"

He said, "Clouds cross the azure of a thousand mountains."

"Why are you in such a hurry?"

"The cries of the geese leaving the water are intense."

Ciming thereupon shouted. The monk shouted too. Ciming struck; the monk struck too. Ciming said, "Look at this blind fellow! Really I should drive you out, but considering you're a newcomer, for now sit and have tea."

He also asked the fundraiser, "I don't ask you about preaching in town; how do you express entering the gate?"

The monk immediately shouted.

Ciming said, "Why do you shout at random?"

The monk shouted again; Ciming struck him.

Ciming asked another monk, "Where have you come from?"

He said, "Yangqi."

Ciming asked, "Where did you spend summer retreat?"

He said, "At Xingjiao."

Ciming asked, "And does the master of Xingjiao have nostrils?"

He said, "Yes."

Ciming thereupon struck him.

[83]

Langya Jiao said to an assembly,

Eliminating bandits and getting rid of robbers still belongs to the realm of effort and achievement.

When the paths of ruler and subject harmonize, and the ocean is calm and the rivers clear, this is still in the realm of the absolute.

What is the basic concern of a Chan practitioner?

The golden fish that's passed through the net is still in the water; the stone horse on the way back gets out of the silken cage.

[Langya Jiao also composed a verse on the story of three pounds of flax:]

> Dongshan's three pounds of flax—
> Brass is not exchanged for gold.
> Buying five colors with a coin,
> He draws an angel on the wall.

[Langya versified the story of the grand master tossing a needle in a bowl of water:]

> Nagarjuna's water in a bowl,
> Kanadeva's needle on down:
> Everyone argues about winning and losing,
> Everybody talks about far and near.
> If you don't see the geese in the clouds,
> How can you know the sand bar's deep?
> A farmer moves a foundation stone,
> And under the stone he finds gold.

TRANSLATOR'S NOTE

The story of three pounds of flax is in *The Blue Cliff Record*. "What is Buddha?" "Three pounds of flax." It might be said that this stands for "being as is" in the broadest sense. The Japanese master Tenkei says, "It is the same everywhere in the universe. Dahui's teacher Yuanwu says of this, "When your defiling feelings, conceptual thinking, and comparative judgments of gain and loss and right and wrong are all cleared away at once, then you will spontaneously understand." The story of tossing a needle in a bowl is in *Transmission of Light*. The Indian patriarch Nagarjuna set out a bowl of water in front of Kanadeva, his successor; Kanadeva tossed a needle into the bowl. The Japanese master Keizan says of this story, "Even if you feel clear and pure," referring to the water, "right then there must be a pervading firmness," referring to the needle.

[84]

Master Zhenjing said to an assembly,

Xuefeng said, "There's a turtle-nosed snake on South Mountain—watch out for it in your comings and goings." Xuefeng had no marks of greatness; so the snake wouldn't go without a head. As for Changqing, responding, "A lot of people lose their lives in this auditorium today," he was like a new bride afraid of her mother-in-law. Yunmen stuck his cane in front of Xuefeng and made a gesture of fright, drawing legs on a snake. Xuansha said, "Why use 'South Mountain'?" If one says one's own perception is closest, one has not escaped just being in a cave. There was no one else with any natural spirit at all. Isn't there anyone here with natural spirit? I dare not hope you will hang another sun of wisdom and individually activate the esoteric influence. Now if you turn to the smelly shirts of the ancients, you can hardly even get a sense of the breath of life.

[85]

A monk asked Nanyuan, "Are the meaning of Chan and the meaning of Buddhism the same or different?"

He said, "Chairman of the board, chief executive officer."

The monk said, "I don't understand."

The master said, "Ox head south, horse head north."

Dahui remarked, "The former answer hit the mark; the latter answer didn't."

[86]

Master Dayu Zhi said to an assembly,

I receive descendants of the Great Hero, the monks of the Chan world race; what gateway is there to race to? How can the striking arrow know the withered tree survives? The withered tree survives, in one year going through springtime twice. Two times spring—behind the curtains, pearls are spread out for people. Spread out for people—even to think is admiring Western Qin.

A monk asked Master Fenzhou, "What is a statement for beginners?" Fenzhou said, "You are a traveling monk." "What is a statement to distinguish a Chan monk?" Fenzhou said, "The sun rises in the West in the morning." "What is a statement of enforcement of the absolute imperative?" Fenzhou said, "Brought a thousand miles, presenting the same old face." "What is an expression stabilizing heaven and earth?" "On the northern continent of Kuru, those who always eat nonglutinous rice have no greed and no anger." I use these four sayings to test all Chan monks, but when you think about it carefully, with these four sayings I've been seen through all at once by all Chan monks.

Dahui remarked, "Do you want to know Dayu? 'One who doesn't change his father's ways for three years can be called respectful.'"

TRANSLATOR'S NOTE

Western Qin was a breakaway kingdom founded by a Turkic general in Chinese service who rebelled against his Chinese employer.

[87]

Master Daning Guan held up his staff to an assembly and said, "High without peril, full without overflowing, in ordinary people and impossible for ordinary people to abandon, in sages and impossible for sages to escape, the ten directions all in one perception, the whole earth without a mote of dust—tell me, what is this? Ha!"

[88]

Master Letan Jun held up his staff to an assembly and said,
     A Chan monk's acrobatic pole accompanies him wherever he goes; he performs wherever he may be. Holding it upside down, lifting it sideways, he's naturally artistic. Thus in ancient times Master Yaoshan asked Yunyan, "I hear you know how to tame lions; is that so?" Yunyan said, "It is." Yaoshan asked, "How many have you tamed?" Yunyan said, "I've tamed six." Yaoshan said, "I too can tame lions." Yunyan asked, "How many have you tamed?" Yaoshan said, "I have only tamed one." Yunyan said, "One is six, six are one." Yaoshan then stopped talking.

Yaoshan and Yunyan take people for fools; both of them together couldn't tame a single lion. If it were me, all I'd have to do is lead myself out, make head into tail and tail into head, revolve two golden eyes, bare some iron-hook claws, and let out a howl making all the wild beasts within a hundred miles disappear, and cause the birds to fall from the sky.

I haven't paraded my lion yet—pay close attention, and first watch me make a secure place.

[Tossing down his staff, he said,] "How many people know what's going on here?"

[89]

Master Fojian said to an assembly,

The supreme Way is without difficulty; just avoid discrimination. Peach blossoms are pink, apricot blossoms are white; who says they're of a uniform color? Swallows twitter, nightingales sing—who says they sound the same? If you don't pass through the barrier of this master teacher, you'll vainly take mountains and rivers for eyes.

[90]

Master Fori Cai versified the story of the cypress tree:

> The cypress tree in Zhaozhou's yard
> Is mentioned to a Chan traveler;
> On the black lacquer screen,
> The pine and the vine are distinct.

[91]

A monk asked Master Yuanzhao, "What is the white ox on open ground?"
He said, "When it's released, there's no place to look for it."

TRANSLATOR'S NOTE

The white ox on open ground, a symbol taken from the *Lotus Sutra*, represents the Ekayana, or One Vehicle, the complete teaching on opening up the knowledge and vision of Buddhas.

[92]

A monk asked Master Datong, "What is the seamless monument?"

He said, "Fog and mist arise back and front; stars and moon circle the pillars holding up the eaves."

"What is the person in the monument?"

"He doesn't bother with the business of purifying society all day long; over the years he occupies a village in the white clouds."

[93]

Master Zihu said,

All things are free—what binds, what restricts? You yourself create your own difficulty and ease therein.

The mind source is a single continuity, pervading the ten directions; to people of the finest faculties it is naturally clear.

Haven't you read Nanquan's statement, "Innocents like this are after all rare in the world"? Clearly they exist; actually everyone is so, but they just lack a robust will—that's what makes them get so tired.

Do you want to understand easily? There has never ever been a single ordinary person or sage appearing before you, and not a single good word or bad word that applies to you.

Why? If you do good, good has no form; if you do evil, evil has no sign.

Since there is no self, what do you take for good or bad? What do you define as ordinary or holy?

Do you believe or not? Do you take responsibility? Where is there to escape? That would be like trying to flee your shadow in the sunlight—can you actually avoid it?

Buddha's teaching is profound and subtle; those who comprehend it motivate themselves, not letting minor circumstances interfere with major tasks. Have you not read the saying "Even if you have to insist on the law all your life, who can forget conditions for even a day?"

Do you want to understand Chan? Let each of you go back to your place and look.

[94]

Master Xuedou Xian addressed an assembly,

"Form arises before it is substantial; terms are produced for the un-named; once form and name have appeared, ambient energy is tur-bid and clear." [Raising his staff:] Everyone, the staff is form and name brought up together; is there any error?

If there is, it's the moon in the water; if not, yet form and name have appeared.

If you can find out, truly it can be said, "When the debt is great, it's hard to repay."

[95]

Gushan said to an assembly,

You all say you travel all around to study and learn. I wonder—study what? Learn what? Is there anything to learn? If there is, come forth and prove it to the assembly.

And do you study Chan, study the Way, study Buddha, study Dharma, study the master of the reality body of Vairocana, study that which is be-yond Buddhahood, or the state beyond nirvana?

If you really study these expressions, that can be considered great error; it is referred to as the mind looking upward never ceasing. This is none of your business.

A monk asked, "What is the great meaning of Buddhism?"

"Spit it out!"

"Whenever there is any expression, it invariably violates the way of Chan. What is the concern of Chan?"

"Shut up!"

[96]

Master Wuzu Yan said to an assembly,

Of old it has been said, "If one discovers reality and returns to the source, all space in the ten directions disappears." I do not concur. If one discovers reality and returns to the source, all space in the ten directions is bumped into everywhere.

[97]

Master Wuzu said to an assembly,

An ancient said, "If I tell you, it'll strip my tongue; if I don't tell you, it'll silence my mouth." Now tell me, is there any help for people in this? Sometimes I try to swallow for you, but it's blocked by my own teeth; sometimes I try to spit out for you, but my throat is too small. So tell me, is there any help for people?

I've always been a purist.

[98]

Master Huanglong Xin eulogized a master teacher:

> The sixth grand master was not a powerful man back then;
> Hiring another to write on the wall, he himself was confused.
> Quite clearly he had a verse saying there is no thing,
> Yet he accepted another's bowl.

Dahui remarked, "Now tell me, is the bowl a thing or not a thing? If you say it's a thing, then old Huanglong isn't a powerful man either. If you say it's not a thing, how does that affect the bowl?"

[99]

Master Yungai Zhi said to an assembly,

Tying on water-repelling shoes, walk over the lakes and rivers; taking hold of iron brambles, roust caves of dragons and tigers. Climbing a tree upside-down, for the final time see there is no creation or destruction. Laughing at old Gautama, in a finger snap go beyond Maitreya.

[100]

Master Fadeng asked Yunji Ji, "Just now someone asked about the meaning of the Chan founder coming from the West. I told him it is neither East nor West. What about you?"

Ji said, "Neither East nor West."

Fadeng said, "How can you get it understanding this way?"

At the time Ji was confused and didn't get the point. That evening he asked for help. Fadeng said, "He naturally has descendants." At these words Ji suddenly attained awakening. He composed a verse, saying,

> Dealing with people to benefit the living is most wonderful;
> Alienating life after all is not good.
> "He naturally has descendants."
> Now that you mention it,
> The application's just right.

[101]

The reply of the national teacher of Qingliang to the imperial crown prince's inquiry about the essentials of mind:

The ultimate way is rooted in the mind; the reality of mind is rooted in nondwelling. The awareness of the nondwelling substance of mind is not obscured; essence and characteristics peaceful, it contains qualities and functions. Comprehending both inside and outside, it is deep and it is broad.

Neither existent nor void, it is not produced and does not pass away. It has no end and no beginning. When you seek it, you cannot get it; reject it, and it still doesn't leave.

If you miss the immediate experience, then the pains of confusion are jumbled; if you realize true essence, then the light of openness is thoroughly clear.

Although mind itself is Buddha, only those who experience it actually know. But if there is "realization" and "knowledge," then the sun of wisdom sets in the land of existence. Yet if there is no illumination and no awakening, then dark clouds cover the gate of emptiness.

If a thought is not produced, then before and after are cut off, and the luminous essence stands alone; others and self are one suchness.

Go directly to the source of mind, and there is no knowledge, no attainment; you neither grasp nor reject, so there is no opposition and no cultivation.

Nonetheless, confusion and enlightenment are interdependent; truth and illusion are relative.

If you seek reality trying to get rid of illusion, that is like wearing out your body to get rid of your shadow; if you realize how illusion is truth, that is like staying in the shade so your shadow disappears.

If you forget perception, not minding, then myriad cogitations disappear; if you spontaneously know dispassionately, here is where all practices come from.

Freed and allowed to go or stay, the quiet mind is aware of the source and stream. Not losing the mystic subtlety whether speaking or silent, action and repose never leave the realm of reality.

In terms of "cessation," it is silent knowing forgetting both; in terms of "observation," it is silent knowing perceiving both. Speaking of experience, it cannot be pointed out to another; speaking of principle, it cannot be understood without experience. Therefore when you realize silence, there is no silence; true knowledge has no knowledge.

With the unified mind in which knowing and silence are not two, harmonize with the centered course in which emptiness and existence merge together. Not dwelling, having no fixation, do not absorb, do not take in; affirmation and negation gone, subject and object are both obliterated.

When this obliteration also ceases, then insight appears.

Insight is not produced outside the mind; the nature of wisdom is originally inherent, but it is basically quiescent and cannot manifest itself. In actuality it depends on achievement of wisdom.

Insight and wisdom complete each other; the basic wisdom and the applied cultivation are really not two entities. When both disappear and you penetrate experientially, then subtle awareness is round and clear.

As beginning and end merge, cause and effect interpenetrate. Being a Buddha in every state of mind, no mind is not the mind of Buddha; realizing enlightenment in every place, there is not a single atom that is not a buddha-land.

So whether truth and falsehood or others and self, when you bring up one, the totality is included. Mind, Buddha, and living beings are as a whole ultimately equal; so we know that when they are deluded, people follow things, and since things have myriad differences people are not the same. But when people are enlightened, things follow people, everyone has one wisdom that clarifies myriad objects.

When words are exhausted and thought is ended, what is effect, what is cause? The essence is fundamentally silent—what is the same, what is different?

Just forget what's on your mind, be empty and clear, and your comings and goings will be peaceful and harmonious, like moonbeams penetrating water, immaterial yet visible, unmindingly mirroring images, reflective yet always empty.

[102]

National Teacher Zhong asked an imperial attendant monk, "What does 'Buddha' mean?"

The imperial attendant said, "It means enlightened."

The national teacher said, "Was Buddha ever deluded?"

The imperial attendant said, "No."

The national teacher said, "Then what's the need for enlightenment?"

The imperial attendant had no reply.

Dahui said in his behalf, "If you don't plunge into the water, how can you be promoted over others?"

[103]

In the process of burning a clearing in the mountains, Master Dasui saw a snake; tossing it into the fire with his staff, he clucked his tongue and said, "You still won't give up this physical body on your own; for you to die here will be like finding a lamp in the dark."

Then a monk asked, "Is there any sin at such a time?"

Dasui said, "When a stone tiger roars, the mountain valleys echo; where a wooden man yells, an iron ox is startled."

Also, he asked a monk, "Where are you going?"

The monk said, "To the western mountains to live in a hut."

Dasui said, "If I call you in the eastern mountains, will you be able to get there?"

The monk said, "No."

Dasui said, "Then you are not yet able to live in a hut."

The monk asked, "What is the master's own way?"

Dasui said, "Painting a winnowing basket with red earth."

"What is the logic of this?"

Dasui said, "The winnowing basket has lips so the rice can't jump out."

[104]

When Master Huanglong Nan was dwelling at Tong-an, he addressed the assembly in these terms:

Today, the eighth day of the fourth month, is our Buddha's birthday, when all the monasteries in the land "bathe baby Buddha." I remember when Cloth Robe Zun was the acting shrine keeper in the congregation at Yaoshan, in the course of the Buddha-bathing rite Yaoshan asked, "You've just managed to bathe this one; can you bathe that one?"

Zun said, "Bring that one."

Yaoshan let the matter rest.

The ancients spoke a word or half a phrase according to the time, and without artifice or mysteriousness. People today try their darnedest to deal with them, without ever reaching their realm.

Some people say "'This one' is the bronze statue, while 'that one' is the reality body. The bronze statue has form and so can be washed, but how can you wash the body of reality? Yaoshan only knew the one, not the two; when Zun pushed back, he could only frown, overcome by shame."

They also say, "When the ancients posed questions, they just wanted to test people. If they ask you about 'that one' and you then talk about 'that one,' this is actually chasing sound and form, gnawing their words, walking into their trap. Yaoshan stopped because he saw he didn't understand."

They also say, "This approach of Yaoshan is already creating an issue where there was none, gouging a wound in healthy flesh. Mr. Zun didn't see the ailment coming up, and added more moxa on top of a cautery scar."

Some say, "When the ancients had attained realization, they performed according to the venue, without any right or wrong, high or low. Both knew what was, but after this people of later times insisted on making up discriminations."

Interpretations like these are due to failure to meet enlightened people. Once they lose the source, they wander off, never to return. That is why they just go by the conscious mind's thinking and comparison, taking this to be the vehicle to the source. What they don't realize is that contrived thought comes from a specific mentality, so to use this thought to discern the sphere of enlightenment is like trying to burn the polar mountain with a firefly's "fire"—it will never kindle, even in a million years.

Therefore high-minded people traveling on foot should look for themselves—what should be done about the perennial concern? What do you use to counter birth and death? Don't let a little bit of flighty and crude conscious vision create an obstacle for you. Buddhism is not this way.

Today I have not avoided verbal activity in order to explain the interaction of these two venerable adepts, showing no winning or losing. Thirty years hence, don't bring it up wrongly.

[105]

Master Yangqi said to an assembly,

Expressions of being and expressions of nonbeing are like vines clinging to a tree; Manjushri and Vimalakirti go home without doing anything about it. Even my speaking thus is also watching a hole being plugged. There is something yet to say—don't misquote.

Dahui remarked, "Profit moves a gentleman."

[106]

When National Teacher Yan first called on Xuefeng, as soon as he entered the gate Xuefeng grabbed him and stopped him, saying, "What is it?" Released, Yan attained enlightenment. He raised his hand and waved it. Xuefeng said, "Are you rationalizing?" Yan said, "What rationale is there?" Xuefeng then gave him the seal of approval.

[107]

Master Zhenjing, in an address to an assembly, held up his staff and said,

"The heart of nirvana is easy to understand; the knowledge of differentiation is hard to clarify."

An ancient said, "If you have support, I give you support; if you have no support, I take your support away." I am not that way. If you have support,

I take your support away. If you have no support, I give you support. Now tell me, which of us is right?

[Tossing down his staff:] What is this?

[Silence.]

This is the Naga girl attaining Buddhahood all at once. Otherwise, it is Sunakshatra, falling living into hell.

TRANSLATOR'S NOTE

The Naga girl is a figure from the *Lotus Sutra*, a young girl who attained Buddhahood instantaneously. Sunakshatra was a disciple of Buddha who thought he had reached nirvana when he entered the fourth stage of meditation, and became so conceited that he "fell living into hell."

[108]

Master Daowu Zhen addressed an assembly,

Dongshan said, "Clouds are steaming rice on Mount Wutai, a dog is pissing skyward in front of the steps to the Buddha shrine. Steaming buns atop a flagpole, three monkeys pitch pennies at night." I do not concur. A three-faced badger treads on the moon; a two-headed ox grabs the mist. A blue rabbit wearing a crown stands on the cypress tree in the yard; a turtle without a shell flies to the sky.

You have seen through my complications; Dongshan's are extremely unusual. Even so, he only managed to go three or four steps, and didn't get past seven or eight leaps. Now tell me, where is the riddle? Today I don't begrudge anything—I'm giving it all away at once.

[Silence.]

Being overly polite diminishes a lord's character; not speaking is truly effective. Even if the ocean changes, it can't be communicated to you.

[109]

Letan Ying said to an assembly,

The stone gate is steep; the iron pass is impregnable. When you look up, there's layer upon layer, a thousand fathoms high. An iron ox without horns bursts through, drumming up waves throughout the ocean of Vairocana.

Now tell me, people, how do you say an expression of not getting into the waves?

[Silence.]

The expression has no time for Asanga's question; even now he is still a monk who sleeps in the meadows.

TRANSLATOR'S NOTE

Asanga was an Indian master, associated with the teaching of *vijnapti-matrata*, "consisting of representation," according to which the world as we conceive it is not objective reality per se but a representation, a mental construction interpreting the data of sense and perception.

[110]

Master Baoning Yong said to an assembly,

People of today use what belonged to people of the past; people of the past made what people have today. Past and present have no back or front; present and past, how many know? Huh? Whoo, whee—when one nine and two nines meet, neither makes a move.

[He also said,]

Seedless spiritual sprouts are planted in fire, iron flowers bloom in the trees. Suddenly a round fruit forms; when it's pointed out to people of the time, they can take care of it.

[111]

Master Huaitang said to an assembly,

The proposition of being and the proposition of nonbeing are like vines clinging to a tree—you people may nod your heads for the moment, but when the tree falls and the vines wither, you have no strategy to challenge the heavens and no tactics to enter the earth. If a spiritually sharp individual can set an eye here, he will see freely in all ways.

[Raising his whisk:] Sunlight fills the eyes—there's not a cloud for myriad miles. If this is under an overturned bowl, how can you blame me?

[112]

Master Huanglong Xin said to an assembly,

Bodhidharma's school of mind has been transmitted up to the present without leaking a drop, without moving a hair. But if it does not move at all, how is it transmitted?

The precious seal stands for the subtlety of the teaching; layer upon layer of brocade, the stitching goes through.

[113]

Guishan asked Yangshan, "Now that you are called a teacher, how do you discern whether those who come from elsewhere know what is or do not know what is; or whether they have transmission from a teacher or not; or whether they are literalists or mystics. Try to tell me."

Yangshan said, "I have a test. Whenever I see monks coming from elsewhere, I stand up my whisk and ask if they expound this elsewhere or not. I also ask what else the elders do elsewhere, leaving this aside."

Guishan said in praise, "This is the tooth and nail of the school of the source since time immemorial."

[114]

Yangshan asked a monk, "Where have you come from?"

The monk said, "The South."

Yangshan held up his staff and asked, "Do they speak of 'This' there?"

The monk said, "No."

Yangshan asked, "If they don't speak of 'This,' do they speak of 'That'?"

He said, "No."

Yangshan called, "Great Worthy, go join in the hall."

But the monk went right off. Yangshan called him again, "Great Worthy!" The monk responded; Yangshan said, "Come here." When the monk approached, Yangshan hit him.

Yunmen remarked, "Without the follow-up words, how could Yangshan have known the man?"

[115]

Master Yunju Ying said to an assembly,

Twenty years ago, when I was living in a hermitage on Three Peaks, Elder Xinghua of Weifu came and asked, "How is it when provisionally using a question for shadow-casting grass?" At that time my mind and thought were slow, and I couldn't give him an answer. Because he had posed the question so remarkably, I dared not offend him. He said, "I think you can't answer this question—it would be better to bow and withdraw." Now as I think of that time, it was hardly worth saying "What's the necessity?"

Later when a fundraiser went to Weifu, Xinghua asked him, "When the teacher on the mountain was living in a hermitage on Three Peaks, I asked him a question he couldn't answer. Has he been able to answer it by now?"

The fundraiser then quoted the foregoing talk. Xinghua said, "In twenty years Yunju has only managed to say 'what's the necessity'? I disagree. How does that compare to saying 'not necessary'?"

Sansheng said, "What it took Yunju twenty years to say is only comparable to half a month's journey for Xinghua."

Dahui remarked, "'What's the necessity?' 'Not necessary'—very tight, very close, meeting the situation face-to-face. If anyone can continue the last word, I'll admit you have met the two venerable adepts."

TRANSLATOR'S NOTE

Shadow-casting grass is used to cast a shadow on water, blocking the reflection of sunlight, in order to see into the water and discern whether there are fish below the surface. Using a question as shadow-casting grass therefore means using a question to probe someone's mind.

[116]

Master Yunfeng Yue addressed an assembly at Cuiyan,
  Is the Way far off?
  Whatever you encounter is reality.
  Is sagehood remote?
  Embody it and you are spiritual.
  Thus sound is used for Buddhist service in this world Endurance, while fragrant rice is used for Buddhist service in the world Accumulation of Fragrance.
  Here, I support and serve the countless Buddhas of past, present, and future in outgoing and incoming breaths, without missing a single one.
  The countless Buddhas of past, present, and future are my attendants; not one of whom fails to show up.
  Anyone who doesn't show up gets thirty blows of the cane.
  But do you understand?
  "Serving countless lands with this profound mind is called requiting the kindness of Buddha."

TRANSLATOR'S NOTE

The world Accumulation of Fragrance, and the use of fragrance to teach, comes from a scene in the scripture *Vimalakirti's Advice*, often cited in Chan literature, where it is emphasized that teaching and learning can take place through all the senses.

[117]

A monk asked National Teacher Zhong, "An ancient worthy said, 'The green bamboos are all the reality body; the clusters of yellow flowers are all transcendent wisdom.' There are those who disagree, calling this a false teaching, while there are also those who believe it, calling it inconceivable. I don't know what to make of it."

The national teacher said, "This is the realm of Samantabhadra and Manjushri, not something that ordinary and lesser people can believe or accept. It is entirely in accord with the sense of the scriptures of complete doctrine of the Great Vehicle.

"So the *Flower Ornament Scripture* says, 'The body of Buddha pervades the cosmos, appearing everywhere, in front of all living beings, going everywhere in sensitive response to conditions, while always on this seat of enlightenment.' Since green bamboo is not outside the cosmos, how could it not be the reality body?

"Also, the *Scripture on Transcendent Wisdom* says, 'Because form is boundless, wisdom is also boundless.' Since yellow flowers are not beyond form, how are they not wisdom?

"The meaning of words that are deep and far-reaching can hardly be construed by those who don't understand them."

Now the Chan traveler bowed and left.

Also, a lecturer on the *Flower Ornament Scripture* asked Master Dazhu, "Why don't you accept the saying that 'the green bamboos are all the reality body, the clusters of yellow flowers are all transcendent wisdom'?"

Dazhu said, "The reality body has no form; it takes shape in the forms of the green bamboos. Transcendent wisdom has no knowledge; it displays characteristics in response to the yellow flowers. It is not that transcendent wisdom and the reality body are in the yellow flowers and green bamboos. Therefore scripture says, 'The Buddhas' true reality body is like space; it shows forms according to things, like the moon reflected in water.' If yellow flowers were wisdom, wisdom would be the same as insentience. If green bamboos were the body of reality, then the green bamboos should be able to function adaptively. Do you understand?"

The lecturer said, "I don't comprehend the meaning."

Dazhu said, "If one has seen the essence, one may say 'yes' and one may also say 'no.' Speaking according to usefulness, one does not get stuck in affirmation or negation. As for people who have not seen the essence, if you mention green bamboo they get fixated on green bamboo; and if you mention yellow flowers they get fixated on yellow flowers. Mention the reality body, and they get hung up on the reality body; mention wisdom, and they don't recognize wisdom. So it all becomes argumentation."

The lecturer bowed, gave thanks, and left.

Dahui remarked, "People in the community, assessing this story, say that 'as the two adepts cut and polished this way, one got the substance and one got the function. Those who get the function set it up on a concrete basis; those who get the substance sweep away by abstraction. As it is said, "The abstract ground of the limit of reality does not admit of a single particle, but nothing is rejected in the context of enlightened service." Master of the truth oneself, one is independent of things; one may put down or lift up, without gain or loss.' This sort of view is referred to as dwarfs watching a play. As for my own view, I want you all to know together. Haven't you read the saying, 'Over the back of a broken-down donkey, there are plenty of green flies hovering'?"

[118]

Master Daning Kuan, addressing an assembly, held up his staff and said,
The essential life of former Buddhas, the encompassing order of later

Buddhas, are entirely herein. Put to use in the present, it makes clouds and rain; it makes auspicious atmospheres and events; it helps humans and angels; it goes out in life and in at death, appearing and disappearing in other worlds, folding and unfolding. Even if one's whole body were a mouth one could not explain it thoroughly; even if one's whole body were an eye one could not see it all. According with it is a moment of mindfulness, and an instant is an eternity.

[119]

Master Dongshan Chu, addressing an assembly, said,

Try to clarify the situation, and you blind yourself; try to stop thinking, and you miss the source. All things are in concert, but neither speech nor silence can express it.

This is not something subjective; don't create all sorts of attitudes. There is a separate discussion apart from the written statement.

But tell me, how do you discuss when detached? Are there any fine points for discussion? Clearly analyzing, clearly demonstrating, clearly expounding, clearly singing, so there is nothing concealed or covered, purely speaking dry-as-a-bone Chan. If you are a spiritually sharp Channist, as soon as you hear it mentioned you will astutely realize the point with your eyes closed. Is this not a matter of having your own perception?

Unfortunately, I rarely encounter such an individual. That is because here my words have no flavor, the food has no flavor, and the teaching has no flavor. Flavorless expression blocks off people's mouths.

Brethren, when you get here it is difficult to stay. If you can see clearly here, then you can tell clearly whether or not the honored abbots all over the land have arrived or not, whether they have penetrated or not.

Why? Because wisdom may be false or true, a path may be genuine or specious. Many just recognize what is in front of the gate or behind the house, using their ordinary mentality and consciousness, learning clichéd complications, piling up a load in their chests, claiming to understand Chan and the Way. Have they ever even dreamed yet of Chan or the Way? This is what is called working without having met an adept, only to become a mere curio in old age. Someday if you should come upon the true heritage, you'll see through past activities and finally regret them, seeing your original birth star.

A monk said, "Where knowledge does not fall into distinctions, please communicate without violation."

"Cake and candy."

"Before the mind is aroused, where are things?"

"When the lotus leaves in the pond move, you can be sure there are fish swimming."

"In the scripture *Vimalakirti's Advice*, all the people of higher goodness expounded the teaching of nonduality, but the layman Vimalakirti remained silent—what is the meaning?"

"If there are no eyes, you don't draw eyebrows."

"Illusion and nonillusion are not yet the ultimate paradigm for a student; what is talk entering into principle?"

"An eighty-year-old man's teeth don't wiggle."

[120]

Master Langya Jiao said,

Propositions of being and nonbeing are like vines clinging to a tree. When the tree falls the vines wither, a fine pile of rotten firewood.

Dahui remarked, "Langya very much appears to be mistaking a thief for his son, but even so it's hard to requite such a huge favor."

[121]

Master Ciming said to an assembly,

When we beat the drum here, the four major continents gather in the same assembly. The staff held sideways, it straightens out the universe and the whole earth. The bowl overturned, it covers worlds as numerous as the grains of sand in the Ganges River. Now I ask you people; where do you settle yourself and live your life? If you know where to settle and live, you eat gruel and rice on the northern continent. If you don't know, you eat gruel and rice on the long bench.

[122]

Master Wuzu Yan said to an assembly,

Those who can say a mouthful paradoxically don't know existence; those who know existence cannot say it. Now tell me, where is the fault? If you want to build a nine-fathom mound, don't begrudge a single basket of earth.

A monk asked Dongshan, "What is the eye of a guide?" Dongshan said, "A paper wick with no oil." Old Dongshan is not entirely lacking, but he sure is poor! If someone asked me what the eye of a guide is, I'd just tell him, "Blind." Why? For the moment I want to match:

> A paper wick with no oil—still quite extraordinary!
> It's not worth bringing up—who would know?
> Turning around, he remembers the road by which he came;
> Buoyant in the moonlight, he follows his feet back home.

[123]

Master Zhenjing said to an assembly,

Once this day has gone, our lives too are less; like fish without enough water, what pleasure is there in this? In the meditation and concentration of the two vehicles of individual liberation, quiescent extinction is pleasure; this they regard as true bliss. For bodhisattvas cultivating insight, delight in truth and joy in meditation are pleasure; they regard this as true bliss. For the Buddhas of past, present, and future, the four infinite attitudes of kindness, compassion, joy, and equanimity are pleasure; they are regarded as true bliss.

Shishuang said, "Cease, desist, be cool." This is called the pleasure of the quiescent extinction of the two vehicles of individual liberation. Yunmen said, "All knowledge penetrates unobstructed," then held up a fan and said, "Shakyamuni Buddha has arrived!" This is called the pleasure of delight in truth and joy in meditation. Deshan's staff and Linji's shout are the pleasure of kindness, compassion, joy, and equanimity of the Buddhas of past, present, and future.

Anything apart from these three kinds of pleasure is not to be considered pleasant. But tell me, is the congregation here within these three kinds or outside them?

The head of the manor has made soup-rice and is giving out cash donations; let's retire to the communal hall and all have tea. Ha!

[124]

Master Shoushan Nian said to an assembly,

Elders, do not shout blindly, or shout at random. Here I always tell you the guest is the guest all along, and the host is the host all along. There is no guest besides the guest, and no host besides the host. If there were two hosts or two guests, they'd be a pair of blind folk.

Therefore when I stand you should sit, and when I sit you should stand. When sitting, I sit with you, and when standing, I stand with you. Even so, here you have to set eyes on it quickly in order to get it. If the pupils of your eyes roll, then you're myriad miles off. Why so? It's like looking through a window at a horse ridden by—a moment's hesitation and you've missed it.

This being so, when you set your mind on this you must be thoroughgoing—don't flail in vain, or someday it'll cheat you. It's up to you. If there is some issue, approach; if not, goodbye.

A monk asked, "How is it when a bodhisattva has not yet become a Buddha?"

"An ordinary being."

"How about after becoming Buddha?"

"An ordinary being. An ordinary being."

"Before the flower of enlightenment has bloomed, how can one distinguish truth?"

"If the winter isn't cold, wait and see after December."

"Isn't this it?"

"Wrong."

"How is it when the signal hasn't yet been sounded?"

"Looking skyward, you don't see the sky."

"How about after it is sounded?"

"Looking earthward, you don't see the ground."

"You are a great teacher; why did you return to Mount Shou?"

"Not sitting on the summit of the solitary peak, I am always at leisure, accompanied by the white clouds."

"The four groups surround you; what doctrine do you preach?"

"Beating the grass to scare the snakes."

"How do you set about it?"

"Nearly could have perished just now."

"Please speak immediately, without using your tongue."

"When I come to this, I can't say anything—let's see you say something."

"That's still using your tongue—please speak otherwise."

"Today Shoushan has lost the advantage."

[125]

Master Shexian Sheng said to an assembly,

Bodhidharma's coming from the West was to communicate to the East direct pointing to the human mind to see its essence and become enlightened, standing out alone in the midst of myriad forms, teaching outside of things. Those who realize it are not obstructed in the slightest. Those who miss it turn their backs on awareness and get mixed up in sense objects; these are people of mediocre and lesser potential. You must be thorough; don't waste time. All of you have this; particularly when we use the meaning of Chan, specially communicated without dogma, the

Way is realized in a single saying, free in all directions, breaking through the skull, lifting off the top of the head—isn't this good?

A monk asked, "Please speak without falling into any relativities."
   He said, "Fallen."
   "What is the seamless memorial tower?"
   "Hair uncombed, face unwashed."
   "What is a home-leaver like?"
   "Tightly turbaned."
   "Then a householder is a home-leaver."
   "Crude hempen sandals."

[126]

Master Cuiyan Zhu said to an assembly,
   Ordinary people are obstructed by their interpretations; bodhisattvas are still not detached from awareness. [Holding up his staff:] The staff is an obstruction; what is awareness?
   If you understand, obstruction by interpretation creates an obstacle and you are not free. If you do not "understand" but return to the source, essence has no duality but expedients include many methods.

[127]

Master Huaitang said to an assembly,
   If you knock on space and make a sound, who can discern the note? If you knock on wood but it makes no sound, it's a waste of effort to lend an ear.
   It is not the phenomena before your eyes; don't create all sorts of attitudes. Occurrence and disappearance do not know each other; herein there is no back or front.
   Where the king of elephants strides, foxes and rabbits leave no tracks. When the moon reflected in the water appears, the wind and clouds are naturally distinct.

When you get here, the universe cannot contain you, heaven and earth do not know your name. A thousand sages stand down—who dares come forth and speak?

Good people, this requires that you sweep away your previous concept of life, your actions and doings, understanding and not understanding. Better you should go back to the mountains always whistling a single note deep in the mist.

[128]

Master Baofeng Ying said to an assembly,

A sage of the past said, "The moon over the river shines on the pines, the wind blows all night. On a clear night, what to do? The Buddha-nature, the pearls of the precepts, the seal of the Buddha-mind; fog and dew, clouds and mist, are clothing on the body."

Chan worthies, though the sage of old spoke in this way, it can be said to be lacking in salt and lacking in vinegar. As for me, I'd say otherwise. The moon over the river shines on the pines; the wind blows all night. On a clear night, what to do? The note of the shepherd boy's flute up on the range startles the crows, and they fly around the trees.

[129]

Master Wuzu Yan said to an assembly,

The Buddhas and Chan masters are born enemies; awakening to the Way is messing with clay. Uncontrived, unconcerned people are as if blind and deaf to sound and form.

So tell me, what would be right?

"Thus" will not do, "not thus" will not do either; so and not so will not do at all.

If someone were to suddenly come forth and say that "thus" will do, "not thus" will do, that so and not so will both work, I would simply say, "I realize you are making a living in a ghost cave."

[130]

Master Baofeng Jun said to an assembly,

The Great Way is everywhere; whatever you encounter, there it is. When the clouds open up, the sun emerges; the waters are aquamarine, the mountains are bluish green. [Suddenly he took his staff and stood it up.] Great Master Yunmen is here. He says that Guanyin Bodhisattva takes a penny to buy a cracker, but when she puts it down it turns out to be a dumpling. People, Yunmen only sees the sharpness of the awl; he does not see the squareness of the chisel. I am otherwise. [He threw down his staff.] Don't serve the king of emptiness midway along the road; make the effort to get home.

Yesterday someone came from Huainan, without news of the roads of Fukien; instead he said the great elephant of Jia province swallowed the iron ox of Xia prefecture.

Ha! What talk is this? It bowls over the land of the cloud-dwelling mountains with laughter.

[131]

Master Yungai Zhi said to an assembly,

"Always profoundly calm, right where you are—if you look for it, obviously you can't see it."

Even though an ancient sage spoke thus, temporarily making a model, if you get hung up on it and can't get out, you just cling to what belonged to an ancient.

If, however, you can get out, then you will have some accord.

I am otherwise. Mounted on a swift horse, I circle the polar mountain; crossing the mountain, I look for ant tracks.

How many are there who know?

[132]

Master Panshan said, "It's like hurling a sword into the air; there's no question about whether it reaches or not. The sphere of the air has no scar, and the blade of the sword is undamaged. If you can be like this, you'll be free from concern in every state of mind."

Dahui remarked, "Tsk, tsk, tsk! 'There's no such sword in my royal storehouse.'"

[133]

The day Master Dongshan Cong opened a teaching center, a monk asked, "A large crowd has gathered; the teacher has mounted the precious chair. Please expound the essential vehicle of transcendence."

Dongshan said, "Even going downhill, unless you run it'll be hard to catch up."

The monk asked, "Whose song do you sing? From whom did you inherit the way of Chan?"

"With a bamboo cane I hold up the moon over a thousand realms; in my bowl I store the clouds of India's five climes."

"When Deshan struck people as soon as they came through the door, this was still building a model, drawing a likeness. When Linji shouted at people as soon as they came through the door, he still did not escape rubbing eyes producing optical illusions. Apart from these two courses, how do you help people?"

"The sky is clear; it hasn't rained for a long time, but some clouds have sprung up in recent days."

"Later on, if people ask me Dongshan's message, how would you have me quote it?"

"The vegetables in the garden are extremely dry; fetch some water to sprinkle on the spinach."

"Where is a rootless tree to be planted?"

"A thousand years' estate is lost in one day."

"Why would a great sage from one state appear in public in another state?"

"If a gentleman wants something, he finds the proper way to obtain it."

"How is it when the ancient mirror is as yet unpolished?"

"It's not far from here to Hanyang."

"How about after polishing?"

"In front of Yellow Crane Pavilion, Parrot Island."

When he sent out a fundraiser, he addressed the assembly in these terms:

The path of leadership belabors the eminent people of the ten directions. "While the ground of reality does not admit of a single particle, in the methods of Buddhist work not a single thing is abandoned." It is for the sake of the pure community that they forgot their fatigue.

So if the whole earth is a single cracker, everyone in the world gets to eat. The only one who doesn't get to eat is the spirit of the desert, who angrily strikes a blow with a cane, such that tiles crumble and ice melts.

[134]

Master Mingzhao led a group to Yao Hermitage, where he held up a sash and said, "It's become too frazzled."

The hermit said, "Don't mistakenly acknowledge the zero point of the scale."

Mingzhao said, "Just right."

[135]

Master Nanyue Rang said to his group, "All phenomena arise from mind. If you reach the ground of mind, your activities will be uninhibited."

A monk asked, "Suppose a mirror molds an image—after the image forms, where has the shine gone?"

He said, "It's like your appearance before you were ordained, Reverend—where's that gone?"

The monk asked, "After formation of the image, why doesn't it reflect?"

He said, "Even if it doesn't reflect, you still can't deceive it at all."

[136]

Master Huayao Ying said to an assembly,

Seventeen, eighteen—say it and you're blind. Nineteen, twenty—people won't believe. I'd wait till a dead tree blooms and a cracker produces soup.

[137]

Luopu was Linji's assistant for a long time. Linji used to praise him, saying, "Who dares to stand up to the point of the lone arrow of Linji's school?"

One day he took leave of Linji. Linji asked, "Where are you going?" Luopu said, "South." Linji drew a line with his staff and said, "If you can cross this, then go." Luopu immediately shouted; Linji struck him once. Luopu bowed.

The next day Linji went up in the hall and said, "There's a red-finned carp who shakes his head, flips his tail, and heads south; I don't know whose pickling jar he'll wind up in."

[138]

Master Yangqi said to an assembly,

The spring wind is like a knife; the spring rain is like a balm. When order is working correctly, all beings are moved. You tell me, how do you express a statement of being truly grounded in reality? Come forth and try to speak where you surge up in the east and sink away in the west. Even if you say it, it's a verse of Liangshan.

Liangshan was a master of the Cao Dong lineage; according to *Transmission of Light*, "Liangshan often spoke of inner being in his teaching."

[139]

When Master Fashang Yu received an invitation while at Twin Ridge, in taking leave of the two assembly leaders Ying and Sheng he said, "We've been together for three years; there's nothing you don't know, but on examination, you're not free from leakage." Drawing a line with his staff, he said, "Leaving this aside for the moment, what about the task of the school of the source?"

Ying said, "The polar mountain rests on the nose."

Fashang said, "If so, you are standing on the edge of a cliff looking at the shoreline, a particularly sad scene."

Ying said, "A celestial spirit glares."

Fashang said, "Nevertheless, though there is no different road for sages and ordinary people, expedient means include many approaches."

Ying said, "An iron snake cannot bore in."

Fashang said, "How can one converse with someone like this?"

Ying said, "It's just because the strength of the roots is slight—don't resent the sunny spring." Then he drew a line too and said, "Leaving aside the work of the school of the source for the moment, what about this matter?"

Fashang slapped him.

Ying said, "This fellow from Zhang province is unable to behave."

Fashang said, "Given a view like this one of yours, if I didn't strike, what better time could I expect?" And he hit him again.

Ying said, "I called it on myself."

Ying and Sheng went together to the mountains to call on Fashang. Ying said, "You always liked to test the teachers all over; now why have you come to make a living in an ancient shrine?"

Fashang said, "Beating the bush is just to scare the snakes."

Ying said, "Better not make people blockheads."

Fashang said, "Why are you sticking your own head in a bowl of glue?"

Ying said, "An ancient said he lived in the mountains because he saw two clay bulls fighting go into the ocean; I wonder, what did *you* see?"

Fashang said, "Someday when you have a bundle of thatch over your head and someone comes and asks you, how will you respond?"

Ying said, "The top of the mountain is not as good as the tail of the range."

Fashang said, "Then you tell me—are you up to the task of living on a mountain?"

Ying said, "Using a hoe does not mean pulling a plow."

Fashang said, "Have you ever even dreamed of the ancients?"

Ying said, "How about you?"

Fashang spread his hands.

Ying said, "A prawn can't leap out of a basket."

Fashang said, "Don't try to compare a three-inch candle to the light of the sun."

Ying said, "And yet the open issue is still there—what about that?"

Fashang said, "Chan followers who try to keep control arbitrarily are very numerous."

Fashang also asked both men, "I wanted to come here to build a teaching hall. Tell me, what approach can be made in that direction?"

Ying said, "The thief is a small man."

Fashang said, "The warrior craps in his pants as soon as he's shaken up."

Ying said, "He's been through the pains of frost and snow."

Fashang said, "Since a bright pearl is naturally valued at a thousand pieces of gold, who would be bagging baby sparrows by the edge of the forest?"

Ying said, "It's like when you're holding your bowl you can't claim not to be hungry."

Fashang then pointed to Sheng and said, "You tell me now—what approach should be made?"

Sheng said, "Originally there is no order of precedence—don't force an arrangement."

Fashang said, "Where will I put you, you ass?"

Sheng said, "Go ahead and knock bricks and hit tiles all you want."

Fashang said, "You too are just an incompetent supervisor."

Ying said, "If there's a treasure worth a thousand pieces of gold, what's the need to bag baby sparrows?"

Fashang said, "When someone of the house to the east dies, the house to the west helps the mourning."

Ying said, "If you see inequality on the road . . ."

[140]

Yunmen said, "The reality body eats food, so the illusory empty body is itself the reality body. Where do the universe and the earth exist? Nothing can be grasped. Emptiness consumes emptiness—if you count on an examination, you'd think there should be such talk."

Dahui remarked, "To start off like a dragon but wind up like a snake earns people's dislike. The reality body eats food, emptiness consumes emptiness—can you call it nothing? My speaking like this, moreover, is making medicine for a dead horse."

[141]

Master Huanglong Xin said to an assembly,

Xuefeng said that the Buddhas of all times turn the wheel of universal teaching in the flames of fire. Yunmen said that the flames of fire expound the teaching while the Buddhas of all times stand there listening. Xuefeng and Yunmen try to outshine each other; but when the fuel is exhausted and the fire goes out, where do the Buddhas listen?

Don't sit clinging to the depths of the white clouds; don't burn people to death with cold ashes.

[142]

Master Dagui Zhen said to an assembly,

On the first night of the lunar cycle, the earth is boundless—who is cramped? On the second night, east, west, north, south, there is no handle. On the third night, Sudhana deliberately heads south to learn.

This is why it is said, when you let go, "thus" spreads its light; when you hold still, "sitting nearby" hides its radiance. Now tell me, is it right to let go, or is it right to hold still?

[A long silence.]

When the three dots of the Sanskrit letter *i* are written vertically, all things are spontaneously renewed.

A monk asked, "What is the Buddha in the city?"

He replied, "One does not stick a signpost in the midst of a crowd of ten thousand people."

"What is the Buddha in the village?"

"A muddy pig, a mangy dog."

"What is the Buddha in the mountains?"

"No people coming and going."

"What is an expression of the special communication outside of doctrine?"

"Can't be translated."

TRANSLATOR'S NOTE

Sudhana is the name of the central character of the pilgrimage story in the final book of the *Flower Ornament Scripture*. The three dots of the Sanskrit letter *i* symbolize the so-called three truths of emptiness, the conditional, and the middle way, a Tiantai Buddhist construct often used in Chan teaching. Verticality means simultaneity.

[143]

As Master Changsha Cen was gazing at the moon with Yangshan, Yangshan said, "Everyone has this; it's just that they can't use it."

Changsha said, "I'll have to employ you to use it."

Yangshan said, "How would you use it?"

Changsha kicked him in the chest.

Yangshan said, "Ha! You're just like a tiger!"

[144]

Zhimen Zuo said to an assembly,

It's been raining a lot for several days now, but tell me—where does the rain come from? If you say it falls from the sky, what is the sky? If you say it comes from the earth, what do you call earth? If you still don't understand, this is the reason an ancient said, "The course of heaven and earth cannot be forcibly altered by any people of the time." If you conceive interpretations here, that's putting an awl in your eye.

[He also said,]

In the blazing sun, self and others; in the clouds and fog, kindness and compassion; in the frost and snow, borrowing a clock; in the hail, hiding the body. But can you hide your body? If you can't hide, you'll get your skull broken by the hailstones.

A monk asked, "When the national teacher called his attendant three times, what did he mean?"

"Feeling sorry for the child, he wasn't aware of unseemliness."

"What does it mean to say that the national teacher disappointed the attendant?"

"Rich food is not for a sated man to dine on."

"What does it mean to say that the attendant disappointed the national teacher?"

"Efforts enough to powder the bones and pulverize the body would still be insufficient repayment."

TRANSLATOR'S NOTE

See below, chapter 163, for the story of the national teacher calling his attendant.

[145]

Master Baoning Yong said,

Shakyamuni Buddha taught for forty-nine years without ever saying a word; Upagupta filled a cave with tallies of initiates without ever initiating a single person. Bodhidharma didn't live on Few Houses Mountain, the sixth grand master didn't dwell in the Cao Valley. Who are the later generations; who are the enlightened predecessors?

This being so, "They are inherently unflawed—do not injure them."

[Slapping his knee, he looked at the crowd.]

Now we're fortunate to have peace in the land.

[146]

Master Baoning Yong composed a verse on the story of the wind and the flag:

> Broad and peaceful, the government highway
> Never prevents people from travel, day or night.
> It's not that the lot of them don't step forward,
> But brambles still spring up right at the start

TRANSLATOR'S NOTE

The sixth grand master, or Sixth Patriarch, of Chan, heard two monks arguing about a flag flapping in the wind. One said the flag was moving, the other said the wind was moving. The master said it wasn't the wind or the flag, but their minds that were moving.

[147]

Master Yunfeng Yue said,

Deshan used to cane students the moment they walked through the door; Linji used to shout at them the moment they entered the gate. See how these two old fellows suffered the same failure.

But things do not occur in isolation; occurrence must have a cause. I'm not taking it easy; I exert the utmost effort for the community. If you people bite the dust on level ground, whose fault is that?

[Silence.]

If you don't settle what should be settled, instead you'll find it in chaos.

[Suddenly he picked up his staff and chased the audience out.]

A monk asked, "Please speak immediately without vagueness."

The master said, "The polar mountain."

The monk hesitated, trying to think of something to say. The master hit him.

A monk asked, "What is the first essential?"

The master said, "A snake goes into a rat hole."

"What is the second essential?"

"A monkey climbs a tree."

"What is the third essential?"

"A villager's sandals."

"What is the substance of wisdom?"

"An arrow piercing a willow leaf."

"What is the function of wisdom?"

"The general loses his post."

"What is the matter under the Chan robe?"

"Bone inside skin."

[148]

Master Dongshan Chu said,

When there is a statement in a saying, this is called the dead word; when there is no statement in a saying, this is called the living word.

What is the living word? When it comes to this point, it's really hard to find people. If it's a matter of saying, "There's no way to set about answering," immediately upon seeing something, without stirring a single particle, without eliminating a single object, who knows how many there are, east, west, north, or south?

If you want to find anyone beyond the mud and water, with the eye to enliven people, expound the way of Chan and bring out the great matter; I don't say that there are none, but still they are few, simply because of failure to arrive at the source and consequently falling into the delusive objectifications of the storage consciousness.

Perceiving what has no name and no concreteness, no right and no wrong, but is everywhere in everything, they say they have attained a state of peace, and seek no more. If they are ever questioned, they knock on their chairs, hold up their fly whisks, and go on ad lib, acting out immediately, bobbing in a pit of foul water, playing with a tailless monkey, until the last day of their lives, when the drum has been beaten to pieces and the monkey has run off—in frantic confusion, they are helpless.

What can regret do then? If you are real Chan practitioners, you would prefer to freeze or starve to death than to ever put on stinking shirts like that.

[149]

The great master of Tiantai, the Wise One, recited the *Lotus of Truth* scripture on Nanyue. Coming to the place in the chapter on the Medicine Master where it says, "This is true diligence, this is called serving the Buddha with real truth," he realized the *samadhi* of the *Lotus of Truth*, attained independent mastery, and saw the whole assembly on Spiritual Mountain, still there.

Dahui commented, "How about those who have not as yet attained independent mastery? Do they see the assembly on Spiritual Mountain? If so, what's the proof? If not, just reciting "this is true diligence, this is called serving the Buddha with real truth" becomes an extraneous matter."

[150]

As soon as the Buddha was born, he pointed to the sky with one hand, pointed to the earth with one hand, walked seven steps in a circle, looked all around the four directions, and said, "In the heavens above and on earth below, I alone am honored."

Yunmen said, "Had I seen him at that moment, I'd have beaten him to death and fed him to the dogs, in hopes that there might be peace on earth."

Yunfeng Yue said, "Although Yunmen has a plan to settle a disturbance, he still has no way of positive self-expression."

Baoning Yong said in a verse,

> When primordial chaos is as yet undifferentiated,
> People are not yet awake.
> As soon as heaven and earth split,
> Phenomena subtly appear.
> Natural-born skills can sure be extraordinary,
> But in the end they lose out to the other's play.

[151]

Master Zhaozhou said,

This matter is clearly evident—even immeasurably great people can't get out of here.

When I went to Guishan, I saw a monk ask, "What is the meaning of the Chan founder's coming from the West?" Guishan said, "Bring me a chair." If one is a real Chan master one has to deal with people on the basis of one's own state.

At that time a certain monk asked, "What is the meaning of the Chan founder's coming from the West?"

Zhaozhou said, "The cypress tree in the yard."

The monk said, "Don't use objects to teach people."

Zhaozhou said, "I'm not using objects to teach people."

"So what is the meaning of the Chan founder's coming from the West?"

"The cypress tree in the yard."

Later Fayan asked Master Guangxiao Jiao, "Where have you come from most recently?"

Jiao said, "Zhaozhou."

Fayan said, "I hear Zhaozhou has a saying, 'The cypress tree in the yard.' Is this so?"

Jiao said, "No."

Fayan said, "Everyone who passes through here says a monk asked Zhaozhou what the meaning of the Chan founder's coming from the West is, and Zhaozhou said, 'The cypress tree in the yard.' How can you deny this?

Jiao said, "The late teacher really said no such thing. Please don't slander the late teacher."

[152]

Master Wuzu Yan said,

Yaoshan asked Shitou, "I have a rough knowledge of the twelve-part teachings of the three vehicles. I hear that in the South you point directly to people's minds to show them their nature so they become enlightened. I do not understand this; please be so kind and compassionate as to instruct me."

Shitou said, "This way will not do, not this way will not do; this way and not this way will not do at all."

When I was a student, I heard brothers discussing this, saying, "Even 'mind itself is Buddha' will not do; denial of 'mind itself is buddha' won't do either." If you talk like this, how dare you call yourselves Channists? Why? You still don't realize that old Shitou was equipped both culturally and martially; he was perfectly able both to hide and to plan.

As for my perception, I want everyone to know in common. If you only see the swelling of the waves, you do not see the dragon palaces in the ocean.

[153]

Master Tangming Hao said,

Manjushri, with his sword, travels freely on Mount Wutai. On the one road of Tangming, I stop the deceits of apparitions. Before the Buddhas of past, present, and future put forth teachings and vehicles, the swimming fish in the bottom of the net cannot cross the Dragon Gate. Fishing in the four oceans is just to hook fierce dragons; mystic talk outside convention is for seeking those who know.

If you bring up the message of Chan, even the polar mountain would shatter; if you explain Buddhahood and Chan mastery, the oceans would evaporate. When the jewel sword is brandished, the light from the hair between the eyes shines ten thousand miles.

I have set out a line of comprehensive explanation for you, choking you; how will you breathe?

A monk asked, "Those of dull faculties take to lesser teachings, not believing they can become Buddhas. How is it after becoming a Buddha?"

"You grab a unicorn in the water."

"Then one ascends to the high seat at once?"

"You ride an ox up to the Thirty-Third Heaven."

"When the ancients held up a gavel or stood up a fly whisk, what did they mean?"

"Riding an ass without shoes on."

TRANSLATOR'S NOTE

The supernal bodhisattva Manjushri represents wisdom; his sword symbolizes cutting through confusion. In China he is associated with the sacred mountain Wutai.

[154]

Master Ciming said,

All saints and sages apply the unconstructed truth, yet there are differences. Before us is Mount An, behind is Mount Zhu—what is the unconstructed truth?

[Silence.]

The following passage is long—I'll put it off till tomorrow.

[155]

Mazu said,

You should each believe your own mind is Buddha. This mind itself is Buddha. The great teacher Bodhidharma came to China from South India, transmitting the supreme vehicle's teaching of one mind, to get you to wake up. He also cited the *Lankavatara Sutra* to seal people's mind ground, lest in your confusion you fail to believe for yourself that each of you has the reality of one mind.

So the *Lankavatara Sutra* has Buddha's talks on mind as its source; the method of denial is the method of teaching. Those who seek the teaching should not be seeking anything—there is no separate Buddha outside of mind, no separate mind apart from Buddha. One does not grasp the good or reject the bad; one does not stick to either extreme of purity or defilement. Realizing the intrinsic emptiness of sin, thought after thought cannot be grasped, having no intrinsic essence.

So the world is only mind; myriad forms are stamped by a single truth. Whatever form you see, you are seeing mind. Mind is not mind of itself; it is there because of form. Just speak in accord with the time, in fact and in principle, and there will be no hindrance at all.

Enlightenment, the result of the Path, is also like this. Whatever is produced in the mind is called form; since you realize form is empty, therefore production is unproduced. If you comprehend the meaning of this, then you can dress and eat according to the season, developing the embryo of sagehood, spending the time according to events. What further concern is there?

If you accept my teaching, listen to my verse:

> The mind ground is explained according to the time
> And enlightenment too is simply peace;
> Free from obstruction, concrete or abstract,
> Creation itself does not create.

A monk asked, "How does one cultivate the Way?"

The master said, "The Way is not in the province of cultivation. If you speak of attainment by cultivation, whatever is developed by cultivation also decays. Thus you are the same as a disciple. But if you say that means no cultivation, you are the same as an ordinary man."

The monk also asked, "By what understanding can one attain the Way?"

The master said, "Your own nature is originally complete; just do not linger over good and bad things, and you can be called a practitioner of the Path. To grasp good and reject bad, contemplate emptiness and enter concentration, is all in the province of contrived effort. If you then seek outwardly, you will become further estranged, increasingly remote.

"Just end mental calculation of the world. A single moment of thought is the root of birth and death in the world. Just don't have a thought, and you remove the root of birth and death. Then you gain the supreme treasure of a sovereign of truth.

"For countless eons, people's illusions, doubts and distortions, falsehoods, egoism, and pride have combined into one mass. Therefore scripture says this body consists of a conglomeration of elements. When it comes into being, it is only elements becoming active; when it passes away, it is only elements becoming quiescent.

"When these elements become active, they don't say, 'We are active,' and when they become quiescent, they don't say, 'We become quiescent.' When preceding thought, succeeding thought, and intervening thought do not await each other, passing away into quiescence moment to moment, this is called oceanic concentration. It takes in all things, just as a hundred thousand different streams return alike to the ocean, all to become ocean water.

"Maintaining a single flavor while containing all flavors, dwelling in the ocean you merge myriad streams, like someone bathing in the ocean, using all the waters.

"Therefore disciples understand confusion, while ordinary people confuse understanding. Disciples do not know that the mind of sages basically has no stages or ranks, cause or result, or conceptions of gradation; cultivating causes to realize results on the basis of false ideas, they dwell in empty concentration for tens of thousands of eons. Even though they are already awakened, having awakened they revert to confusion. The enlightening beings look upon this as like the pains of hell, failing to see Buddha-nature because of sinking into voidness and stagnating in quiescence.

"People of superior faculties awaken as soon as they hear a real teacher's guidance, suddenly realizing the fundamental essence without going through steps, stages, or ranks. Therefore it is said, 'Ordinary people have changeable minds, whereas listeners do not.'

"Enlightenment is spoken of in contrast to delusion; since there is fundamentally no delusion, enlightenment does not stand either. Everyone has been absorbed in the nature of things for countless eons, never leaving absorption in the nature of things as they dress, eat, converse—the functions of the six sense organs, and all activities, are all the nature of things.

"If you do not know how to return to the source, but pursue labels and descriptions, delusive sentiments arise at random, and you initiate all sorts of actions. If you can reflect back for a moment, the whole being is the enlightened mind.

"You should individually realize your own mind—don't memorize my words. Even if you can explain countless principles, the mind is still not more; and even if you cannot explain at all, the mind is still not less. What can explain is your mind, and what can't explain is your mind as well.

"Even if you can project duplicates of your body, radiate light, and manifest eighteen transformations, that is not as good as going back to the dead ashes of self. Having drenched the dead ashes so they have no energy is a metaphor for disciples' mistaken cultivation of cause and realization of result. Since they have not drenched the dead ashes, they still have some energy. This is a metaphor for the work enlightening beings do on the Way as they mature unadulterated, so that evils do not influence them. "If you talk about the three treasuries of the Buddha's provisional teachings, you could talk for countless eons without exhausting them—like links in a chain, they never end. But if you realize the enlightened mind, there is nothing else."

Dahui remarked, "During the Jianyan [1127–1131], when I was leading the assembly at Bowl Peak, in the assembly leaders' dormitory there were two collections made by Chan Master Dongshan Cong, *Essentials of Chan* and *Halls of the Masters*. At the end of *Essentials*, words of the two masters Shitou and Mazu are cited as exemplars. An extract from a lecture of Mazu said, 'Therefore the *Lankavatara Sutra* has Buddha's talks on mind for its source; the methodology is the method of negation.' So we know there can be no doubt that later people mistakenly changed it to 'the *Lankavatara* says "Buddha said, 'Mind is the source.'"'"

"Chan master Yongming Shou, in his *Source Mirror Collection*, and Chan master Tianyi Huai, in his *Communication of Enlightenment* collection, followed the latter reading, so later students frequently followed it too, not knowing the original. They even went looking for this supposed quotation in the scripture. What a laugh! Don't they realize the *Lankavatara Sutra* is just a book about Buddha's talks on mind? Mazu's statements indicate the main message of the scripture; they are not sayings from the scripture itself. Tianyi said, 'When it comes to the method of negation, you can only employ it methodically.' This is Tianyi's indication that the expression 'method of negation' is not a scripture quote. So the *Source Mirror* and *Communication of Enlightenment* collections made by the two sage teachers were not necessarily wrong; probably these are simply errors of later transmitters. As a proverb says, 'When one word is copied three times, a *horse* and a *house* become a *hose*.' How true it is! If literate people read the *Lankavatara* and find there is no such saying, they will consider the citation in Chan Master Dongshan Cong's *Essentials of Chan* to be correct."

[156]

Master Shending Yin said,

A monk asked Shoushan, "How is it when nary a wisp has appeared?"

He said, "Meeting the founder of Chan on the road."

"What about after appearing?"

"Don't tarry in doubt anymore."

A monk once asked me how it is when nary a wisp has appeared; I said to him, "White clouds over the ridge." When he asked me how it is after appearing, I said, "Water flows at the bottom of the gulch."

These two sayings are worth gnawing on, looking at them from all angles. As for my sayings, they are like chewing on a piece of wood or tile, truly flavorless. You will only get them by seeing on your own and realizing on your own.

Understand?

The sky is high in the southeast; the earth is slanted to the northwest.

[157]

Master Tianyi Huai said,

Two thousand years ago, the greatly awakened World Honored One wanted to take a group of saints up to the Sixth Heaven to expound the *Great Collection Scripture*. He commanded the humans and angels of this and other worlds, as well as all the evil demons and spirits, to gather all together and accept instruction from the Buddha to protect the true teaching.

Any who didn't go were chased to the gathering by hot iron discuses hurled by the kings of the four skies. Once all had assembled, none did not follow the Buddha's directions, each vowing to protect the true teaching.

There was, however, a demon king who said to Buddha, "Gautama, I will aspire to enlightenment when all beings have attained Buddhahood, all realms of beings are emptied, and even the names of beings no longer exist."

One whose mind and heart do not change when facing danger is one with true integrity. How would you express a saying to put forth energy on behalf of Gautama? Ordinary spiritual powers, subtle capacities, intelligence, and eloquence are totally useless here.

Everyone loves Buddha, but when you get here, what is Buddha, what is a demon? Can anyone distinguish?

Do you want to know the demon? Open your eyes and you see light. Do you want to know the Buddha? Close your eyes and you see darkness.

With my staff I have pierced the noses of both demon and Buddha at once.

Dahui commented, "This critique by old Tianyi is indeed extraordinary, but even so he hasn't avoided dualism in speech. If he had stopped at the point where he asked what is Buddha and what is a demon, he would undoubtedly have caused people to wonder. But then he went on to say, "Want to know the demon? Open your eyes and you see light. Want to know the Buddha? Close your eyes and you see dark." This is quite indulgent. He also said he had pierced the noses of both demon and Buddha with his staff—this is adding frost to snow.

"I myself will say a word on Gautama's behalf. When the demon king said he would aspire to enlightenment when all realms of beings are emptied and even the names of beings no longer exist, I would say, 'I almost mistakenly called you a demon king.' This saying has two contradictions: if you can find them out, then it must be admitted you have Chan perception."

[158]

National Teacher Shao said,

The true source is but one; myriad virtues have no words. When confronting light straight on, it's like a diamond sword. This is how those who realize suchness attain true awakening in all places—on swordlike mountains, in forests of blades, in cauldrons of boiling water, in embers of fireplaces, at the impact of staves, at the sound of shouts.

Thus there is not the slightest appearance of change in the alternation of action and stillness, going and coming, coming to life and passing away; there is no appearance of difference. And there is no more understanding in terms of perception and consciousness.

Why? Good people, this is what is called the natural potential of the subtle essence, beyond the circuit of yes and no.

This is the basis of the saying "If you give life, I too give life; if you kill, I too kill"—the capacity of the universal ruler to give life and to kill interacts like a thunderbolt.

[159]

Master Daowu Zhen said to an assembly,

When a lion roars, a colt of even the finest breed jumps. Clear in the mirror of the ancient Buddhas, the solitary moon over the three mountains shines bright.

[Then he did a jig and got down from the platform.]

. . .

A monk asked, "How is it when one understands immediately upon con-centration?"

"A pestle tied to a rat's tail."

"What is Buddha?"

"Dongting is his parasol."

"An ancient said, 'When we came, we brought nothing; when we leave, we take nothing.' What does this mean?"

"Three lifetimes, or sixty eons, is still not a long time."

The monk said nothing. The master asked, "Understand?" The monk said he didn't. The master said, "Dongting extends hundreds of miles, but that still isn't big."

"What is the substance of being as is?"

"A demon bends its knees; the pupils of the eyes are black."

"What is the function of being as is?"

"A diamond pestle smashing iron mountains."

TRANSLATOR'S NOTE

Dongting is a large lake.

[160]

Lingyun awakened to the Way on seeing peach blossoms. He composed a verse on the occasion:

> For thirty years I sought a swordsman;
> How many times have the leaves fallen and shoots sprouted!
> But ever since seeing the peach blossoms once,
> I have never doubted anymore.

When he quoted this to Guishan, Guishan said, "Those who gain ac-cess through objects never backslide; keep it well."

Xuansha said, "He's quite correct, but I'll bet he's not done yet."

. . .

Dahui commented, "When something comes up in one house, a hundred houses are busy."

[161]

Master Yangqi said to an assembly,

When body and mind are pure, objects are pure; when objects are pure, body and mind are pure. Do you know what I'm getting at? The coin that was lost in the river must be retrieved from the river.

[162]

Master Deshan said to an assembly,

What concerns do you have, from morning to night? Isn't it that you want to show off by questioning me? I'm not afraid of you, but I wonder what doubts you have.

Recently, in this time of degenerate teaching, there are lots of groups of ghosts who run off at the mouth to others, claiming to be Chan teachers. I wonder how much Chan you have managed to learn—come tell me about it!

Your blind baldies at various centers have taught you to "practice"— how many Buddhas have you produced running to irrelevancies?

If there is nothing to learn, then what are you after? If you have learned anything, then try to show me what you've learned. But you'll have to be ready to take a beating if you say anything wrong.

You've been charmed by the old baldies in centers all over into claiming you are "practitioners" and rigidly posturing as if you were like enlightened people.

Don't use your mind whimsically; revolving in endless mundane routines is all because of state of mind. Why? Because when the mind is aroused all sorts of things arise.

If you can refrain from producing a single thought, you'll be forever freed from birth and death, and will not be bound up by birth and death.

You go when you want to go and sit when you want to sit—what further concern is there?

I see that wherever you go you determine to learn Buddhism in the assembly of some old baldy, taking on a load without concern for your body or life. All of you have had your eyes nailed shut and your root of life severed. You're like two or three hundred whores.

You say your regal sway sets up the banner of the teaching to open the eyes of later generations; but can you even save yourselves?

You talk of "practice" like this, but haven't you heard that Buddha went through three long eons of cultivation? And where is he now? He died after eighty years—how was he different from you?

Don't go crazy; I suggest to you that it would be better to stop and not be obsessed with anything. The moment a thought flashes through your mind, you're a minion of the devil, an immoral worldling.

You see me appearing in the world, and you all want to get together in groups of five and ten and come challenge me with difficult questions, hoping to tongue-tie and silence me. You're puppets! Why don't you come forth now?

If you fill a burlap sack with awls, you'd be quite skilled if none of them stuck out. I'd like to ask you what's true—don't be mistaken. You impulsively run elsewhere claiming to understand Chan and the Way, boasting and putting on airs. When you get to this point, you'll have to vomit it all out before you can realize freedom.

Just do not stick to sound and form externally, and do not conceive of subject and object internally. In essential being there is neither ordinary nor holy—what more would you learn? Even if you learn a hundred thousand marvelous doctrines, you're just a sore-sucking ghost; it's all mere fascination.

This void of mine might be said to exist, yet it is not existent; it might be said not to exist, yet it is not nonexistent. You might call it ordinary, but it is not ordinary; you may call it holy, but it's not holy. It cannot be placed anywhere, but it is the teacher of all your myriad things.

I do not mean to slander him about this, but this is why Buddha spewed out so much spittle of expedient means, to teach you to be free. Don't search outside. As long as you don't acquiesce, you want to collect unusual sayings and store them in your chest, so you can talk cleverly, getting by on glibness, hoping to be acknowledged by people as a Chan master, wanting to obtain a position of prominence.

If you entertain such views, someday you'll go to hell where your tongue will be pulled out.

Everywhere you go, you look for people to say you are a member of the school of the Chan founder, but when you are questioned about the fundamental matter, your mouths are like a wooden bolt, immediately shooting off about bodhi, nirvana, thusness and liberation, extensively quoting the verbal teachings of the triplex canon, claiming this is Chan, this is the Way, fooling the people at large.

What relevance has this? You are bringing our spiritual forebears into disrepute.

My perception is not that way. Here I have no Buddha and no Dharma. Bodhidharma was a smelly old foreigner; the bodhisattvas of the tenth stage are dung haulers; the equally and subtly enlightened are immoral worldlings; bodhi and nirvana are donkey-tethering stakes; the twelve-part canonical teachings are ghost tablets, paper for wiping pus from sores; those who have attained the four fruitions, the three ranks of sages, and those from initial inspiration to the tenth stage are ghosts haunting ancient tombs, unable to save even themselves; Buddha was an old foreigner, a piece of crap.

Good people, don't make the mistake of putting on a garment of sores.

What are you studying? Having eaten your fill, you talk about thusness and nirvana—do you have blood under your skin? You have to have a strong character before you can attain: don't be infatuated with sages, for "sage" is an empty name. Anyone who can present you anything from anywhere for you to cling to obsessively, produce interpretations for, keep carrying around and caring for, has in any case become delusive and aberrant.

This is the result of insisting there is something to acquire by learning. This is what is meant by sprites haunting grasses and trees, and wild foxes.

Here I have no doctrine at all to give you to interpret. I don't understand Chan myself, and I am no teacher. I don't understand anything at all; I just consume and excrete. What else is there?

I urge you to be free from concerns, promptly stopping your search: don't learn aberration and madness. Everybody carries around a corpse, traveling, licking up the slaver of the old baldies wherever you go. Imbibing their drivel, you immediately proclaim that you are going into *samadhi*, cultivating capacities, accumulating good deeds to nurture the embryo of sagehood in hopes of fulfilling the realization of Buddhahood.

I see such people as having poison arrows in their hearts, blinding needles deranging their eyes. They are the antithesis of our spiritual ancestors; they cause the plan of our school to stagnate. They say they are renunciants, but this way they consume the donations of patrons everywhere without being able to digest even water.

Don't calculatingly claim you venture to travel in foreign lands, not taking care of your parents at home—do you think there is no fault in that? Don't misuse your mind—the lord of the underworld will dun you for the cost of your footgear someday, put a ring through your nose and hitch you to a post to make you pay back the cost of your lodging. Don't say I didn't tell you!

You people sure seem lucky, meeting me coming out in public to untie you, uncage you, and unburden you, so you can be decent people. No state of being in any realm can contain you. There is no special doctrine besides.

This radiant void is unobstructed, free: it is not something you can attain by embellishment. From the Buddha and from the Chan founders, all have transmitted this teaching, whereby they attained liberation; the doctrines of the whole canon just put it in orderly arrangements.

You are people of the present time; don't seek somewhere else. Even if Bodhidharma were to come here, he would just tell you to be without affectations; he would tell you not to be contrived. Dressing, eating, excreting, there is no more "birth and death" to be feared, and no nirvana to be attained, no enlightenment to be realized. You're just an ordinary individual, without affectations.

Most important of all, don't fold your hands and pretend to be a Chan teacher, looking for a place to appear in public, talking cleverly to seduce the younger generation in hopes of getting people to call you an elder. Totally alienated from your real self, you only know a flood of subjective consciousness, hoking up oddities day and night, never ceasing, claiming famous names, titles, and heritage. I am not one of your gang: if I see a great master failing to discern good and bad, I criticize him for it.

As for you, just don't get obsessed with thoughts of reputation and appearance, terminology and rhetoric, maxim and meaning, objective representation, function and principle, good and bad, ordinary and holy, grasping and rejection, focus on objects, defilement and purity, light and darkness, being and nonbeing. If you get it this way, only then are you an unaffected individual. Then even Buddha cannot compare to you; even the Chan founders cannot compare to you.

Don't go running off flattening your feet—there is no special Chan path to study. If anything is attained by study, it is secondary or tertiary, an externalist view.

There are no psychic powers or capacities of altered manifestation to attain either. You say psychic powers are wisdom, yet angels, wizards, cultists with the five powers, and titans also have psychic powers—but are they enlightened?

Suppose you live alone on a solitary mountain peak, eat but once a day, sit constantly without lying down, practice prostration and recitation six times a day, and try to fend off birth and death with that: Buddha had a saying, "All activities are impermanent—this is the law that whatever is created must perish."

If you say you can attain by entering concentration, stilling the spirit, quieting down thoughts, well, some cultists have also managed to get into states of tremendous concentration seeming to last eighty thousand eons, but are they enlightened? Obviously they are mesmerized by false notions.

Buddha was not a holy man; Buddha was an old foreigner, a piece of crap. What I want of you is to distinguish good and bad; don't get stuck on personality and ego. Then you will avoid the language of "holy men" and the language of "enlightenment," becoming liberated.

Wonderful sayings and principles drown you and bind you. Why? If the deluded mind isn't stopped for a moment, this is how birth and death will continue.

Time does not wait for anyone: don't pass the days wavering and shilly-shallying. Time should be valued.

I'm not expecting you bumpkins to carry baggage—if you agree, then trust; if you don't agree, well, everyone has his own bowl of crap—take it away!

I also don't seek after your old baldies all over the place who occupy a site and preach Chan and Tao. You rush to learn from them and quote from them, but here I don't have any doctrine at all to give you.

You take what you get by question and study to be knowledge and understanding, but I can't go to the hell for liars, where tongues are pulled out—if anyone has anything at all to teach you, or says "there is the Buddha," "there is the doctrine," "there is the world to escape," they are all foxy charmers.

Do you want to know? It's just a void, with nothing to attain, pure and clear everywhere, radiant with light, thoroughly translucent inside and out. There is no affectation, no dependence, nothing to dwell on. What are you concerned with?

I'll just be an old beggar all my life, until the day I die. Though I live in the world, I'm not affected by it—where would I want to escape from? Even if there were someplace to go, that too would be a cage, where bedevilment can get at you.

Don't belabor your body and mind, for there is nothing to attain. All that is necessary is to avoid belaboring sound and form at all times; just set aside your activities hitherto, and you will suddenly shed bridle and chain, and forever remove cover and wrapping. When a single thought is not produced, then linear succession is cut off: without cogitation, without thought, there is nothing at all that can affect your feelings.

How can you even attempt to express this in words? You have a lot of intellectual understanding, but have you ever perceived "It" face-to-face? Renunciants and others up to the tenth-stage bodhisattvas with satisfied hearts cannot even find a trace of "It." That is why the celestial angels celebrate, the earth spirits offer support, the Buddhas of the ten directions sing praises, and the king of demons wails. Why? Because this void, leaping with life, has no root, no dwelling place.

If your eyes waver at this point, then you miss it.

Don't seek Buddha, for Buddha is a mass-murdering robber who has seduced who-knows-how-many people into the pits of the demons of lust. Do not seek Manjushri or Samantabhadra, for they are bumpkins. What a pity to be a fine, upstanding individual but take someone else's poison and then try to imitate the appearance of a Chan teacher, seeing spirits and seeing ghosts.

After that you'll go crazy, running around to other houses looking for gypsy women to tell fortunes. You have been slipped "fortunes" by ignorant old baldies who tell you to bow to the ghosts of "patriarchs," the ghosts of "Buddhas," the ghost of "enlightenment," the ghost of "nirvana."

The little whores who don't understand them ask, "What is the meaning of the patriarch's coming from the West?" The old baldies then hit their meditation benches, pretending that is objective representation; or hold up a fly whisk and say, "Fine weather, nice rain, good lamps," using clever words to create arbitrary categories, saying there is a "mystic path," a "bird's path," and an "outreach." If you hold on to explanations like this, that is like putting filth in a precious vessel, like using human waste for incense.

You are grown adults, just as others are—who should you be afraid of? You spend whole days slurping the snivel and drool of old baldies elsewhere, and wind up without conscience and shameless. How miserable—they make you crazy.

The result of this cause is clear. As water buffaloes, you will pull plows, your eyes bulging; your strength unable to rise to the occasion, you will be beaten on the back. This is for having stolen food and clothing from Buddhism, claiming you were "practicing."

If you do not understand the great principle, even if you pass through Buddha's belly, you're just a walking piece of crap. Never having met a good person, you readily accept the scenery at the doors of the six senses, spouting clichés as if they were mysterious words and marvelous sayings, colorful and fresh, without having any attainment of your own—it's just the snivel and drool of other people.

There is also a type who gather in twos and threes for discussion—where is freedom from affectation preferred?—winter and summer they glibly talk about Chan, with intellectual interpretation for understanding meanings and principles. You all entertain views like this, looking for some advantage. Is there any true principle like this? You'll go to hell someday; don't say I didn't tell you.

Wherever you go, you don't harvest a single vegetable, you don't gather a single bundle of firewood—one day when your luck runs out, you'll be eating nothing but grass. Consuming the donations of the faithful in vain, you only arbitrarily claim to be studying, even pretending to be Chan masters.

This is of no benefit to people. For your own part, in all your activities twenty-four hours a day your mind will stick to things; when you see people, you only want to seduce them, wagging your tail, pointing to one thing and talking about another. In the eyes and in speech unable to see in actuality, you just want to use imitative sayings to check understandings.

How am I different from you? Don't take the glibness of the moment and wind up ingesting others' poison, becoming like greedy whores with no morals, blind baldies and herds of sheeplike monks perverting other people and leading them into hell.

Don't read books in a trivializing way, pursuing slogans and mottoes, looking for competition. When one after another passes stuff like this along, when will you ever stop?

What I am encouraging is not a bad thing. You must have your own eyes to discern the pure and the polluted—are they words of a Buddha, or words of a demon? Don't let others confuse you.

The most wonderful sayings are all temporary expedients of Buddha. What is essential is to stop—don't rely on anything, or take in the words of others for intellectual understanding, discriminating near and far, forging superficial falsehoods, memorizing the idle words and long talks of others—all of this is conjectural thought.

I'm afraid you'll fall into a pit doing superficial acts of piety, robbed by mere talk, getting little but considering it enough, stationary in quietude, unwilling to progress further. Confused by things yourself, you get other people mixed up. You follow myriad doctrines because you don't believe there is fundamentally nothing concrete to the void; you can't augment it or diminish it.

You people are like crows, with bodies in the sky but minds in the trash, just looking for carrion to eat. Don't say I've never engaged in community discussion, that I holler mercilessly, without fear of the consequences. It's just because you don't keep to your own lot but race off to the four quarters to stand by others' doors, like banshees relating statements and passing on sayings, making up interpretations according to obsessions, tracks of mind not forgotten.

Not even standing on your own, you carry a corpse around all the time, wearing stocks and chains, traveling five hundred or even a thousand miles to come here and stand in front of me, as if you lacked the way of Chan—"Master, explain for us, instruct us!" I act with my whole being, clobbering and warding off you bumpkins, hollering at you thieving pieces of crap. You may put on impressive appearances, but you don't know good from bad.

For you to come to me is like meeting someone from the bayous and cooking up a mess of fish chowder. What I am aiming at for the time being is for you to put down your heavy burden, take off your stocks and chains, to be decent people. Do you consent?

If you consent, then stay. If not, go off wherever you will. Fare well. Goodbye.

[163]

The national teacher called his attendant three times. The attendant answered three times. The national teacher said, "I thought I was letting you down—who would have known you'd let me down!"

Dahui commented, "Did the national teacher see the attendant? Did the attendant see the national teacher?"

[164]

Master Xuedou said to an assembly,
    One who can fill a cloth bag with awls without any sticking out is an expert. My awls are sticking out—isn't there a Channist standing by who disapproves? Come forth! [A long silence.] Since you've all drawn in your heads, now listen to critical examination of the centers all over.

[165]

One day Xuedou asked a monk, "Have you bathed?"
    The monk said, "I am not going to bathe in this life."
    The master asked, "What is your purpose in not bathing?"
    The monk said, "Today I've been exposed by the master."
    The master said, "A robber doesn't strike a poor man's house."

[166]

Master Linji said to an assembly,
    Those who study Buddhism in the present time should seek truly accurate perceptive understanding for now. If you attain truly accurate perceptive understanding, then birth and death do not affect you; you are free to go or to stay. Don't seek the extraordinary, for the extraordinary comes of itself.

Past worthies since ancient times all had ways of developing people. What I teach people just requires you not to allow yourself to be confused by others. Act when necessary, without further hesitation.

Where is the ailment of students of the present time who do not attain realization? The ailment is in their failure to trust themselves. If you cannot trust yourself enough, you will frantically pursue all sorts of objects, spun around and changed by those myriad objects, unable to be free.

If you stop your mind from rushing, seeking thought after thought, then you are no different from Buddhas and Chan masters.

Do you want to know what a Buddha or a Chan master is? It's what's right there in your presence listening to the teaching.

When students cannot trust in this, they seek outside. Even if you get something by seeking, it's all just literary terminology and description—after all you don't get the meaning of living Chan mastery.

If you don't find it this time, you will go on changing, experiencing different states and conditions for a thousand lifetimes over myriad eons, pursuing good and bad objects, being reborn in the bellies of donkeys and oxen.

My vision is no different from Shakyamuni Buddha's; every day, in your various activities, what is missing?

The sixfold spiritual light has never been interrupted. If you can see this way, you'll be an unaffected individual for the rest of your life.

The world is unstable, like a house on fire. This is not a place you stay forever. The killer demon of impermanence is instantaneous, and makes no distinction between aristocrats and commoners, or between the old and the young.

Do you want to be no different from Buddha and Chan masters? Just don't seek outside.

The moment the light of mind is clear, this is the elemental embodiment of Buddha in your house.

The moment the light of mind is free of discriminatory thought, this is the blissful embodiment of Buddha in your house.

The moment the light of your mind is free of division, this is the temporal embodiment of Buddha in your house.

These three embodiments are you, the people present listening to the teaching. You have these capacities only by virtue of not seeking outside.

According to academics, the three embodiments are the ultimate ideal. In my view that is not so. These three embodiments are descriptions. They are also a kind of dependency.

An ancient said, "Embodiment is defined depending on meaning, while the land is defined on the basis of substance. For the embodiment of the essence of things there is the land of the essence of things." So obviously these are reflections of a light. You should apprehend that which is dealing with the reflections—this is the original source of all Buddhas; your homecoming takes place everywhere.

Your physical body cannot expound the teaching or listen to the teaching; your spleen, stomach, liver, or gall bladder cannot expound the teaching or listen to the teaching. Empty space cannot expound the teaching or listen to the teaching.

What is it that can expound the teaching and listen to the teaching?

It is something quite evident, right here, an individual independent light—this can expound the teaching and listen to the teaching.

If you can see in this way, then you're no different from Buddha and Chan masters. Just don't interrupt it anymore, at any time—whatever meets the eye is "It."

Yet, because "when feelings arise, wisdom is blocked; as mental images change, substance differs"—that is why you revolve in mundane routines, undergoing all sorts of suffering.

In my view, nothing is not extremely profound, nothing is not liberation. The element of mind has no form, but pervades the ten directions—in the eyes it is called seeing, in the ears it is called hearing, in the nose it smells, in the mouth it speaks, in the hands it grips, in the feet it walks.

Basically it is a single spiritual light, differentiated into a sixfold collective. With the whole mind void, you are liberated wherever you are.

When I speak in this way, where is my intention? It is just because you cannot stop the mind from compulsively seeking everywhere that you get into the idle devices of the ancients.

If you take my view, you preside over the psychic and magical Buddhas; the tenth-stage bodhisattvas with fulfilled hearts are like migrant laborers; the equivalent and sublime illuminates are peasants wearing stocks and chains; the saints and solitary illuminates are like sewage; enlightenment and nirvana are like donkey-tethering stakes.

Why so? It's just because you haven't realized the emptiness of the incalculable eons that you have these obstacles. If you were real true people of the Way, you wouldn't be like that.

Just be able to dissolve past habits according to circumstances, going when you need to go, sitting when you need to sit, without any thought of seeking Buddhahood. Why so? An ancient said, "If you're going to act in contrived ways to seek Buddhahood, then Buddhahood is a major sign of birth and death."

Time is to be valued. You just depend on others, superficially studying Chan, studying Tao, learning names and terms, seeking Buddhas, seeking masters, seeking spiritual guides, measuring conceptually.

Make no mistake about it—you only have one father and mother; what more do you seek? Turn your awareness back on your self and look.

A man once saw the back of a mirror and thought he'd lost his head—only when he stopped looking for it was he relieved.

Be ordinary—don't put on appearances.

There's a kind of baldy who cannot distinguish good from bad, who sees spirits and ghosts, points to one thing and describes another, makes the best of fair weather and foul—someday people like this will have to pay their debts, swallowing hot iron balls in front of the king of the underworld. Men and women of good families get charmed by these foxy devils, then hoke up wonders. Blind fools, they will be dunned for their food bills someday.

It is urgent that you seek truly accurate perceptive understanding.

Then you can go freely through the world, avoiding physical and mental derangement at the hands of this type of spiritual charmer.

Don't contrive anymore; just be normal. As soon as you form a mental urge, you're already mistaken. Just don't seek Buddhahood—"buddha" is a term. Rather, do you know what it is that is seeking?

The Buddhas and Chan masters of all times and all places only emerge because of quest for truth. People today who study the Way only do so in quest of truth. Only when you get the truth are you done; as long as you haven't gotten it, as before you revolve in mundane states.

What is the truth? The truth is the element of mind. The element of mind is formless, and all-pervasive. It is being used right here and now, but people cannot trust it fully, so they learn terms and expressions, seeking their conceptual assessments in writings. They are as far from the Way as the earth is from the sky.

When I speak of the teaching, what teaching do I expound? I expound the teaching of the mind ground, which can enter into purity, into defilement, into the ordinary, into the holy, into the absolute, into the conventional; and yet is not your absolute or conventional, ordinary or holy. It can give names to all the absolute and the conventional, the ordinary and the holy, but no absolute or convention, nothing ordinary or holy, can affix a name to it.

If you can lay ahold of it, then use it—don't fiddle around anymore. Only then will you accord with the mystic message.

My teaching is distinct from everyone else. Even if a Manjushri and a Samantabhadra were to come forth, each manifesting an incarnation before my eyes, and ask about the teaching, as soon as they addressed me I would already have distinguished them.

How can I do this? Because my vision is distinct—outwardly I do not grasp the ordinary or the holy, while inwardly I do not dwell in the fundamental. I see through the basic reality, and no longer doubt or err.

[167]

The Twenty-Fifth Grand Master of Buddhism, Vasasita, debated with the Hindu Venerable Anatman. The Hindu said, "Please discourse silently, without using words." The Buddhist master said, "If words are not used, who will know who won?" The Hindu said, "Just get the proposition." The Buddhist master said, "What is your proposition?" The Hindu said, "My proposition is there is no mind." The Buddhist said, "If there is no mind, how can you have a proposition?" The Hindu said, "The mindlessness I preach ought to be called a non-proposition." The Buddhist said, "You say mindlessness ought to be called a non-proposition; I say non-mind ought to propose a non-term." The Hindu said, "If you're going to propose a non-term, who can understand the proposition?" The Buddhist said, "You use the term non-proposition—what term does this designate?" The Hindu said, "It is to define non-proposition; this term has no designation." The Buddhist said, "Since the term is not a designation, the proposition is not a proposition either. Who understands, and what is to be understood?" They went back and forth like this fifty-nine times before the Hindu was silenced, believing in the Buddhist and acquiescing.

Dahui remarked, "Why was Vasasita so troubled? If I had been asked by the Hindu for silent discourse without using words, I would have immediately said, 'Your proposition has fallen through.' Now is there anyone who wants to debate silently with me? If someone comes up and says, 'Your proposition has fallen through,' I know you're making a living in a ghost cave."

[168]

Master Daning Kuan said to an assembly,

No thought is the source, no dwelling is the basis, true emptiness is the substance, ethereal being is the function. That is why it is said that the whole earth is true emptiness, the whole universe is ethereal being.

Now tell me, who can apply this?

The four seasons go on and on, the sun and moon are always light; reality basically never changes, the Way has no location. Adapt to conditions and you will be free; pursue objects and you will rise and fall.

In this land and other regions, you enter the ordinary and the holy, but tell me, how do you express going into a village and adapting to its customs?

[A long silence.]

Sanskrit in India, Chinese in China.

[169]

Master Yuanming said to an assembly,

The bequest of Spiritual Mountain has been transmitted to the ten directions. When Buddhas emerge in the world, that is called setting up a site of enlightenment and turning the wheel of universal teaching. This teaching is right in the immediate present; it is still far from the school of living Chan. Why don't the most advanced followers ask any questions?

[A monk came forward, but Yuanming said,] "Go, go! The road to India is very, very long!"

The monk asked, "What is the meaning of the assembly on Spiritual Mountain?"

"The initial illusion reaches right to the very present."

"What is the very first proposition?"

"Three lifetimes, sixty eons."

"Does someone who's experienced a great awakening have any faults?"

"Iron mountains stand across the road. Cut off the sunlight and sky and earth are dark. Those in a frantic hurry circle the earth, throughout every clime. At such a time, if Buddhas or Chan masters appeared they'd deserve a beating. But even so, 'while officially not even a needle is admitted, privately a horse and carriage can get through.'"

[170]

Master Jiangshan Fang said to an assembly,

It's not a matter of being able to say it or not; everywhere they take it for a marvel. Hanshan lit a fire, his hair got full of ashes; he laughingly scolded Fenggan, this old brigand.

"How is it when the lotus blossom has not yet emerged from the water?"

"When threading a needle, you don't like the eye to be too small."

"How about after it emerges?"

"Relaxing sorrowful brows all day long."

"What is the immutable icon?"

"Walking through town wearing a cotton shirt."

"I don't understand."

"Riding a donkey stepping through the waves of Lake Dongting. Passing through the three levels of waves, I single-mindedly listen for one peal of thunder. When you extend your hand, you can't even see your palm."

"Can I go forward or not?"

"You're stamping the earth while calling to the sky."

"A cloth drum is hard to sound at the gate of thunder."

"An embroidered ball can't be used to sew a scarlet banner."

"This saying will circulate widely after thirty years."

[Fang thereupon struck a blow.]

"A rushing stream crosses sword blades, fast flames pass spear points—do you allow your students to be tentative?"

"When the weather is cold and the days are short, the nights are even longer."

"The embroidered curtains are sewn with mandarin ducks—passersby cannot see."

"Inside the skull, the mettle to challenge the heavens."

"Teacher!"

"A chicken head but a phoenix tail."

"Everyone else washes in mud, but you produce a picture."

"I'm the guest today; I hope you'll be attentive. Even so, it won't do to let go."

[The master smacked the meditation platform once and got down.]

[171]

Master Xinghua said to an assembly at the opening of a hall,

This stick of incense is basically for Sansheng, but Sansheng was too strict for me, so it is appropriate for me to succeed to Daxue. Daxue was very generous to me. With Sansheng I learned expressions of host and guest—if I hadn't met Daxue, they'd have misled me all my life. At Daxue's, taking a beating I saw the logic of spiritual grandfather Linji getting a beating at Huangbo's. This stick of incense I offer to the late master Linji.

What did Buddha and Kasyapa discuss at the Shrine of Many Children?

When one person conveys a falsehood, ten thousand people pass it on as truth.

[172]

Master Wuzu Yan said to an assembly,

"Suchness," the "ordinary," and the "holy" are all dream talk; "Buddha" and "sentient beings" are both excess verbiage. If someone were to come forth and say, "What about the elders of Panshan?" I would just say to him, "If not for the early blooming of the flowers on the outskirts of the capital city, how could we have the orioles alighting on the willow branches?" If he went on to ask, "What about the elder of Wuzu?" I would say to myself, "Yes! Keep awake!"

[173]

As Zihu was hoeing the ground, he pressed down on the hoe. Turning around, he looked at Shengguang and said, "It's not that there's nothing to do, but if you've got an attitude, you err."

Shengguang immediately asked, "What is there to do?"

Zihu kicked him in the chest, knocking him down. At this Shengguang was enlightened.

[174]

Master Fahua Ju said to an assembly,

If you open your mouth, you're saying too much. Even if you don't open your mouth, that's still excess talk.

The imperial monarch hands down decrees, but the custom of a rustic shop is different.

[175]

Master Xuansha said to an assembly,

The true school of the ancient Buddhas always manifests in response to people, adapting with dignity, shedding light everywhere, evenminded in concealment as in the open, thoroughly aware of high and low.

This is why the eye of the Way is primary; merge with the fundamental and clarify the mind, for this alone is the end.

Myriad forms are one body, from the same source: when you open up, there is no boundary—who speaks of getting stuck?

The phenomena of countless ages are all in the immediate present, but people of the time have developed opposition to the eternal essence over the course of long years. Perceiving things with confused minds, they thereby turn away from the true source, fixated on being or stuck on emptiness.

Failing to meet good friends, or companions on the Way, they only go by their own subjective interpretations; even if they hold discussions, it is all speculative.

Even when it comes to finding out the ground of principle, you do not distinguish true from false—of course you have never fished out your self in everyday life.

As for the ancient worthies, sages of yore, they knew their own times. Mastering themselves, pressing on with their work, they lived in mountain caves.

An ancient worthy said, 'If your feelings retain a sense of holiness, you still fall into religious materialism. If your view of self hasn't been forgotten, it turns into affliction.'

It cannot be said that you will hit the mark by fasting, discipline, constant sitting without reclining, stopping the mind, meditating on emptiness, freezing the spirit, or entering concentration—what connection is there?

Cultists in India can go into trances lasting eighty thousand eons, freezing the spirit in utter silence, closing their eyes, mortifying their bodies and annihilating their intellects; but when that period is up, they cannot escape repeating mundane routines, all because their perception of reality is not clear and they have not broken through the root source of birth and death.

The unattached are not like this. They cannot be the same as those cultists; all of them truly understand and have great knowledge and vision, able to penetrate like the Buddhas, silently aware, forgetting conceptual knowledge, taking in myriad forms without resistance.

Right now, where is not you? Where is not clear? Where is not evident? Why don't you understand this way?

Without this state, what can you do about the various kinds of impulse? It all turns into falsehood—where is your everyday empowerment?

If you really haven't had an awakening yet, then you need to be urgent about it at all times, even if you forget to eat and lose sleep, as if you were saving your head from burning, as if you were losing your life. Concentrate deeply to liberate yourself—cast aside useless mental objects, stop mental discrimination, and only then will you have a little familiarity.

Otherwise, one day you will be carried away by consciousness and emotion—what freedom is there in that?

Now there's no comparison to the clarity of the exposition of inanimate objects. The earth, the trees, the stones—they expound the teaching with exceptional veracity; it's just that few people can hear it.

If you do hear this exposition, only then can you discuss it.

But tell me, how do you discuss the teaching expounded by the inanimate? Let's see you try to say. Don't tell me they have "no speech, no explanation, no seeing, no hearing." And don't tell me they "explain without being asked, lauding their own course."

Haven't you read [in the *Flower Ornament Scripture*] how the youth Sudhana visited fifty-three advisers, finally meeting Maitreya? In a finger snap he gained entry through the door; once he had entered the door, it shut by itself.

Inside the tower he saw the past deaths and reincarnations of a hundred thousand Buddhas, and one hundred and twenty advisers on whom he called, as projected scenes inside the tower, all appearing at the same time, witnessing and testifying to enlightenment for him. Sudhana's doubts ceased all at once.

Anyone who has this discovery of true reality can discuss it. Then being in the rough and tumble of the ordinary world is the same as being in the pure lands of the Buddhas. What birth and death would you fear anymore?

Who knows that all the teachings have no real substance?

Even Kasyapa's inner hearing at the assembly on Spiritual Peak was like talking about the moon.

The saying of the ancient worthy, "Don't think good or bad at all" is the same as pointing at the moon.

All the practices and stages of the three vehicles, liberation, bodhisattvas, nirvana, holy virtues, and sanctification are all like flowers in the sky, horns on a rabbit.

Haven't you heard it said, "When you come back and observe the world, it's like something in a dream." Contrived mental states are not to be relied upon; over the long run, they are of no benefit.

It is just because you veer away from reality and abandon the root that you try to detach from ordinary feelings and break down your mind on a religious path. If you entertain views like this, you will not get out of their limitations and won't be able to dispense with their mental and physical elements.

Haven't you heard it said, "All activities are impermanent—this is the law that whatever is originated passes away." You just try to forge ahead—how can you understand what's right here?

Only when you have penetrated can you know this.

If you have not yet found out, you should know they are all vain, mundane, unbelievable things. Only if you have great basic capacity can you understand them.

If you can just penetrate now, it'll be thus forever. An ancient worthy said, "You should finish in this life—who can take on leftover misfortune for eons on end?"

[176]

Master Langya Jiao said to an assembly,

Go forward and you die; retreat and you perish. If you neither advance nor retreat, you fall into the realm of indifference.

Why so?

"Although the capital city is fun, it's not a place for a long stay."

Dahui remarked, "Weeping tears of blood is no use; it's better to get through the rest of spring keeping your mouth shut."

[177]

Master Yangqi Hui held up a staff and said to an assembly,

One is all, all are one. [Drawing a line:] Mountains, rivers, the whole earth, and all the old masters in the world are shattered—what are your nostrils? [A long silence.] A sword is drawn from the jeweled scabbard on account of iniquity; medicine is taken out of the gold bottle on account of illness.

[178]

Master Guanxi Xian said to an assembly,

There are no walls in the ten directions, and no gates in the four quarters; bare, naked, there is nothing to grasp.

"Why did the founder of Chan come from the West?"

"A bowl full of rice, a container full of soup."

"I don't understand."

"When hungry, eat; when full, stop."

"Long have I heard of Guanxi, the Pouring Stream, but now that I get here I only see a flax-soaking pond."

"You only see the flax-soaking pond, not the pouring stream."

"What is the pouring stream?"

"Swift as an arrow."

[179]

Elder Huo called on Deshan. As soon as Deshan saw him, he made as if to take out his seat cloth. The elder said, "Leaving this aside for the moment, if someone comes with mind and environment unified, what would you say to him to avoid being criticized everywhere?"

Deshan said, "You're still three steps short of past days; come back as an independent individual."

The elder thereupon shouted.

Deshan didn't reply.

The elder said, "I've choked the old fox."

Guishan heard this story told. He remarked, "The elder may have gotten the advantage, but nevertheless he was covering his ears to steal a bell."

[180]

An, "the Iron Lion," was at Fengxue, sitting by the fireside, when a certain minister of education came to visit. Seeing An there, he immediately asked, "How do you get out of the burning of the world?"

An picked up a poker and stirred the fire. The minister tried to think of something to say. An said, "Minister of education, minister of education."

[181]

When Sansheng called on Deshan, as he was about to spread out his seat cloth to bow, Deshan said, "Stop—don't spread your picnic cloth here; we have no leftovers to give you."

Sansheng said, "Lucky there are none—if there were, where would you put them?"

Deshan hit Sansheng. Sansheng caught the cane and pushed Deshan over. Deshan laughed. Sansheng cried, "Heavens!" and left the audience hall.

The chief monk asked, "High-minded people on pilgrimage should attain objective proof of the fundamental way; what is objective proof of the fundamental way?"

Sansheng said, "What did you say?"

The chief monk asked again. Sansheng hit him with his seat cloth and said, "Ignoramus! How many decent people have you offended?"

As the chief monk was about to exchange courtesies, Sansheng walked past him to the second-ranked monk and extended his courtesies to him.

[182]

Master Dayu Zhi, addressing an assembly, quoted Panshan's verse, saying, "The light is not illumining objects, and the objects are not even there. When light and objects are both forgotten, then what is this?" Now the master held up his whisk and said, "The lights of Buddhas numerous as atoms are all here, irradiating your hearts, livers, and guts. Don't speak of it in the presence of a Chan monk; you'd best watch your mouth!"

At an informal gathering, he said to an assembly, "The reverberations of a single clang, crystal clear, resound throughout the universe; even as one who knows lends an ear, the enemy has already crossed the river. Understanding thus is like taking a donkey saddle ridge for your father's lower jawbone."

[183]

Master Cuiyan Zhen quoted a story about Huangbo when he was the head of the assembly at Nanquan's and the workman Gan Zhi requested a distribution of money. Huangbo said, "Disbursal of money and teaching are equal." The worker carried the money out of the hall. In a moment he came back and again asked for a distribution of money. Huangbo said, "Disbursal of money and teaching are equal." Now the workman went around handing out the cash.

Master Cuiyan Zhen said, "As for the workman, 'a clever lad loses his profit.' As for Huangbo, when did he ever dream of material giving?"

Dahui commented, "The run of the mill follow perverts and criminals; this cloud-dwelling saint is a bit better."

[184]

Master Gushan said to an assembly,

If you have not yet mastered the great task, and have not tapped the artery of the source, avidly memorizing words and phrases is making a living in conceptual consciousness. Haven't you read the saying "Conception is a robber; consciousness makes waves in which everyone is drowned, without any freedom."

If you have not yet penetrated the great matter, it's best to stop, ceasing all striving, so body and mind are simple and serene. Refrain from fixation at all times, and the matter will actually be easily revealed.

This is something I say to you by way of encouragement, just because I have no choice. The ancients called it medicine for a dead horse. If it is a realized individual, talking to someone this way is like talking in your sleep.

Now what about you—can you actually use a single word from the twelve-part teachings? Can you actually use a single phrase from the sayings of the adepts? If it is the twelve-part teachings, which teaching are you in? If it is the sayings of the adepts, in what saying will we find you?

Therefore it is said that the twelve-part teachings cannot express it, ordinary and sacred cannot contain it, the passage of time cannot move it, verbal expression cannot cover it.

Talk like this is generally for people who've gotten their heads stuck in doctrine, to free them up; but if you talk this way to someone who's never given a hint of that, he'll grab you and ask why you're babbling nonsense—and you can't blame him.

You must be very discerning. Do not fail to distinguish the auspicious from the ominous. If anyone can distinguish, come forth and demonstrate it.

[185]

Master Huanglong Nan said to an assembly,

Haklena appeared in disguise in the sky; Manora pointed to the earth and produced a spring. In Deshan's school, that's incomparable, but in Linji's school it only gets one side. [A long pause.] What is the Other Side?

TRANSLATOR'S NOTE

Haklena and Manora were Indian forerunners of Chan. Their enlightenment stories are retold in *Transmission of Light*.

[186]

A monk asked Nanyuan, "Where have the sages since time immemorial gone?"

He replied, "If not to heaven, then to hell."

The monk asked, "What about you, Master?"

He replied, "Do you know where I'll wind up?"

The monk hesitated, trying to think of something to say. The master hit him with his fly whisk. Then he told the monk to approach and said, "The command is for you to exercise," and he hit him again.

Xuedou said, "Since the command went into effect on its own, the whisk was ignorant of the reason. I say 'Blind!' just to add frost to snow."

Dahui commented, "Balancing the three essentials and three mysteries of Linji must be credited to that Nanyuan—then why does Xuedou say the whisk was ignorant of the reason? I too say 'Blind!' just hoping both can get to meet."

[187]

Baizhang asked Zhaozhou, "Where have you just come from?"

Zhaozhou said, "Nanquan."

Baizhang asked, "What statements does Nanquan have?"

Zhaozhou said, "People who have not yet attained should simply be still."

Baizhang immediately shouted.

Zhaozhou made a gesture of fright.

Baizhang said, "Fine stillness!"

Zhaozhou danced a jig and left.

[188]

When Chan Master Jing of Mount Sikong was questioned by students, he would answer with verses. Here are three that are recorded:

The four gross elements have no owner; like flowing water,
They meet the crooked and the straight without "that" or "this."
When minding neither purity nor pollution,
How could blockage or free flow divide consciousness?
When coming in contact with the world of objects, just be like
        water;
In the world without minding, what problem is there one way or
        another?

Seeing, hearing, awareness, knowledge—there is no obstruction.
Sound, scent, flavor, feeling—these are perpetual *samadhi*.
Neither grasping nor rejecting, no love or hate,
If you can respond to situations basically not minding,
Then you can finally be called independent observers.

Only when you've seen the Way do you practice the Way—
If you don't see, what do you practice?
The emergence of the Way is like space—
What is there to cultivate in space?
Those who practice the Way by all kinds of contemplation
Are stirring fire looking for foam.
Just observe the manipulation of the puppets—
When the strings are cut, it all stops at once.

[189]

Deshan asked the administrator, "How many people are here for the first time today?"

The administrator said, "Eight."

Deshan said, "Call them and we'll try them all at once."

[190]

Master Zhenjing said to an assembly on disbanding the summer retreat,

Does anyone have any questions? [Hitting his meditation bench once with his fly whisk:] The natural mechanism of the universe includes negative and positive, life-giving and death-dealing.

The shining of the sun and moon is sometimes bright and sometimes dim, sometimes hidden and sometimes clear.

The flow of rivers may be high or low, constricted or free.

In the governments of enlightened rulers, there is leadership and administration, there is ceremony and music, there is reward and punishment.

In the existence of Buddhas in the world, there are sudden and gradual, there are temporary and true, there are joining and disbanding.

The joining is on the fifteenth day of the fourth month, when all the holy and ordinary of the whole world, even the plants and the rocks [tapping to his left with the whisk] join together all at once from *here* [holding up the whisk]. They're all on the whisk—see? [Shouting once, he continued:] As for the fifteenth day of the seventh month, the rocks and the trees throughout the world, and the holy and the ordinary [tapping to his right with the whisk] disband all at once from *here*. [Shouting, he continued:] How about before the fifteenth day of the fourth month and after the fifteenth day of the seventh month? Is it in session or out? [Holding up the whisk:] It's all on the whisk—do you see?

[Then he shouted and said,] Eminent worthies, in these three shouts, there is one shout that is an adamantine diamond sword, one shout that is a crouching lion, and one shout that is a test. If people can distinguish each one of them, then they can see the great master Linji's way goes beyond ordinary sense—even Huangbo got slapped, even Dayu got punched. Even though two or three centuries have passed since then, I would admit that you can personally become his direct heirs.

After that, you can open up the door of nonduality, balancing the paths of the various masters, smashing falsehood and revealing truth, supporting the school and establishing the teaching, repairing the deteriorated order, freely exercising great knowledge and vision, with the eye of universal truth shining, decisively defeating the army of the devil without stirring from the fundamental state.

[Shout.] You should know there's a shout that doesn't act as a shout. When you get here, you have to have the adamantine eye to suddenly pick up before making a mess.

But tell me, eminent worthies—pick up what? [After a long silence, he shouted one shout.]

[191]

Master Letan Jun said to an assembly,

This morning is the tenth day of the twelfth month. Last night it snowed, and the ridges are all white, as far as the eye can see, high and low; the green bamboo and pines are hard to distinguish. Next year's silkworms will mature and the wheat will ripen and everyone will rejoice, drumming their bellies and singing and laughing unceasingly, taking up panpipes, playing wildly, dancing around, forgetting themselves.

[Shouting a shout:] When Chan travelers meet, they just snap their fingers; how many people can know what this means?

[192]

A Hindu king asked Parati, "What is Buddhahood?"

Parati said, "Seeing nature is Buddhahood."

The king asked, "Do you see nature?"

Parati said, "I see the nature of Buddhahood."

The king asked, "Where is the nature?"

Parati said, "The nature is in function."

The king asked, "What function is this? I don't see it now."

Parati said, "It is functioning now; it's just that you yourself don't see."

The king asked, "Does it exist in me?"

Parati said, "If you do anything, it is there; if you don't use it, though, the substance is invisible."

The king asked, "When it is used, how many places does it appear?"

Parati said, "If it appears, there must be eight."

The king said, "Please explain those eight appearances for me."

Parati said, "In the womb, it is called the body. In the world, it is called the person. In the eyes, it is called seeing. In the ears, it is called hearing. In the nose, it distinguishes smells. In the tongue it talks. In the hands it grips; in the feet it steps. It manifests everywhere, including the universe, concentrating it in an atom; those who know realize it is the Buddha-nature, while the undiscerning call it the spirit."

When the king heard that, his mind opened up and awakened.

Dahui commented, "Right now I dare ask you all—which is Buddha-nature, which is spirit?"

[193]

Devadatta slandered Buddha and so fell into hell while still alive. Buddha had Ananda relay a message to him: "Are you comfortable in hell?" Devadatta said, "Even though I'm in hell, I'm as blissful as in the third meditation heaven." Buddha also had Ananda ask, "Do you want to get out?" Devadatta said, "When the Buddha comes, then I'll leave." Ananda said, "The Buddha is the teacher of the whole world—how could he have any place in hell?" Devadatta said, "How could I have any place out of hell?"

Cuiyan Zhen remarked, "Familiar words come from the mouth of the familiar."

[194]

Yunmen asked Caoshan, "What is purifying practice?"

Caoshan said, "Eating the crops of the endowment."

Yunmen asked, "How is it when going on just so?"

Caoshan said, "Can you accumulate stores?"

Yunmen said, "What is hard about dressing and eating?"

Caoshan said, "Why don't you talk about wearing fur and bearing horns?"

Yunmen then bowed.

[195]

A Confucian scholar who read the scripture *Names of a Thousand Buddhas* asked Master Changsha, "Of the hundreds and thousands of Buddhas, we only hear the names—what lands do they live in, and do they teach people?"

Changsha said, "Cui Hao wrote a poem on the Yellow Crane Pavilion; have you ever written a poem on that subject?"

The scholar said, "No."

Changsha said, "When you have nothing to do, write one."

Huanglong Xin eulogized,

In front of Yellow Crane Pavilion
At the time of religious war
The hundred thousand Buddhas fly the flag of surrender—
If they have no lands, where will they return?
At least they won a poem from a scholar.

[196]

In an address at Baiyun, Master Wuzu Yan quoted, "Xuefeng asked Deshan, 'What doctrine have the sages since antiquity taught people?' Deshan said, 'Our school has no verbal expression, and not a single doctrine to give people.' Xuefeng had an insight from this. A monk asked Xuefeng, 'When you saw Deshan, what did you attain to enable you to have peace?' Xuefeng said, 'I went empty-handed and returned empty-handed.'

"Today I am speaking to those who have yet to pass through. Suppose two people come from Loyang, but when you ask where they're from they say Suzhou. When you ask them how things are in Suzhou, they say everything's as usual. Even so, they can't fool me. Why? Because their pronunciation is different.

"Ultimately? The wheat of Suzhou, the lotus of Shaobai."

In another address to an assembly, he cited, "A monk asked Caoshan, 'How is it when the Buddha has not yet emerged in the world?' Caoshan said, 'I am not comparable.' 'What about after emergence in the world?' 'Not comparable to me.' If you view this from the standpoint of conventional truth, Caoshan deserves twenty blows. If you view this from the point of view of the Chan path, I deserve twenty blows. Even so, there's an eye on the cane; both men get hit, but one completely agrees while one completely disagrees. If you can tell them apart, I'll admit you have half an eye."

[197]

When Xingyang Jing first called on Xiyuan, he asked, "When about to question but not yet having questioned, then what?"

Xiyuan immediately hit him. Jing remained silent. Xiyuan said, "If you call it a cane, your eyebrows and whiskers will fall out."

Jing was greatly awakened at these words.

[198]

Master Langya Jiao said to an assembly,
My late teacher composed a verse:

> Three mysteries, three essentials—
> the actualities are hard to differentiate.
> When you get the meaning, forget the words,
> and the Way is easy to approach.
> When one statement is clear, it includes myriad forms;
> On the ninth day of the ninth month, chrysanthemums
> bloom anew.

[Shouting once, Langya said,] Which mystery is this? [After a long pause, he said,] You are infinitely sorry, and I too am infinitely sorry.

A monk asked, "What is Buddha?"
    Langya said, "Bronze head, iron forehead."
    The monk said, "I don't understand."
    Langya said, "Bird beak, fish gills."

[199]

A monk asked Master Dalong, "The physical body deteriorates and decomposes; what is the indestructible body of reality?"
    Dalong said, "The mountain flowers, blooming, resemble brocade; the valley stream, brimming, is deep as indigo."

Dahui remarked, "If you take these two lines to explain the body of reality, you'll fall living into hell."

[200]

When Master Cuiyan Zhen was the assembly leader in the community of Master Guizong Nan, Nan asked him, "I hear you always use the story of the girl coming out of concentration to help people—is that so?"
    Zhen said, "No."
    Nan said, "When extravagant, one is not sparing; when sparing, one is not extravagant. Why do you say no?"
    Zhen said, "Even if they're genuine Chan monks, you can't let them lack salt and broth."
    Nan then turned and called to an attendant to tell the cook to make only plain gruel the next day.

TRANSLATOR'S NOTE

The story of the girl coming out of concentration appears in the *Wumen-guan*. A girl remained in concentration after an assembly had dispersed. Manjushri, who represents transcendent insight, tried to rouse her but was unsuccessful. Buddha then summoned a bodhisattva named Netted Light, who was able to rouse the girl from concentration at a finger snap. This stands for the principle that *prajna*, transcendent insight, intuits emptiness, or the absolute, while *jnana*, knowledge, here represented by Netted Light, distinguishes conditional existence or relative truth.

[201]

As Master Xuansha was attending Xuefeng on a walk, Xuefeng pointed to the earth in front of them and said, "This spot of ground is good for building a seamless monument."

Xuansha said, "How high?"

Xuefeng looked up and down.

Xuansha said, "In the matter of human and divine rewards for virtue, I don't deny you; but when it comes to the prophecy of Spiritual Mountain, you haven't even dreamed of it."

Xuefeng said, "What would you say?"

Xuansha said, "Seven or eight feet."

Langya Jiao remarked, "When a country is pure, talented people are valued. When a family is rich, the children are delicate."

[202]

On an occasion when monks came to call on Fayan, he pointed to a bamboo blind. Two monks went and rolled it up. Fayan said, "One gain, one loss."

[203]

Longji asked a monk, "Where are you coming from?"

The monk said, "From Cuiyan."

Longji asked, "What has Cuiyan been saying to followers?"

The monk replied, "He always says, 'Meet Maitreya when you go out the gate; see Shakyamuni when you go in the gate.'"

Longji said, "How can you say that?"

The monk asked, "What about you, Master?"

Longji said, "Going out the gate, meet 'who'; going in the gate, see 'what.'"

At these words the monk had insight.

[204]

When Master Dacheng Zun was in the assembly of Cizhao, one day he asked, "What was the meaning of the ancient in asking for fire?"

Cizhao said, "Let it go out."

Dacheng asked, "After it's out, then what?"

Cizhao said, "The thirty-first day of the first month."

Dacheng said, "Then it's a good time."

Cizhao said, "What principle do you see?"

Dacheng said, "All tired out today."

Cizhao thereupon struck him. Dacheng then composed a verse:

> The opportunity for seeking fire is really fast!
> The subtle function with the hidden edge, few people suspect.
> If you want to understand my teacher's personal message,
> When the fire goes out in the crimson furnace, he doesn't add
> more fuel.

TRANSLATOR'S NOTE

The story of the master asking for fire is recounted in a later segment of this collection. One day Guishan was standing by Baizhang. Baizhang said, "Who is it?" He said, "Lingyou." Baizhang said, "Stir up the brazier to see if there is any fire or not." Guishan stirred it up and said, "There is none." Baizhang got up himself, stirred deeply, and found a little fire. Showing it to him, he said, "Is this not fire?" Guishan was thereupon enlightened.

[205]

Master Guanghui Lian said to an assembly,

When the Chan imperative goes into effect, the tracks of humans and divinities disappear; when a pathway is opened up, we temporarily talk of complications. Why so? In the interval of an urge to deliberate, you've already lost your life.

I do not shrink from the criticisms of others—I go into mud and water for your sake. Doesn't anyone understand? For the moment, let me try to convey a message. [Silence.] Look, look—everyone's living in the world of bedevilment!

[Then he held up his staff and said,] Speak quickly! Speak quickly!

[The group hesitated; he then shouted a shout.]

A monk asked, "What is a true human with no position like?"

He said, "Wood above, iron below."

The monk said, "Then the fault is in being."

The master said, "The judge tosses down his pen."

The monk bowed. Lian said, "Haul him out!"

[206]

Master Luohan Chen asked a monk from Baofu, "How is Buddhism taught there?"

The monk said, "Baofu sometimes says to the group, 'Block your eyes so you can't see; block your ears so you can't hear; stop your conceptual faculty so you can't discriminate.'"

Chen said, "I ask you, if you don't block your eyes, what do you see? If you don't block your ears, what do you hear? If you don't stop your conceptual faculty, how do you discriminate?"

The monk had insight at these words.

Dahui remarked, "Wealth despises a thousand mouths as too few; poverty resents one body as too much."

[207]

When Master Touzi was in Tongcheng county, Zhaozhou asked him, "Aren't you the master of Touzi hermitage?"

Touzi said, "Donate some cash to me for tea and salt."

Zhaozhou went back to the hermitage before Touzi. Come evening, he saw the master return carrying oil. Zhaozhou said, "Long have I heard of Touzi, but now that I've arrived I only see an old oil vendor."

Touzi said, "You only recognize an old oil vendor—you don't recognize Touzi."

Zhaozhou said, "What is Touzi?"

Touzi held up the oil jar and said, "Oil, oil!"

[208]

Caoshan questioned the Paper-Robed Wayfarer when the latter visited: "Aren't you the Paper-Robed Wayfarer?"

The wayfarer replied, "I do not presume."

Caoshan asked, "What is the phenomenon in the paper robe?"

The wayfarer said, "Once a fur garment is put on the body, myriad things are *thus.*"

Caoshan asked, "What is the function in the paper robe?"

The wayfarer stepped forward, said, "Yes!" and then passed away right then and there.

Caoshan said, "Since you know how to go this way, why don't you come this way?"

The wayfarer suddenly opened his eyes and asked, "How is it when the real essence of the one spirit does not avail itself of a womb?"

Caoshan said, "This is not yet sublime."

The wayfarer asked, "What is sublime?"

Caoshan said, "Borrowing without dependence."

The wayfarer said farewell, then sat down and died. Caoshan then composed a verse:

> The essence of awareness, complete and clear, is a formless
> body:
> Don't mistake far and near based on intellectual opinion.
> When thoughts differ, you're blind to the substance of the
> mysterious;
> When mind diverges, you're not neighbor to the Way.
> When subjectively discriminating myriad things,
> You get submerged in the objects before you;
> When conscious awareness is fragmented,
> You lose the basic reality.
> If you understand such expressions with complete clarity,
> You'll wind up unburdened, as you were before.

A monk asked, "How is it when one ox drinks water and five horses don't neigh?"

Caoshan replied, "I know how to keep my mouth shut!"

TRANSLATOR'S NOTE

The one ox stands for mind; the five horses stand for the primary senses.

[209]

Zhaozhou said to an assembly,

Brethren, those who come from the South, I unload, while those who come from the North, I load. This is why it is said, "If you approach a superior person to ask about the Way, you lose the Way; if you approach an inferior person to ask about the Way, you find the Way."

Brethren, when a true person expounds a false doctrine, the false doctrine accordingly becomes true. When a false person expounds a true doctrine, the true doctrine accordingly becomes false. Everywhere else they are hard to see but easy to know; here I am easy to see but hard to know.

[He also said to an assembly,]

This matter is like having a brilliant jewel in the palm of your hand: when a foreigner comes, a foreigner is reflected; when a native comes, a native is reflected.

I take a blade of grass and use it as the sixteen-foot golden embodiment of Buddha; I take the sixteen-foot golden embodiment and use it as a blade of grass. Buddhahood is identical to affliction; affliction is identical to Buddhahood.

[210]

A monk asked Zifu, "What is 'entering correct concentration on a single atom'?"

Zifu assumed a posture of meditation.

The monk asked, "What is 'rising from concentration on all atoms'?"

Zifu said, "Who are you asking?"

Yunmen remarked, "This teacher got trapped in words without even realizing it." He added, "The first act was already complication; then he even says, 'Who are you asking?'"

[211]

Nanquan asked Huangbo, "'When concentration and insight are learned equally, you can see the Buddha-nature clearly'—what is the principle here?"

Huangbo said, "One only gets it when not leaning on anything twenty-four hours a day."

Nanquan asked, "Is this your view?"

Huangbo said, "I don't presume."

Nanquan said, "Never even mind the fee for soup and water for now—who will you have pay the cost of footgear?"

Huangbo stopped.

Dahui remarked, "Haven't you read the saying—'When you meet a swordsman on the road, you'd better show your sword; don't present a poem to someone who's not a poet.'"

[212]

A monk asked Master Shexian Sheng, "Suppose a total incorrigible came to you; would you try to help him?"

The master said, "When a law is outdated, it becomes corrupt."

The monk asked, "Where is the compassion?"

The master said, "The years turn into devils when you get old."

"How is it when the precious sword hasn't been drawn from its scabbard?"

"Smacks you in the face."

"How about after it's drawn?"

"Pulls out your teeth."

"How is it when 'speaking of the immediate, not leaving any traces'?"

"When midnight strikes at high noon, a stone man tilts his head to listen."

"What about 'speaking of the gradual, countering the conventional to conform to the Way'?"

"The question is clear; it is presented right to your face."

"What is action transcending a teacher?"

"How much have my eyebrows grown?"

"What is the 'solitary body revealed in sense objects'?"

"The thousand-man ships north of the pass, the ten-thousand-bushel vessels south of the river."

"Then it is not an object of sense."

"Literalists write ten thousand lines in one letter."

"What is the master's deepest point?"

"A cat has the ability to stop bleeding; a tiger has the power to raise a corpse."

"Is this it?"

"The pestle pounds southeast, the grindstone rolls northwest."

[213]

A monk asked Master Shimen Cong, "Days and months come and go, with movement and change; before we realize it, we are deteriorating with age. Is there anyone who does not grow old?"

The master said, "There is."

"How is the one who does not grow old?"

"A young dragon is powerful, roaring loudly; later on, refinement and spirituality grow more and more."

"What is the most profound point for a student?"

"A turtle withdraws its head, feet, and tail in the depths of the water."

"What is it like there?"

"Someone traveling on the road has no way of knowing."

"I hear there is an ancient saying, 'Just *this*—now who moves his mouth?' What does this mean?"

"Don't mistake the ridge of a donkey saddle for your father's lower jawbone."

[214]

A monk asked Master Baoen Cong, "How is it when the lion has not come out of the cave?"

He said, "Weapons cannot attack it."

"How about after it comes out of the cave?"

"No way to hide."

"How about when on the verge of coming out?"

"Life hangs by a thread."

"What about what's passing?"

"Pressure."

[215]

Master Cuiyan Zhen said to an assembly,

A monk asked Master Baling, "What is the Way?"

He replied, "Someone with clear eyes falls into a well."

The monk also asked Baoying, "What is the Way?"

He replied, "In front of Five Phoenix Pavilion."

The monk also asked Shoushan, "What is the Way?"

He replied, "Where you stand, three feet deep."

Of these three sayings, one "stands like a mile-high wall," one "transports a boat over dry land," and in one "host and guest interact." Can anyone distinguish them? Try to say.

If not, for now practice the compassion of arhats to break through bondage; practice the compassion of bodhisattvas to bring peace to living beings; practice the compassion of Buddhas to realize the character of suchness.

[216]

Wayfarer Kefu asked Linji, "What is 'removing the subject but not the object' like?"

Linji said, "The warm sun produces growth, spreading over the earth like brocade; a baby's hair hangs down, shiny as floss."

"What about 'removing the object but not the subject'?"

"The royal command has already gone into effect all over the land; the general beyond the pass is free from smoke and dust."

"What about 'removing neither subject nor object'?"

"The king ascends the precious throne; old peasants sing songs."

"What about 'removing both subject and object'?"

"The states of Bing and Feng incommunicado, occupying one region alone."

Kefu understood the message at these words. Entering deeply into the doors of the three mysteries, three essentials, and four statements, he helped the mystic teaching greatly.

TRANSLATOR'S NOTE

Fenyang describes the three mysteries as follows:

> The first mystery: the reality realm is boundlessly vast; inter-connections and myriad forms are all complete within a mirror.
>
> The second mystery: Shakyamuni Buddha questioned Ananda; the learned one answered according to the issue. Response according to capacity is unlimited.
>
> The third mystery: directly emerging before the emperors of antiquity, outside the four propositions and hundred negations [all formal philosophy], a villager questions a sage.

He also defined the three mysteries as follows:

> The first mystery: personally transmitted before Kasyapa [the first Indian patriarch of Chan, regarded as successor to the Buddha]

The second mystery: beyond definition, apart from verbal
explanation.
The third mystery: a clear mirror reflects without bias.

Fenyang describes the three essentials in these terms:

The first essential: no fabrication in speech.
The second essential: a thousand sages enter mysterious depths.
The third essential: outside the four propositions and hundred
negations, walking through the paths of Cold Mountain.

The four statements are the four relations of subject and object referred
to here.

[217]

Fayan pointed to a chair and said, "If you know the chair, there's plenty
of room."
Yunmen said, "If you know the chair, you're as far off as sky from earth."
Tianyi said, "If you know the chair, it's made of maple and cedar wood."

Dahui remarked, "If you know the chair, you'd better shave your head and
wash your feet. Even so, there are many people who still misunderstand."

[218]

Master Deshan, one day when the meal was late, took his bowl and left
the hall. At that time Xuefeng was in charge of preparing the rice. As
soon as he saw Deshan, he asked, "The bell hasn't rung yet, old fellow, the
drum hasn't sounded yet—where are you going with your bowl?"
Deshan thereupon returned to his room.
Xuefeng told Yantou about this. Yantou said, "Even the great Deshan
doesn't understand the last word."

When Deshan heard this reported, he had an attendant call Yantou to him. He asked, "You don't approve of me?" Yantou secretly expressed his meaning.

The next day Deshan gave a talk that was not the same as his usual talk. Yantou clapped and laughed in front of the hall, saying, "Happily the old fellow in the hall understands the last word! Hereafter no one in the world will be able to oppose him. Even so, he only has three years."

After three years Deshan did in fact pass away.

[219]

Prime Minister Yu Di asked Siyu, "I ask the teacher for a word on the ultimate principle of Buddhism."

Siyu said, "Prime Minister, the ultimate principle of Buddhism requires you to get rid of your subjective rationales."

The prime minister said, "Then I ask you to get rid of your subjective rationales."

Siyu said, "Go ahead and ask a question."

The prime minister asked, "What is Buddha?"

Siyu called, "Mr. Prime Minister!"

The prime minister responded.

Siyu said, "Don't seek elsewhere."

Later Yaoshan heard of this story and said, "What a pity! Prime Minister Yu was buried alive at the foot of Siyu Mountain!"

The prime minister heard of this and made a special visit to Yaoshan. He asked, "What is Buddha?"

Yaoshan called to him, "Mr. Prime Minister!"

The prime minister responded, "Yes?"

Yaoshan said, "What is this?"

Now the prime minister had an insight.

Shaoqing brought this up with Luoshan and said, "Equally they are saying, 'What's special?' But there is a vast difference."

Luoshan said, "Even though you are a great master, still you shouldn't be hasty. At that time it was lucky to meet Prime Minister Yu: here if he rousted a tiger with a burning tail from a nest of weeds, where would Yaoshan be?

Shaoqing said, "How so?"

Luoshan said, "Did you know Minister Yu had done refining gold?"

[220]

Master Xuedou said, "'There are no walls in the ten directions, no gates in the four quarters'—where did the ancients meet guests? If you can utter a line taking hand in hand, then I'll allow you 'the heavens above and the earth below.'"

[221]

Yunmen went to Tiantong. Tiantong said, "Can you be sure?"

Yunmen said, "What are you saying?"

Tiantong said, "If you don't understand, you're wrapped up in the immediate present."

Yunmen said, "If you do understand, you're wrapped up in the immediate present."

Dahui remarked, "At the crossroads, he took his stand with unyielding daring."

[222]

Master Tianyi Huai composed two verses on matter and emptiness:

> Matter is empty; emptiness is matter; the emptiness of
>   matter is empty.
> It blocks the Tong Pass, so the road is impassable.

When the eonic fire rages, every wisp is consumed.
The green mountains, as before, are in the white clouds.

East, west, south, north,
Ten myriad, eight thousand;
Even Subhuti is at a loss—
Lotuses sprout within fire.

[223]

Baofu asked a monk, "What Buddha is it in the shrine?"

The monk said, "Let the master try to determine."

Baofu said, "Shakyamuni Buddha."

The monk said, "Better not treat people like fools."

Baofu said, "It's you who are treating me like a fool."

Baofu also asked a monk, "What is your name?

The monk said, "Xiance" [which means "benefiting all like moisture"].

Baofu said, "Suppose you meet a desiccant; then what?"

The monk said, "Who's the desiccant?"

Baofu said, "I am."

The monk said, "Better not treat people like fools, Master."

Baofu said, "It's you who are treating me like a fool."

Baofu also asked the rice cook, "How wide is the cauldron?"

The cook said, "Let the master try to measure it himself."

Baofu made a gesture of measuring with his hands.

The cook said, "Better not treat people like fools."

Baofu said, "It's you who are treating me like a fool."

Also, when Baofu saw a monk he said, "What work have you done to get so big?"

The monk said, "How much shorter are you, Master?"

Baofu hunched, making as if he were shorter.

The monk said, "Better not treat people like fools, Master."

Baofu said, "It's you who are treating me like a fool."

[224]

Master Zhaozhou asked Touzi, "When someone who has undergone the great death returns to life, then what?"

Touzi said, "One cannot go by night; it is necessary to get there when it's light."

[225]

When Luoshan was at Heshan, as he saw off Elder Ju, a fellow traveler, when they went out the gate Luoshan poked in front of him with a staff. The elder did not respond.

Luoshan said, "A stone ox blocks the ancient road; one horse spawns a pair of colts."

Later a monk quoted this to Sushan. Sushan said, "A stone ox blocks the ancient road; one horse spawns three tigers."

[226]

Master Letan Ying said to an assembly,

When Shakyamuni pointed to the sky with one hand and the earth with the other and said, "In the heavens above and on earth below, I alone am the sole honored one," you may say he was acting as if there were no one around. If a clear-eyed Chan monk had been there at the time, he would have caused Shakyamuni to find no road up to the heavens and no gateway into the earth. Even so, the bronze dish lamp must be filled with oil before this is possible."

Dahi remarked, "It could be valued; it could be denigrated."

[227]

A monk asked Jianfu Si, "When the ancient shrine has no Buddha, then what?"

He replied, "Where does the pure voice come from?"

The monk also asked, "How can one attain fulfillment without resorting to cultivation and realization?"

He replied, "If you cultivate realization, you don't attain fulfillment."

[228]

Chan master Fayan's verse on the theme of the triplex world being only mental:

> The three realms are merely mental;
> Myriad things are but representation.
> Only representation, only mental—
> Sound to the eye, form to the ear.
> Form does not reach the ear;
> How can sound contact the eye?
> Form to the eye, sound to the ear—
> Myriad things are in order.
> Myriad things are not mental objects—
> How can you view them as illusory?
> Earth, mountains, and rivers—
> Who is enduring, who changes?

Also, his verse on the six characteristics of the *Flower Ornament* teaching:

> The *Flower Ornament* principle of the six characteristics:
> Within sameness there is still difference;
> If difference is different from sameness,

That is not Buddha's teaching at all.
In the meaning of the Buddhas,
When have totality and distinction
Ever had sameness and difference?
When entering concentration in a male body,
No attention's focused on the female body.
When no attention's focused,
There are no names;
Myriad forms are distinctly clear,
Neither abstract nor concrete.

TRANSLATOR'S NOTE

The six characteristics of the *Flower Ornament* teaching are descriptions of the universe and all things in terms of sameness and difference, totality and distinction, formation and disintegration.

[229]

Qingyuan asked Shenhui, "Where are you coming from?"
　　Shenhui said, "From Caoqi."
　　Qingyuan asked, "What have you brought?"
　　Shenhui shook himself and stood there.
　　Qingyuan said, "You're still carrying rubble."
　　Shenhui said, "Don't you have any gold to give people, Teacher?"
　　Qingyuan said, "Even if I had, where would you put it?"

[230]

Master Luohan Nan said to an assembly,
　　Scarlet mist penetrates the sky, white herons dot the isle of immortals. I am not the man of Cold Mountain; at times at the ancient ford riding a swift steed I gallop to a high tower; jade globes roll in the Milky

Way, ten thousand miles. Trying to understand true liberation separately is looking for bubbles in fire.

He also instructed an assembly,

Chan is not Chan, Tao is not Tao. The tongue seeps at random. Last night the solar disc floated cassia flowers; this morning the lunar cave produces mushrooms and herbs. Ah, ha, ha! Ten thousand ounces of pure gold—there's nowhere to look. When one statement cuts off thinking, things do not reach each other.

[231]

Xuefeng said, "There are people who starve to death sitting by a basket of food; there are folks who die of thirst on the bank of a river." Xuansha said, "There are people who starve to death inside a basket of food, people who die of thirst with their heads in the water." Yunmen said, "The whole body is food; the whole body is water."

Citing this, Dahui shouted and said, "Talkative teachers are irrepressibly outstanding indeed. 'The whole body is food; the whole body is water'— where does this information come from?"

[232]

Great Master Bodhidharma's *Teaching on Peace of Mind* says,

When people are deluded, they follow things; when people are liberated, things follow them. If you're liberated, then consciousness absorbs form; if you're deluded, form absorbs consciousness.

As long as there is conscious discrimination making comparative assessments of the immediate experience of your own mind, it is all dreams. If the conscious mind is silent, without any stirring thought, this is called true awareness.

What is the immediate experience of your own mind? When you see all things existing, their existence is not existence of itself, but your own mind conceives of them as existing. When you see all things as nonexistent, their nonexistence is not nonexistence of itself; your own mind conceives of them as nonexistent.

This is how it is with everything—in every case it is your own mind construing them as existing or not existing.

Also, even if people have done all sorts of things wrong, once they see the spiritual ruler in themselves they will attain liberation.

Those who attain liberation through actual events are robust in strength. Those who see the teaching in the context of actual events never lose mindfulness wherever they are. Those whose understanding comes from writings are weak. Those to whom the teaching and actual events are identical are deep.

No matter what you do—leap and dance, or stumble and fall—none of it is outside the realm of reality. Anyone who tries to use the realm of reality to enter into the realm of reality is an ignoramus. Whatever you do is never outside the mind of the realm of reality. Why? Because the substance of mind is the realm of reality.

People of the world study various branches of learning—why don't they attain enlightenment? Because they see themselves—that's why they don't attain enlightenment. The self means the ego; perfected people are not troubled when they experience misery, and are not delighted when they experience pleasure, because they don't see self.

The reason they are not concerned by pain or pleasure is that they are selfless and therefore attain supreme emptiness. If even the self is not there, what would not disappear?

If all things are empty, who cultivates the Path? If you have a "who," then you need to cultivate the Path. If there is no "who," then you don't need to cultivate the Path. "Who" is the ego; if you are egoless, then you don't create judgments as you encounter things.

When you affirm something as so, that is your own affirmation, not that the thing itself is so. When you deny something as not so, that is your own denial, not that the thing itself is not so.

As long as you are mindless even as you are mindful, this is considered attainment of Buddhahood. When you apprehend things directly without creating views, this is called attaining the Path. One who, on encountering things, directly apprehends their source is one whose eye of insight is open.

Those with wisdom let things be as they may, but not themselves, so they have no grasping and rejecting, opposition and accord. Fools let themselves be as they may, but not things, so they have grasping and rejection, opposition and accord.

Not seeing a single thing is called seeing the Way; not practicing anything is called practicing the Way.

When you're one with all places, you have no place; when you're one with all activities, you have no activity.

The state of nonstriving is seeing Buddha. When you look at appearances, then you see ghosts everywhere. By grasping appearances, you fall into hell; by observing reality, you attain liberation.

If you see conceptually, you experience things like boiling water and burning coals, witnessing the appearances of birth and death. If you see the nature of the universe, it is the nature of nirvana. Have no conceptual thought, and there is the nature of the universe.

The mind is not material, so it is not existent; yet it functions, so it is not nonexistent. Also, while it functions yet it is always empty, so it is not existent; while empty it always functions, so it is not nonexistent.

[233]

Master Shimen Cong said to an assembly,

Questions and answers must make supposition and refutation complete; if you have a dragon's head but a snake's tail, you're fooling yourself. It's like a king wielding a sword—it's up to the king's will. It resembles a mirror on a stand—it calls for an excellent view. As soon as you open your mouth, you're a million miles away; if you lower your head in thought, there are myriad barriers. If you direct people without true insight, the least that will happen is becoming a wild fox.

. . .

A monk asked, "What is the mind of the ancient Buddhas?"

The master replied: "Stepping on a balance weight, hard as iron."

"What is the meaning?"

"The bright sun tells you."

"I don't ask about the verdant mountains and aquamarine waters—how do you express intensity?

"The hands reach past the knees; the ears droop to the shoulders."

[234]

Master Guanghui Lian said to an assembly,

There's originally nothing to Buddhism; the sages since time immemorial have all been hoking up wonders, creating programs, oppressing free people and making them menials, burying their posterity. Then there were Yunmen, Zhaozhou, Deshan, and Linji; deadly dull, they suffered injustice all their lives.

Here I am not that way. Even if old Shakyamuni Buddha were to show up, I'd banish him to another world, so there would be no trace of him. Why would I do this? So I wouldn't have to worry about losing my posterity.

When I speak this way, how do you people understand? If you can understand here, won't that be joyous? It will get you to shed your hair shirt so you can be clean and free. If you don't understand, next year there will be more new stipulations, disturbing the spring wind, with never an end.

A monk asked for more instruction in a private interview, saying, "The master just said that even if old Shakyamuni Buddha came up you'd banish him to another world . . ." Before he had finished quoting, Lian said, "If you understand this way, you'll go to hell like an arrow." The monk said, "Then how should I understand?" Lian hit him. The monk hesitated, trying to think of something to say. Lian said, "Understand?" The monk said, "No." Lian said, "Today I have explained to you without trying to avoid being censured everywhere; to serve infinite lands with this profound heart is called requiting the blessings of Buddha."

Dahui cited this and said with scorn, "Decent people are unwilling to do it; you have to lie in your piss."

[235]

Master Zhenjing said,

The ancient caves of Xinfeng—myriad layers pierced; the true trail of Wuben—a thousand forests thickly clustered. In beautiful places past and present, Buddhist service long flourishes. Therefore in days of old the great teacher Wuben once said in a lecture, "Only the enlightenment of Buddhas is a real resort." Then he shouted and said, "Still behaving this way." Chan worthies, what did the great teacher mean by "still behaving this way"? Do you know what it comes down to? There are many in monastic communities who discuss this. Some say, "Listening to Buddha, listening to the teaching, is like a born enemy; how much the more so having a resort! Therefore it is subject to the great teacher Wuben's critical examination." Some say, "Wuben just wanted people to stop." Some say, "Wuben just saw the sharpness of the awl; he didn't see the squareness of the chisel." When have such ilk seen the ancient even in dreams? Since it is not like this, then how is it?

Chan worthies, this matter requires close attention; don't be crude minded. First-class study of Chan ultimately gets to the bottom of it; the thousand differences and myriad distinctions in the school of the source, the different routes of concealing and revealing, only those of great wisdom understand. Ever since, no one has fathomed this, and so many hug a child who isn't crying, hit a clean ball, hold the mooring rope while launching the boat, hold on to a bridge pillar to wash. Everyone is capable—who has no share? If you understand all at once, you drive off the plowman's ox, take away the hungry man's food, enter fire without burning, enter water without drowning, not lingering anywhere, fulfilled everywhere, spiritual light shining alone, clearly distinct. This can be called being clear and free, raising the sail to cross over to the shore, setting in motion the boat that carries people over, appearing and disappearing in the heaps of foaming waves in the ocean of birth and death, going and coming, roaming independently. [Shouting:] Let others slander, let others repudiate; wearing both rain hat and raincoat in the rain, now I temporarily part from the moon at the strait and for the moment carry fish back to market.

TRANSLATOR'S NOTE

The names Xinfeng and Wuben both refer to the great master Dongshan Liangjie, ancestor of the Cao Dong school of Chan.

[236]

Hu, "the Nail," called on Master Baoshou. Baoshou asked, "Aren't you Hu the Nail?" Hu said, "I don't presume." Baoshou said, "Can you nail space?" Hu said, "Please pound it in, Master." Baoshou thereupon hit him. Hu the Nail didn't agree. Baoshou said, "Later there will be a talkative teacher who will point it out for you." Subsequently he called on Zhaozhou. Zhaozhou aid, "Aren't you Hu the Nail?" Hu said, "I don't presume." Zhauzhou said, "Can you nail space?" Hu said, "Please pound it in, Master." Zhaozhou said, "For the moment I'll nail this gap." Hu then mentioned the story of Baoshou using his cane. Zhaozhou said, "My speaking this way is thousands of miles away from that Baoshou."

[237]

A monk asked Master Shuilu, "What should a student apply his mind to?" Shuilu said, "To apply the mind is to miss." The monk said, "How is it when not arousing a single thought?" Shuilu said, "A useless fellow." The monk said, "How is this thing preserved?" Shuilu said, "Beware." The monk asked, "When meeting on a narrow road, what then?" Shuilu grabbed him by the chest and gave him a shove.

[238]

Master Jinfeng said to an assembly, "Twenty years ago I had an indulgent heart; twenty years later I have no indulgent heart." A monk asked, "How was it having an indulgent heart twenty years ago?" He said, "When asked about the ordinary, I answered about the ordinary; when asked about the holy, I answered about the holy." The monk said, "How is it having no indulgent heart twenty years later?" He said, "When asked about the ordinary, I don't answer about the ordinary; when asked about the holy, I don't answer about the holy."

[239]

Master Huangbo said to an assembly, "You people are all gobblers of dregs; if you travel like this, where will you have Today? Do you know there are no Chan teachers in all of China?" Then a monk asked, "What about those who order followers and lead groups everywhere?" Huangbo said, "I don't say there's no Chan, just that there are no teachers."

Guishan asked Yangshan about this. Yangshan said, "A king goose picking out milk [from water] is sure no duck." Guishan said, "This is truly hard to distinguish."

[240]

Master Yungai An asked Shishuang, "I don't ask about myriad doors being closed; how is it when myriad doors all open?" Shishuang said, "What about the business inside?" An said, "No one greets him." Shishuang said, "You've said quite a bit all right, but you've only managed to say eighty percent." An said, "I ask you to say, please, Master." Shishuang said, "No one knows him."

Dahui remarked, "A pair of iron hammerheads with no holes; one of them is heavier."

[241]

Master Langya Jiao said to an assembly,

"Originally there is not a single thing" crushes people of the world. Even if you understand immediately, you're sitting in a cesspit. What is the one route to pass through to freedom? Subtle sound, observing the sound of the world, the sound of purity, the sound of the ocean tide.

In a verse on the story of Baizhang's fox, he said,

> The clear mirror on its stand, those who emulate it are rare:
> When Chan people get here, they try to figure it out.
> Even if you can point out the moon in the autumn sky,
> After all you're just a wild fox.

In a verse on Qingping's saying about the Great Vehicle and Lesser Vehicle, he said,

> When mountains are high, the sun's emergence is early;
> In a steep fastness the green pines grow old.
> Trampling the flowering apricot branches,
> Let the cold wind sweep.

In a verse on the story of the wind and the flag, he said,

> "It is not the wind, and not the flag"—
> No talkative professor can explain.
> If you seek mystic understanding with clever words,
> You'll be separated by a thousand mountains, blocked by myriad
>   mountains.

TRANSLATOR'S NOTE

For the story of Baizhang's fox, see chapter 648 below. See also *Wumen-guan*, example 2, in Cleary, *Unlocking the Zen Koan*.

[242]

Master Letan Jun said to an assembly,

The mainspring of the founding teacher is hidden in mystery; few people know it. How can it be brought up to those who don't understand mind? [Shouting once:] What am I saying? If it were only thus, the whole school of Bodhidharma would have been wiped off the face of the earth. Therefore when the World Honored One first realized this matter, he thereupon opened the gate of expedient means to show the manifestation of reality and enable every Tom, Dick, and Harry everywhere to understand this matter.

Today I cannot but open the gate of expedients in emulation of the ancients. [Hitting the Chan seat once with his whisk:] The gate of expedients is opened—what is the manifestation of reality? [A long pause.] Eight out of ten, nine out of ten ignorant people run at night.

[243]

Master "Conquering Demons" Zang called on Master Xiu of the Northern School. Xiu asked, "You're called 'Conquering Demons'—there are no mountain sprites or woodland spooks here. Are you going to turn into a demon?" He said, "Where there are Buddhas, there are demons." Xiu said, "If you are a demon, you must be dwelling in the state of the inconceivable." He said, "Here even Buddhas are empty—what state is there?"

[244]

Master Shitou said to an assembly,

My teaching is the transmission of past Buddhas; it does not discuss meditation or diligence, just arriving at the knowledge and insight of Buddhas. Mind itself is Buddha—mind, Buddha, living beings, enlightenment and affliction—the names are different but the essence is one. You should know the spiritual essence of your own mind is beyond annihilation and eternity, not defiled or pure, profoundly calm and perfectly complete, equal in ordinary people and saints. Its responsive function has no standard method; it is beyond thought, ideation, and cognition. The three realms and six courses of existence are only manifestations of your own mind. How could the moon in water or images in a mirror have any origin or passing away? If you are able to know this, you lack nothing.

A monk asked, "What is liberation?" He said, "Who binds you?" The monk said, "No one binds me." He said, "Who seeks liberation?"

He asked a monk, "Where are you coming from?" The monk said, "From Jiangxi." He said, "Did you see Great Master Ma?" The monk said, "Yes." Shitou then pointed to a piece of firewood and said, "How is Master Ma like this?" The monk had no reply. He went back and quoted this to Great Master Ma. Ma said, "Did you see how big the log was?" He said, "Immeasurably large." Ma said, "You are very strong." The monk said, "How so?" Ma said, "You carried a log all the way here from Nanyue—doesn't that take strength?"

[245]

Yantou went with Xuefeng and Jinshan to call on Linji. On the way they encountered Elder Ding. Yantou asked him where he was coming from; Ding said, "From Linji." Yantou asked, "Is the master well?" Ding said, "The master has passed away." Yantou said, "We three were going just to pay respects to him; now we find the master's passed away. We're unfortunate, not seeing the master; pray tell, what sayings did he have? Please cite one or two examples." Ding then cited Linji saying, "'In the mass of naked flesh there is a true human with no status, always going out and in through our senses. Those who have not yet witnessed this, look, look!' At that time there was a monk who asked, 'What is the real human with no status?' Linji got down from the Chan seat, grabbed him, and said, 'Speak, speak!' The monk hesitated; Linji then pushed him away and said, 'A true human with no status—what a piece of crap.' Then he returned to his quarters." Yantou unconsciously stuck out his tongue. Jinshan said, "Why didn't he say, 'In the mass of naked flesh is not the true human with no status'?" Ding then grabbed him and said, "How far apart are a true human with no status and not a true human of no status? Speak quickly! Speak quickly!" Jinshan just turned green and yellow, unable to speak. Yantou and Xuefeng urged him, "This novice has offended you, Elder; please be merciful." Ding said, "If not for these two old fellows, I'd have beaten this bed-wetting imp to death."

[246]

Master Baiyun Duan said to an assembly,

"A clay Buddha does not get through water; a wooden Buddha does not get through fire; a metal Buddha does not get through a furnace. The real Buddha sits within." Zhaozhou's twelve sets of bones and eighty-four thousand pores have been thrown into your chest all at once. Today, seeing injustice on the road, I will put forth energy for the man of old. [Rapping the seat once.] You should know that seas and mountains belong to an enlightened ruler; it's not certain that heaven and earth fall to a good person.

[247]

A monk asked Yangshan, "Can the reality body teach?" Yangshan said, "I can't say—someone else can say." The monk asked, "Where is the person who can say?" Yangshan pushed out a pillow. Guishan heard of this; he said, "Yangshan uses the business of the sword blade."

Dahui commented, "Guishan truly 'took pity on his son, mindless of being unseemly.' When Yangshan pushed out the pillow, this was already indulging; to further put a name on it, calling it the business of the sword blade, misleads literalists, who will thus accept vanity and continue an echo, circulating it further. Although I seem to be borrowing water to offer flowers, essentially there is no crooked determination of truth. Now is there no bystander who does not agree? Come forth; I want to ask you—does pushing out the pillow amount to the reality body teaching or not?"

[248]

Master Wuzu Yan said to an assembly,

The Buddhas of the ten directions, the six generations of patriarchs, and the teachers all over the land all share this tongue. If you know this tongue, only then do you understand great liberation. Then you say mountains, rivers, and earth are Buddha; plants, trees, and forests are Buddha. If you don't know this tongue, you'll only achieve minor liberation and will have a lot of work to do in the future.

When I speak thus, is there any reality to it or not? What is the reality? Return to the hall and drink tea.

[249]

When a certain nun was going to open a hall, Master Tankong tested her, saying, "A nun has five obstructions and can't open a hall." The nun said, "When the Naga girl became a Buddha, how many obstructions did she have?" Tankong said, "When the Naga girl became a Buddha, she manifested eighteen transformations; let's see you try to transform." The nun said, "I'm not a wild fox spirit—what would I transform?" Tankong then hit her. Later the teaching master of Zhenzhou heard of this and said,

"Did the master's staff break, trying to help someone with this understanding?" Cuiyan Zhi said, "Tell me, did the nun have eyes or not? Just carrying a broken cash string, how could one understand?"

[250]

When Master Sansheng was in the community of Yangshan, an official came to see Yangshan. Yangshan asked him what his official post was, and he replied that he was a provincial judge. Yangshan raised his whisk and said, "Can you judge this?" The official was speechless. Yangshan had the whole community present sayings, but none of them were fitting. Sansheng was unwell and was in the nirvana hall trying to rest; Yangshan had an attendant go ask him to present a saying. Sansheng said, "Just say the master has an issue today." Yangshan then had the attendant go ask what the issue was. Sansheng said, "A second offense is not permitted."

[251]

When Master Xinghua was in Sansheng's assembly, he always used to say, "When I traveled around the South, my staff never rousted a single one who understood Buddhism." Later he went to Dajiao's place, where he was asked to be superintendent of the monastery. One day Dajiao called him out, "Superintendent, I hear you say that when you traveled around the South your staff never rousted a single one who understood Buddhism. On what principle do you base this?" Xinghua shouted; Dajiao hit him. Xinghua shouted again, and Dajiao hit him again. The next day in the teaching hall Xinghua called out, "Superintendant, I am dubious of these two shouts of yours." Xinghua shouted again, as before; Dajiao hit him. Xinghua shouted again, and Dajiao hit him again. Xinghua said, "When I was at Sansheng's place I learned the expressions of guest and host, but it's all been broken down by you, older brother. I say to you, give me a method of peace and ease." Dajiao said, "You blind ass! You come here and suffer defeat. Take off your patchwork robe and I'll give you a drubbing."

[252]

Master Jingqing said to an assembly,

If you have a boat but no oar, that won't do. If you have an oar but no boat, that won't do either. If you have both an oar and a boat, that still won't do. "Still won't do" won't do either. How is it with you?

One time he said,

If one person arrives, that still won't do. If one person doesn't arrive, that still won't do. If both arrive, that won't do either. "Won't do" won't do either. How about you? This is the subtlety within the subtle; wiping clear the blue sky, throughout the sky there is no obstruction.

[253]

Master Yangqi said to an assembly,

The scenery suddenly clear, beings' feelings relax. Taking a step—a thousand embodiments of Maitreya. Going into action—Shakyamuni everywhere. Manjushri and Samantabhadra are both here. If there are any in the group who are not fooled by others, they will say I am selling flour mixed with bran. Even so, they are filling a cloth bag with awls.

[254]

One day Yunmen said, "Dividing into two, splitting into three, where are the needle tube nostrils? Try to bring them up for me one by one." He answered himself, "Upper, middle, lower."

Dahui commented, "Leaning against the gate, standing by the door, he plays with the spirit."

[255]

The Fourth Patriarch said to meditation master Rong,

The hundred thousand teachings revert alike to the heart; wonderful virtues as numerous as sand grains in the Ganges River all abide in the wellspring of mind. All methods of discipline, methods of concentration, methods of insight, spiritual powers and manifestations, are all inherent, not apart from your mind. All afflictions and obstacles of habit are originally void; all causes and effects are like dream illusions. There is no triplex world to leave, no enlightenment to seek. Humans and nonhumans are equal in essence and characteristics. The Great Way is empty and open, beyond thought, beyond cogitation. Now that you have gotten such principles, you lack nothing anymore; how are you different from Buddha? There is no special doctrine beyond this. Just let your mind be free; don't do contemplative exercises, and don't try to settle your mind either. Don't conceive greed or hostility; don't think of sorrow or worry. Clear and unobstructed, free as you will, not contriving virtues, not perpetrating evils, walking, standing still, sitting, lying down, whatever meets the eye, in any circumstance, is all the subtle function of Buddha. It is called Buddhahood because of happiness without sorrow.

[256]

Lecturer Liang called on Mazu. Mazu asked him, "I've heard you're quite a lecturer on scriptures and treatises; is this so?" Liang said, "I do not presume." Mazu said, "What do you lecture with?" He said, "I lecture with mind." Mazu said, "'Mind is like an artisan, ideas are like apprentices'—how can this lecture on scriptures?" Raising his voice, Liang said, "If mind cannot lecture, can space lecture?" Mazu said, "Indeed, space can lecture." Liang disagreed and left; as he was about to go down the stairs, Mazu called him, "Professor!" Liang turned his head, and was suddenly greatly enlightened. He then bowed. Mazu said, "This dull-witted preacher! What are you bowing for?" Liang went back to his monastery and told his audience, "I thought no one could match the scriptures and treatises I lecture on; today, at one question from Mazu, my whole life's effort has dissolved." He went straight into the western mountains and there was never any trace of him anymore.

[257]

Master Yunfeng Yue said to an assembly,

When speech does not leave nests, how can the path get out of enclosures? A cloud across a valley mouth misleads how many people from the source of the stream. Therefore it is said that words do not set forth facts and speech does not accord with situations, those who accept words are lost, those who linger over sayings are astray. When you get here, how will you speak of understanding? [Pause.] If you want to avoid action with immediate consequences, don't slander the Realized One's wheel of true teaching.

He also said to an assembly,

The whisk has swallowed the polar mountain. In ordinary discourse Deshan set up a sign in a bustling marketplace—how do you deal? [Pause.] Officially not even a needle is admitted; privately even a horse and carriage can pass.

[258]

Master Daming Kuan said to an assembly,

The perennial matter is not gotten from Buddhas, not sought from patriarchs. The inborn essence of great people is fundamentally naturally real of itself. Orderly in action and repose, going and coming without fixation, it is like a fish in water, surfacing and diving according to its nature, like a bird flying in the sky with no obstruction at all. Who understands such talk? [Pause.] One energy contains myriad forms without speaking; where do myriad spirits leave the impersonal?

. . .

A monk asked, "In the teachings it speaks of coming to know that all beings are originally Buddhas; why are there afflictions and enlightenment?"

He said, "Sweetgrass is sweet, coptis root is bitter."

The monk said, "After all they turn out to be two."

He said, "You sure understand, all right."

The monk asked, "Given that it's one true reality realm, why are there then a thousand differences and myriad distinctions?"

He said, "When the roots are deep, the foliage flourishes."

The monk said, "Then is it possible to get out of this?"

He said, "Playing clever turns out clumsy."

The monk asked, "Doing, stopping, letting go, and annihilation are four illnesses in the teaching; how should beginners proceed?"

He said, "An expert craftsman wielding an ax does not follow a plumb line when cutting wood."

[259]

Master Longhua Yu said to an assembly,

When Matanga entered China, he was already involved in prolixity; when Bodhidharma came from the West, he didn't keep to his place. Now when I speak thus, this too is prolonging ignorance for others' idle issues.

When I was traveling, I met Master Wuzu Jie. He asked, "How do you say the one statement that doesn't fall on the lips and mouth?" I said, "So venerable, so great, yet you don't even know a saying?" Jie then shouted. I shouted too. Jie picked up a cane, and I knocked it out of his hand. Jie said, "There's still something to talk about." I put my seat cloth over my shoulder and immediately left without looking back.

[260]

Master Nanquan said to an assembly,

The Burning Lamp Buddha said it—if what is thought up by mental descriptions produces things, they are empty, artificial, all unreal. Why? Even mind has no existence—how can it produce things? They are like shadows of forms dividing up empty space, like someone putting sound in a box, and like blowing into a net trying to inflate it. Therefore an old adept said, "It is not mind, not Buddha, not a thing," teaching you how to practice. It is said that tenth-stage bodhisattvas abide in the concentration of heroic progress, gain the secret treasury of teachings of all Buddhas, spontaneously attain all meditations, concentrations, liberations, spiritual powers, and wondrous functions, go to all worlds and manifest physical bodies everywhere, sometimes present the appearance of attaining enlightenment, turning the wheel of the great teaching, and entering complete extinction, causing infinity to enter into a pore, expound a one-line scripture for countless eons without exhausting the meaning, teach countless billions of beings to attain acceptance of the truth of no origin; yet this is still called the folly of knowledge, the folly of extremely subtle knowledge, completely contrary to the Way. It's very difficult, very hard; take care.

[261]

Master Nanyuan said to an assembly, "In the mass of naked flesh stand like a wall a mile high." A monk asked, "'In the mass of naked flesh stand like a wall a mile high'—isn't this a saying of yours?" He said, "Yes." The monk then overturned the Chan seat. Nanyuan said, "Look at this blind fellow acting rebelliously." The monk hesitated; Nanyuan hit him and drove him out.

Dahui said, "I now guarantee you this matter is ultimately not in vain."

[262]

Master Longshan asked a monk, "Where have you come from?" The monk said, "From an old adept." Longshan asked, "What sayings did the old adept have?" The monk said, "When he spoke, a thousand statements, ten thousand statements; when he didn't speak, not a single word." Longshan said, "Then a fly lays eggs." The monk bowed. Longshan hit him.

[263]

Master Dongshan Liangjie got lost and came upon Longshan, so he called on him and paid respects. Longshan asked, "This mountain has no roads; where did you come from?" Liangjie said, "Leaving aside for the moment the fact that there are no roads, where did you enter from?" He said, "I've never wandered." Liangjie asked, "How long have you been here?" He said, "Time is irrelevant." Liangjie asked, "Was this mountain here first, or were you here first?" He said, "I don't know." Liangjie asked, "Why don't you know?" He said, "I don't come from among humans or celestials." Liangjie then asked, "What is the host within the guest?" He said, "Never goes out the door." Liangjie asked, "What is the guest within the host?" He said, "The blue sky is covered by white clouds." Liangjie asked, "How far apart are guest and host?" He said, "Waves on the Long River." Liangjie asked, "When guest and host meet, what is said?" He said, "A clear breeze sweeps the bright moon." Liangjie also asked, "What principle did you see that you came to live on this mountain?" He said, "I saw two clay bulls fighting go into the ocean, never to be heard of since." Then he spoke a verse on the subject:

> I've dwelt all along in a three-section reed house;
> In a single beam of spiritual light, myriad objects are at rest.
> Don't bring right and wrong to judge me;
> The scrutiny of the ephemeral world is irrelevant.

[264]

Master Touzi said to an assembly,

You people come here looking for fresh sayings, to gather flowers and collect brocade, considering it important to have something to say. I'm an old man, with diminished energy, slow in speaking. If you question me, I reply accordingly, but I have no mysterious subtleties for you. And I don't have you dwell on figuring. I never speak of transcendence or immanence, or the existence of Buddha, or Dharma, or ordinary or holy. And I don't maintain sitting to bind you people. A thousand kinds of manifestations are all your conception of interpretations, which you carry around on your own, experiencing yourselves what you yourselves have created. Here there's nothing to give you; I don't dare deceive you. There is nothing external and nothing internal that can be expressed to you. Do you know?

At that time a monk asked, "How is it when not taken in by either the external or the internal?" The master said, "Do you want to dwell on this trying to figure it out?" The monk asked, "Is there anything special in the canonical teachings?" The master said, "Recite the canonical teachings."

[265]

Master Baoming Yong said to an assembly,

There is a fellow with a suspicious gut, hateful eyes, and a straight nose, ragged and craggy, who faces south to see the North Star, knows how to make the gold crow [the sun] call at noon, make an iron ox bellow at midnight, so heaven and earth spin, mountains and rivers run, birds and beasts lose their territories; he finds Manjushri and Samantabhadra appearing and disappearing here and there, free in every way, through ten thousand experiences over a thousand lifetimes. Suddenly he meets Gautama Buddha, who without reservation pats him on the head again and again, giving him the prediction of enlightenment—"Good, good! You're doing a lot of Buddhist service; wonderful, wonderful!" At this he himself is ashamed and alarmed; he hides his head and pulls back his hands. Hey, everyone! If this talk circulates widely, what's the need to trudge on after thirty years?

[266]

Master Huaitang, addressing an assembly, knocked the seat once and said,

As soon as a mote of dust arises, the whole earth is contained in it. All your ears are in one voice; one voice extends to everyone's ears. If you are swift hawks brushing the sky, then you should take advantage of the time; if you are tired fish staying in a pond, it's a waste of effort to make waves.

[267]

Master Zhaozhou said to an assembly, "Things fundamentally have no origin and presently have no extinction; there is no more to say. As soon as you speak, this is origination; and if you don't speak, this is extinction. People, what is the principle of no origination and no extinction?"

A monk asked, "Are plants unborn and undying?" He said, "This fellow only recognizes the dead word."

A monk asked, "What is the sixteen-foot golden body?" He said, "Putting a neckband on sleeves, boring a collar at the side." The monk said, "I don't understand." He said, "If you don't understand, borrow someone else's tailoring."

Someone asked, "What was the intention of the coming from the West?" He said, "Gapped teeth grow fur."

Someone asked, "Does an oak tree have Buddha-nature?" He said, "Yes." "When will it become a Buddha?" He said, "When the sky falls to earth." "When will the sky fall to earth?" He said, "When an oak tree becomes a Buddha."

[268]

When Master Cuichan was in Ding province, he lectured in the provincial government headquarters: holding up his staff, he said, "Come forth, and I strike; don't come forth, and I also strike." A monk came out and said, "Cuichan!" Cuichan threw down the staff and said, "You've been standing a long time, Governor; take care."

[269]

A monk asked Wayfarer Kefu, "What is the guest within the guest?"

He said, "Leaning on the gate, standing by the door, is like a drunk speaking out blowing off steam without shame or diffidence."

"What is the host within the guest?"

"Verbally remembrancing Amitabha, with a pair of staffs a blind man doesn't show up."

"What is the guest within the host?"

"Holding the seal of the patriarchs high, action appropriate to potential benefits people; it should be known that what is said is compassionate."

"What is the host within the host?"

"Wielding the sharpest sword sideways, fulfilling right order, in a realm of great peace cutting down the ignorant."

"If it is a realm of great peace, why then cut down the ignorant?"

"It is not permissible to travel at night; as soon as you take up a torch you must go to the road to let people see."

[270]

Master Xinghua one day called to a monk. The monk responded, "Yes!" Xinghua said, "If you arrive, you don't check." Xinghua called to another monk; the monk said, "What?" Xinghua said, "If you check, you haven't arrived."

A monk asked, "When there are comers from all directions, then what?" Xinghua said, "Hit the one in the middle." The monk bowed. Xinghua said, "Everyone, yesterday I went to a village feast; halfway back I ran into a sudden storm and took shelter in an ancient shrine."

[271]

Master Zhimen Zuo said to an assembly,

Nanquan said, "Since youth I have been tending a water buffalo. When I try letting it go east of the valley, it inevitably eats the water plants of that country's king. When I try letting it go west of the valley, it inevitably eats the water plants of that country's king. It's better to take in a little bit everywhere without being seen at all." Therefore the great master Yunmen said, "On level ground the dead are countless; those who can get through a forest of thorns are the experts." Even if you can cut off ordinary and holy and terminate being and nothingness, you're just a rat going into a rice jar, and still don't know the opening beyond.

At that time a monk asked, "What is the opening beyond?" Zuo hit him and said, "I've already smeared you with a piece of crap; why do you still come to bite my hand?" The monk hesitated; the master drove him off.

[272]

Master Puming of Qingliang said to an assembly,

The founder's teaching of mind is all-pervasive, constant through all time. It is like this naturally. The truth is spontaneously realized without depending on cultivation, fulfilled of itself without depending on attainment. Totally present, it is called the immovable ground. Even when in use it is not existent; when unused, it is not nonexistent. The subtle essence is profoundly still, constant and unchanging. The essence is combined with subtle function, fully responsive without contrivance, reflecting infinite forms and features interacting.

Mind has no nature of its own; it manifests fully in contact with phenomena. Without stirring from the site of enlightenment it is omnipresent in all worlds. For the moment turn attention around to this realm; if you turn away from awareness to get involved in sense objects, you mistakenly construe reflected phenomena.

The meaning of this concern is like a royal highway; if you travel on it, that's it, but even if you don't travel on it, you're still on the road.

A discourse like this is still an expression of teaching method. If we were to bring out the vehicle of the aim, all we could do would be to disperse at once.

[273]

Yangshan asked Sansheng, "What is your name?" Sansheng said, "My name is Huiji." Yangshan said, "Huiji? That's me!" Sansheng said, "My name is Huiran." Yangshan laughed out loud.

Dahui commented, "Two fellows hiding their bodies while revealing their shadows—they pay no attention to onlookers."

[274]

Master Linji said to an assembly,

Followers of the Way, Buddhism has no place for exerting effort; it's just being without issues in everyday life, dressing, eating, excreting, lying down when tired. Foolish people laugh at me, but the wise know this. An ancient said, "Those who make efforts outwardly are all ignoramuses." You just be the master wherever you are, and wherever you stand is reality; no objects at all can jerk you around. Even if you have preexisting habit energies, acts that bring on immediate consequences, all of it becomes an ocean of liberation.

Those who study Chan in the present time do not know the teaching; they are like sheep in the grass, putting whatever they come upon in their mouths. They do not distinguish servant from master, do not differentiate guest and host. People like this enter the Path with perverted minds, so they cannot be called genuine leavers of home; they are actually ordinary worldly people. Those who leave home must be able to distinguish constant truly accurate perceptive understanding, distinguishing

Buddhas, distinguishing demons, distinguishing truth, distinguishing falsehood, distinguishing the ordinary, distinguishing the holy. If they can make such distinctions, they are called genuine leavers of home. If they cannot distinguish demons from Buddhas, they are actually leaving one home to enter another home; they are called people who create karma—they cannot be called genuine leavers of home.

Right now there is an identity of Buddha and demon. Clear-eyed wayfarers strike both demon and Buddha. If you love the holy and hate the ordinary, you bob endlessly in the ocean of birth and death.

At that time a monk asked, "What is the Buddha demon?"

The master said, "A moment of doubt in your mind is the Buddha demon. If you can realize that myriad phenomena have no origin, and mind is like an illusory projection, there is not a single atom or a single phenomenon anymore; everywhere is pure. Then there is no Buddha demon."

[The master continued,]

Buddha and sentient beings are two states, defilement and purity; according to my perception, there is no Buddha, no sentient beings, no past, no present. Those who get it get it immediately, with no restriction of time. And there is no cultivation or realization either, no gain and no loss. At all times there is nothing special beyond; even if there is anything beyond this, I say it is like a dream, like an illusion.

What I am talking about is just your solitary light clearly evident before your eyes right now, listening to the teaching. This person does not linger anywhere, independent everywhere, entering into all different states without being jerked around. In an instant one penetrates the universe, speaking of Buddhas when meeting Buddhas, speaking of patriarchs when meeting patriarchs, speaking of saints when meeting saints, speaking of hungry ghosts when meeting hungry ghosts, everywhere traveling lands teaching people, without departing from the moment, pure and clear everywhere, light penetrating the ten directions, myriad things as one.

Followers of the Way, powerful people, now you know there is fundamentally no issue. Just because your faith is insufficient, you race around seeking, thought after thought, discarding your head seeking a head, unable to stop yourself. Bodhisattvas of the complete all-at-once teaching, for example, enter into the reality realm and manifest bodies in pure lands, weary of the ordinary and delighting in the holy. Such types have not yet forgotten grasping and rejecting, still minding defilement and purity. As for the perceptive understanding of the Chan school, it is not so—it is right here and now, no other time.

What I say is all temporary opposition of medicine to illness, with no real truth at all. If you see this way, you are genuine leavers of home; you can consume ten thousand ounces of gold a day.

Followers of the Way, don't go from one to the next, to be stamped by teachers everywhere and claim you understand Chan and understand the Way, glib as a waterfall—this is all behavior creating hell. If you are authentic students of the Way, you don't see the faults of the world; you urgently seek real true perceptive understanding. If you arrive at the true mind, and realize its essence is complete illumination, only then will you be done.

Someone asked what real true perceptive understanding is. The teacher said,

You just enter the ordinary, enter the holy, enter the defiled, enter the pure, enter the lands of all Buddhas, enter Maitreya's tower, enter Vairocana's world, all of it—every place manifests lands becoming, abiding, decaying, and empty; Buddhas appear in the world, turn the wheel of the great teaching, and enter nirvana without remainder: you do not see that there is any appearance of going or coming; looking for birth and death, you cannot find them. Then you enter the reality realm with no origination, roaming in lands everywhere; you enter the flower bank world, and see all things completely real, all of them truth. There is only the independent wayfarer listening to the teaching—this is the matrix of all Buddhas. Therefore Buddhas are born from independence; if you realize independence, even Buddha has no attainment. If you can see this way, this is real true perceptive understanding. When students don't understand, they cling and construe terms and expressions; they are obstructed by those terms ordinary and holy. Therefore they block their eye of the Way and cannot attain clarity.

As for the twelve-part teachings, they are all representational expressions; when students don't understand, they conceive interpretations of representational terms and statements. All of these are dependent, and fall into cause and effect, still not escaping birth and death in the triple world.

If you want to attain freedom to leave or stay in birth and death, right now discern the person listening to the teaching, with no form, no appearance, no root, no basis, no abode, leaping with life. This must be the function of myriad kinds of facility, but it has no location. Therefore if you seek after it, you become further estranged; if you look for it, all the more you turn away, calling it a mystery.

Followers of the Way, don't give recognition to a dreamlike illusory accompaniment; while you are losing time being dilatory, you will return to impermanence. What are you looking for in this world as liberation? You pass the time seeking a mouthful of food to eat and mending clothing, but you should visit good teachers. Don't shilly-shally, wasting your life pursuing comfort, dying in vain. Time should be valued; every moment is fleeting. In crude terms you are oppressed by the four gross elements of earth, water, fire, and air, and more subtly by the four appearances of birth, abiding, change, and passing away, without any end in sight. Followers of the Way, for now you need to discern the four kinds of formless state to avoid being battered by conditions of the environment. What are the four kinds of formless state? When you have a thought of attachment in your mind, you are drowned by water. When you have a thought of hostility in your mind, you are burned by fire. When you have a thought of doubt in your mind, you are impeded by earth. When you have a thought of delight in your mind, you are blown away by wind. If you can discern in this way, you can avoid being affected by states or objects; in every situation you can utilize states and objects, welling up in the east and sinking away in the west, welling up in the south and sinking away in the north, welling up in the center and sinking away in the periphery, welling up in the periphery and sinking away in the center, walking on water as if it were earth, walking on earth as if it were water. How so? Because of realizing the four gross elements are like dreams, like illusions.

Followers of the Way, what is now listening to the teaching is not your four gross elements, but can use your four gross elements. If you can see this way, then you are free to go or stay.

According to my perception, there is nothing to reject. If you despise the ordinary and love the holy, you are bound by holy and ordinary states. There is a kind of student who goes to Mount Wutai looking for Manjushri to appear. They have already gone wrong. There is no Manjushri on Mount Wutai. Do you want to know Manjushri? Your present functioning with never any aberration, unobstructed everywhere—this is the living Manjushri. The undifferentiated light in your mind in each moment wherever you are is all Samantabhadra. The ability of your mind in a single moment to be independent, liberated wherever you are—this is the reality of the concentration of Avalokitesvara. They are principal and companion to one another; when manifest they are manifest at the same time, and when hidden they are hidden at the same time. One is three and three are one. Only when you understand this way should you read the teachings.

[275]

Yunmen said, "'In the lands in the ten directions there is only the truth of one vehicle'—but tell me, is the self within the truth of one vehicle or outside the truth of one vehicle?" He answered himself, "Entry."

Dahui commented, "A particularly sad situation."

[276]

Master Baiyun Duan said to an assembly,

The body of Buddha fills the realm of reality, manifest in the presence of all living beings, reaching the senses according to conditions, omnipresent yet always on the seat of enlightenment. Everyone, how do you explain this principle of reaching the senses according to condition? In a snap it fully responds to the faculties and potentials of all living beings on earth, yet without ever moving a hair. This is called reaching the senses according to conditions while always on this seat. How about when I am invited by Dharma Blossom monastery, part from this community to lodge in Pine prefecture, open a teaching hall, then return to this temple—tell me, do I leave "this seat" or not? If you say I leave, worldly truth prevails; if you say I haven't left, how do you see this phenomenon of not leaving? Is it not the realms of infinite lands, one's own and others, not being separate on a hair tip, all times not being apart from the immediate moment? Or is it not simultaneously pervading all spontaneously, without thought? If so, this is waving a stick to hit the moon.

Here you must awaken before you get it; and after awakening you also need to meet someone else. If you say you can rest once you've awakened, then why do you need to meet someone else? If you have met someone after awakening, when you reach out expediently you will naturally have a way to succeed in every case; you will not blind students. If you just realize a dry turnip, you'll not only blind students, you yourself will also tend to be the first to run afoul of the point and hurt your hand.

Look—my teacher Yangqi asked his teacher Ciming, "When hidden birds twittering leave the clouds and go into the scattered peaks, then what?" He answered, "I walk in wild weeds and you enter a recondite village." Yangqi said further, "'Officially not a needle can get in'—let me ask another question." His teacher shouted. He went on to say, "A fine shout." His teacher shouted again. My teacher also shouted. His teacher then shouted twice in a row. My teacher finally bowed. Everyone, you should know that one who meets someone else after having awakened is shaking hands atop a thousand peaks when encountering people at a crossroads, and when meeting atop a thousand peaks is at a crossroads shaking hands. For this reason I once composed a verse, saying,

> Where others dwell, I do not dwell:
> Where others go, I do not go.

It's not that I can't live with others;
In general, monks and lay folk must be distinct.

Here as I am about to go, I've opened up my cloth bag and spread everything in front of you. Those who have eyes should not be mistakenly suspicious. Take care.

[277]

Master Dagui Zhenru said to an assembly,

The ancient Buddha said that in the past he taught the four truths at Benares—he fell into a pit—then currently expounds the most subtle unexcelled great teaching—he adds mud to dirt. Now is there anyone who can transcend convention independently without going through steps? [Pause.] Appear beyond the heavens—who is the person here?

A monk asked, "When the Buddha Victorious by Great Penetrating Knowledge sat on the site of enlightenment for ten eons, why couldn't he attain Buddhahood?"

The master replied, "Torments people to death."

A monk asked, "How was Niutou before he met the Fourth Patriarch?"

The master replied, "Hair standing up in the cold."

The monk asked, "How about after meeting?"

The master replied, "Forehead breaking out in a sweat."

[278]

Master Huanglong Nan said to an assembly,

"Where people of the time dwell, I do not dwell; where people of the time go, I do not go." To perfectly understand the intended meaning here, you must know how to enter a pit of fire with your whole body. [Drawing a line with the whisk:] Foul smoke fumes, red flames rage. But those whose eyes are not yet clear are all inside. The ancient sages since time immemorial have all gone into the pit of birth and death, into the fire of ignorance, to lift out sentient beings. As for you people, how will you go in? If people can go in, they can be said to be in fire without burning, in water without drowning. If they can't enter, not only can they not help themselves, they can't help others either. If you can't help yourself or help others, there's no benefit to a shaven head and monastic robes. [After a long silence, he called to the group; when they raised their heads, he said,] Going out with an ox head, coming back with a horse head.

[279]

Vice Minister Yang and the imperial attendant Li had a dialogue with Master Mingsong of Tang.

Question: "Amitabha spreads the teaching in the West; Bodhidharma communicated mind in the East. When a foreigner comes, a native appears; where water reaches, a stream forms. The five holy mountains stabilize, high and steep; a hundred valleys go to the source, immeasurably vast. The essence of one spirit manifests forms depending on the environment. In the three realms of existence, based on what is life established?"

Mingsong said, "A male immortal has no wife; a female immortal has no husband."

Yang said, "When a nun shaves her head, she no longer bears children."

Mingsong said, "The iron ox of Xia prefecture can bellow; the colossus of He province recites 'Maha.'"

Li said, "A sideways leap to a mountain top."

Mingsong said, "Riding an ox, one doesn't wear shoes."

Guanghui Lian said, "Goading an elephant, he turns the spear around."

Fenyang Zhao said, "Straightening his body, he splits his face."

. . .

Dahui commented, "Watch the play with the snow lion in the moonlight."

Question: "Xuansha didn't leave the mountain, Baoshou didn't cross the river. Sudhana called on fifty-three teachers, Huiyuan formed a group of eighteen monks and laymen. Xuefeng went to Touzi three times, Zhiyi lectured on the *Lotus Sutra* for ninety days. Were these six fellows foxes crying or lions roaring? Speak quickly, speak quickly!"

Mingsong said, "When the water flows swiftly, the fish are slowed down; where the peak is high, birds don't nest."

Yang said, "The great sage of Si province [thought to be a manifestation of the archetypal bodhisattva Avalokitesvara]."

Mingsong said, "Adding another layer of mud on top of dirt."

Li said, "The tongue is covered with gold coins."

Mingsong said, "Song and music at play in the middle of the night—who can appreciate the tune?"

Guanghui Lian said, "The streets are full of song—everybody looks."

Fenyang said, "Seeing a picture on a wall, people laugh."

Dahui commented, "Foxes cry, lions roar."

Question: "Fengxue held up the seal, Nanyuan passed on the robe, Mr. Zhao spread the teaching in West River, Master Song leads disciples in Binglu—the teaching of the Southern School flourishes greatly in the north. But tell me, whose benevolent power did each two teachers receive?"

Mingsong said, "He doesn't go into the Lotus Pond to bathe, but lazily roams in the Himalaya Mountains."

Yang said, "In the Clear Cool Mountains, ten thousand bodhisattvas."

Mingsong said, "In Vimalakirti's congregation, the saints gather."

Li said, "Carrying dry firewood on his back, he encounters a wildfire."

Mingsong said, "The mouth is the gateway of disaster."

Guanghui Lian said, "'Zang's head is white, Hai's head is black.'"

Fenyang Zhao said, "Addressing heaven, his hands press the earth; phew!"

Dahui commented, "Monkeys ride on a turtle's back."

Question: "The heaven of thirty-three deities is above the sun and moon; in the fourth meditation there are no disasters of wind or fire; at Sanjiao the cart of an iron ox is ridden, at Linru the seal of complete presentation is gripped; a monkey has an ancient mirror; a cat has spiritual radiance reaching ten thousand miles—who is it that directly understands?"

Mingsong said, "In the morning he looks southeast; in the evening he looks northwest."

Yang said, "Cats and cows do know of existence."

Mingsong said, "Fatally stuck in reeds on a grave."

Li said, "Heating an oil pot in the moonlight."

Mingsong said, "A stone man's belt."

Guanghui Lian said, "Straw-sandal Chan, Diamond Zhou."

Fenyang Zhao said, "Pleated Robe again meets Hu, 'the Nail.'"

Dahui said, "A small excursion, a big meeting."

Question [writing the word "tail" inside a circle]: All Buddhas are inside: move, and you're bereft of your body and life; stare, and you're blind on both sides. When you hesitate, a thousand mountains, ten thousand rivers; even if you understand immediately, you're sitting on the ground in a storehouse of coal. If there's anyone who doesn't spare his eyebrows, convey the message."

Mingsong said, "Shattered."

Yang said, "I never lie."

Li said, "Leaving its burrow, the rabbit runs into a net."

Mingsong said, "No impediment east or west, free north and south."

Guanghui Lian said, "Brandishing his staff, he goes down into hell."

Fenyang Zhao said, "Boring through mountains, penetrating stone walls, his nose is bleeding."

Dahui commented, "One experiences the results of one's own actions."

[280]

Master Huanglong Xin said to an assembly,

An empty valley transmits echoes; time and again you hear what you haven't heard. Adhesive within color is clear; everywhere you see without seeing. Since there is no seeing in seeing, and what has not been heard is heard, this is called the door of absorption in the inexhaustible treasury, the door of spiritual powers of the inexhaustible treasury, the door of wisdom of the inexhaustible treasury, the door of liberation of the inexhaustible treasury. If one can know and see thus, believe thus, cultivate and realize thus, awaken and enter thus, I say this person has reached the source of the Buddha-mind, entered the knowledge and vision of Buddhas. Since this is entering the knowledge and vision of Buddhas, is this subjective perception or objective perception? If it is objective perception, what do you take to be the subject? If it is subjective perception, what do you consider the object? If you consider that both subjective and objective perception are not the Buddha vehicle, what is the Buddha vehicle?

Therefore the Realized One is not intellectually clever; the Realized One is the source of wisdom. The founding teacher is not comprehended by subtlety; the founding teacher is the essence of subtlety. Once the source and essence are distinguished, clarity and pollution are self-evident. Once you understand clarity and pollution, substance and function are both complete. Once you are complete in substance and function, you attain great freedom. The precious sword of Spiritual Peak is always openly present, able to kill people and also able to give people life. Trying to advance results in loss of life; trying to retreat turns against the person concerned. But tell me, how do you express not advancing and not retreating? [Pause.] The pines in the valley, a thousand years old—cranes come and gather. The red cassia on the moon—phoenixes nest.

[281]

The enshrouding demon king led his cohorts following Diamond Navel bodhisattva for a thousand years but couldn't find out where he appeared. Suddenly the demon got to see him one day and asked, "Where do you abide?" The bodhisattva said, "I don't abide in an existent abode, and I don't abide in no abode. I abide this way."

Fayan said, "Granted that the enshrouding demon king didn't see Diamond Navel, what about Diamond Navel—did he see the enshrouding demon king?"

Dahui said, "Since they couldn't find the place of appearance, what were they following for a thousand years? Diamond Navel said, 'I don't abide in an existent abode, nor abide in no abode; I abide like this.' They fooled each other. Fayan said, 'Granted that the enshrouding demon king didn't see Diamond Navel, did Diamond Navel see the enshrouding demon king?' Such a critique is seeing a hole and putting a stopper in it. Right now isn't there anyone who knows where I appear? [Following up with a shout:] Why are you talking in your sleep?"

[282]

Master Zhou of Guangde monastery in Rang province said to an assembly,

Before the bell just now had rung, you elders must have known the time; why should you show up? Holding a symbol of authority at my chest actually serves to submerge and cramp you elders. This being so, I've strewn sand in your eyes. The Buddhas of past, present, and future are on your noses turning the wheel of the great teaching—look, look! [Pause.] The rites of spring are being carried out in winter.

[283]

A monk asked Master Yi of Taizi monastery in Fen province, "What is the realm of Fenyang like?" He said, "The Helu mountains are covered by clouds and mist; the water of West River, rushing, pours into the ocean." The monk asked, "What is the person in the realm like?" The master said, "The local noble enforces proper order; beware of violating his dignity." The monk asked, "What should a student be familiar with?" The master said, "Sitting straight, mindful of the characteristics of reality." The monk asked, "What is the point of turning around?" The master said, "The head of the street, the tail of the alley." The monk asked, "Where is effort to be applied?" The master said, "A thousand-pound load sways on both sides." The monk asked, "I've gotten your instructions on three propositions; is there anything beyond?" The master said, "There is." The monk asked, "What is beyond?" The master struck him. The monk asked, "One tune has no notes—how can I harmonize?" The master said, "Three times nine is twenty-seven; play a pipe at the fence." The monk said, "The musical scale is not related to the subtle; a stone man claps and laughs." The master said, "Only one on the same path will know."

[284]

A monk asked Master Guo of Dacheng monastery in Tang province, "What is the thing that has been transmitted since time immemorial?" The master said, "A gold dish is presented—everyone look!" The monk asked, "What is the meaning of the coming from the West?" The master said, "When the sky clears, the sun comes out." The monk said, "I don't understand." The master said, "When rain falls, mud forms."

[285]

Master Dayu Zhi said to an assembly,

Vertically it comprehends past, present, and future; horizontally it pervades the ten directions—pick it up, and the emperor of gods is startled; put it down, and the earth spirits are shaken. If you don't pick it up and don't put it down, what do you call it? [He answered himself:] A frog.

He also said to the group,

The Buddhas of past, present, and future do not know existence; cats and cows do know existence. [Then he held up his whisk and said,] Cats and cows are all here, radiating light and shaking the earth. Why is it so? The two stages are not the same.

Dahui commented, "If Dayu had not made the latter statement, he might have had his eyes replaced by cats and cows. Even so, he still didn't escape a back-and-forth of balance weights."

[286]

Master Bajiao said to an assembly,

Suppose someone traveling suddenly comes upon a ten-thousand-fathom pit in front of him, while a wildfire is approaching him from behind. On both sides are thickets of thorns. If he goes ahead, he falls into the pit; if he retreats, the wildfire burns him. If he turns to either side, he is obstructed by a forest of thorns. Now how can he escape? If he can escape, he must have a way out. If he can't escape, he is a fallen dead man.

[287]

Master Linji asked the monastery superintendent, "Where have you been?" He said, "I've been to town to sell yellow rice." Linji drew a line with his staff and said, "And did you manage to sell this?" The superintendent shouted; Linji hit him. The chief cook came, and Linji recounted this to the cook. The cook said, "The superintendent didn't understand what you meant." Linji said, "What about you?" The cook bowed; Linji hit him too.

Huanglong Nan said, "When the superintendent shouted, it would not do to let him go. When the cook bowed, he let go what wouldn't do. Linji carried out the imperative. As for my two 'wouldn't do,' after twenty years there will be someone who will explain."

[288]

Nanquan asked a lecturer, "What scripture can you lecture on?" He said, "The scripture on Maitreya's incarnation." Nanquan said, "When will Maitreya be incarnated?" He said, "Now he's in heaven, yet to come." Nanquan said, "There is no Maitreya in heaven, and no Maitreya on earth."

Dongshan cited this and asked Yunju about it. Yunju said, "If there is no Maitreya in heaven, and no Maitreya on earth, who gives the name?" At this question, Dongshan's seat shook; he said to Yunju, "When I was at Yunyan's I questioned the old man, and the brazier shook; today, questioned by you, my whole body runs with sweat."

Ming-an said, "Now I cite this; if there is anyone who can pose a question, do so." Then he said, "The earth is shaking."

Dahui commented, "I don't deny that the seat shook, the brazier shook, and the earth shook, but if these three old fellows want to see Nanquan, they'll have to wait until Maitreya is incarnated. If someone comes forth and says, 'If there is no Maitreya in heaven and no Maitreya on earth, then who would you have incarnated?' how would you reply? I would just tell him, 'My fault.'"

[289]

Master Xuedou cited an ancient who said: "Sand can't get in the eyes, water can't get in the ears—if there is someone who can trust completely and hold still, and not be fooled by others, what sound of a hot pot are the verbal teachings of patriarchs and Buddhas?

"Then let him hang up his bowl bag and break his staff—he is definitely a wayfarer without issues. Also an ancient said the polar mountain can fit in the eyes, the water of the ocean can fit in the ears, ordinary folk listen to others' deliberations, the verbal teachings of patriarchs and Buddhas are like dragons taking to water, like tigers in the mountains; then it is necessary to pick up the bowl bag and carry the staff—this too is a wayfarer without issues. It is also said this way won't do, not this way won't do either; after that, there's no connection. Of these three wayfarers with no issues, you need to choose one to be your teacher."

Dahui commented, "Which among these three people can be a messenger? I want to call him to wash my feet. Xuedou is this way; I am not this way. If a patchrobed monk comes forth and says they should be charged on the same indictment, you can't suspect him."

[290]

The Twenty-Seventh Patriarch Prajnatara showed Bodhidharma a priceless pearl given him by a king of southern India and asked, "This pearl is round and bright—is there any that could match this?" Bodhidharma said, "This is a worldly treasure, not fit to be considered supreme; of all treasures, the treasure of Dharma is supreme. This is worldly luster, not fit to be considered supreme; of all luster, the luster of wisdom is supreme. This is worldly brilliance, not fit to be considered supreme; of all brilliance, the brilliance of mind is supreme. The lustrous brilliance of this pearl cannot shine of itself; it needs the light of knowledge to discern it. Once one discerns this, one knows this is a pearl; once one knows it's a pearl, then one understands it's a treasure. If one understands it's a treasure, the treasure is not a treasure of itself. If one discerns the pearl, the pearl is not a pearl of itself. The pearl is not a pearl of itself in that one must use the pearl of knowledge to distinguish a worldly pearl. That a treasure is not a treasure of itself means that it is necessary to depend on the treasure of wisdom to understand the treasure of Dharma. So you have the Way, Teacher, thus the treasure appears. When people have the Way, the same is true of the treasure of mind."

The reverend Prajnatara knew Bodhidharma was his Dharma successor, and subsequently entrusted the treasury of the eye of truth to him. He said in verse,

> The mind ground produces seeds;
> It also produces principles based on facts.
> When the fruit is complete, enlightenment is fulfilled;
> When the flowers blossom, the world arises.

Dahui commented, "He explained the principle; you should take refuge in Buddha, Dharma, and Sangha."

[291]

Chan master Yangqi Zhenshu said to an assembly,

All human consciousnesses have one source, provisionally called Buddha. When the physical body comes to an end, this does not perish. Metal may liquefy, simplicity may be lost, but this is always there. In the ocean of essential nature, golden waves rise spontaneously without wind. The vital spirit of mind has no sign, but myriad forms are equally perceived. Those who comprehend these principles reach everywhere without speaking; their work assists mystic influence without exertion. How can you turn away from awareness and instead get mixed up in the toil of the senses, mistakenly imprisoning yourself in the clusters and elements?

[292]

Master Shitou asked Layman Pang one day, "How are your everyday affairs since you met me?" He replied, "If you ask about everyday matters, there's simply no way to say." Shitou said, "I knew you were thus; that's why I asked." The layman then presented a verse, saying,

> Everyday affairs are no different;
> It's just that I myself am in harmony.
> At no point is it a matter of grasping or rejecting;
> Nowhere is there any reaching out or turning away.
> Who gives titles of nobility?
> There's not a speck of dust in the mountains.
> Spiritual powers and marvelous functions—
> Hauling water and carrying firewood.

Shitou approved of this.

[293]

Master Fahua Ju said to an assembly, "One, two, three, four, five; you may cite them in reverse. When have pillars and lamps ever become Buddhas and patriarchs? Those who do not spare their eyebrows, say it right away." A monk asked, "Say what?" The master said, "Outside of the light dress of midnight to ten, a jug and wool cloak." The monk said, "At just such a time, then what?" He said, "Meditating at night, the solitary moon is cool; arising in the morning, a fleck of cloud is high." The monk hesitated, trying to think of something to say. The master said, "Understand?" The monk said, "No." So the master composed a verse to teach him, saying,

> Thirty, fifty—why cite anymore?
> Adapting successfully to square and round,
> Eliminate Buddhas and patriarchs.

Before they have made the names known
I cannot grasp them.

[294]

Master Jiuling Yuan called on Changqing. Changqing asked, "What is your name?" He said, "Mingyuan." Changqing said, "What about the matter of the Other Side?" He said, "I retreat two steps." Changqing said, "Why do you pointlessly retreat two steps?" Yuan had nothing to say. Changqing said in his stead, "If I do not step back, how can I know Mingyuan?" Yuan thereupon got insight.

Later a monk asked, "When there is not a single thing ahead and responsive function lacks nothing, then what?" Yuan held up a firebrand; that monk got insight.

[295]

The Hindu ascetic Dirghanakha, soliciting a debate with the Buddha, said, "I would debate with you; if my doctrine is refuted, I'll cut off my own head." The Buddha said, "What is the basis of your doctrine?" The ascetic said, "I take total nonacceptance to be fundamental." The Buddha said, "Do you accept this view?" The ascetic abruptly left. On the way he reflected and said to his disciples, "I should go back and cut off my head to apologize to the Buddha." His disciples said, "You should hopefully gain victory in the presence of humans and deities—why cut off your head?" The ascetic said, "I would rather cut my head off before a man of wisdom than gain victory before ignoramuses." Then he said regretfully, "My doctrine fails on two points. If I accept this view, my failure is crude; if I do not accept this view, my failure is a fine point. No humans, deities, or followers of the two vehicles know the point of failure of my doctrine; only the Buddha and the great bodhisattvas know the failure of my doctrine." He went back to the Buddha and said, "My doctrine fails on two points, so I should cut off my head to apologize to you." The Buddha said, "There is no such thing in my doctrine of enlightenment. You should change your mind and aim for enlightenment." At this the ascetic and his group of five hundred disciples all submitted to the Buddha at once, became monks, and realized sainthood.

Master Tianyi Huai said in verse,

> If he accepts this view, he disbands his school;
> If he doesn't accept this view, with whom will be debate?
> The carrying pole suddenly breaks; both sides fall off.
> Heaven and earth appear on the tip of a hair.

[296]

Dongshan said to an assembly, "Brethren, at the beginning of autumn, the end of summer, you go east and go west; you should just go where there is not a single inch of grass for ten thousand miles." He also said, "But how do you go where there is not an inch of grass for ten thousand miles?"

Later a monk cited this to Shishuang. Shishuang said, "As soon as you go out the gate there's grass."

Dahui commented, "Haven't you heard it said that a single drop of lion's milk disperses ten gallons of donkey milk?"

[297]

The master known as the Oven Breaker did not reveal his name or surname. His speech and action were inscrutable. He lived in seclusion on Mount Song. The mountain villagers had a shrine they considered most sacred. In it there was only an oven. People far and near constantly held ceremonies, cooking many living creatures to death. One day the master, accompanied by attendant monks, went into the shrine; he knocked the oven three times with his staff and said, "Tsk! This oven is just a construction of clay and brick; where does the holiness come from, whence does the sanctity arise, to cook living creatures to death this way?" He knocked it three more times, and the oven collapsed. The master said, "It's broken, collapsed!" In a trice someone in a blue robe and tall hat appeared and bowed to him. The master said, "Who are you?" He said, "I was originally the spirit of the oven of this shrine. For a long time I have been subject to consequences of action. Now that you've explained the principle of no origin to me, I've been freed from this place and born in heaven; I came just to thank you." The master said, "This is your inherent nature, not my imposed explanation." The spirit bowed again and disappeared. The attendant monks asked, "We've been attending you for a long time, but have not received expedient direction. What indication of method did the spirit get to be born in heaven right away?" The master said, "I just said to him, 'This is a construction of clay and bricks; where does the holiness come from, whence does the sanctity arise?' I had no reasoning for him besides this." The attendant monks stood there thinking. The master said, "Understand?" They said, "No." The master said, "Why don't you understand inherent nature?" The attendant monks were enlightened at once. Later there was a Chan master Yifeng who cited this to the national teacher An. The national teacher said in praise, "This guy thoroughly understands the oneness of beings and self. He can be said to be like the bright moon in the sky, visible to all. It's hard to fathom the line of his speech."

[298]

Linji asked Xingshan, "What is the white ox on open ground?" Xingshan imitated the lowing of an ox. Linji said, "Shut up." Xingshan said, "What about you, old brother?" Linji said, "This animal!" Xingshan gave up.

[299]

Master Jiashan had a disciple who attended him for a long time; he sent him traveling, and he made the round of Chan shops. Later he heard that his teacher had gathered a group and his way had become very famous. He returned to visit him and asked, "If you had something so extraordinary, Master, why didn't you tell me before?" Jiashan said, "When you steamed rice, I lit the fire; when you served the food, I set out the bowls—how did I let you down?" From this the disciple became enlightened.

[300]

Chan master Chang called on the Sixth Patriarch. The patriarch asked, "Where do you come from? What are you seeking?" Chang said, "I recently went to Mount Baifeng, paid respects to Master Datong, and was taught the doctrine of seeing essential nature and realizing Buddhahood; I have not yet resolved my doubts, and hope you will be so kind as to take me in." The patriarch said, "What did he say? Try to quote it to me, and I will testify for you."

Chang said, "I had been there for three months and still had gotten no instruction. In my eagerness for the teaching I went to the abbot's room alone, paid respects, and pleading, asked, 'What is the fundamental essence of my original mind?' He said, 'Do you see space?' I answered, 'Yes.' He said, 'Do you see that space has any appearance?' I said, 'Space is formless—what appearance does it have?' He said, 'Your fundamental essential nature is like space; look back into your own essential nature— nothing can be seen at all. This is called right seeing. There is nothing knowable at all—this is called true knowledge. There is no blue or yellow, long or short—you only see the complete illumination of the essence of awareness, clear and pure at its fundamental source. This is called seeing essential nature and realizing Buddhahood. It is also called the world of bliss. It is also called the knowledge and vision of the Realized.' Though I heard this explanation, I am not yet sure; I implore you to instruct me so that I won't be stuck."

The patriarch said, "That teacher's explanation still maintains perception and knowledge; that's why it makes you uncertain. I will now teach you a verse."

Not seeing a single thing but maintaining a view of nothingness
Is like floating clouds blocking the face of the sun.
Not knowing a single thing yet keeping to recognition of
  emptiness
Is like flashing lightning occurring in the vast sky.

"This knowledge and perception produce mistaken recognition at a glance—when have you ever understood expedient means? You should instantly acknowledge your error; your own spiritual light is always manifest. Always heed the verse, and your mind will be open." Then he uttered a verse, saying,

Producing intellectual interpretation with no basis,
Seeking enlightenment fixated on descriptions,
If you keep a single subjective thought of enlightenment,
How can you transcend past confusion?
The inherent source of awareness is basic;
If you follow perception, you flow madly along;
If you don't enter the room of the founding teacher,
You absentmindedly head in both directions.

[301]

Master Langya Jin held up his staff and said to an assembly, "Panshan said, 'The one road upward is slippery.' Nanyuan said, 'Standing like a mile-high wall is inaccessible.' Linji said, 'Sparks and lightning are slow.' I have a statement that settles heaven and earth; let everyone set their sights high, set their sights high." Standing up his staff, he got down from the seat.

He also said to an assembly, "Understanding in a statement, a wandering son returns home; understanding in mind, only then can one serve in the hall of honor. If you can be like this, only then are you able to step forward from the top of the hundred-foot pole. No mind in a statement, no statement in mind—once you can be like this, then how do you turn around and put forth energy? If you don't understand, the staff will put out energy for you." Standing up the staff, he got down from the seat.

[302]

Yunmen said, "Do you want to know the founding teacher?" Pointing with his staff, he said, "The founding teacher is hopping on your head. Do you want to know the founding teacher's eyes? The founding teacher's eyes are under your feet." He also said, "This is tea- and rice-feasting ghosts and spirits. Even so, ghosts and spirits are insatiable."

Dahui commented, "Haven't you heard it said that residual illusion gives luster to life?" At that time a monk standing by coughed. Dahui said, "What's wrong with my speaking this way?" As the monk tried to come up with something to say, Dahui hit him.

[303]

Changsha Cen said to an assembly,

If I were to bring up the teaching of the source completely, the weeds would be ten feet deep in front of the teaching hall. It is because I have no choice that I tell you people that all worlds in the ten directions are a single eye of the ascetic; all worlds in the ten directions are the whole body of the ascetic; all worlds in the ten directions are one's own light; all worlds in the ten directions are within one's own light; in all worlds in the ten directions there is no one who is not oneself. I always tell you that the Buddhas of all times together with the beings of the whole universe are the light of great wisdom; before the light emanates, where do you understand? Before the light emanates, there is not even any information of Buddhas or beings—where do you find mountains, rivers, and lands?

At that time a monk asked, "What is the eye of an ascetic?"

The master said, "Impossible to ever get out." He also said, "It is impossible to get out by becoming a Buddha or a master, and it is impossible to get out revolving in the six paths of existence."

The monk asked, "Impossible to get out of what?"

The master said, "Seeing the sun in daytime, seeing the stars at night."

The monk said, "I don't understand."

The master said, "The colors of the wonderfully high mountain are green upon green."

Dahui said, "A familiar place is hard to forget."

[304]

Master Lingshu was asked by a monk, "What is the way of your house?" He said, "A thousand-year field, eight hundred owners." The monk asked, "What is a thousand-year field with eight hundred owners?" He said, "A ramshackle house no one repairs."

Dahui said, "Sad man, don't talk to sad people."

[305]

When Xiangyan was in the community of Baizhang, his natural intelligence was brilliant and swift, but he couldn't attain Chan. After Baizhang passed away he went to Guishan. Guishan questioned him, "When you were at our late teacher Baizhang's place, you had ten answers for every question, a hundred answers for every ten questions. This was your brilliance and mental acuity, conceptualization of intellectual interpretation, the root of birth and death. Try to tell me something about before your parents gave birth to you." At this one question, he was simply at a loss. He went back to the dormitory and looked over the writings he used to read, looking for a saying to use for a reply. Ultimately he couldn't find one, and he lamented to himself, "A picture of a cake cannot satisfy hunger." He respectfully went up to the hall and begged Guishan to explain for him. Guishan said, "If I explained it to you, later on you'd revile me.

What I say is mine, and has nothing to do with you." Xiangyan finally took all the writings he'd collected and burned them. Then he said, "I won't study Buddhism in this lifetime; for now I'll work as a perpetual server monk and avoid belaboring mind and spirit." Then he tearfully took leave of Guishan and went straight to Nanyang; seeing the ruins of National Teacher Zhong's abode, he stayed there and built a hut. One day as he was clearing away weeds and brush, rubble hit some bamboo and made a sound; he was suddenly awakened. He went right back, bathed, and lit incense; bowing to Guishan from afar, he said in praise, "The master's great kindness surpasses that of parents; if you had explained for me back then, how could this have happened today?" Then he said in verse,

> At one impact, I forgot what I knew;
> I no longer depend on practice.
> My conduct upholds the ancient path,
> Not falling into passivity.
> Everywhere there are no tracks or traces
> In manners outside sound and form.
> Those who arrive at the Way
> All call this the supreme key.

When Guishan heard of this, he said, "This fellow is through." Yangshan, who was standing by, said, "This is composed by mental machination, conceptual consciousness; wait till I have personally tested him." Subsequently Yangshan met Xiangyan and said, "The master has praised your discovery of the great matter. Try to explain." Xiangyan then recited the foregoing verse. Yangshan said, "This comes from memory of earlier learning. If you have truly become enlightened, let's see you give another explanation." Xiangyan composed another verse, saying,

> Last year's poverty was still not actually poverty;
> This year's poverty is poverty indeed.
> In last year's poverty I still had ground to stick an awl;
> This year I'm so poor I don't even have an awl.

Yangshan said, "I'll grant that you understand the Chan of Buddhas, but you still haven't even dreamed of the Chan of patriarchs." Xiangyan composed another verse:

> I have a device;
> It's seen in the blink of an eye.
> If people don't understand,
> Call a novice besides.

Yangshan then reported this to Guishan and said, "Happily Xiangyan understands patriarchs' Chan."

Dahui said, "Guishan in his later years was good at directing plays; he made this set of live puppets admirable. But what was admirable? Each watched the movements of each other's hands and feet; how could it be known the speech was in someone else?"

[306]

When Master Judi was dwelling in a hermitage, there was a nun who came right up with a hat on and circled his meditation seat and said, "If you can speak appropriately, I'll take off my hat." Judi had no reply; the nun thereupon went off. Judi said, "Why don't you stay a while?" The nun said, "If you can speak appropriately, I'll stay." Judi again had no reply. After the nun left, Judi lamented to himself, "Though I'm a grown man, I don't have a manly spirit." He was going to abandon his hermitage to go traveling around seeking, but that night the spirit of the mountain said to him. "You don't need to leave the mountain: a living mahasattva will come and explain the teaching for you." As it turned out, in ten days Master Tianlong arrived at the hermitage. Judi welcomed him courteously and told him all about what had happened. Tianlong raised a finger to show him. Judi was immediately greatly enlightened.

After that, whenever he was asked a question, Judi would just raise a finger. There was a boy working as a food server who whenever asked anything would also respond by raising a finger. Someone said to Judi, "This boy surely can't also understand Buddhism. Whenever anyone questions him, he always raises a finger like you." Having heard this, one day Judi concealed a knife in his sleeve and called the boy to him; he asked, "I hear you also understand Buddhism; is this true?" He said, "Yes." Judi said, "What is Buddha?" The boy immediately raised a finger. Judi cut it off. The boy ran out screaming. Judi called him back; when the boy turned his head, Judi said, "What is Buddha?" The boy unconsciously made to raise his hand; when he didn't see his finger, he was suddenly greatly enlightened.

Judi always used to say, "I attained Tianlong's one-finger Chan and used it all my life without exhausting it."

Langya Jiao said in verse,

> Judi's one finger I report for you to know;
> A newly hatched hawk takes to the skies and flies.
> If you don't have the strength to lift a cauldron and uproot a
>   mountain,
> A horse that gallops a thousand miles isn't easy to ride.

[307]

Master Sanjiao said to an assembly, "If we discourse on this matter, in lowering and raising the eyebrows you've already stumbled past." At that time Magu came forth and asked, "I don't ask about lowering and raising the eyebrows; what is 'this matter'?" Sanjiao said, "Stumbled past." Magu then overturned the Chan seat. Sanjiao immediately hit him.

Changqing said, "Dispirited."

Dahui said, "He stumbled past Magu without even knowing it."

[308]

Master Zhimen Zuo said to an assembly,

There's been quite a lot of spring rain for the last two or three days, a veritable downpour. Ordinary people see water as water, celestials see water as crystal, fish see water as a dwelling, hungry ghosts see water as fire. What do you patchrobed monks call it? If you call it water, you're the same as ordinary people. If you call it crystal, then you're the same as celestials. If you call it a dwelling, you're the same as fish. If you call it fire, you're the same as hungry ghosts. So what is usual for you? This is why it is said that if one has attained, one speaks of fire without burning the mouth, speaks of water without drowning. When you eat rice every day, can you lack a single grain? Also, an ancient spoke of wearing clothes and eating rice all day long without ever chewing a single grain or ever putting on a single thread. Even so, you must really arrive here before you can accomplish this. If you have not yet arrived at this state, don't try to fake it.

A monk asked, "In the clear purity of omniscient knowledge, do hells still exist?"

The master said, "The king of hells is not created by ghosts."

"What is Buddha?"

"Wearing out straw sandals, go on barefoot."

"What is beyond Buddha?"

"Hanging the sun and moon on the tip of a staff."

"How is it when the lotus has not yet emerged from the water?"

"Lotus blossoms."

"How about after emerging?"

"Lotus leaves."

[309]

Master Shoushan Nan said,

If you want to attain intimacy, first of all don't come questioning with questions. Do you understand? The question is in the answer, and the answer is in the question. If you question with a question, I am under your feet. If you hesitate, trying to come up with something to say, then you're out of touch.

At that time a monk came forward and bowed. Shoushan immediately hit him. The monk asked, "How is it when one hangs up one's staff deep in the mountains?" He said, "Wrong." The monk said, "Wrong." Shoushan hit him.

[310]

Master Baiyun Xiang said to an assembly,

Do you people understand? Just get an understanding in the streets, at the end of the market, among butchers and brokers, in the hot water of the cauldrons of hell. If you understand this way you can be teachers of humans and celestials. If in the school of patchrobed monks, you're as far away as sky from earth. There is another type who just become good people on a bench. Tell me, which of these two kinds of people is superior?

[311]

Luzu used to immediately face the wall whenever he saw a monk come. When Nanquan heard of this, he said, "I usually tell monks to get an understanding before Buddhas appear in the world, and still can't find one or a half. This way, he will go on till the year of the donkey."

Baoju asked Changqing, "In the case of Luzu, where was the embellishment, that he was spoken of this way by Nanquan?" Changqing said, "Not one in ten thousand can withdraw himself and defer to others."

Dahui said, "If not for Nanquan, Luzu might stare right through the wall."

[312]

After Luopu had finished traveling around, he went right to the Anshan peak of Mount Jia and built a hut. After some years Jiashan came to know of this and composed a letter, which he sent a monk to deliver. Luopu received it, then sat down and extended his hand again, as if seeking something. The monk had no reply; Luopu then hit him and said, "Go back and tell your teacher about this." The monk went back and related this to Jiashan. Jiashan said, "If this monk reads the letter, he will surely come within three days. If he doesn't read the letter, this man cannot be saved." Jiashan then had someone watch for him to leave his hut, and then burn the place. As it turned out, after three days he left the hut and came. Someone told him his hut was on fire, but Luopu didn't even look back; he went directly to Mount Jia to see Jiashan. Without bowing, he stood there in front of him with folded hands. Jiashan said, "When a chicken roots in a phoenix nest, it is not of the same kind—go away." Luopu said, "I've come from afar with the wind—please meet with me once." Jiashan said, "There is no you before me, no one here." Luopu shouted. Jiashan said, "Wait, wait—don't be careless and hasty. Clouds and moon are the same, mountains and valleys are different. It's not that you can't cut off the tongues of everyone on earth, but how can you get a tongueless man to be able to speak?" Luopu stood there thinking; Jiashan then hit him.

Xinghua said, "Just know how to be Buddha—what sentient beings will you pity?"

[313]

National Teacher Zhong asked a Chan practitioner where he'd come from. He said, "From the South." The teacher said, "What teachers are there in the South?" He said, 'The teachers are quite numerous." The teacher said, "How do they teach people?" He said, "The teachers there directly point out to students that mind itself is Buddha—Buddha means awareness, and you presently are fully equipped with the nature of perception and cognition. This nature is able to raise the eyebrows and blink the eyes; its functions, going and coming, pervade the body—in the head, the head knows; in the feet, the feet know. Therefore it is called accurate pervasive knowledge. There is no Buddha apart from this. This body has birth and death, but the nature of mind has never ever been born or passed away. The birth and death of the body is like a dragon changing its bones, a snake shedding its skin, a person leaving an old house. So the body is impermanent, while that nature is permanent. Teaching in the South is generally like this."

The teacher said, "If so, it's no different from the outsider Sanjaya. He said there is a spiritual nature in this body; this nature can recognize pain and itch. When the body disintegrates the spirit leaves, like the owner of a house getting out when the house burns down. The house is impermanent, while the owner is permanent. Clearly those with such a view cannot distinguish falsehood from truth. How can this be right? When I was traveling around I saw a lot of this type; recently they've become especially abundant. They gather groups of three to five hundred cloud gazers, saying this is the message of the Southern School, taking the *Platform Scripture* and altering it, adding confused drivel and excising what the sage meant, deluding followers. How can this be the verbal teaching? Ouch! Our school is lost! If perception and cognition were the Buddha-nature, Vimalakirti would not have said, 'The truth is beyond perception and cognition; if you act on perception and cognition, this is perception and cognition—it is not seeking truth.'"

The monk also asked, "The definitive doctrine of the *Lotus of Truth* opens up the knowledge and perception of Buddhas—what about this?"

The teacher said, "This doesn't even speak of bodhisattvas or the two vehicles—how could the ignorant confusion of sentient beings be considered the same as the knowledge and perception of Buddhas?"

The monk also asked, "What is the Buddha-mind?"

The teacher said, "Fences, walls, tiles, and pebbles."

The monk said, "This is very much at variance with scripture. The

Nirvana Scripture says, 'It is other than inanimate things like fences and walls, therefore it is called Buddha-nature.' Now you say these are the Buddha-mind—are mind and nature different or not?

The teacher said, "When confused, they're different; when enlightened, they're not different."

The monk said, "Scripture says Buddha-nature is permanent, while mind is impermanent; now you say they're not different—why?"

The teacher said, "You're just going by the words, not by the meaning. It is like water freezing into ice during the cold months, and ice melting into water when it's warm. When people are confused, this freezes nature into mind; when people are enlightened, this melts mind into nature. If you cling to the inanimate having no Buddha nature, scripture shouldn't say the triplex world is only mental. So it is you yourself who are at variance with scripture, not me."

The monk asked, "If inanimate things have the nature of mind, can they teach?"

The teacher said, "They are clearly always teaching, uninterruptedly."

The monk said, "Why don't I hear them?"

The teacher said, "You yourself don't hear."

The monk said, "Who can hear?"

The teacher said, "The saints can hear."

The monk said, "Have common people no part in it?"

The teacher said, "I teach for common people, not for saints."

The monk said, "I am deaf—I do not hear the teaching of inanimate things. You must hear it."

The teacher said, "I don't hear it either."

The monk said, "If you don't hear it, how do you know inanimate things teach?"

The teacher said, "Lucky I don't hear it—if I could hear it, you wouldn't hear my teaching."

The monk said, "Can common people ultimately get to hear it?"

The teacher said, "If common people hear it, then they are not common people."

The monk said, "What scriptural basis is there for the teaching of the inanimate?"

The teacher said, "Haven't you read the *Flower Ornament* saying, 'Lands teach, beings teach, everything in all times teaches'?"

The monk said, "Beings are sentient, aren't they? You've only said inanimate things have Buddha-nature—what about sentient beings?

The teacher said, "Since it is true even of the inanimate, how could it not be true of sentient beings?"

The monk said, "If so, then the teachers of the South who say that perception and cognition are Buddha-nature should not be classified as being the same as outsiders."

The teacher said, "I'm not saying they have no Buddha-nature. How could outsiders have no Buddha-nature? It's just that their view is wrong; they conceive of one reality as dual, so I repudiate them."

The monk said, "If both have Buddha-nature, well, if you kill sentient beings that is binding action subject to retribution, but I've never heard that there is retribution for damaging inanimate things."

The teacher said, "Sentient beings are subjective; they think of self and possession, and form resentments, so there are consequences of wrongdoing. Inanimate things are objects and have no feelings of resentment, so it is not said that there is retribution."

The monk said, "In the teachings we only read that sentient beings become Buddhas; we do not see inanimate things receiving the prediction of enlightenment. And which of the thousand Buddhas in the eon of intelligence was an inanimate Buddha?"

The teacher said, "It is like a crown prince is just an individual before he has inherited kingship, but after he inherits the throne the whole land belongs to the king—is the land enthroned separately? Now when a sentient being receives the prediction of attaining Buddhahood, all lands in the ten directions are the body of Locana Buddha—how can there be inanimate objects receiving the prediction in addition?"

The monk said, "If all beings live on the body of Buddha, then they befoul the body of Buddha with excrement, they excavate and tread upon the body of Buddha. How could there be no wrongdoing?"

The teacher said, "The totality of beings is Buddha; who do you want to consider at fault?"

The monk said, "Scripture says the body of Buddha is unobstructed; now you take compounded solid things to be the body of Buddha—doesn't this contradict the holy teaching?"

The teacher said, "The major scripture on transcendent insight says you cannot speak of the uncompounded apart from the compounded. Do you believe form is empty?"

The monk said, "It is the true word of Buddha—how could I not believe?"

The teacher said, "If form is empty, how could there be any obstruction?"

The monk said, "If sentient beings' Buddha-nature is the same, it only takes one Buddha's practice for all sentient beings to be liberated at that time. Now this is not so; where is the significance of sameness?"

The teacher said, "Haven't you seen the *Flower Ornament* doctrine of six characteristics, which states that there is difference in sameness and sameness in difference and that this is true of all the categories of becoming and decay, totality and distinction? Although sentient beings and Buddhas have the same one nature, this does not preclude separate individual cultivation and individual attainment. I have never seen that when others eat I am full."

The monk said, "There are teachers who indicate to students that if they just know their own nature, when they die and slough off this leaking shell, the intelligent nature affixed to the spiritual dais departs, and this is called liberation. What about this?"

The teacher said, "I have already said this is still a judgment of the two vehicles and outsiders. The two vehicles reject birth and death and delight in nirvana. Outsiders also say, 'I have great trouble because I have a body' and aim for oblivion. People who have entered the stream spend eighty thousand eons; those of the other three attainments spend sixty, forty, and twenty thousand eons; and pratyekabuddhas spend ten thousand eons absorbed in space, while outsiders dwell for eighty eons in neither perception nor nonperception. The two vehicles, when these eons are complete, can still shift their minds to the Great Vehicle, while outsiders return to cyclic existence."

The monk said, "Is Buddha-nature of one kind, or different?"

The teacher said, "It cannot be of one kind."

The monk said, "How so?"

The teacher said, "There is the completely unborn and undying, and the half born and half dying, half not born or dying."

The monk said, "Who makes this interpretation?"

The teacher said, "Here with me Buddha-nature is completely unborn and undying; with you in the South, Buddha-nature is half born, half dying, and half not born or dying."

[314]

Dongshan went to Guishan and asked, "I recently heard that National Teacher Zhong held that inanimate things teach; I have not yet plumbed that subtlety." Guishan said, "Here I also hold this, but it's hard to find suitable people." Dongshan said, "Do tell, Master." Guishan said, "The mouth born of my father and mother will never explain for you." Dongshan said, "Is there anyone who sought the Way at the same time as you?" Guishan said, "There is a series of caves from here; there is a wayfarer, Yunyan—if you can watch the wind by the way it blows the grass, he'll certainly be esteemed by you."

When he got to Yunyan he asked, "Who can hear the teaching of the inanimate?" Yunyan said, "The inanimate can hear." Dongshan said, "Can you hear?" Yunyan said, "If I could hear it, you wouldn't hear my teaching." Dongshan said, "Why don't I hear?" Yunyan stood up his whisk and said, "Do you hear?" Dongshan said, "No." Yunyan said, "You don't even hear my teaching; how could you hear the teaching of the inanimate?" Dongshan said, "In what scripture is the teaching of the inanimate?" Yunyan said, "Haven't you read the Amitabha scripture saying, 'Water birds and woods all remembrance Buddha and remembrance Dharma; inanimate plants and trees pipe and sing in concert'?" At this Dongshan had insight. He then produced a verse, saying,

Wonderful, wonderful!
The teaching of the inanimate is inconceivable.
If you listen with your ears you'll never understand;
When you hear their voice with your eyes, only then will you know.

Later, when he left Yunyan, he asked, "After you die, if someone asks whether I can describe your likeness, how shall I reply?" Yunyan was silent for a long while, then said, "Simply say, 'Just this is it.'" Dongshan sank into thought. Yunyan said, "Having gotten this matter, you really have to be thorough." Dongshan left without saying anything. Later, as he was crossing water, he saw his reflection and only then was he suddenly enlightened. Then he produced a verse, saying,

Just avoid seeking from others,
Or you'll be estranged from self.
I now go on alone; everywhere I meet It.
It now is really I; I now am not It.
Only when understanding this way
Can one accord with suchness as is.

[315]

Linji said to an assembly,

There is someone who is on the road yet not away from home; there is someone away from home who is not on the road—which one deserves the support of humans and celestials?

Dahui said, "The thief's body is already exposed."

[316]

Master Shexian Sheng said to an assembly,

Journeying Chan followers must be deliberate. Study requires the eye to study, the state of perception must find expression of the state of perception; only then do you have some familiarity, and only then will you not be confused by objects and not fall into evil ways. Ultimately, how do you understand? Sometimes expression reaches but mind does not—you mistakenly focus on phenomena that are reflections of thought about present sense data. Sometimes mind reaches but expression does not—you are like blind people touching an elephant, each describing it differently. Sometimes mind and expression both reach—breaking through heaven and earth, light illumines the ten directions. Sometimes neither mind nor expression reach—people with no eyes run hither and thither, and suddenly fall unawares into a deep pit.

He also said to an assembly,

The bloodline of the teachers of the school, the ordinary or holy, Nagarjuna, Vasubandhu, heaven, hell, boiling water in cauldrons, coals of furnaces, oxhead soldiers of hell, myriad forms, sun, moon, stars and planets, other regions, this land, sentient beings, inanimate things—[drawing a line with his hand] all enter this school. In this school it is possible to kill and also possible to give life. To kill you need a killing sword; to give life you need a life-giving expression. What are the killing sword and life-giving expression? Anyone who can say, come forth and try to tell everyone. If you can't say, you are failing your everyday life.

A monk asked, "If one has not yet understood oneself, what can be used as a test?" The master said, "Striking the signal to sleep in a bustling marketplace." The monk asked, "What does that mean?" The master said, "Lighting a golden lamp at noon."

[317]

Master Zhenjing said to an assembly,

In the school of Dongshan, sometimes we mix with mud and water, sometimes we stand like a wall a mile high. If you people try to see Dongshan in mixing with mud and water, Dongshan is not in mixing with mud and water. If you try to see Dongshan in standing like a wall a mile high, Dongshan is not in standing like a wall a mile high. If you try to see Dongshan everywhere, Dongshan is not everywhere. If you don't want to see Dongshan, Dongshan has you by a nose halter. If you try to go to sleep, he gives the halter a yank, making your eyes spin without you even knowing it. I don't need you to know Dongshan—if you just get to know yourself, that will do.

[318]

Master Baofu Huo was asked by a monk, "How is it when a house that is poor gets robbed?" He said, "It cannot be wiped out." The monk asked, "Why can't it be wiped out?" He said, "The thief is one of the family." The monk said, "If he is one of the family, why does he become a thief?" He said, "Since there is no response inside, he can do nothing outside." The monk asked, "When the thief is suddenly caught, where is credit due?" He said, "I've never even heard of a reward." The monk said, "Then it is effort without achievement." He said, "It's not that there is no achievement; it is accomplished without resting on it." The monk asked, "Since it is a successful achievement, why not rest on it?" He said, "Haven't you heard it said that peace is originally achieved by the general, but it is not permitted for the general to see peace?"

Dahui said, "Wrapped up in fooling."

[319]

Master Lumen Tan was asked by a monk, "What is the noumenal ground of ultimate reality?" He said, "The southern continent, the northern continent." The monk said, "Then things are the same unity." He said, "They're still separated by the polar mountain."

[320]

Master Deshan said to an assembly,

Having no issues in regard to self, don't seek at random. Attaining something by random seeking isn't attainment. Just have nothing on your mind; when you have nothing on your mind, you are openly aware, sublimely unoccupied. Even the slightest course of speech is all self-deception; even the slightest fixation of thought is active causation of the three mires [of hells, hungry ghosts, and animality]; even a flicker of emotional arousal is a fetter for myriad eons. The names of the holy and the epithets of the ordinary are all empty sounds; exceptional appearances and inferior shapes are all illusory forms. If you want to seek these, how can you not be burdened? But then if you reject them, that too becomes a great affliction. In the end there is no benefit.

[321]

Master Dazhu said to an assembly,

You people are luckily naturally fine people without issues; why do you suffer fatally contriving to wear stocks and go to prison? Every day until nightfall you run fitfully, saying you're studying Chan, learning the Way, understanding Buddhism. This way you become increasingly out of touch. This is just pursuing sound and form—when will you stop? I heard Master Mazu say, "Your own treasury is totally complete—use it freely; it isn't based on external seeking." From this I came to rest at once; my own treasure is available for use wherever I am. This can be called happiness. There is nothing to grasp, and nothing to reject. I do not see any sign of origin or destruction in anything; I do not see any sign of coming or going in anything. Throughout the worlds in the ten directions, there's not a single atom that's not your own treasury. Just carefully examine on your own the three treasures in one body in your own mind. This is always spontaneously evident, without doubt. Don't pursue thought, don't seek; the essence of mind is originally pure. Therefore the *Flower Ornament Scripture* says, "All things are unborn, all things are undying. If you can understand this way, the Buddhas will always be present." Also, the scripture *Vimalakirti's Advice* says, "Contemplate the true characteristic of the body; the Buddha is also thus." If you do not follow sound and form-stirring thoughts, and do not pursue appearances, conceiving interpretations, you will naturally have no issues. Don't keep standing there—goodbye. [The assembly remained without dispersing; Dazhu said,] Why are you people staying here, not leaving? I have already made a presentation to your face; will you stop? What is there to doubt? Don't misuse your mind, madly wasting your energy. If you have feelings of doubt, you may ask whatever you want.

A monk asked, "What is Buddha? What is the teaching? What is the community? What are the three treasures in one body?"

The master said, "Mind is Buddha; you don't need to use Buddha to seek Buddha. Mind is the teaching; you don't need to seek the teaching by means of the teaching. Buddha and the teaching are not two; their combination is the community. This is the three treasures in one body. Scripture says, 'Mind, Buddha, and living beings—these three have no distinction.' Purity of body, speech, and mind is called Buddha appearing in the world; impurity of their actions is called Buddha passing away. For example, it is like when angry there is no joy, and when joyful there is no anger—it is just one mind; actually there are no two entities. When basic wisdom naturally without fault manifests, it is like a snake transforming into a dragon, without changing its scales; when people turn their minds around to become Buddhas, they don't change their faces. Essential nature is fundamentally pure, and doesn't depend on cultivation to become so. Having realization and cultivation is the same as conceit. True emptiness has no blockage, responsive function is inexhaustible, beginningless, endless; those of keen faculties suddenly awaken, function without compare—this is unexcelled enlightenment. Mind has no form or appearance—this is the subtle body; having no appearance, it is itself the reality body as it really is. Nature and characteristics are inherently empty—this is the boundless body of space. The array of myriad practices is the reality body of virtue. The reality body is the basis of myriad transformations;

they are named according to the situation. The function of wisdom is inexhaustible—this is called the inexhaustible treasury. It can conceive myriad truths—this is called the treasury of fundamental truth. It is endowed with all-knowledge—this is called the treasury of insight. Myriad things are ultimately as such—this is called the treasury of those who arrive at suchness. Arrival at suchness means the suchness of all things. All things in the world, becoming and disappearing, are without exception ultimately thus."

He was asked, "Scripture says, 'Those six teachers of outside paths are your teachers; you left home relying on them. When those teachers fall, you too fall along with them. Those who donate to you are not called fields of blessings; those who support you fall into the three evil paths. Slandering Buddha, tearing down the teaching, not entering into the numbers of the community, ultimately not allowing transcendence in extinction—if you are like this, then you can take food.' Now I request the Chan master to clearly explain this."

Dazhu said, "Randomly going along with the six sense faculties is called the six teachers. Seeking Buddha outside mind is called outside paths. Possessing something to donate is not called a field of blessings. Intentionally accepting offerings falls into the three evil ways. 'If you can slander Buddha' means not seeking with fixation on Buddha. 'Tearing down the teaching' means not seeking with fixation on the teaching. 'Not entering the numbers of the commnity' means not seeking with fixation on community. 'Ultimately not attaining transcendence in extinction' means the function of knowledge is present. If there are any who can understand this way, they obtain the 'food' of delight in truth and the bliss of meditation."

He was also asked, "A scripture on insight speaks of liberating all kinds of sentient beings so they all enter nirvana without remainder; it also says there are really no sentient beings attaining liberation in nirvana. How can these two passages of scripture be reconciled? Everyone says it means actually liberating sentient beings without grasping the features of sentient beings. I've always wondered about this and am still uncertain; please explain to me.

He said, "All kinds of sentient beings are inherent in one body; they develop according to actions. Therefore ignorance constitutes birth from eggs, being wrapped up in afflictions constitutes birth from wombs, immersion in the water of affection constitutes birth from moisture, and suddenly occurring affliction constitutes birth from transformation. When enlightened, one is a Buddha; when deluded, one is called a sentient being. Bodhisattvas just consider successive thoughts sentient beings; to undertand successive thoughts are essentially all empty is called liberating sentient beings. The insightful liberate before formation in their own original state; since before formation is empty, they know there really are no sentient beings attaining liberation by extinction."

[322]

Yunmen held up his staff and cited the teachings, saying, "Ordinary people actually consider this existent, the two vehicles analyze it and call it nonexistent, those awakened to conditionality call it illusory existence, bodhisattvas identify its essence with emptiness, and patchrobed monks see a staff and just call it a staff—when they walk they just walk, and when they sit they just sit, totally unshakable."

Dahui said, "Bitter gourd is bitter to the root; sweet melon is sweet to the stem."

[323]

Master Lingquan Ren was asked by a monk, "What was the intention of the founding teacher?" He said, "Facing upward, raising his eyebrows alone; turning his head, clapping by himself." When asked, "What is your family style?" he said, "Riding an ox wearing a hat of woven vines, crossing water wearing shoes and a shirt."

[324]

Master Sheng of Mount Da'an was asked by a monk, "Please speak apart from the four propositions and beyond the hundred negations." The master said, "There is no such sword in my armory." He was asked, "How is it when there are multiple locks and no information gets through?" He said, "How did you manage to get here?" The questioner said, "What about after arriving?" He said, "How are things therein?" He was asked, "What is the real of the real?" He said, "A clay Buddha at a crossroads."

[325]

Master Lumen Zhen was asked by a monk, "What is your family style?" He said, "There is salt, no vinegar." He was asked, "What is a wayfarer like?" He said, "The mouth is like the nose." He was asked, "Suppose a guest comes; how do you treat him?" He said, "Thanks for passing by this rustic shack." He was asked, "What is Chan?" He said, "A phoenix goes into a chicken coop." He was asked, "What is the Path?" He said, "A lotus fiber leading a huge elephant." He was asked, "When the eon disintegrates, does *this* disintegrate too?" He said, "Facing a bank, looking at the edge, is particularly sad." He was asked, "What is your turning point?" He said, "Last night at midnight I lost my pillow."

[326]

Master Letan Jun said to an assembly,

Drilling a precious pearl or sawing a jade slab is easy; seeing a hole and putting in a stopper is hard. The color of the moon merged with the clouds is white; the sound of the pines soaked in dew is cold—I don't ask you people about this; but tell me: what did Elder Maudgalyayana and Subhuti discuss? [Silence.] The handle of the dipper in the house to the east is long; the handle of the dipper in the house to the west is short.

[327]

Master Dongshan Chu said to an assembly,

Here at Dongshan, ordinarily in the abbot's room it's not like the Chan path or Buddhism subjectively expounded elsewhere, one coming, one going, humming and buzzing. I have always explained fully to you, spoken fully, held forth fully, sifted fully; there's no room for you to block or cover up one way or another. I have turned it all out at once; how do you Chan worthies understand? Try to tell the assembly. It's like the case of insects being able to land anywhere but not being able to land on flames of fire. You get the sweet talk of old baldies elsewhere dealt out to you, saying 'This is Chan,' 'This is the Way,' 'This is enlightenment, nirvana,' 'This is reality as is, liberation.' Your eyes are bunged with stoppers two-foot-eight long, yet you do not know, are not aware; coming here to Dongshan, you don't know what I'm talking about. Can you understand? Even if you understand reality as is, nirvana, bodhi, and liberation—it makes no difference—you're tied up by the feet and can't get loose. If you are spiritually sharp patchrobed monks, you'll bite right through and be free and clear. Wouldn't that be pleasant? If you chomp and chomp and can't chew through, as before you enter an antique shop. When will you ever get out? I cannot help but make effort for you as a bystander.

[328]

Master Tiantong Qi asked Master Fulong, "Where have you come from?" He said, "From Fulong [meaning "subdued dragon"]." Qi said, "And did you manage to subdue the dragon?" Fulong said, "I never subdued this beast." Qi said, "Go have some tea."

Also, the great worthy Jian asked, "The student comes standing out, requesting the teacher to be clear and to the point." The master said, "Here I crap once, and that's all—what 'outstanding' or 'clear and to the point' are there?" Jian said, "Answering like this, you'd better buy straw sandals and go traveling again." The master said, "Approach." Jian approached;

the master said, "What is wrong with my answering this way?" Jian had no reply. The master hit him.

[329]

Jiashan said to an assembly, "Remain the master, and you don't fall into a second view." Master Baiyuan Tong came forth from the crowd and said, "It should be known that there is one person who doesn't join company." Jiashan said, "This is still a second view." Tong overturned the Chan seat. Jiashan said, "What about you, old brother?" He said, "When my tongue rots I'll tell you."

Another day Tong asked, "'There is nothing before the eyes. The mind is before the eyes. *This* is not before the eyes. It is not within reach of ear or eye'—is this not a saying of yours?" Jiashan said, "Yes, it is." Tong then overturned the Chan seat and stood there with hands folded in a salute. Jiashan got up and hit him with his staff. Tong then withdrew.

Fayan said, "Why didn't he leave as soon as he overturned the Chan seat? Why did he insist on waiting for Jiashan to hit him before leaving?"

[330]

Master Liutong Shao went to Tongquan. One day he burned off the weeds for a new field; when he came back, Tongquan asked him, "Where have you been?" He said, "Burning off a field." Tongquan said, "How are things after the fire?" He said, "An iron snake can't bore in."

[331]

Master Yungai Han was asked by a monk, "What are waves flooding the skies on a mountain peak?" He said, "Manjushri is making a ruckus." "How is it when making a ruckus?" "Not extending great compassion before an opportunity."

[332]

Jianfeng said to an assembly, "Bringing up one, don't bring up two. If you let the first move go, you fall into the secondary." Yunmen came forth from the group and said, "Yesterday there was someone who came from Tiantai and went to Jingshan." Jianfeng said, "Don't do chores tomorrow."

Dahui said, "Each one brings out the family disgrace; luckily there are no witnesses."

[333]

Master Ciming said to an assembly,

"The body of reality is formless; it manifests forms in response to beings." [Holding up his staff:] This is a staff—what is the reality body? Leaving this complication aside, the communal hall and Buddha shrine have gotten into your nostrils, the waters of the four great oceans are on your heads, the dragon kings are under your fingernails—do you feel them? If you feel them, you go three thousand by day, eight hundred by night, smoke rising under your feet, fire rising on your heads. If you don't know, eat when hungry, sleep when tired. [He planted his staff once.]

[334]

Master Wushi Guan kept his door closed and sat alone. One day Xuefeng knocked on the door, and he opened it. Xuefeng grabbed and held him and said, "Is this ordinary or holy?" Guan spat and said, "This wild fox spirit," and pushed him out and shut the door again. Xuefeng said, "I just wanted to know the old brother."

[335]

Master Shuangling Zhen asked Daowu, "Why are the tracks of a bodhisattva without spiritual powers impossible to follow?" Daowu said, "Only one on the same path would know." Zhen said, "Do you know?" Daowu said, "I don't know." Zhen said, "Why not?" Daowu said, "Go away—you don't know what I'm saying."

[336]

Master Daowu was first enlightened when he heard a shamaness in a village hut propitiating a spirit saying, "Consciousness of the spirit has no teacher." Later he called on Master Guannan Chang, who confirmed his understanding. He also went to Deshan's school; whenever there was a lecture, he'd put on a lotus blossom hat, bare his chest, take a bamboo strip, beat a drum, play a flute, and call out, "Stupid third son!" Sometimes he'd say, "I beat Guannan's drum, sing Deshan's song." Someone asked, "What was the intention of the founding teacher coming from the West?" Saluting with the bamboo strip, he said, "Yes." Once he asked Guanxi, "How are you?" Guanxi said, "No position." He said, "Isn't this the same as space?" Guanxi said, "This butcher! Where there are living beings to kill, he doesn't weary."

[337]

Master Jingshan Yin was asked by a monk, "How is it when shutting down to be like ashes?" He said, "This is still the work of people at the time." The monk asked, "What about after it's done?" The master said, "The plowman's field is not seeded." The monk asked, "What about the ultimate end?" The master said, "When the grain is ripe, not managing the field."

[338]

Master Yangqi said to an assembly,

Snow, snow everywhere, shining bright, white and pure. The Yellow River freezes shut, stopping the slightest flow. In the light of the blazing sun it must burst out. Must burst out, chewing thorns atop the head of the three-faced spirit king, bleeding under the feet of the thunderbolt bearer.

He also said,

Treading on a balance beam, it is hard as iron. When a mute has a dream, who will he tell? On the peak of the polar mountain, waves flood the sky; at the bottom of the ocean, one meets the heat of fire.

[339]

Venerable Parshva asked a boy, "Where do you come from?" The boy said, "My mind does not go." The patriarch said, "Where do you dwell?" The boy said, "My mind does not stay." The patriarch said, "Are you unsettled?" The boy said, "So are the Buddhas." The patriarch said, "You're not the Buddhas." The boy said, "The Buddhas too are not."

Dayu Zhi said, "Each question of the ancestral teacher, and each answer of the boy, all lacked understanding. Now how do you people understand?"

Dahui said, "Even if you can understand now, study for three more lifetimes, sixty eons."

[340]

Yaoshan asked Shitou, "I have a rough knowledge of the twelve-part teachings of the three vehicles; I've heard that in the South they point directly to people's mind to see its essential nature and realize Buddhahood. I really do not understand, and humbly hope for your compassion and guidance." Shitou said, "'Thus' won't do, 'not thus' won't do either;

'thus and not thus' won't do at all. What about you?" Yaoshan stood there thinking. Shitou said, "Your affinity is not here. In Jiangxi there is a great master Ma; go there, and he should explain for you."

When he got there, he posed the same question as before. Ancestor Ma said, "Sometimes I have him raise his eyebrows and blink his eyes; sometimes I don't have him raise his eyebrows and blink his eyes. Sometimes having him raise his eyebrows and blink his eyes is right; sometimes having him raise his eyebrows and blink his eyes is not right." At this, Yaoshan had insight. He thereupon bowed. Ancestor Ma said, "What principle have you seen?" Yaoshan said, "When I was at Shitou's, I was like a mosquito on an iron ox." Ancestor Ma said, "Now that you are like this, you should keep it well."

One day Ma said, "How are you these days?" Yaoshan said, "Skin shed completely, only true reality remains." Ma said, "Your attainment can be said to accord with the essence of mind and pervade your four limbs. Since you are capable of being like this, gird your belly with three strips of bamboo skin, and go dwell on a mountain wherever you are." He said, "Who am I to presume to speak of dwelling on a mountain?" Ma said, "It's not like that. There's no going forever without staying, and no staying forever without going. If you want to help, yet no one's helped; and if you want to act, nothing gets done. You should be an ark; don't stay here forever." With this, Yaoshan respectfully took his leave and went back to Shitou.

One day as he was sitting, Shitou came, saw him, and asked, "What are you doing here?" He said, "I'm not doing anything at all." Shitou said, "Then you're sitting idly." He said, "If I were sitting idly, that would be doing something." Shitou said, "You say you're not doing—not doing what?" He said, "Even a thousand sages do not know." Shitou then composed a verse:

> All along living togther, I don't know his name.
> Helping each other whatever happens, we go on just so.
> Even the lofty sages since antiquity don't know—
> How can the hasty common type understand?

Dahui said, "Goods are real value; money is variable."

[341]

Master Fojian said to an assembly,

Matters before the fifteenth day of the month—spreading flowers on brocade. Matters after the fifteenth day of the month are like a bubble in the ocean. Right on the fifteenth day is much like a one-foot mirror reflecting a thousand miles of forms. So even though real emptiness is trackless, nevertheless the oceanic reflection radiates light. Even if the exposed pillars blossom with flowers, what hundredfold ugliness of Buddha's face do you talk about? Why is it like this? "Wherever I go, the frosty night's moon descends as it will into the valley ahead."

[342]

Master Dayu Zhi said to an assembly, "You swallow the ocean on your side, I carry the polar mountain on my back; tell me, how far apart are you and I? Do you understand? Where the royal rule is rather strict, it is not permitted to plunder the markets."

A monk asked, "What is your statement for people?"

He said, "Four corners, eight surfaces."

"What does that mean?"

"Eight depressions, nine protrusions."

"What is Buddha in a city?"

"A stone flag at a crossroads."

"What is the Way?"

"Eight bushels, four pecks."

"How about the person on the Way?"

"Boiling gruel, cooking rice."

"What is Buddha?"

"Sawing apart a balance beam."

"What was the intention of the founding teacher in coming from the West?"

"Burning the ground in broad daylight and lying down, burning the ground at night and sleeping."

"People of old distinguished soils from sprouts, knew people based on their words; I come up asking the teacher to discern."

"Flowers embellish the earth."

"What is the meaning of the founding teacher's coming from the West?"

"When the weather is cold, the days are short."

"What about before Bodhidharma came?"

"He was in India."

"What about after coming?"

"He was in China."

[343]

Master Zhenjing said to an assembly,

A lion does not eat the leavings of an eagle; would a hawk attack a dead rabbit? Let out Linji's great dragon; pull out Yunman's glance. [Finally, holding up his staff, he said,] Where dragons go, rain comes; three plants, two trees.

[344]

One day Guishan was standing by Baizhang. Baizhang said, "Who is it?" He said, "Lingyou." Baizhang said, "Stir up the brazier to see if there is any fire or not." Guishan stirred it up and said, "There is none." Baizhang got up himself, stirred deeply, and found a little fire. Showing it to him, he said, "Is this not fire?" Guishan was thereupon enlightened. He bowed in thanks and presented his understanding. Baizhang said, "This is just a temporary byway. Scripture says, 'If you want to know the meaning of Buddha-nature, you must observe time and conditions.' When the time has come, it is like having been confused then suddenly understanding, like having forgotten then suddenly remembering. Then you realize your own thing is not gotten from another. Therefore an ancestral teacher said, 'Having become enlightened, it is the same as before enlighten-ment; there is no thought and no doctrine.' It is just that there is no vain thought of ordinary or holy; the original state of mind is inherently com-plete. Now that you are thus, carefully preserve it on your own."

Another day he accompanied Baizhang on a walk on the mountain. Coming to a woods, Baizhang said, "Cook, did you bring fire?" He said, "I did." Baizhang said, "Where is it?" Guishan then picked up a twig, blew on it twice, and handed it to Baizhang. Baizhang said, "Like insects eating away at wood."

Dahui said, "If Baizhang hadn't made that last statement, he might have been made a fool of by the cook."

[345]

When the master known as the Boatman parted with his fellow student Daowu, he said to Daowu, "In the future, if there is a spiritually sharp lecturer, direct one to me." Subsequently he drifted around Huading in a small boat. Hence he was called the Boatman Monk in those days. Sub-sequently Daowu went to Jingkou and came upon Jiashan lecturing. A monk asked, "What is the reality body?" Jiashan said, "The reality body has no form." The monk asked, "What is the eye of reality?" Jiashan said, "The eye of reality has no flaw." Daowu unconsciously let out a laugh. Jia-shan then got down from the chair and asked Daowu, "There must have been something wrong with my answer to this monk to make you laugh. I hope you will not begrudge compassion." Daowu said, "You're estab-lished in a way, but you still haven't had a teacher. Go to Huading and call on the Boatman." Jiashan said, "Will I be able to find him?" Daowu said, "This man doesn't have a single tile over his head or any ground under his feet."

Jiashan then changed his vestments and went directly to Huading. As soon as the Boatman saw him, he asked, "Great Worthy, what temple do you dwell in?" He said, "If it conforms, I don't dwell; if I dwell, it doesn't conform." The Boatman said, "Where did you learn?" He said, "It's not within reach of ears or eyes." The Boatman said, "A fitting statement is a ten-thousand-eon donkey-tethering stake." He also asked, "Letting down a line a thousand fathoms, the intent is in the depths. Three inches away from the hook, why don't you speak?" As Jiashan was about to open his mouth, the Boatman knocked him into the water with a pole. As soon as he climbed up into the boat, the Boatman again said, "Speak, speak!" As he was about to open his mouth, the Boatman hit him again; Jiashan was suddenly greatly enlightened. He then nodded three times. The Boatman said, "You may play with the line on the pole, but the meaning is distinct of itself without invading the clear waves." Jiashan followed up with the question, "What is your intention in casting the line and hook?" He said, "The line is lowered into the clear water; the bobber is intended to tell whether anything is there or not." Jiashan said, "Speech carries with it the mystery, but has no course; the tongue speaks without saying anything." The Boatman said, "I have fished throughout the river waves; this is the first time I've come across one with golden scales." Jiashan covered his ears. The Boatman said, "Right, right."

Finally he instructed him, "Hereafter you should just have no tracks where you hide, but do not hide where there are no tracks. In twenty years with Yaoshan, I only understood this. Now that you have attained, hereafter do not dwell in cities or villages, just seek out one or a half by a hoe deep in the mountains to continue the lineage, not letting it end." Jiashan then took leave and went. He looked back again and again; finally the Boatman called to him, and when Jiashan turned his head the Boatman stood up an oar and said, "Do you think there's something else?" Then he capsized the boat and disappeared into the water.

[346]

Master Baiyun Duan, teaching a group, cited Yunmen bringing up a verse by Sanping: "'This very seeing and hearing is not seeing and hearing'— what do you call seeing and hearing? 'There is no other sound and form to present to you'—what verbal sound and form are there? 'Here, if you comprehend, there is no issue at all'—what issue is there? 'Substance and function may be separate or not separate'—speech is substance; substance is speech. [He went on to hold up his staff and say,] The staff is substance, the lamps are function—are they separate or not separate? Haven't you read the statement that omniscient knowledge is pure?" [Baiyun said,] "Everyone, Yunmen can only draw Mount Omei based on a likeness; I am not this way. 'This very seeing and hearing is not seeing and hearing; there is no other sound and form to present to you'—eyes are eyes, ears are ears. 'Herein, if you comprehend, there is no issue at all. Substance and function may be separate or not separate'—four or five hundred rows of flowering willows, two or three thousand music pavilions."

A monk asked, "What is Buddha?" Baiyun said, "There is no cool spot in a cauldron of boiling water." The monk asked, "What is the great meaning of Buddhism?" Baiyun said, "Pressing down a gourd in water." The monk asked, "What is the meaning of the founding teacher's coming from the West?" Baiyun said, "Crows fly, rabbits run."

[347]

Nanyuan asked Fengxue, "How do you evaluate the staff of the South?" Fengxue said, "I make an exceptional evaluation." Fengxue then asked Nanyuan back, "How is it evaluated here?" Nanyuan picked up his staff, lay it across his shoulder, and said, "Acceptance of no origin under the staff; not seeing a teacher when facing a situation."

Dahui said, "At that time Fengxue should have unrolled his seat cloth and made a prostration, or else overturned the Chan seat." Then he turned to Zhongmi and said, "You tell me, at that time would it have been right for Fengxue to bow, or would it have been right to overturn the Chan seat?" Zhongmi said, "The brigand in the bush is busted." Dahui said, "Look at this blind fellow," and hit him.

[348]

Master Fahua Ju went to Master Dayu Zhi's place. Dayu asked, "What is the meaning of the man of old seeing peach blossoms?" Fahua said, "The crooked does not hide the straight." Dayu said, "Granting that for the moment, what about 'This'?" Fahua said, "Having picked up gold on a big street, how can those around know?" Dayu said, "Do you know?" Fahua said, "Meeting a swordsman on the road, show your sword; do not present a poem to one who is not a poet." Dayu said, "A master poet!" Fahua said, "Two people pull a single red thread." Dayu said, "And what about Xuansha's saying, 'Right, quite right'?" Fahua said, "When the ocean dries up, at last you see the bottom, but a person's heart is never known, even until death." Dayu said, "That's so." Fahua said, "A tower reaches the clouds; mountain peaks are piled in layers of green." He also presented a verse, saying,

> A phoenix, returning, leaps spontaneously into the sky;
> An old crow roosts in Lingyun's peach tree.
> Past and present stop versifying the meaning of the peach
>   blossoms;
> In heaven above or the human world, no one can add to it.

[349]

Master Zhaozhou said to an assembly,

A gold Buddha does not get through a furnace, a wooden Buddha does not get through fire, a clay Buddha does not get through water. The real Buddha sits within—bodhi, nirvana, suchness, and Buddha-nature are all clothes sticking to the body. This is also called affliction. If you don't ask, there is no affliction. Now where is the noumenal ground of reality placed? When one mind is not aroused, myriad things have no fault. You just sit investigating the principle for twenty or thirty years; then if you don't understand, cut off my head. It's a waste of effort to grasp dreams, illusions, flowers in the sky. If the mind does not differ, myriad things are one. Since it is not obtained from outside, why cling anymore? You are like goats randomly putting things in your mouth. I see Master Yaoshan said that if anyone posed a question he'd just have them shut their doggish mouth. I too have people shut this doggish mouth. Grasping self is defilement, not grasping self is purity. Like hunting dogs, you just want to eat something. Where is Buddhism? Here, a thousand people, ten thousand people, are all seeking Buddhism—I can't find even one wayfarer. If you are a disciple of the king of emptiness, don't make your mind sick— this is most difficult to cure. Before there was the world there was already this nature; when the world disintegrates, this nature won't disintegrate. Once you have seen me, you are none other than the master; why seek this outside any further? At precisely such a time, don't turn your head around and exchange your brain; if you turn your head around and exchange your brain, you'll lose it.

At that time a monk asked, "I understand you to say that when the world disintegrates this nature does not disintegrate; what is this nature?" He said, "The four gross elements and five clusters." The monk said, "These are still subject to disintegration; what is this nature?" He said, "The four gross elements and five clusters."

Fayan said, "Are these one or two? Do they disintegrate or not? How do you understand? Try to decide."

Dahui said, "A celestial king in a military camp."

TRANSLATOR'S NOTE

The four gross elements and five clusters refer to the physical and mental constituents of the human being.

[350]

Master Dahui Zhen said to an assembly,

Fenzhou said, "If you know the staff, the task of travel is finished." [Then he raised his staff and said,] This is a staff; what is the task of travel? Even if you can see here, in the school of patchrobed monks you're just a rank novice. If you don't know, divine this way and that in a village of three families; even if you hit upon a determination, it's still uncertain.

[351]

At Zihu's school he set up a sign saying, "Zihu has a dog that takes people's heads on top, takes people's hearts in the middle, and takes people's legs below. Hesitate and you lose your body and life." A monk asked, "What is Zihu's dog?" The master howled. Two monks from Linji's congregation came to call; as soon as he raised the blind, the master said, "Look out for the dog!" The monks turned and looked; the master immediately went back to his quarters.

[352]

In India bells and drums were prohibited, so this was called a purge [of Buddhism]. After seven days, the honorable Deva used supernatural power to go up into a tower and ring the bell. A crowd of outsiders gathered at the bell tower and found the door locked. Then they shouted, "Who is up in the tower ringing the bell?" Deva said, "Deva" [meaning "god"]. The outsiders said, "Who is the god?" He said, "I" ["Self"]. They said, "Who is Self?" He said, "You." They said, "Who is 'you'?" He said, "Dog." They said, "Who is a dog?" He said, "You." They said, "Who are 'you'?" He said, "I" ["Self"]. They said, "Who is Self?" He said, "God." They went back and forth like this seven times; the outsiders all realized they were defeated, and petitioned the king to ring bells and sound drums again, promoting Buddhism.

TRANSLATOR'S NOTE

This story plays on the Hindu identification of *atman* and *Brahman,* as self and deity, or individual and universal soul.

[353]

Master Huayao Ying, teaching an assembly, held forth his staff and said,

I now guarantee this matter for you—it is ultimately not in vain. The great enlightened World Honored One was a speaker of truth, who told of reality, who told it like it is, not fooling, not contradicting, not cheating you people. But can you actually believe? [Shouting once, he said,] Nothing to grab on to, climb up above; no self below; sky and earth both emerge from within the mind. Over ten thousand miles, the eighth and ninth months; on one body, the northwest wind. [He planted the staff.]

[354]

Datian was asked by Shitou, "What is your mind?" He said, "What manifests speech." Shitou then shouted him out. After ten days Datian asked, "If what I said earlier was not right, other than this, what is mind?" Shitou said, "Excluding raising the eyebrows and blinking the eyes, bring forth mind." He said, "I have no mind—how can I bring it forth?" Shitou said, "You've always had a mind—how can you say you've no mind? Negating mind is just the same as slander." At these words Datian awakened.

Dahui said, "Tell me, what did Datian realize?"

[355]

Master Ni of White Horse Mountain was asked by a monk, "What is the pure reality body?" He said, "A frog in a well swallows the moon." "What is the true eye of White Horse?" "Facing south gazing at the North Star."

[356]

Master Baoming Yong said to an assembly, "The great square has no out-side; the great circle has no inside. No inside, no outside, holy and ordi-nary everywhere congregate. Tiles and pebbles radiate light; the polar mountain shatters into smithereens—innumerable teachings, a hundred thousand absorptions." [Raising his staff:] "It's all here—understand? Sulu sulu, sheelee sheelee."

He also said to an assembly, "The manifestation of reality has no form; indicating form, manifesting form, a thousand oddities, ten thousand descriptions. Appearing from this, when joyful, the whole face is radiant; when angry, both brows stand up. Not ordinary, not holy, sometimes so, sometimes not—humans cannot assess; no celestials can fathom. Even if one can bring it up directly, one is still not great. If one does not turn his head when called, don't mistakenly suspect him."

[357]

A monk asked Shishuang, "Why does one not see the teacher's face close up?" Shishuang said, "I say the whole world has never hidden it." The monk later asked Xuefeng, "What is the meaning of 'the whole world has never hidden it'?" Xuefeng said, "What place is not Shishuang?" The monk went back and related this to Shishuang. Shishuang said, "What is this old fellow's rush?" Xuansha said, "The old fellow on the mountain has stumbled past."

[358]

Master Yunju Ying said to an assembly,
    Those who attain aren't flippant; those who understand don't act meanly. Those who know don't bemoan; those who understand have no contempt. What comes down from heaven is poverty; what springs up

from the earth is wealth. Establishing oneself within the school is easy; leaving the school within oneself is hard. Move, and you bury yourself ten thousand feet deep; don't move, and you produce sprouts where you are. Transcend to freedom at a single saying, and you stand out alone in your time. Speech should not be much; if there's a lot, it has no use.

[359]

Master Jingshan Feng said to an assembly,

Piercing the clouds not crossing waters, crossing waters not piercing the clouds, heaven and earth—holding still, not holding still; space—letting go, not letting go. Three horizontal, four vertical; now separating, now joining. It's not that there is no using the long to make up for the short. People, "cooked rice is rice" makes a statement, but it is hard to say. [Pause.] Private affairs don't get official response.

A monk asked, "What is entering concentration in a single atom?"

He said, "A snake bites a rat's tail."

"What is emerging in all atoms?"

"A turtle bites a fishing pole."

The monk said, "Then east and west are not distinguished, south and north are not distinguished."

He said, "A single lamp to light the night in front of the hall, several stalks of shining green bamboo outside the blind."

"How is it before the Buddhas appear in the world?"

"Not inscribing the wine shop's sign."

"How about after they appear in the world?"

"Giving three taps aboard a fishing boat."

[360]

Master Deshan Yuanming said to an assembly,

Just study the living word, don't study the dead word. If you understand from the living word, you'll never be bogged down in doubt. "Each atom is a Buddha-land, each leaf is a Buddha"—these are dead words. Raising the eyebrows, blinking the eyes, raising a finger, standing up a whisk—these are dead words. "Mountains, rivers, and earth have no further mistake"—these are dead words.

A monk then asked, "What is the living word?"

He said, "A Parsi looks up."

The monk said, "Then I'm not mistaken."

Yuanming thereupon hit him.

[361]

Master Yunmen said to a newcomer, "Master Xuefeng said, 'Clear the way—Bodhidharma's coming!' I ask you what you make of this." The monk said, "Bumping into the master's nose." Yunmen said, "The earth spirit explodes, taking the polar mountain, leaps to the Brahma heaven, and smacks the emperor of gods in the nose; why do you hide your body in Japan?" The monk said, "Better not fool people, Master." Yunmen said, "What about bumping into my nose?" The monk had no reply. Yunmen said, "I knew you were just a literalist."

Dahui said, "Carrying a load of confusion, one exchanged it for a load of curios. Weighing it out on a scale with no markers, one handed it over to a lacquer bucket of ignorance. Now tell me, what will the lacquer bucket of ignorance use it for? If you can utter an independent living statement, I'll admit you see Yunmen in person."

[362]

Master Kaixian Zhi said to a group,

Aim and instruction are provisional expressions; Buddhas and patriarchs are imposed terms. Receiving instruction and communicating mind are both vanities; seeking reality and searching for truth get even further off. If you take your self and your own mind to be ultimate, there is necessarily something else and someone else in contrast.

At that time a monk asked, "What would be right?"

He said, "'Right' means there is 'wrong.'"

"How does one gain entry?"

"When were you ever outside?"

[363]

Master Wuzu Yan said to an assembly,

Yesterday I went into the city and saw a puppet show. I couldn't help approaching to watch, and I saw some exceptionally fine looking, others unbearably ugly. Having seen them individually moving around, walking and sitting, blue, yellow, red, and white, when I looked closely it turned out there was someone behind a blue curtain. Unable to restrain myself, I asked the puppet master's name. He said, "Old monk, just watch—why ask for a name?" At this remark of his, I simply had no reply, no reason to give. Can anyone speak for me? Yesterday I lost my reserve over there; today I pay back the principal here.

He also said,

Baiyun doesn't know how to explain Chan. The three gates open out to both sides. There is someone moving the mechanism: two sides—east flap, west flap.

He also said,

Lingyun's verse on awakening on seeing peach blossoms says, "For thirty years I've sought out a swordsman; how many times have the trees shed their leaves and again sprouted twigs! Ever since seeing peach flowers once, right up till now I've never doubted anymore." Xuansha said, "Right, quite right, but I dare say the elder brother is not yet through." What "right" is he talking about? It'll take thirty more years of study to get it.

[364]

Master Muzhou said to a group,

Have you people found an entry yet? If you haven't found an entry yet, you should find an entry. If you have found an entry, henceforth don't let me down.

He also said,

I tell you very clearly yet you still don't understand, let alone if I cover up.

At that time a monk came forth and bowed and said, "I would never dare let you down."

Muzhou said, "You've already let me down."

Dahui said, "Tsk! Has he complicated it or not?"

[365]

Master Longya said to an assembly,

People who investigate the mystery must pass beyond Buddhas and patriarchs before they can get it. Master Dongshan said, "Only when the verbal teachings of the patriarchs and Buddhas are like born enemies do you have a part in study." If you cannot pass beyond, you will be fooled by the patriarchs and Buddhas.

A monk then asked, "Do the patriarchs and Buddhas have any intention of fooling people?"

The master said, "You tell me—do rivers and lakes have any intention of obstructing people?" He also said, "Though rivers and lakes have no intention of obstructing people, because people cannot cross them at the time, rivers and lakes turn out to obtruct people, so you can't say rivers and lakes don't obstruct people. Although patriarchs and Buddhas have no intention of fooling people, because people of the time cannot pass beyond, patriarchs and Buddhas turn out fooling people; so you can't say patriarchs and Buddhas don't fool people. If one can pass beyond patriarchs and Buddhas, this person is beyond patriarchs and Buddhas. Only then does one realize the intent of patriarchs and Buddhas. Then one is the same as transcendent people. If one has not passed beyond, and only studies Buddhas and seeks patriarchs, then one will never get out in a million years."

The monk then asked, "How does one avoid being fooled by patriarchs and Buddhas?"

The master said, "The Way must simply be realized on one's own."

Someone asked, "What is the meaning of the founding teacher's coming from the West?"

The master said, "When a stone turtle can talk, then I'll tell you."

"The turtle is speaking."

"What does it tell you?"

"What did the ancients attain so that they came to rest?"

"It's like a thief entering an empty house."

[366]

Master Baoci Yu was asked by a monk, "What is it like when meeting with the mind's eye?"

He said, "What does it say to you?"

"What is true seeing?"

"Nothing interposed."

"This way it's immediate seeing."

"Southern Spring is a very good place to go."

"What is the meaning of the coming from the West?"

"Last night in the middle of the night I accompanied him across the river."

"How is it when applied as the situation arises?"

"East of the ocean is a fruit tree pith."

[367]

Master Xiquan Xi was asked by a monk, "Buddha was delivered by Maya; whose son are you?"

He said, "Raising a red flag over the water."

"Of the thirty-six strategies, which way is most subtle?"

"Not making the first move."

"What if suddenly confronted?"

"It's not hard to put your back on the ground."

[368]

Elder Taiyuan Fu was managing the bath house at Xuefeng. In the course of a visit by Master Xuansha to Xuefeng, Xuefeng said, "I have an old rat here—now he's under the bath house." Xuansha said, "Wait till I check him out for you." As soon as he went there, he saw Elder Fu putting in water; he said, "A new arrival has come to see you." Fu said, "We've already met." Xuansha said, "In what eon have we ever met?" Fu said, "Don't snooze." Xuansha went back and told Xuefeng, "I've checked him out." Xuefeng said, "How did you check him out?" Xuansha related the foregoing talk. Xuefeng said, "You ran into a brigand."

Dahui said, "One more's been checked out."

[369]

Zhu Shiying, edict attendant, once asked Master Zhenjing in a letter, "Buddhism is extremely subtle—how does one concentrate in the midst of daily affairs; how does one study? Please be so kind and compassionate as to point this out."

Zhenjing replied, "The ultimate subtlety of Buddhism is nondual, but until you have reached the subtlety there is comparative superiority and inferiority. When one reaches the subtlety, then the person who understands mind actually knows one's own mind is ultimately originally

enlightened, is actually independent, is actually at ease, actually liberated, actually pure, and in daily affairs just uses his own mind. If you can
take hold of the transformations of your own mind, then use it, without
asking if it's right or wrong. If you set your mind to thinking, already
you don't know. If you don't take on an attitude, it is naturally real in
every particular, clear and sublime in every particular, in every particular like a lotus blossom to which water does not adhere. The purity of
mind transcends that, so if you're confused about your own mind you
are a common creature, while if you understand your own mind you're a
Buddha. So common creatures are Buddhas, and Buddhas are common
creatures—it is due to confusion or enlightenment that they are one or
the other.

"Now many people who study the Way do not trust their own mind,
do not understand their own mind, are not able to use the clarity and
subtlety of their own mind, and do not attain the ease and liberty of their
own mind. They mistakenly seek Chan and the Way externally, mistakenly set up wonders, and mistakenly create grasping and rejection. Even
if they cultivate practice, they fall into the nihilistic states of outsiders
or the two vehicles. So-called practice may fall into the pit of annihilation or eternity. Those with nihilistic views extinguish the original subtle
clear nature of their own mind—they just stick to voidness outside mind
and remain in meditative stillness. Those with the view of eternity do
not realize the emptiness of all things, and they cling to the existents of
the world as realities, considering them ultimate."

[370]

Master Xitang Zang was asked by a layman, "Are there heavens and hells
or not?" He said, "There are." The layman said, "Do the treasures of
Buddha, Dharma, and Sangha exist or not?" He said, "They do." The layman asked many more questions, and the master answered them all in
the affirmative. The layman said, "Are you not mistaken in saying so?"
He said, "Have you seen an adept?" The layman said, "I have called on
Master Jingshan." He said, "What did Jingshan tell you?" The layman

replied, "He said it's all nonexistent. The master said, "Do you have a wife?" The layman said, "Yes." The master asked, "Does Master Jingshan have a wife?" The layman said, "No." The master said, "For Master Jingshan, it's right to speak of nonexistence."

[371]

Prime Minister Li asked a monk, "What verbal teaching does Grand Master Ma have?" The monk said, "Sometimes he says mind is Buddha; sometimes he says it is not mind, not Buddha." Li said, "It's all beyond 'this side.'" Li instead asked Master Xitang Zang, "What verbal teaching does Grand Master Ma have?" Zang called, "Prime Minister!" Li responded. Zang said, "The drums and horns directing the army have gone into action."

[372]

When Nanquan Puyuan came to Letan, he saw Master Letan Xing facing a wall. Nanquan patted him on the back. Xing asked, "Who are you?" Nanquan said, "Puyuan." Xing said, "How are you?" Nanquan said, "As usual." Xing said, "Why are you so busy?"

Dahui said, "He wanted to check."

[373]

Chan master Yan of Oxhead Mountain had been a commandant of a Soaring Hawks garrison during the Great Works era of the Sui dynasty. He always had a water-straining bag hung from his bow, and he used it to draw water wherever he went. He went on expeditions with the major general and repeatedly served meritoriously in combat. During the Martial Virtue era of the Tang dynasty, when he was forty years old, he finally sought to become a renunciant. He went into the Huangong mountains in Shu province and followed Chan master Baoyue, becoming his disciple. Once when he was in a valley, he went into concentration, tranquil and undisturbed by the rising mountain waters, and the water receded of itself.

There were two men who in the past had served in the army with him, who heard Yan had gone into seclusion and went together into the mountains to look for him. When they found him, they said to Yan, "Commandant, are you crazy? Why are you living here?" He replied, "My madness is about to clear up; your madness is just starting. Indulging in materialism, craving glory and greedy for favor, you whirl around in birth and death—how can you get yourselves out?" The two men, edified, sighed in admiration and left.

Later Yan went into Oxhead Mountain, called on Chan master Rong, and discovered the great matter. Rong told him, "I received the true secret from Great Master Daoxin. Whatever I had attained disappeared. Even if there were something beyond nirvana, I'd say it too is like a dream illusion. When a single mote of dust flies, it blocks out the sky; when a single mustard seed falls, it covers the earth. You have already gone beyond this perception—what more is there for me to say?"

[374]

The Sixth Patriarch heard a monk quote a verse by Wolun saying, "Wolun has a skill, able to cut off a hundred thoughts; when mind is not aroused in face of objects, enlightenment grows day by day." The patriarch said, "This verse does not clarify the ground of mind; if you practice based on this, it increases bondage." Accordingly he presented a verse, saying, "Huineng has no skills, does not cut off a hundred thoughts. Mind is aroused repeatedly in face of objects; how can enlightenment grow?"

[375]

A monk came to Master Sushan about building a monument. Sushan asked him, "How much money are you going to give to the builder?" The monk said, "It's entirely up to you, Master." Sushan said, "Are you going to give the builder three coins, two coins, or one coin? If you can answer, build the monument for me yourself." The monk had no reply.

At that time Master Luoshan was living in a hermitage on Dayu Ridge. That monk went to Luoshan, who asked him where he'd come from. He said he'd come from Sushan. Luoshan asked him what sayings Sushan had uttered recently, and the monk repeated what Sushan had said. When Luoshan heard this account, he said, "Has anyone been able to tell?" The monk said no one had been able to speak. Luoshan said, "Go back to Sushan and tell him that I heard about this on Dayu and said, 'If you give the builder three coins, the master will surely never get a monument in all his lifetime. If you give the builder two coins, the master and the builder together will put forth one hand. If you give the builder one coin, you'll burden the builder and his eyebrows and whiskers will fall out.'" The monk then went back and quoted this to Sushan. Hearing this statement, Sushan bowed ceremoniously toward Dayu Ridge and said in praise, "I thought there was no one; on Dayu there is an ancient Buddha radiating light reaching all the way here." Then he told the monk, "Go to Dayu and say he's like a lotus blossom in winter." The monk then took this statement to Luoshan. Luoshan said, "Turtle hair has already grown several yards."

[376]

Long ago a certain monk went to see Cuiyan, but he was absent at the time. So the monk saw the superintendent. The superintendent asked if he'd visited the master hitherto; he said he hadn't. The superintendent then pointed to a dog and said, "If you want to see the master, eminent, just bow to this dog." The monk was speechless. Later Cuiyan returned and heard about this. He said, "How would one avoid being speechless like this?" Yunmen said, "If you want to observe the teacher, first observe the disciple."

Dahui said, "At that time, if I were this monk I'd have bowed to the dog."

[377]

The Eighteenth Patriarch Jayashata went to the country of Visha. He met the [future] Nineteenth Patriarch Kumarata, who asked, "What is this group?" The patriarch said, "Buddhist disciples." When he heard the epithet "Buddha," he got scared and immediately shut his door. After a while the patriarch knocked on the door. He said, "No one's home." The patriarch said, "Who is answering?" Hearing his words as unusual, he finally opened the door.

Fenyang Zhao said in his stead, "It just so happens I've forgotten."

[378]

Master Sushan Ren held a wooden snake; a monk asked, "What is that in your hand?"

Sushan held it up and said, "A daughter of the Cao family."

"What is the master's family style?"

"A foot-and-a-half turban."

"What is a foot-and-a-half turban?"

"Inside a circle can't be grasped."

He also cited a saying of Xiangyan and asked Jingqing, "'Agreement can't be total'—how do you understand?" Jingqing said, "It totally depends on agreement." Sushan said, "What about 'agreement can't be total'?" Jingqing said, "In this there is no way of agreement." Sushan said, "You've finally satisfied me."

[379]

When Cloth Robe Zun came to the foot of Mount Shao, he met Master Shaoshan Pu. Zun asked, "Which way is the road up Mount Shao?" Shaoshan pointed it out and said, "Oh, it goes into that deep green darkness." Zun went up and grabbed him and said, "Long have I heard of Shaoshan; isn't that you?" He said, "Yes, indeed, I am; what's your business?" Zun said, "I would pose a question; will you answer?" Shaoshan said, "Considering that you aren't a master archer, how will you shoot a general?" Zun said, "A phoenix goes right into the misty sky; who's afraid of a wild sparrow in the woods?" Shaoshan said, "You may go ahead and beat the drum drawn in the hallway; try to set forth your way for me." Zun said, "A single statement goes beyond a thousand sages; the vines on the pines are not on the same level as the moon." Shaoshan said, "Even if you are beyond the prehistoric Buddha, you're still half a month's journey behind me." Zun said, "Where is my fault?" Shaoshan said, "Exceptional sayings, people of the time know to exist." Zun said, "So then real jade is distinct in the mud, not eliminating the dust of myriad workings." Shaoshan said, "You're exercising skills in vain at the workshop of a master craftsman." Zun said, "I am just thus; how about you?" Shaoshan said, "An immortal girl tosses a shuttlecock at night, weaving brocade in the home to the west." Zun said, "Isn't this your way?" Shaoshan said, "When a farmer makes a jade water-clock, it's not the work of a specialist." Zun said, "This is still literary talk—what is your way?" Shaoshan said, "Lying across the universe, who is it that shows up?" Shaoshan also said, "You have a spirit soaring to the sky; I have strategy going into the earth. You swallow the ocean; I carry the polar mountain. You come on wielding a sword; I await you thrusting a spear. Hurry up and tell me the one road beyond." Zun said, "A clear mirror is on its stand—please take a look." Shaoshan said, "I won't look." Zun said, "Why not?" Shaoshan said, "In shallow water there are no fish; it's useless effort to let down a hook." Zun had nothing to say. Shaoshan then hit him.

Dahui said, "They'd make Muzhou laugh his head off."

[380]

Master Langya Jiao said to an assembly,

A monk asked Mazu, "What is Buddha?" He said, "Mind is Buddha." The monk asked, "What is the Way?" He said, "Not minding is the Way."

The monk asked, "How far apart are Buddha and the Way?" He said, "Buddha is like an open hand; the Way is like a closed fist." That man of old was not without expedients, but I too have a bit here. If no one buys, I'll sell myself and buy myself. What is Buddha? There are a multitude of auspicious herbs in front of the crag. What is the Way? There are plenty of spiritual sprouts below the valley stream. How far apart are Buddha and the Way? Several bits of white clouds enshroud an ancient temple; a single stream of aquamarine water encircles the green mountain.

He also said to an assembly,

The former Liangshan said, "Those who come from the South, I give thirty blows; those who come from the North, I give thirty blows. Even so, this does not amount to the fundamental vehicle." Liangshan's fine piece of real gold he turns into hard iron to sell off. I do not concur. Those who come from the South, I give thirty blows; those who come from the North, I give thirty blows; let all the patchrobed monks on earth detract.

[381]

Master Letan Jun said to an assembly,

"If you want to know the meaning of Buddha-nature, observe time and season, causes and conditions." As I recall, in olden times a monk asked Yunmen, "What is the song of Yunmen?" Yunmen said, "The twenty-fifth day of the last month of the year." The monk asked, "How about the one who sings it?" Yunmen said, "Easygoing for the moment." Chan worthies, is this not time and season? How do you understand Yunmen's meaning? Where the clear sound of the song of Yunmen penetrates, it encompasses the ten directions. Those who join in can hardly match; it is not the same as the six notes. Therefore it is said, "When the family to the east sings songs, the family to the west can't sit silent." For me today a fleeting opportunity is hard to catch up with; I'll sing a round to offer the community—listen clearly, listen clearly. [Then, drawing out his voice, he sang:] La la li li lila. It's a cold day; for now I'll say half—go back to the hall and have tea.

Also, on a day when the earth spirits are celebrated after the autumn equinox, he said to the assembly,

Myriad kinds of setups do not compare to normalcy, which doesn't startle people and is always as usual. It is like when the autumn wind comes it has no intention of chilling people, but people naturally feel chilly. Sweet melon is sweet to the stem; bitter gourd is bitter to the root. This morning everyone in the land pays respect to the shrine god and shrine goddess. Only the king of the entire year is totally rough in the chill.

[382]

The Ground-Hitting Monk got the essence from Mazu. He concealed his name. Whenever a student posed a question, he'd just hit the ground with a stick; in his time he was called the Ground-Hitting Monk. One day a monk hid his stick and asked him a question; he turned around looking for his stick, but didn't see it. He said, "If it were here, I'd be able to apply a stroke of the stick." Someone asked one of his disciples what he meant when he just hit the ground whenever he was asked a question. His disciple immediately took a piece of kindling out of the stove and tossed it in the pot.

Dahui said, "When an adopted son is not as good as his father, the family declines in a single generation."

[383]

Gushan asked Master Xiuqi, "Sound and form are pure reality—what is the Way?" Xiuqi said, "Why are you speaking arbitrarily?" Gushan crossed from east to west and stood there. Xiuqi said, "If you're not thus, it's a disaster." Gushan then crossed over to the east. Xiuqi then got off the Chan seat; just when he had gone one or two steps, Gushan grabbed and held him and said, "Sound and form are pure reality—what about this fact?" Xiuqi slapped him. Gushan said, "In ten years you won't even have anyone to pour tea, even if you want." Xiuqi said, "Why would I want old Gushan?" Gushan laughed aloud three times.

[384]

A monk came to call on Master Hualin; just as he unrolled his seat cloth, Hualin said, "Slowly, slowly." The monk said, "What do you see?" Hualin said, "It would be a pity if you bumped into the bell tower." The monk became enlightened from this.

[385]

Master Huangbo Hui called on Master Sushan Ren. When he first arrived, he found Sushan sitting in the teaching hall accepting inquiries. Hui first looked over the great assembly, then asked, "How is it when leaving instantly?" Sushan said, "Space is full; how will you leave?" He said, "If space is full, it's better not to leave." Sushan then stopped. Hui left the hall and called on the chief monk. The chief monk said, "I just watched you replying to the master; what you said was quite extraordinary." Hui said, "I just blurted it out; really it just happened that way. Please be so kind and compassionate as to instruct me in my ignorant confusion." The chief monk said, "In an instant is there any hesitation?" Hui was greatly enlightened at these words.

[386]

When Master Panshan was in the community of Great Master Ma, he went out into the marketplace to preach; he happened to see a customer buying pork saying to the butcher, "Cut a pound of the fine stuff for me." The butcher put down his cleaver, saluted, and said, "Inspector, which is not fine?" Panshan had an insight from this. Later, one day he went out and saw a funeral procession; a cantor was ringing a bell and saying,

"The crimson disc surely sinks in the west—where will the spirit go?" The pious son inside the curtains cried, "Alas, alas!" Panshan then became greatly enlightened. He went back dancing, and Ancestor Ma confirmed his realization. When Panshan was about to pass away, he said to the community, "Can anyone depict my likeness?" Some of the group drew portraits of him and presented them, but none were found suitable. Then Puhua came forth and said, "I can depict the master's true likeness." Panshan said, "Show me." Puhua did a somersault and left. Panshan said, "Where will this little pisser get a grip on craziness?"

[387]

In Jiashan's community there was a monk who went to Shishuang; as soon as he stepped across the threshold he said, "How are you?" Shishuang said, "Not necessary, Professor." The monk said, "If so, then goodbye." That monk also went to Yantou's place, and as before said, "How are you?" Yantou made a sighing sound. The monk said, "If so, then goodbye." As the monk turned around, Yantou said, "Though this one is young, still he can stay focused." The monk returned and related this to Jiashan. Jiashan went up in the hall and said, "Let the monk who went to Yantou and Shishuang earlier come forth and cite it factually." When the monk had finished his recital, Jiashan said, "Everyone, do you understand?" No one in the community had a reply. Jiashan said, "If no one can say, I won't spare my eyebrows but go ahead and say. Though Shishuang has the sword that kills, still he lacks the life-giving sword. Yantou also has the killing sword, and he has the life-giving sword as well."

Dahui said, "Don't speak of a dream in front of the ignorant."

[388]

Master Wuzu Fayan said to an assembly,

If you solely go thus, the road is cut off and the people are few; if you solely come thus, you turn against sages of the past. If you leave these two roads, patriarchs and Buddhas cannot get near. Even if you are born the same and die the same as me, that still doesn't amount to normality. Why? A phoenix is not an ordinary bird; it won't roost on any but a phoenix tree.

He also said to an assembly,

So, so—a shrimp cannot leap out of a basket. Not so, not so—playing at cleverness turns out clumsy. Soft as iron, hard as mud—twelve pairs of adamantine eyes. In the hands of a patchrobed monk, the balance lowers; there is a price, with no bargaining. How does one with no nostrils smell fragrance?

A monk asked, "What is the business of the Linji lineage?"

He said, "A criminal hears thunder."

"What is the business of the Yunmen lineage?"

"A crimson flag flashing."

"What is the business of the Cao Dong lineage?"

"Sending a letter, it doesn't get home."

"What is the business of the Gui Yang lineage?"

"A broken sign lies across an ancient road."

The monk bowed. Wuzu said, "Why didn't you ask about the business of the Fayan lineage?"

The monk said, "I leave that to you, Master."

Wuzu said, "A watchman stays up at night."

[389]

Master Changqing Leng called on Lingyun. Leng asked, "What is the great meaning of Buddhism?" Lingyun said, "Before the business of the ass has passed, the business of the horse comes up." Leng went back and forth from Xuefeng to Xuansha for twenty years this way but still hadn't understood this matter. One day as he rolled up a blind he was suddenly greatly enlightened. Thereupon he said in verse, "Wonderful, wonderful—rolling up a blind, I see the whole world. If anyone asks what religion

I understand, I'll pick up a whisk and whack him the moment he opens his mouth." Xuefeng quoted this to Xuansha and said, "This guy has penetrated." Xuansha said, "Not yet—this is an expression of intellectual perception; I'll have to test him further." In the evening when the monks came up to ask questions, Xuefeng said to Leng, "Xuansha still doesn't approve of you; if you really have true enlightenment, bring it up before the assembly. Leng said in another verse, "In myriad forms, the body revealed alone—only when people spontaneously acknowledge it is it familiar. In the past I mistakenly sought on the road—as I view it today, it's ice within fire." Xuefeng turned to Xuansha and said, "This can't be another expression of intellectual perception."

Later he dwelt at Changqing. In his community there was a superintendent in charge of buckets who was always talking to the monks. One day Leng went into the dormitory and saw him; he asked, "What are you doing blabbering every day?" The superintendent said, "A day without working is a day without eating." Leng said, "Then draw a bow and shoot an arrow." He said, "I'm just waiting for the garrison commander to come." Leng said, "After the garrison commander has come, then what?" He said, "Wait for his tendons and bones to be strewn over the ground and his eyeballs to pop out." Leng then left.

[390]

Meditation master Mengshan Ming followed Workman Lu to the Dayu Ridge. When the workman saw Ming come, he placed the robe and bowl on a rock and said, "This robe represents faith—is it worth fighting over? Go ahead and take it." Ming tried to pick it up but it felt heavy as a mountain and wouldn't budge. Stymied and frightened, he said, "I came seeking the Dharma, not the robe. Please teach me." The patriarch said, "Not thinking of good, not thinking of evil, at precisely such a time what is your original face?" Ming was thereupon greatly enlightened. His whole body running with sweat, he tearfully bowed and asked, "Outside of the foregoing esoteric saying's esoteric meaning, is there any further point?" The patriarch said, "What I said to you just now is not esoteric; if you look back into your own face, the secret is in you." Ming said, "Though I went along with the community at Huangmei, I really didn't see into my own face. Now that I've had a way in shown to me, I'm like someone drinking water who knows for himself if it's cool or warm. Now you are my teacher." The patriarch said, "If you are thus, you and I both had Huangmei as a teacher. Keep it well yourself."

[391]

A monk asked Master Duofu, "What is the bamboo grove of Duofu like?" He said, "One or two canes slanted." The monk said, "I don't understand." He said, "Four or five canes curved."

Dahui said, "Granted your 'one or two canes slanted, four or five canes curved,' give me back the bamboo grove of Duofu. And how can you undersand verbally?"

[392]

A monk asked Master Shoushan Nian, "How is it when myriad machinations die out?" He said, "Stagnant water does not contain a dragon." The monk said, "How about after activation?" Shoushan said, "The blue-eyed foreign monk smiles and nods." The monk asked, "What is the road of right practice?" Shoushan said, "A pauper doesn't eat a variety of foods." The monk said, "He lets go and returns home." Shoushan said, "Never smelled fragrance or odor." The monk asked, "What is talk transcending Buddhas and going beyond patriarchs?" Shoushan said, "The wind and frost north of the border are intense; the snow south of the river isn't cold." The monk asked, "I've heard there's an old saying, 'Ever since seeing peach blossoms, I've never had a doubt'—what does this mean?" Shoushan said, "Two people carry a three-foot staff." The monk said, "Am I allowed to carry it?" Shoushan said, "Put it down." The monk asked, "What is the substance of reality as such?" Shoushan said, "Knocking brick, hitting tile." The monk asked, "What does this mean?"

Shoushan said, "Avoid stepping on it." The monk asked, "What is the student's original body?" Shoushan said, "Not leading an ox into town."

[393]

Master Zhenjing said to an assembly,

In the school of Dongshan you go when you need to go, sit when you need to sit; shitting in a bowl, puking in a pitcher; cultivating practice attached to dogma is like an ox pulling a millstone.

He also said to an assembly,

Ascetic Peak is covered with moss; Pen-Toss Peak is wrapped in vines. At Arhat Cloister three workers are ordained in a year; in Guizong monastery tea is taken after inquiries.

A monk asked, "What is Buddha?" The teacher laughed out loud. The monk said, "What's there to laugh about?" The teacher said, "I'm laughing at you conceiving interpretation pursuant to words." The monk said, "I happen to have lost the advantage." The teacher said loudly, "Don't bow." The monk then went back to the group. The teacher laughed again and said, "You're conceiving interpretation pursuant to words."

[394]

When Master Mingzhao came to Elder Tan's place in Quan province, Tan said, "For intensive study, one should go where there is even one person, and should go where there is even half a person." Mingzhao then asked, "I don't ask about where there is one person; what about where there is half a person?" Tan had nothing to say. Subsequently he sent a novice to ask; Mingzhao said, "Do you want to know where half a person is? It's just a fellow playing with a mud ball."

[395]

When two senior monks, Shen and Ming, came to the Huai River, they saw someone pulling in a net; there was a fish that got through and out. Shen said, "Brother Ming—how clever—it's just like a patchrobed monk!" Ming said, "Even so, how is this as good as not getting snared in the net in the first place?" Shen said, "Brother Ming, you still lack enlightenment." In the middle of the night Ming finally understood.

Dahui said, "As for what Elder Ming understood, was it what was in the net or what got out of the net?"

[396]

Yantou took leave of Deshan along with Xuefeng and Jinshan. Deshan asked, "Where are you going?" Yantou said, "Temporarily leaving you to go down off the mountain." Deshan said, "What about after that?" Yantou said, "I won't forget you." Deshan said, "Based on what do you say this?" Yantou said, "Haven't you heard the saying that to have knowledge equal to the teacher diminishes the teacher's virtue by half; only when knowledge surpasses the teacher is one qualified for transmission?" Deshan said, "So it is. So it is. Keep it well yourself."

With this, the three men took leave. When they reached Li province, Jinshan stayed there. The other two were stopped by snow when they came to Tortoise Mountain. Yantou just slept every day, while Xuefeng just sat in meditation. Xuefeng called to Yantou, "Brother, brother! You're just sleeping." Yantou yelled at him, "Get some sleep! Seated every day, you're like a village earth spirit; someday you'll charm other people's sons and daughters." Xuefeng pointed to his chest and said, "I'm not yet at peace here; I don't dare fool myself." Yantou said, "I had thought you'd someday build a grass hut atop a solitary peak and broadcast the great teaching, but still you talk like this. If you're really like this, tell me each of your insights." Xuefeng said, "I first went to Zhezhong and met Master Yanguan; he brought up the meanings of form and emptiness, and I got an entry." Yantou said, "Avoid bringing it up for thirty years hence." Xuefeng said, "Also when I read the verse of Master Dongshan on realizing the Way on crossing water, I got an insight." Yantou said, "This way you still wouldn't be able to thoroughly save yourself." Xuefeng said, "I also asked Deshan if I have a part in the business of the immemorial school of the source; Deshan hit me and said, 'What are you saying?' At this point I opened up like the bottom falling out of a bucket." Yantou shouted and said, "Haven't you heard it said that what comes in through the gate is not the family treasure?" Xuefeng said, "What would be right?" Yantou said, "Later on, if you want to broadcast the great teaching, let every particular flow from your own chest, covering heaven and earth for me." At these words Xuefeng was greatly enlightened. He jumped down, prostrated himself, then rose and shouted repeatedly, "Elder brother, today on Tortoise Mountain I've finally attained the Way! Today on Tortoise Mountain I've finally attained the Way!"

[397]

When National Teacher Shao was still a householder he asked Longya, "How is it when the sky cannot cover you and the earth cannot support you?" Longya said, "A wayfarer ought to be like this." Shao asked seventeen times. Longya said, "Wayfarer, if I told you, afterward you'd revile me." Later, when Shao was dwelling on the Mastering Mysteries peak of Mount Tiantai, he suddenly had an insight into this previous conversation as he was taking a bath. He then ceremoniously lit incense and bowed toward Longya at a distance and said, "If he had explained it all to me at that time, today I would surely revile him."

Dahui said, "Right now you're doing it quite a bit."

[398]

When meditation master Da bowed to the Sixth Patriarch, his head did not touch the ground. The patriarch scolded him, "How is bowing without touching the ground as good as not bowing at all? There must be something in your mind—what have you been practicing?" He said, "I recite the *Lotus of Truth Scripture*; I've already done it three thousand times." The patriarch said, "If you recite it ten thousand times and get the meaning of the scripture, and yet don't consider that excellent, then you go along with me. Now you are taking pride in this practice, totally unaware of your error. Listen to my verse."

> Bowing is basically to break the flagstaff of pride—
> Why should your head not go to the ground?
> When you are egotistic, fault then comes to be,
> Nullifying merit incomparably.

The patriarch also said, "What is your name?" He said, "Fada." The patriarch said, "Your name means 'Attainment of Dharma'—when have you ever attained the Dharma?" He again uttered a verse, saying,

> You're now named Attainment of Dharma;
> You recite diligently, never ceasing.
> Vain repetition just follows sound;
> When clarifying mind one is called a bodhisattva.
> You now have a chance; that's why I'm talking to you.
> Just believe Buddha has no words;
> Lotuses will spring from your mouth.

When Fada heard the verses, he repented of his error and said, "From now on I will humbly respect everyone. I only pray you will be so kind as to briefly explain the principles in the scripture." The patriarch said, "You recite this scripture—what do you take to be its aim?" Fada said, "I am stupid; all along I've just recited it literally; how would I know its aim?" The patriarch said, "Recite it for me, and I'll explain it to you."

Fada then recited the scripture out loud; when he came to the chapter on expedients, the patriarch said, "Stop—this scripture basically has causal emergence in the world as its aim. Even if it tells many sorts of similes, none go beyond this. What is the cause? Just one great matter. The one great matter is the knowledge and vision of Buddhas. Be careful not to misinterpret the meaning of the scripture. Where you see it speaking of demonstration and realization, since it is the knowledge and vision of Buddhas, you think you have no part in it—if you interpret it this way, that is slandering the scripture and destroying the Buddhas. Since they are Buddhas, they already have knowledge and vision—what would be the need to reveal it anymore? Now you should trust that the knowledge and vision of Buddhas is just your own mind—there is no other entity. It is because all sentient beings shroud their light themselves, greedy for sense objects, getting involved outwardly and agitated inwardly, accepting compulsion, that trouble Buddhas to rise from concentration and take the trouble to encourage them to stop; don't seek outside, and you are no different from Buddhas—so this is called revealing the knowledge and vision of Buddhas. You just labor to keep reciting, considering this a meritorious exercise—how is that different from a long-haired ox admiring its tail?"

Fada said, "Then should I just understand the meaning and not trouble to recite the scripture?" The patriarch said, "What's wrong with the scripture? What would prevent you from reciting it? It's just that delusion and enlightenment are in the individual; loss and gain depend on you. Listen to my verse."

> When the mind is deluded, the *Lotus of Truth* repeats;
> When the mind is enlightened, it repeats the *Lotus of Truth*.
> If you recite for a long time without understanding yourself,
> You become an enemy of the meaning without thoughts;
> When recitation is correct, with thoughts recitation becomes
>   wrong.
> When neither existence nor nonexistence are thought up,
> You always ride the white oxcart.

Fada, having heard this verse, went on to declare, "The scripture says that even if the great listeners, and even the bodhisattvas, all used all their thinking to assess it, they still could not fathom of the knowledge of Buddhas. Now you would have ordinary people just understand their own minds, and call this the knowledge and vision of Buddhas; one who does not have superior faculties will still not avoid doubt or denial. Now, the scripture speaks of an oxcart among three carts as well as a white ox- cart—how are they distinguished? Please explain further."

The patriarch said, "The meaning of the scripture is clear; you miss it by yourself. As for the fact that the people of the three vehicles cannot fathom Buddhas' knowledge, the trouble is in trying to measure. Even if they use all their thinking collectively to try to figure it out, they get fur- ther and further away. Buddhas basically teach for ordinary people, not for Buddhas. Those who will not believe this principle are allowed to leave the audience; what they don't realize is that they are sitting in the white oxcart yet still seek the three carts outside the door. Indeed, the text of the scripture clearly tells you there is no second, and no third; why don't you see that the three carts are artificial, for the past, so the one ve- hicle is real, for the present. So it just teaches you to leave the artificial and resort to the real. After resorting to the real, even the real has no name. You should know that all the valuable assets belong to you; once you get to use them, you don't conceive of father, and don't conceive of son, and have no conception of use. This is called holding the *Lotus Scripture*, never letting go from age to age, always keeping it in mind day and night."

Having been thus instructed, Fada jumped for joy and celebrated with a verse, saying,

> Three thousand recitals of the scripture
> Have disappeared at one statement from Caoqi.
> As long as one hasn't understand the meaning of appearance in
>   the world,
> How can one stop the madness of multiple lifetimes?
> The goat, deer, and oxcarts are provisional setups;
> Beginning, middle, and final are expedient propositions.
> Who knows that inside the burning house
> Has been the king of Dharma all along?

The patriarch said, "From now on you can finally be called a monk who recites the scripture."

TRANSLATOR'S NOTE

The goat, deer, and oxcarts represent the Buddhist vehicles of hearers, who strive for nirvana; pratyekabuddhas, who enlighten themselves; and bodhisattvas, who strive for universal enlightenment. The symbolism comes from a story in the *Lotus Sutra*: a man finds his house is on fire and urges his children to get out. The children, however, preoccupied with their playthings, don't listen. As an expedient, the man tells them he has carts outside for them; because he knows they have different inclinations, he offers three kinds of carts to suit each one. When they finally leave the burning house, they find there is only one kind of cart, here referred to as the white oxcart, symbolizing the Ekayana, or One Vehicle, the way to the knowledge and vision of Buddhas.

The image of the father and son and valuable assets is also from the *Lotus Sutra*. A rich man's son leaves home and falls into destitution. After long wandering, he happens to come to the estate of his father, now in another land. He doesn't recognize his father, but his father recognizes him; in disguise, the father approaches his long-lost son and offers him a job cleaning a cesspit on the estate. After twenty years of diligent labor, the son is given the position of steward, yet maintains humility and returns to his bed of straw each night. Finally, on the father's deathbed, he reveals that the steward is actually his son and bequeaths his entire fortune to him. This story symbolizes progression from delusion to purification to enlightened knowledge.

[399]

Master Xuansha asked Xuefeng, "Now I am totally functional—how about you?" Xuefeng tossed out three wooden balls. Xuansha then made a gesture of chopping down a signpost. Xuefeng said, "You can only be like this if you were personally on Spiritual Peak." Xuansha said, "It's only my business."

Dahui said, "I only allow the old foreigner's knowledge; I don't allow the old foreigner's understanding."

TRANSLATOR'S NOTE

In Chan mythology, Spiritual Peak was where the Buddha passed on to Kasyapa the "special transmission outside doctrine" identified with Chan.

[400]

Jianyuan accompanied Daowu to a funeral. Jianyuan patted the coffin and said, "Alive? Dead?" Daowu said, "I won't say alive, and I won't say dead." Jianyuan said, "Why won't you say?" Daowu said, "I won't say, I won't say." Halfway back, Jianyuan said, "Tell me right away, Teacher; if you don't say, I'll hit you." Daowu said, "Hit me if you will, but I won't say." Jianyuan then hit him. When they got back to the monastery, Daowu said, "You'd better leave here—you'll be inconvenienced if the superintendent finds out." Jianyuan went to Shishuang, where he cited the foregoing story and asked for help. Shishuang said, "I won't say alive, and I won't say dead." Jianyuan said, "Why won't you say?" Shishuang said, "I won't say, I won't say." With this, Jianyuan had an insight. After Daowu passed away, Jianyuan took a hoe and crossed the teaching hall west to east and east to west. Shishuang said, "What are you doing?" Jianyuan said, "I'm looking for the sacred relics of the late teacher." Shishuang said, "The enormous waves are huge; the white-capped billows flood the sky—what sacred relics of the late teacher are you looking for?" Jianyuan said, "Just right for applying effort." Shishuang said, "Here even a needle won't go in—what effort will you apply?" Jianyuan left with the hoe over his shoulder.

. . .

Master Baoning Yong versified,

> Waiting by the door all day, leaning on the building;
> How many times has the clear mirror reflected combing the head?
> Once you've been in the service of a celebrity,
> You can be shameless in front of others.

[401]

Master Huitang said to an assembly,

Not being companion to myriad things is absorption in noncontention. When you go right on this way, unavoidably when the strings of a musical instrument are too tight, the sound is shortened. If you can scatter pearls inside a violet gauze curtain, you will not necessarily bring on a bad result from a good cause.

He also said to an assembly,

Where there is impediment is not a wall; where there is free passage is not empty space. If you can understand this way, mind and matter are fundamentally one. The whisk is matter—what is mind? As soon as a spiritually sharp fellow hears it brought up, seeing horns on the other side of a fence he already knows it's an ox. If you hesitate anymore, thinking, white clouds extend for a thousand miles, ten thousand miles.

[402]

Master Lingyun was asked by Changsheng, "How is it when primordial chaos is not yet differentiated?" He said, "The exposed pillars get pregnant." Changsheng said, "How about after differentiation?" Lingyun said, "Like a fleck of cloud dotting the clear sky." Changsheng said, "But is the clear sky subject to being dotted?" Lingyun didn't reply. Changsheng said, "Then life does not come about." Again Lingyun didn't reply. Changsheng said, "How is it when absolutely clear and spotless?" Lingyuan said, "This is still the real eternal flowing." Changsheng said,

"What is the real eternal flowing like?" Lingyuan said, "Like a mirror always being clear." Changsheng said, "Is there anything beyond?" Lingyun said, "There is." Changshen said, "What is beyond?" Lingyun said, "Break the mirror and I'll meet with you."

[403]

Master Yunmen once said, "The lamp is yourself. Take a bowl and eat food; the food is not yourself." A monk then asked, "How about when the food is oneself?" Yunmen said, "This wild fox spirit, a fellow in a three-family village." He also said, "Come on, come on—you're not saying food is yourself." He said, "I am." Yunmen said, "You'll see in a dream in the year of the ass, a fellow in a three-family village."

Dahui said, "Using his own mind to the full, he laughs off another person's mouth."

[404]

Shimen Cong said to an assembly,
   If you can say the first statement, you burst forth from within a rock. If you can say the second statement, you press on ahead. If you can say the third statement, you cannot even save yourself.

He also said to an assembly,
   Five white cats have sharp claws; when you raise them, there are no pests running around the house. Clearly climbing trees is a way of safety; avoid last words accepting forgetting life. What is an expression of forgetting life? Don't misquote.

A monk entered the room and said, "At precisely 'such' a time, is there still a teacher?" Shimen said, "The lamp shines all night—what place is not illuminated?" The monk said, "What is the ultimate concern?" He said, "Tomorrow is the Cold Food holiday."

"What is the meaning of a burr on a rapids?"

"When the roof is wrecked, you see the sky."

"What is the meaning of seeing the sky when the roof is wrecked?"

"All the way above and below."

[405]

Baoci, hearing the coo of a pigeon, asked a monk, "What is that sound?" He said, "A pigeon." Baoci said, "If you want to avoid committing a crime with immediate consequences, don't slander the Realized One's wheel of true teaching."

[406]

Master Dongshan Chu's verse on an ox says,

> Tending an ox by myself,
> It has no corral to go out and in.
> Released into the fragrant grasses
> Its color can then show.
> Going in the morning, no one chases it;
> Returning in the evening, no one calls it.
> Its strength cannot be matched;
> It has horns, but no tether.
> Without being driven, it goes free.
> When driven, it goes along;
> There are no ruined fields in the land.
> These are all developments of the ox.
> If anyone looks for it,
> It runs to the horizon.
> Led back, it resembles you all;
> I ask you—do you see or not?

[407]

Master Yunfeng Yue said to an assembly,

In the teachings it says, "This perception and objects are fundamentally the body of sublime pure light of enlightenment." It also says, "Forests, trees, lakes, and wetlands all broadcast the sound of Dharma. Interlacing lights weave together like a network of jewel threads." How wondrous are the Chan worthies!—this kind of talk of ancient sages is called turning to objects of sense to open up expedients indirectly. So it says, "It is like my pressing the symbol of the ocean with my finger, radiating light. The moment you arouse your mind, toil over sense objects arises first." Understand? The whisk is temporarily used to direct the world; the staff is provisionally for people who respond. [He gave a whack with the whisk.]

He also said to an assembly,

The basis of sentient beings rests on the ocean of knowledge as its source. The stream of conscious creatures has the whole body of reality as its substance. It's just that knowledge is blocked when feelings occur and substance differs when conceptions change. When you arrive at the basis, feelings disappear; and when you know the mind, substance is collective. Do you understand? The ancient Buddhas and exposed pillars merge; the Buddha shrine and celestial kings bump heads. If you don't understand, the single and the multiple cancel each other.

[408]

Layman Pang asked Mazu, "Without obscuring the original human, please set your eye on high." Mazu looked straight down. The layman said, "One kind of stringless lute—what master can play it beautifully?" Mazu looked straight up. The layman then bowed. Mazu went back to his room. The layman followed him in and said, "Playing at being clever turns out clumsy."

[409]

Master Yaoshan said to an assembly,

The ancestral teachers only taught preservation; if greed or hostility arise, it is imperative to ward them off and not let them touch you. If you want to know how to do this, you must bear up like dead wood or stone. There really are no ramifications to attain. Even so, you still must see for yourself. Don't eliminate speech entirely. I am not speaking these words to you to reveal the unspoken. That originally has no features such as ears or eyes.

At that time a monk asked, "How is it that there are six courses of mundane existence?" The teacher said, "Although I am within this circle, I am basically not affected."

Someone asked, "How about when one does not comprehend the afflictions in one's person?" The teacher said, "What are afflictions like? I want you to consider. There is even a type who just memorize words on paper; most are confused by scriptures and treatises. I have never read the books of scriptures and treatises. You have fluctuating minds simply because you are confused by things and go through changes, at a loss, inwardly unstable. Even before you have learned a single saying or half an expression, a scripture or a treatise, already you talk this way about 'enlightenment,' 'nirvana,' the mundane and the transmundane; if you understand this way, then this is birth and death. If you are not bound by this gain and loss, then there is no birth and death. You see teachers of rules talking about stuff like *naihsargika* and *dukkata*—this above all is the root of birth and death. Even so, when you examine birth and death thoroughly, it cannot be grasped. From the Buddhas above to insects below, all have these differences of excellence and inferiority, good and bad, big and small. If it doesn't come from outside, where is there some idler digging hells to await you? Do you want to know existence in hell? It is boiling and broiling right now. Do you want to know existence as a hungry ghost? It is presently being more false than true, so people can't trust you. Do you want to know existence as an animal? It is presently disregarding justice and humanity and not distinguishing friend from stranger—isn't this wearing fur and horns, being butchered and hung upside down? Do you want to know humanity and divinity? It is present pure conduct. You should guard against falling into these states. First of all, don't abandon this. This is not easily attained: you must stand atop the peak of the highest mountain and walk on the bottom of the deepest ocean. This is not easy to practice, but only then will you have some accord. Those who come forth now are all people with many issues. I'm looking for a simpleton but cannot find one. Don't just memorize sayings in books and make them out to be your own perception and knowledge, looking with contempt upon those who don't understand—people like this are all incorrigible heretics. This mentality simply doesn't hit the mark—you must examine carefully and understand thoroughly. This kind of talk is still within the bounds of the world. Don't waste your lives under a patch robe. At this point there is even more subtlety and detail. Don't consider it idle, for you should know it. Take care."

[410]

A monk asked Master Cuiyan, "Whenever there are verbal statements, they're all defilement; what is the actuality beyond?" He said, "Whenever there are verbal statements, they're all defilement."

"When the ancients raised a gavel or stood up a whisk, what was the meaning?"

"A false teaching is unsupportable."

"Why couldn't Sengyao depict Mr. Zhi's true likeness?"

"How could it be matched absolutely?"

"In dangerous bad paths, what serves as a bridge?"

"Yaoshan told of it repeatedly."

[411]

Master Guanghui Zhen was asked by a monk, "What is the realm of Guanghui?" He said, "In front of a mountain temple, after providing for a celebration."

"What is the master's family style?"

"A spade holding a hoe."

[412]

One day Fengxue asked the gardener Zhen, "At the time of the persecution of Buddhism, where did the good spirits protecting the Dharma go?" He said, "They were always in the streets, but no one saw them." Fengxue said, "You have penetrated."

Dahui said, "You tell me—has Fengxue himself penetrated or not?"

[413]

Master Huanglong Ji was asked by a monk, "What is your family way?"

He said, "The crystal bowl has no bottom."

"What is the sword of a ruler?"

"It does not wound myriad species."

"How about the one who carries it?"

"Blood sprays the heavens."

"A fine 'not wounding myriad species'!"

Ji hit him.

"A hair engulfing an ocean and a mustard seed containing a mountain is not the proper business of a student; what is the proper business of a student?"

"Stamping a prognostication chart and holding it up to view in the marketplace."

"I come to you urgently requesting the teacher to communicate some information."

"Fire burns the undergarment belt."

"What is someone with great doubt like?"

"Sitting face-to-face in a circle, a bow falls into a wine cup."

"What about someone who doesn't doubt?"

"Sitting again in a circle, a bow falls into a wine cup."

"How is it when the wind is quiet and the waves are stilled?"

"Atop a hundred-foot pole, five ounces hang down."

TRANSLATOR'S NOTE

A bow falling into a wine cup alludes to a famous simile for mistaking mental construction for objective reality. A bow hung on a wall reflected in a cup of wine appears to the drinker as a snake in the wine; the drinker becomes sick to his stomach, thinking he has swallowed a snake. When he looks up and sees the bow hung on the wall and realizes the "snake" was a reflection of the bow in the wine, his stomach upset disappears.

[414]

Ministry President Li Ao admired the way of Yaoshan and made a special trip to the mountain to pay his respects, punctiliously observing the courtesies of a guest. He went straight up to the seat; Yaoshan, reading a scripture in a dignified manner, didn't even look at him. Li then said, "Seeing the face is not as good as hearing the name" and brusquely left. Yaoshan then called, "Ministry President!" Li turned his head. Yaoshan said, "How can you value ears and devalue eyes?" Li then made a prostration; rising, he asked, "What is the Way?" Yaoshan pointed to the sky and pointed to a water pitcher. Li said, "I don't understand." Yaoshan said, "Clouds are in the sky; water is in the pitcher." Li then bowed in thanks. He presented a verse, saying,

> He's refined his physical form like the body of a crane;
> Under a thousand pines, two boxes of scriptures.

I came to ask the Way, nothing else;
Clouds are in the sky; water is in the pitcher.

[415]

Master Shoushan Zhi asked Master Nian, "What is the meaning of Deshan's cane and Linji's shout?" Nian said, "You try to say." Zhi immediately shouted; Nian picked up a cane. Zhi pointed to the cane and said,
"Don't act at random." Nian threw down the cane and said, "Someone
with clear eyes is impossible to fool." Zhi said, "The brigand is busted."

A monk asked, "What was the purpose of the founding teacher's coming
from the West?"
    The master said, "A three-foot staff breaking an earthenware bowl."
    "What is Buddha?"
    "The bottom of a bucket falling out."
    "What statement have the sages since time immemorial had?"
    "'Thus have I heard.'"
    "I don't understand."
    "'Believing, accepting, putting into practice.'"

TRANSLATOR'S NOTE

"Thus have I heard" is the standard introduction to Buddhist scripture;
"believing, accepting, putting into practice" is the standard conclusion.

[416]

Master Baishui of Jiazhou was asked by a monk, "What was the meaning
of the coming from the West?"
    He replied, "There is no abode in the four seas; one drop moistens
heaven and earth."
    "On the one road of Caoqi, what is to be discussed?"

"Thousand-year-old cranes come and gather in the valley pines; phoenixes return to the fragrant cassia on the moon."

Dahui said, "And you say Caoqi has no mundane talk."

TRANSLATOR'S NOTE

Caoqi is the Sixth Patriarch of Chan, from whom most Chan masters traced their spiritual descent, hence emblematic of Chan teaching.

[417]

National Teacher Gushan Yan said to an assembly,

If the spiritually sharp stop as soon as they're challenged, folks like this are thousands of miles away—what salvation is there for them? Going ahead and falling back, taking in a "how?" they are like drunks. What breath of patchrobed monks do people like this have? This being so, then what about the business in the school of the source? Here you must be suitable people—it's really not easy. Brethren, I'm not sparing words to tell you it doesn't depend on memorizing a single letter and doesn't need any effort; you don't need to blink and don't need to puff: sitting massively, you succeed to it right away. But tell me, what do you succeed to? Do you consider it succeeding to the Buddha, succeeding to the Dharma, succeeding to the Way, succeeding to what is beyond Buddha, the expression after nirvana? If you succeed to this expression, it can be considered a great delusion; this is called the mind looking upward not ceasing. It is irrelevant to you, brethren. For your part, how do you succeed? I invite everyone to try to see: What is this? Is it ordinary? Is it holy? Is it the teacher of Vairocana, master of the reality body? Where does it abide? For how long? Is there any square or round to it, broad or narrow, long or short, large or small? Try to say. Is there anything as big as a thread or a hair that can cover it? Is there the slightest gap? Where is it copied; where is it written? It is so evident, so basic—

why don't you get it right away? Instead you stick your heads into the statements of others, studying in intellectual consciousness. What connection is there? Haven't you seen the saying that intellect is a thief and consciousness is waves? Running off in search, you'll never have any rest. If you have no eyes yourself, you go to others, selectively excerpting and copying from books. Even if you take in the oceanic canon with its billion statements at once, this is all others' and has nothing to do with your self. This is also called dependent understanding through conceptual learning. This is like jellyfish depending on shrimp for eyes—there's no independence. It's also like the blind distinguishing colors based on what other people say, therefore not being able to discern the true characteristics of color. If you study the scriptures, codes, and treatises, there are already people for that; this is why I always say the scriptures have teachers of scriptures, the codes have teachers of codes, the treatises have teachers of treatises. They are organized, categorized, and classified, and there are already people who transmit and memorize them day and night, at bright windows and by lamplight. What about Chan masters? Can anyone say? Try to come forth and speak.

At that time a student asked, "What is the presently evident potential?"

The master said, "What are you saying?"

The monk asked again; the master shouted him out.

[418]

Ehu asked some distinguished clerics, "Walking, standing, sitting, lying down—ultimately what do you consider the Way?" They answered, "The knower is it." He said, "'It cannot be known by knowledge, cannot be recognized by cognition'—how can the knower be it?" Some replied, "Nondiscrimination is it." He said, "'Be able to distinguish the characteristics of things without moving from the highest truth'—how can nondiscrimination be it?" Some replied, "The four meditations and eight concentrations are it." He said, "'The body of Buddha is not constructed and doesn't fall into any categories'—how can it be in the four meditations and eight concentrations?" Now the whole group shut their mouths.

Dahui said, "When we're reviling each other, you may lock beaks; when we're spitting at each other, you may spray water."

[419]

Master Yangshan asked a monk, "Where are you from?" He replied, "From Yu province." Yangshan said, "Do you still think of that place?" He said, "I'm always thinking of it." Yangshan said, "That place is full of buildings, woods, gardens, people, and houses—think back to what thinks; are there so many kinds of things there?" The monk had an insight at these words; he said, "Here I don't see that any of it is there." Yangshan said, "Your understanding is still in an object; it is right at the stage of faith, but not at the stage of personality." The monk said, "Don't you have any other instructions?" Yangshan said, "Whether there is any in particular or not misses the mark. According to your view, you only attain one mystery, getting the seat and wearing the robe—hereafter, see for yourself."

TRANSLATOR'S NOTE

The "seat" and "robe" are symbols from the *Lotus Sutra*, representing emptiness and forbearance.

[420]

Panshan said to an assembly, "The one road beyond has not been transmitted by a thousand sages; students toil over forms like monkeys grabbing at reflections." Langya Jiao said, "He has come forth and extolled a boundless sound basis."

[421]

When Wuyi first went to Shitou's place, he said, "If we agree in a single statement, I'll stay; if we don't agree, I'll leave." Shitou remained seated. Wuyi then left. Shitou called to him. Wuyi turned his head. Shitou said, "From birth to death, it's just this; why are you turning your head and revolving your brain?" Wuyi was greatly enlightened at these words; he then broke his staff.

[422]

Master Yunju You said to an assembly,

People engaged in study need to attain the basis of enlightenment, discovering the ground of mind. If you realize the master of the reality body, then the whole earth, plants and trees, take refuge in the Buddha, Dharma, and Sangha. If you realize the teacher of Vairocana, the realm of space takes refuge in the Buddha, Dharma, and Sangha. But tell me, what do you call the master of the reality body? What do you call the teacher of Vairocana? Do you want to understand directly? Radiate light in your eyes, manifesting auspicious signs; turn the great wheel of Dharma in your ears.

He also said to an assembly at the commencement of a summer retreat,

In formless light there is a real human with no status appearing and disappearing in the triple world, whirling in the five courses of existence, not abandoning the ten bad actions, not realizing the heart of nirvana, not hating breaking precepts, not respecting keeping precepts, not passing winter, not passing summer. Do you know where this goes? [Pause.] In the sun's flames for ninety days the spiritual body is completed.

[423]

Duan ["the Lion"] Shizi's two verses on reading the *Heroic Progress Scripture*:

Looking for the mind in seven places, the mind does
    not finish;
Befuddled Ananda does not get a glimpse.
Even if by seeking you see no mind,
This is still washing a clod of earth in mud.

The teaching of eight references was delivered long ago;
Since ancient times teachers of the school have each analyzed it.
Even if you can refer to what is no reference,
This is still a shrimp leaping not getting out of the basket.

TRANSLATOR'S NOTE

Looking for the mind in seven places is an exercise given by Buddha to his disciple Ananda in the *Heroic Progress Scripture*. The seven places are inside, outside, hidden in the sense faculties, in darkness, wherever encountered, in between sense faculties and sense data, nonattachment.

The eight references are another *Heroic Progress* exercise, examining the nature of perception: light is traced back to the sun, darkness is traced back to the new moon, transparency is traced back to doors and windows, obstruction is traced back to walls and roofs, objects are traced back to discrimination, indistinguishability is traced back to space, density is traced back to sense data, pure light is traced back to clarity.

[424]

Master Yaoshan asked Yunyan, "Where have you come from?" He said, "From Baizhang." Yaoshan asked, "What sayings does Baizhang have?" he said, "Sometimes he says to the assembly, 'I have a statement containing a hundred flavors.'" Yaoshan said, "Salty is salty, bland is bland—neither salty nor bland is normal flavor. What is the statement containing a hundred flavors?" Yunyan had no reply. Yaoshan laughed and said, "What can you do about present birth and death?" Yunyan said, "There is no birth and death present." Yaoshan said, "You were with Baizhang for twenty years and still haven't gotten rid of mundanity." The next day Yaoshan also asked, "What else does Baizhang teach?" Yunyan said, "Sometimes he says, 'Understand outside the three statements; realize outside the six statements.'" Yaoshan said, "Happily there is no connection." He again asked, "What else does he teach?" Yunyan said, "Sometimes he goes up in the hall, then when the assembly has gathered, he chases them out with his staff; then he calls to them, and when they turn their heads he says, 'What is this?'" Yaoshan said, "Why didn't you say so before?" Yunyan had insight at these words.

Dahui said, "It's not that he didn't get an insight, but he still didn't get out of the cave of complications."

[425]

Liangya Jiao said to an assembly,

You people are here with me passing the summer; I will point out five kinds of sickness to you. One, don't go to where there isn't so much as an inch of grass for myriad miles. Two, don't lodge alone on a solitary peak. Three, don't draw a bow and nock an arrow. Four, don't settle yourself outside of things. Five, don't get stuck in enlivening and killing. Why? If there is lingering in any one place, it's impossible to save yourself. If you pass through all five states, only then are you called a guide. If you people go to other places and meet clear-eyed adepts, pass on a message for me, so that the ancestral way will not fall. If they are ordinary followers, then you should snooze. Why? If you take pride in dressing up in a country where people go naked, I think you really don't know timing.

Also, in a verse on the story of the cypress tree, he said,

> Zhaozhou's cypress tree in the yard—
> No patchrobed monks can fathom it.
> The whole hall of itinerant monks
> Are all visitors of the ten directions.

[426]

Emperor Zhongzong of the Tang dynasty sent the court attendant Xue Jian to deliver an imperial summons inviting the Sixth Patriarch, hoping the teacher would be so kind as to hasten to the capital. The patriarch offered up an excuse of illness, wishing to end his days in the forest at the foot of the mountain. Jian said, "The Chan worthies in the capital city all say that if we want to get understanding of the Way we need to sit and meditate and practice concentration, that no one has ever attained liberation but by means of meditation concentration. What about the teaching you expound?"

The patriarch said, "The Way is realized by mind—how could it be in sitting? Scripture says, 'If you see the Realized One as sitting or lying down, you are going on a false path.' Why? Because there is no whence or whereunto—if there is neither production nor destruction, this is the pure meditation of the realized. The emptiness of all things is the pure sitting of the realized. Ultimately there is no realization, how indeed in sitting!"

Jian said, "When I return to the capital, the emperor will surely question me—please be so kind and compassionate as to point out the essentials of mind."

The patriarch said, "The Way has no light or dark; light and dark mean alteration. An endless succession of lights still has ending."

Jian said, "Light symbolizes wisdom; dark symbolizes affliction. If people who practice the Way don't use wisdom to shine through affliction, how can beginningless birth and death be escaped?"

The patriarch said, "If you use wisdom to shine through affliction, this is a small view of the two vehicles, potentials for the goat and deer carts. Those of higher knowledge and great potential are not like this at all."

Jian said, "What is the understanding of the Great Vehicle?"

The patriarch said, "Enlightenment and ignorance are essentially nondual. Nondual essence is true essence. True essence is not less in the ordinary and ignorant, and not more in the wise and sagacious. It is not destroyed in the midst of afflictions, and not at rest in meditation concentration. It does not end or persist, does not go or come, is not in the middle, or inside or outside. Not born, not passing away, essence and characteristics as such, always abiding unchanging—this is called the Way."

Jian said, "How is 'not born and not passing away' different from outsiders?"

The patriarch said, "The 'not born and not passing away' preached by outsiders means using extinction to stop production, using birth to show annihilation. Even annihilation is not extinguished; birth explains nonproduction. The 'not born and not passing away' that I teach means there is fundamentally no origination of itself, and presently no annihilation. Therefore it is not the same as outsiders. If you want to know the essence of mind, just do not think of any good or bad, and you will naturally gain entry into the pure essence of mind. It is calm, always quiet, with countless wondrous functions."

Having received this teaching, Jian was greatly enlightened.

[427]

Master Xiangyan said, "Suppose someone is up in a tree, holding onto a branch by his mouth, his hands not gripping any branch, his feet not set on the tree. Someone asks him the meaning of the coming from the West. If he doesn't reply, he's evading the question, but if he does reply he loses his life. At such a time, what would be right?"

A certain elder Hutou said, "I don't ask about climbing up a tree; please tell us about before climbing the tree." Xiangyan laughed out loud.

Xuedou said, "It's easy to talk about up in the tree, hard to talk about under the tree. I'll climb the tree; bring on a question."

Baoning Yong said in verse,

> The old awl sets up many methods indirectly;
> Moreover, he produces branch upon branch.
> Best be like a good horse seeing the shadow of the whip;
> One who chases a clod isn't a lion cub.

    . . .

Dahui said, "Even having swallowed a thorny chestnut and passed through an unbreakable enclosure, when you look at this kind of talk you're still a Confucian seeing a legendary sage ruler."

[428]

When two monks came calling on Chan master Yongming Shou, he asked the first inquirer, "Have you ever been here?" He said, "Yes." Then he asked the second monk if he had been there, and he said he hadn't. Shou said, "One gain, one loss." In a while, an attendant asked, "Of the two monks who just came, which one lost and which one gained?" Shou said, "Have you ever known these two monks?" The attendant said, "Never." Shou said, "In the same pit there's no different dirt."

[429]

Master Luohan Nan said to an assembly,

"The very wise appear to be ignorant; the very skillful appear to be inept." Don't say today, midautumn, is an auspicious day, the same air in all quarters, the same moon in a thousand ponds, for thirty years white flowers have reflected snow; if you understand this way, your brain will shatter.

He also said to the assembly,

It's windy, and the chrysanthemums at the foot of the fence are now yellow; their subtle talk of the western patriarch's meaning tinkles like jewels. I don't know who can hear this speech—it can set the standard for the school. Then you see my whisk displaying great spiritual powers, turning into [the supernal bodhisattvas] Manjushri, Samantabhadra, Avalokitesvara, and Mahasthamaprapta, piercing your skulls. Surely if you thoroughly know the source, you can be said to provide support for countless Buddhas in exhaling and inhaling. If you don't know, I'll turn it over to Deshan and Linji to strike a blow.

[430]

Changqing said, "It's better to say that saints have the three poisons than to say the Realized One has two kinds of speech. I don't say the Realized One says nothing, only that he doesn't have two kinds of speech." Baofu said, "What is the Realized One's speech?" Changqing said, "How can a deaf man hear?" Baofu said, "I knew for sure you were speaking of the secondary." Changqing said, "What is the Realized One's speech?" Baofu said, "Go have some tea."

[431]

Master Jinfeng Zhi held up a head rest and said, "Everyone calls it a head rest; I say it is not so." A monk said, "What do you call it?" Zhi held up the head rest. The monk said, "Then you act accordingly." Zhi said, "What do you call it?" The monk said, "A head rest." Zhi said, "You've fallen into my pit."

[432]

When Master Xuansha wanted to travel around to call on teachers, he took his bag to leave the mountain. He stubbed his toe, drawing blood and causing intense pain. He lamented, "This body is not existent; where does the pain come from?" So he then returned to Xuefeng. One day Xuefeng asked him, "What are you?" He said, "I'll never dare deceive people." Another day Xuefeng called him and said, "Why don't you travel around to study?" He said, "Bodhidharma didn't come to China; the Second Patriarch didn't go to India." Xuefeng approved of this. Xuansha also read the *Heroic Progress Scripture* and discovered the ground of mind. Henceforth his response to potentials was swift, in subtle accord with the scripture. Xuefeng praised him, calling him a reincarnation.

[433]

One day the Sixth Patriarch said to his students, "I want to return to Xinzhou; prepare a boat at once." His students said, "After you leave here, when will you come back?" The patriarch said, "Fallen leaves return to the root; when I came I had no mouth."

Fayun Xiu said, "Not only did he have no mouth when he came; when he left he had no nostrils either."

[434]

When Zhaozhou heard a novice announce his arrival, he told an attendant, "Have him leave." As soon as the attendant told him to leave, the novice said goodbye. Zhaozhou said to a monk standing by, "The novice has entered the gate; the attendant is outside the gate."

[435]

Master Guanghui Lian asked Master Nian, "The student having personally arrived at a mountain of jewels, how is it when he returns empty-handed?" Nian said, "A torch in front of the door of every house." Lian was greatly enlightened at these words; he said, "I do not doubt what the old masters all over the land say." Nian said, "How would you explain your understanding to me?" Lian said, "Panning on the ground." Nian said, "You understand." Lian then bowed.

Dahui said, "Tell me, did Master Nian agree with Guanghui or not? If you say he agreed with him, why didn't he hit him? If you say he didn't agree with him, why didn't he hit him? If anyone can say, I'll hit you."

[436]

Master Yongguang Zhen said to an assembly,

If the point of speech misses, you're myriad miles from home. You simply must let go over a sheer cliff, allowing yourself to accept it, and come back to life after annihilation—then you can't be fooled. How can people hide an extraordinary message?

[437]

When Master Jishan Zhang was with Touzi, he was in charge of firewood. As he was drinking tea, Touzi said to him, "All forms are in this cup of tea." Zhang then turned over the tea and said, "Where are myriad forms?" Touzi said, "What a waste of a cup of tea." Later Zhang called on Xuefeng. Xuefeng asked, "Aren't you Zhang the superintendent of firewood?" Zhang made a chopping gesture. Xuefeng approved of this.

[438]

When Master Xiangcheng first called on Master Tong, he asked, "How is it when one seems like two?" Tong said, "One fools you." Xiangcheng thereupon had an insight. A monk asked, "How is it when there is not a thread to tie an ant in a bag, and not enough meat and rice in the kitchen to gather flies?" Xiangcheng said, "Daily relinquishment, not seeking; craving comes from confusion."

[439]

Master Mingzhao asked Sushan, "A tiger sires seven cubs—which one has no tail?" Sushan said, "The seventh one has no tail."

[440]

As Yaoshan was roaming in the mounains with Daowu and Yunyan, they saw two trees, one dead and one flourishing. Yaoshan asked Yunyan, "Is the withered one right, or is the flourishing one right?" He said, "The flourishing one." Yaoshan said, "Then clearly light will blaze everywhere." He also asked Daowu; Daowu said, "The withered one is right." Yaoshan said, "Then clearly everywhere will be austere." In a little while novice Gao came; Yaoshan also asked him. Gao said, "Let the withered one be withered; let the flourishing one flourish." Yaoshan turned and looked at Yunyan and Daowu and said, "Not right, not right."

[441]

When Master Nanyue Rang first called on the Sixth Patriarch, the patriarch asked, "Where have you come from?" He said, "From Mount Song." The patriarch said, "What thing has come this way?" He said, "To speak of it as a thing would not be accurate." The patriarch said, "Does it take cultivation and realization?" He said, "It's not that there is no cultivation or realization, but if defiled it can't be successful." The patriarch said, "It is just this nondefilement that the Buddhas keep in mind. You are now like this; I too am like this."

[442]

Master Zhimen Zuo said to an assembly,

Xuefeng's rolling balls, Luohan's writing, Guizong's cutting a snake, Dasui's burning off a field—tell me, what do they illustrate? Can anyone clarify? Try to say. If you cannot clarify, this is why it is said that to cut a snake you need to be able to cut a snake; to burn off a field you need to be able to burn off a field. As soon as subjective data arise, that produces false views. If you have no sinew in your eyes, you'll be poor all your life.

. . .

A monk asked, "What is the Buddha Victorious by Great Penetrating Knowledge?"

He said, "Speech has no second echo."

The monk asked, "What is sitting at the site of enlightenment for ten eons?"

He said, "Calamities do not occur alone."

The monk asked, "What is the state of Buddhahood not manifesting?"

He said, "'Though gold dust is precious . . .'"

The monk said, "What is not managing to attain Buddhahood?"

He said, "'. . .it cannot stick in the eyes.'"

[443]

Master Puhua used to go to town ringing a bell and saying, "Come in light and I'll strike in light; come in darkness and I'll strike in darkness. Come in all directions and I'll strike like a whirlwind. Come in space and I'll flail around."

One day Linji had a monk grab him and say, "When not coming any such way, then what?" Puhua pushed him away and said, "Tomorrow there's a ritual feast in the monastery of Great Compassion." The monk returned and told Linji about this. Linji said, "I had doubted this fellow hitherto."

[444]

A monk traveling to Taishan asked a woman, "Which way is the road to Taishan?" The woman said, "Right straight ahead." As soon as the monk had gone a few paces, the woman said, "A fine monk, and so he goes." Someone told Zhaozhou about this. Zhaozhou said, "Wait till I go check out this woman." The next day he went and questioned her the same way; and the woman answered the same way. Zhaozhou went back and said to the group, "I've checked out the woman of Taishan for you."

Dagui Zhe said in verse,

The old adept of the community has no peer;
His awesome dignity affects the four hundred princes.
At one blow the barrier has been shattered;
His benevolence is so great it can hardly be repaid with rain
  and dew.

[445]

A monk asked Fayan, "What is one drop of water from the wellspring of
Chan?" Fayan said, "It is one drop of water from the wellspring of Chan."
When National Teacher Yuan heard this, he had insight at these words.
Later, when he dwelt on Lotus Peak, he composed a verse, saying,

The peak of penetrating mystery
Is not in the human world;
Outside mind there are no things.
Filling the eyes, green mountains.

When Fayan heard this verse, he said, "It just takes this one verse to
naturally continue our school."

[446]

The Sixth Patriarch said to an assembly,

Good friends, each of you clean your mind and listen to my teaching.
Your own mind is Buddha—don't doubt anymore. There is not a thing
you can establish outside—it is all the basic mind conceiving all sorts of
things. Therefore scripture says, "When thought is produced, all kinds of
things are produced; when thought passes away, all kinds of things pass
away." If you want to develop knowledge of all kinds, you need to attain
absorption in unity, absorption in one practice. If in all places you do
not dwell on appearances, do not conceive aversion or attraction to any
of those appearances, and have no grasping or rejection, do not think of

such things as benefit, fulfillment, or destruction, and you are at peace, calm, open, aloof, this is called absorption in oneness. If in all places whether walking, standing, sitting, or lying down, your pure unified direct mind does not move from the site of enlightenment, truly making a pure land, this is called absorption in one practice. If people are equipped with these two absorptions, it is like the earth having seeds, able to store, develop, and perfect their fruits. Unity and unified practice too are like this. My teaching now is like timely rain moistening the earth; your Buddha-nature is like the seeds—when watered, they will sprout. Those who take up my teaching will certainly attain enlightenment; those who follow my practice will certainly realize the sublime result.

[447]

Master Qingyuan asked Shitou, "Where did you come from?" He said, "From Caoqi." Qingyuan then held up his whisk and said, "Does Caoqi have this?" He said, "Not only Caoqi—it's not even there in India." Qingyuan said, "Have you ever been to India?" He said, "If I had, it would be there." Qingyuan said, "Not yet—speak again." He said, "You too should say half, Master. Don't rely wholly on me." Qingyuan said, "I don't decline to tell you, but I'm afraid afterward no one would get it."

[448]

Master Muping first called on Luopu. He asked, "What is before a single bubble has emerged?" Luopu said, "To move a boat, become familiar with the current; raising the oar, distinguish the waves." Muping didn't get it; next he called on Panlong and asked the same question. Panlong said, "Moving a boat, you don't distinguish the waters; raising an oar, you lose the source." Muping was initially enlightened by this.

Yunfeng Yue said, "If Muping had understood at Luopu's words, that still would have amounted to a little bit; too bad he drowned in Panlong's stagnant water." Someone asked, "How was Muping?" Yunfeng replied, "He didn't bother with the ax; after all he just stayed here. Chan worthies, whenever you set out to travel around, you must distinguish false and true, discern reality and artifice, have a bit of eye sinew. Even so, this is drawing the bow after the thief has gone."

Dahui said, "These words of Yunfeng can blind people and also can open people's eyes."

[449]

Master Muping picked up his staff, showing it to the assembly, and said, "If I pick it up, you then turn to before picking up to construct a theory; if I don't pick it up, you then turn to when it's picked up to construe mastery. Now tell me, where is my effort to help people?" At that time a monk came out and said, "I don't presume to arbitrarily create a gap." The master said, "I know you're not out of your depth." The monk said, "The lowest place, when leveled, is more than enough; the highest place, when gazed upon, is lacking." The master said, "You're creating gap upon gap." The monk had nothing to say. The master said, "If you cover your nose to steal incense, you'll uselessly get penalized."

[450]

Master Yangshan went to Dongsi. Dongsi asked, "Where are you from?" Yangshan said, "I'm from Guangnan." Dongsi said, "I've heard that there is a bright pearl that stills the sea in Guangnan. Is this true?" Yangshan said, "Yes." Dongsi said, "What is this pearl like?" Yangshan said, "It is hidden when the moon is dark and appears when the moon is bright." Dongsi said, "And did you bring it?" Yangshan said, "I brought it." Dongsi said, "Why don't you show me?" Yangshan joined his hands, stepped forward, and said, "Yesterday I went to Guishan and was also asked for this pearl; I simply had nothing to say in reply, no principle to set forth." Dongsi said, "You are truly a successor to Guishan, well able to roar. You're like a bug making a nest on a mosquito's eyelash, standing at a crossroads yelling that the land is vast, with hardly any people, and those met with are few."

[451]

When Baizhang called on Mazu a second time, as he stood by Mazu looked at the whisk at the corner of the meditation seat; Baizhang said, "Do you identify with this function or detach from this function?" Mazu said, "Later on, when you open your lips, how will you benefit people?" Baizhang took the whisk and stood it up. Mazu said, "Do you identify with this function or detach from this function?" Baizhang hung the whisk where it was before. Mazu drew himself up and shouted; Baizhang was deafened for three days. Fenzhou said, "If he was enlightened, the matter rests there; what more 'deafened for three days' is there to talk about?" Shimen said, "If he wasn't deafened for three days, how could he become enlightened?" Fenzhou said, "My speaking thus compares to that Shimen's half-month journey." Donglin Cong said, "When you should speak, you don't shrink from cutting off the tongue; when you're in charge of a furnace, you don't shrink from sparks flying. How can Buddhism crookedly follow human sentiments? Today I go to the black dragon's cave to fight for the pearl; it's not that Baizhang was not deafened for three days, but how could Fenzhou and Shimen avoid both being blind? What about these three elders—did they become enlightened or not? [After a pause he said,] If the ancestors do not finish, the calamity comes to their descendants."

Also, Fenyang's verse says,

> It's always because of having nothing to do he attends the
>   teacher's presence;
> The teacher points to what's hung at the corner of the rope
>   seat.
> Picking it up, putting it down, he's returned it to its original
>   position:
> Distinctly clear, one shout is transmitted even now.

Zhenjing's verse says,

The visitor's sense step by step rolls along with another;
He has a great luster of dignity but cannot show.
Suddenly a single shout and both ears are deaf;
A demon king's eyes open on Huangbo's face.

[452]

A monk asked Muzhou, "Can the entire canon be recited in one breath?"
Muzhou said, "What pastries do you have? Set them right out!"

Dahui said, "When you get up early in the morning, there are also people
who've been traveling by night."

[453]

Master Letan Ying said to an assembly,

Nanquan, Guizong, and Magu went together to pay respects to National Teacher Zhong. Halfway there, Nanquan drew a circle on the
ground and said, "If you can speak, we'll go; if not, we won't." Guizong
sat in the circle; Magu curtseyed. Nanquan said, "So then we won't go."
Guizong said, "What mental activity is this?" Bodhisattvas learning
wisdom must reach this state before they can. It's like filling a gold bowl
with pearls—they roll without being pushed. Even so, when Nanquan
said, "So then we won't go," where was the gain and loss? Is there anyone
who can say? Try to come forth and say. If not, I will add a footnote for
you. [Silence.] Unless you go into the immense waves, how can you reveal the person sporting in the tide?

[454]

Master Fachang Yu brought up to Master Nan the minister Chang's contemplation of the saying about circumstances of birth. Fachang said,
"Why not give him an immediate end?" Nan said, "Legs were drawn for

a snake, but he didn't get a glimpse." Fachang said, "How did you help him?" Nan said, "Chewing up raw ginger, drinking up vinegar." Fachang said, "Commonplace preacher—you too go this way." Nan said, "What is your idea?" Fachang picked up his whisk and hit him. Nan said, "This old fellow has no human feelings."

Fachang also brought up having asked Xinghua when in Hunan, "Where does someone who knows existence go?" Xinghua said, "Sudhana's staff." Fachang said, "I'm not asking about Sudhana's staff—tell me, where does someone who knows existence go?" Xinghua said, "Sometimes climbing mountains, sometimes crossing rivers." Fachang said, "You only know how to go higher with every step; you don't know how to let go from the sky." Xinghua said, "Though I am old, still I don't turn my back on opportunities that come up." Master Nan said, "What did you do then?" Fachang said, "I mistakenly suspected Xinghua." Nan said, "Now that you know, tell me, where are you going from?" Fachang said, "Who are you asking?" Nan said, "Why pretend to be deaf and dumb?" Fachang said, "Even so, I don't turn my back on opportunities that come up."

TRANSLATOR'S NOTE

"Circumstances of birth" is one of the so-called three barriers of Huang-long Huinan: "How is my hand like a Buddha's hand?" "How is my leg like a donkey's leg?" "Everyone has circumstances of birth—what are your circumstances of birth?" Regarding "Sudhana's staff," Sudhana is the name of the central figure of the last book of the *Flower Ornament Scripture*, which tells the story of his journey to call on teachers.

[455]

Master Panshan said, "The mind-moon solitary and full, its light engulfs myriad forms. When the light is not shining on objects, the objects are not there either. When light and objects are both gone, then what is this?"

Dahui said, "A thousand years' supplies, one morning's community."

[456]

Master Gaoan Benren said to an assembly, "Ordinarily I don't want to stir up people's sons and daughters before sound or after expression. Why? Sound isn't sound, form isn't form." At that time a monk asked, "How is it that sound isn't sound?" The master said, "Can you call it form?" The monk said, "How is it that form isn't form?" The master said, "Can you call it sound?" The monk bowed. Benren said, "Tell me, did I explain to you; did I answer what you said? If anyone can discern, he's got an entry."

[457]

Zhaozhou went to a hermit's place and asked, "Is there? Is there?" The hermit raised his fist. Zhaozhou said, "Where the water is shallow is not the place to moor a ship," and he left. He went to another hermit's place and said, "Is there? Is there?" That hermit also raised his fist. Zhaozhou said, "Able to let go, able to take away; able to kill, able to give life," and then he bowed.

Jiangshan Ai said, "Zhaozhou only sees the sharpness of the awl."

Yunju Shun said, "Zhaozhou was quite spunky at that time, but even so his nose is in the hands of the two hermits."

[458]

Magu asked Linji, "Of the Great Compassionate One's thousand hands and eyes, which is the true eye?" Linji said, "Of the Great Compassionate One's thousand hands and eyes, what is the true eye? Speak quickly, speak quickly!" Magu pulled him off the Chan seat and sat in it himself. Linji then approached and said, "How are you?" Magu hesitated. Linji then shouted, dragged him off the Chan seat, and sat down. Magu thereupon went out.

. . .

Daguan said, "Chan worthies, these two venerable adepts acted like this; tell me about it. People these days all speak of illumination and function; illumine what bowl? Everyone just knows how to ride a horse by themselves to go catch a brigand, wield a sword themselves to kill a brigand; these two men were able to take away a brigand's horse to catch the brigand, snatch away the brigand's sword to kill the brigand. Even so, though Linji got the advantage, after all this was losing the advantage."

[459]

Master Baiyun Duan said to an assembly,

It is very clearly known that the Way is just *this*—why can't people pass through? It is just because when they see someone open his mouth they immediately call it verbal expression, and when they see someone keep his mouth shut they immediately call it silence.

He also said,

All activity and talk in all worlds is without exception oneself. So it is said that falling along the way subtly embosoms past aversion. Have you not seen how the great master Yunmen said, "Hearing sound, awaken to the Way; seeing form, understand the mind," then raised his hand and said, "Guanyin Bodhisattva brings a coin to buy a cake," then lowered his hand and said, "After all it's a bun." And haven't you seen how when I was at Fahua I once pointed out to the assembly, "Chan master Wuye said that if the slightest subjective thought of ordinary and holy is not yet terminated, one cannot avoid entering into a donkey's womb or a horse's belly. Everyone, even if the slightest subjective thought of ordinary and holy is terminated at once, you still won't escape entering into a donkey's womb or a horse's belly. Blind blokes, just look at it this way. Inquire!"

[460]

The workman Gan Zhi went to Nanquan, donated gruel, and requested a recitation. Nanquan then sounded a signal and said, "Recite *Mahaprajna-paramita* for cats and cows." Gan Zhi abruptly left. After gruel, Nanquan asked the cook, "Where is the workman?" The cook said, "He immediately left at that time." Nanquan broke the pot.

[461]

Master Huanglong Xin said to an assembly,

There are no phenomena outside mind; thus things can be understood. There is no mind outside phenomena; thus mind can be comprehended. Comprehensible, understandable, mind and phenomena fulfill the aim. Fulfill the aim, and everything is the aim; make mind complete, and every state of mind is mindless. Since there is no mind in mind, you go directly to the source. When you find the source, when you manifest a great body, it fills space; and when you manifest a small body, not an atom is established. How is it when not an atom is established? [Silence.] One drop of ink in two places completes a dragon.

[462]

Master Guanghui Lian said to an assembly,

In the olden days, in the assembly of Linji, when the chief monks of the two halls encountered each other, they looked at each other and each gave a shout, then stopped. Tell me, people, were there still guest and host? If you say there were guest and host, you are just a blind fellow. If you say there was no guest or host, you are still a blind fellow. If there was not, yet not that there wasn't, this is myriad miles away. If you can speak here, you still deserve thirty blows. If you can't speak, you still deserve thirty blows. When patchrobed monks get here, how can they get out of my corral? [Silence.] Ouch! A frog and a worm jump up to the Thirty-Third Heaven, bump into the polar mountain, and shatter it. [Raising his staff:] You bunch of holeless hammerheads, withdraw at once! Withdraw at once!

Someone asked, "What was the intention of the founding teacher in coming from the West?"

He replied, "Waving a red flag on a bamboo pole."

[463]

When Elder Huo came to study with Master Rirong Yuan, Yuan clapped three times and said, "A fierce tiger is in the house—who can oppose it?" Huo said, "A swift hawk soars into the sky—who can catch it?" Yuan said, "That one and this one are hard to match." Huo said, "Stop for now; this case isn't decided yet." Yuan took his staff and danced back to his quarters. Huo had nothing to say. Yuan said, "Did this fellow have to die?"

[464]

Master Tianyi Huai said to an assembly,

An ancient said, "A single space on the mountain of five clusters—we go out and in the same door without meeting each other. For countless ages dwelling in a rented house—after all we never know the landlord."

An old adept brought this up and said, "Since we don't know him, who do we ask to rent to begin with? Bringing it up this way is still far off. Why? You should know that on the road of the dead there is a place for the living to emerge; on the road of the living the dead are innumerable. Which is the innumerable dead on the road of the living, and which is the place for the living to emerge on the road of the dead? If you can find out, you remove your greasy headgear and shed your stinking shirt."

Dahui said, "The ancient Buddha Tianyi is indeed fine, but not yet good. Let patchrobed monks with eyes try to distinguish."

[465]

Master Huangbo went to the kitchen, saw the superintendent of meals, and asked him what he was doing. "Selecting the rice for the community," he said. Huangbo said, "How much do they eat in a day?" The superintendent said, "Two and a half piculs." Huangbo said, "Isn't that too much?" The superintendent said, "I'm afraid it's still too little." Huangbo then hit the superintendent. He told Linji about this, and Linji said, "I'll test this old fellow for you." As soon as he went to stand in attendance on Huangbo, Huangbo recounted the foregoing conversation; Linji said, "The superintendent didn't understand; please say something on his behalf." Then he posed the question, "Isn't that too much?" Huangbo said, "Why didn't he say, 'They'll eat another time tomorrow'?" Linji said, "Why speak of tomorrow—eat right now." Having said this, he slapped Huangbo. Huangbo said, "This lunatic still comes here to grab the tiger's whiskers." Linji gave a shout and left.

Guishan said, "Only when you've raised children do you know your father's kindness." Yangshan said, "It is much like bringing in a thief who ransacks the house."

[466]

Master Touzi was asked by a monk, "'All sounds are the voice of Buddha'—is this so?" He said, "Yes." The monk said, "Master, don't make a sound farting." Touzi then hit him. The monk also asked, "'Coarse words and fine speech all return to ultimate truth'—is this so?" He said, "Yes." The monk said, "Can I call you an ass?" Touzi then hit him.

Dahui said, "Two outlaws are foiled." He also said, "But tell me, which one is a bush bandit, and which one is a true rebel?"

[467]

Master Wuzu Yan said to an assembly,

The grandee Lu Geng asked Nanquan, "There is a stone in my garden; it has sat up, and has lain flat. I want to sculpt it into a Buddha—can I?" Nanquan said, "You can." Lu said, "Can't I?" Nanquan said, "You can't." To be a teacher, one must clarify choices; why does he say it's possible when someone else says it's possible, and say it's impossible when someone else says it's impossible? Do you know where Nanquan is at? I do not spare my eyebrows to give you an explanatory footnote. Who says it's possible, and who says it's impossible? If you still don't understand, tonight I'll make a similitude for you. [Raising his hand:] Take the triple world and twenty-eight heavens and make a Buddha's head; with the sphere of metal and region of water make the Buddha's legs; with the four major continents make the Buddha's body. Though you've made this Buddha, you are still living therein. Do you understand yet? I'll make a second similitude. Take the eastern continent to make a Buddha; make the southern continent a Buddha; make the western continent a Buddha; and make the northern continent a Buddha. Plants, trees, and forests are a Buddha; animate creatures are a Buddha. This being so, then what do you call sentient beings? Do you understand yet? Better to return the eastern continent to the eastern continent; return the southern continent to the southern continent; return the western continent to the western continent; return the northern continent to the northern continent; return plants, trees, and forests to plants, trees, and forests; return animate creatures to animate creatures. This is why it is said, "These phenomena abide in the normative state; the features of the world are always there." This being so, then what do you call Buddha? Do you understand? If this fellow suddenly comes forth and says I should stop talking in my sleep, let everyone remember this recital.

[468]

Yunmen said, "The eyelashes extend horizontally through the ten directions; the eyebrows penetrate heaven and earth above and penetrate the underworld below. The polar mountain blocks off your throat. Does anyone understand? If there is anyone who understands, drag out Cambodia to butt heads with Korea."

Dahui said, "'This is a great spiritual spell, a spell of great knowledge, an unexcelled spell, an unequaled spell, able to eliminate all suffering, really true not in vain.' Do you want to know Yunmen? Haven't you heard it said, 'Everyone must be stirred by party music'?"

[469]

Master Mingzhao composed two verses:

> Smashing open golden chains, the eyes are like bells;
> Brushing the eyebrows up, they grow over the head.
> Only then is one called an heir to the Dharma King,
> Naturally allowed to travel freely throughout the land.
>
> A lion teaches its cub the secret of the wanderer;
> As it goes to leap forward, it's already turned around.
> Where sword points cross interlocked,
> Hawk's eyes, when the time comes, have lost the trail.

[470]

The Clam Monk lived in no fixed place. After he was acknowledged by Dongshan, he blended in with the populace along the Min River. He used to follow the riverbank gathering clams to eat. At night he would sleep in the paper money offerings at White Horse Shrine. The local residents called him the Clam Monk. Master Huayan Jing heard of him

and wanted to determine if he was real or fake; he buried himself in the
paper money ahead of time, and when the Clam Monk came back to settle late that night he grabbed him and asked, "What is the meaning of the
founding teacher's coming from the West?" The Clam Monk immediately replied, "The bowl on the wine stand in front of the spirit."

[471]

Jingqing asked Xuefeng, "What about the ancient worthies—didn't they
communicate mind by mind?" Xuefeng said, "Also they didn't establish
writings or verbal statements." Jingqing said, "What about not establishing writings or verbal statements—how is that transmitted?" Xuefeng remained silent. Jingqing bowed in thanks. Xuefeng said, "Wouldn't it be
better to ask me another question?" Jingqing said, "I ask the master a
question." Xuefeng said, "Just so; do you think there is some discussion
besides?" Jingqing said, "For you, 'just so' will do." Xuefeng said, "How
about you?" Jingqing said, "Totally disappointing."

[472]

Master Reclining Dragon from Korea was asked by a monk, "What are
the signs of a great person?" He said, "Not reaching out inside purple
gauze curtains." The monk asked, "Why not reach out?" He said, "He is
not noble." The monk asked, "How should one apply the mind twenty-
four hours a day?" He said, "A monkey eating caterpillars."

[473]

Master Baiyun Zang was asked by a monk, "What is the deepest state?"
He said, "A midget crosses a deep valley stream." The monk asked, "What
about when barefoot?" He said, "Why not strip?"

[474]

The scholar Zhang Cho ["Cho" means "unskilled"] called on Shishuang. Shishuang asked, "What is your surname?" He said, "Cho's surname is Zhang." Shishuang said, "When you look for skill, it cannot be found—where does 'unskilled' come from?" At these words Zhang had an insight; he then set forth a verse, saying,

> Light shines silently, pervading countless worlds;
> Ordinary and holy animate beings are collectively my family.
> When a single thought is not produced, the total being appears;
> As soon as the six senses stir, they are blocked by clouds.
> Removing afflictions doubly increases sickness;
> Heading toward reality as such is all in error.
> Going along with the multitude of conditions, there is no obstruction;
> Nirvana and birth and death are flowers in the sky.

Yunmen asked a monk, "'Light shines silently, pervading countless worlds'—aren't these the words of the scholar Zhang Cho?" The monk said, "Yes." Yunmen said, "This is the failure of talk."

Dahui said, "A donkey picks out a wet spot to piss."

[475]

Master Baiyun Duan said to an assembly,

In ancient times, in the assembly on Spiritual Mountain the World Honored One held up a flower and Kasyapa smiled. The World Honored One said, "I have the treasury of the eye of truth; I impart it to Kasyapa the Elder. Transmit it successively; don't let it die out." It has come down to the present day. Everyone, if it is the treasury of the eye of truth, old Shakyamuni had no part himself—what did he impart, what did he transmit? What does this mean? Each one of you on your own part has the treasury of the eye of truth yourself. Everyday getting up is it; affirming what is so and negating what is not, distinguishing south and distinguishing north, all sorts of activities, are all reflections of the treasury of the eye of truth. When this eye opens, the universe, the whole earth, sun, moon, stars, and planets, myriad forms, are right before you, but you do not see that there is the slightest definition. When the eye is not yet open, it's all in the pupils of your eyes. Those whose eye is already open are not within these limitations; for those whose eye is not yet open, I will spare no effort to open the treasury of the eye of true teaching for you: look! [He then raised his hand, putting up two fingers.] Look, look! If you can see, everything is one. If not, I cannot but reiterate in verse:

> Everyone's treasury of the eye of truth—
> A thousand sages cannot match it.
> Communicating a line for you,
> Its light fills the country.
> The polar mountain runs into the sea;
> Severe frost comes down in the sixth month.
> Though the flower of truth speaks this way,
> There is no statement to discuss.

Everyone, after having spoken fully, why is there no statement that can be discussed? [He shouted.] Divide your body into two places and see.

[476]

Master Tianyi Huai said to an assembly,

"Skillfully able to distinguish the characteristics of all things without moving from the ultimate truth"—how do you explain this principle of distinguishing? I will try to distinguish: the four directions are it; in the mountains is it; the communal hall, Buddha shrine, kitchen, triple gate, and "here" are it; in the teaching hall is it; the whole land is it; monks are monks; the laity is the laity. How do you explain the ultimate truth?

If you can understand here, you pierce old Vimalakirti's nostrils. If you don't understand, wait till Aniruddha emerges in the world.

TRANSLATOR'S NOTE

Aniruddha was one of Gautama Buddha's top ten disciples, foremost in clairvoyance. To emerge in the world means to emerge as a Buddha.

[477]

Master Shunji was asked by a monk, "What is someone engaged in great practice like?" He said, "Wearing stocks and chains." The monk asked, "What about someone creating a lot of karma?" He said, "Practicing meditation, entering concentration." The monk was speechless. Shunji then said, "You ask me about good—good does not follow evil. You ask me about evil—evil does not follow good. Therefore it is said that good and evil are like floating clouds, arising and disappearing, both having no abode." The monk was enlightened at these words. Later the Oven Breaker heard of this and said, "My son has thoroughly understood all things have no origin."

Dahui said, "What can be done about forming false imaginations in front of the skull?"

[478]

Master Yunju You said to an assembly,

A monk asked Zhaozhou, "What is the meaning of the founding teacher's coming from the West?" Zhaozhou said, "The cypress tree in the yard." The monk said, "Don't use an object to teach people." Zhaozhou said, "I'm not using an object to teach people." The monk said, "What is the meaning of the founding teacher's coming from the West?" Zhaozhou said, "The cypress tree in the yard."

Extraordinary! When ancient sages gave out a saying or half a phrase, they could be said to have cut off the doorway of holy and ordinary, and directly shown the eyes of Maitreya, never degenerating over time. Among the communities are many ways of different interpretation, a multiplicity of evaluations, burying the essential meaning, mistakenly analyzing the terms and words. Some say, "The green, green bamboo is all reality as such; the flourishing yellow flowers are without exception wisdom." Some say, "Mountains, rivers, plants and trees—every thing is a manifestation of the true mind, not just the cypress tree in the yard. Dust, hair, tiles, and pebbles are in totality the infinite interrelations in the one reality realm, principle and phenomena completely merging." Some say, "The cypress tree in the yard—as soon as it is brought up, get it directly. The substance we face is complete reality—when you hesitate you fall into sense objects. It requires the action of the person involved, meeting at the moment, whether beating, shouting, or holding up a fist, or abruptly leaving—this eye is like a spark, like lightning." Some say, "The cypress tree in the yard—what further issue is there? Zhaozhou was helping directly, speaking realistically: when hungry, eat; when tired, sleep—all activities are your own experience of it."

Views like this are numerous, plentiful—all of them are of the family of the celestial devil, aberrant doctrines. They just take discriminations of the subjectivity of consciousness, applying their minds to grasping and rejecting, making forced intellectual views, transmitting them mouth to ear, fooling and confusing people, hoping for fame and profit. What kind of behavior is this, sullying the way of the ancestors? Why don't they travel around looking for good teachers to settle their bodies and minds, to be something like a patchrobed monk?

Since ancient times there have naturally been guides and exemplars of the school of the source. Our Buddha-mind school is respected and trusted by the celestials; even the three grades of sages and ten ranks of saints cannot fathom its source. [Raising his whisk:] If you understand here, the mountains, rivers, and earth are fellow seekers with you. [Looking right and left:] How dare I degrade decent people?

[479]

A monk asked Yunfeng, "Is there any Buddhism on mountain peaks and sheer cliffs?" He said, "There is." The monk asked, "What is the Buddhism on mountain peaks and sheer cliffs?" He said, "Monkeys climbing trees upside-down."

Dahui said, "If people can accept and apply this, their lifetime's study is finished."

[480]

Master Langya Jiao said to an assembly,

As I read the ninth section of the *Flower Ornament* "Golden Lion" essay, on formation by the operation of mind, with the explanation that it is like a foot-high mirror containing multiply multiplied images, if so, you can say they exist and you can say they are nonexistent, you can deny and you can affirm; even so, you still need to know there is an opening on a staff. If you don't know, the staff snakes through a lamp and enters the Buddha shrine, bumping into Shakyamuni and knocking over Maitreya; the pillars clap and laugh. Tell me, what are they laughing at? [He planted his staff.]

[481]

National Teacher Shao asked Longya, "Why can't the powerful noble be approached?" Longya said, "It's like fire with fire." Shao said, "Suppose it comes upon water—what then?" Longya said, "Wayfarer, you don't understand." Next he asked Sushan, "A hundred times around, a thousand layers—whose realm is this?" Sushan said, "A rope of strands twisted to the left ties up a demon." Shao went on to say, "Please speak without falling into past or present." Sushan said, "I won't say." Shao said, "Why not?" Sushan said, "Herein being and nothingness are not distinguished."

[482]

Master Yunmen said to an assembly,

I cannot help but tell you to be free of concerns at once; this is already burying you away. You still want to step forward seeking sayings, pursuing statements, seeking understanding, setting out challenges in a thousand different ways with myriad distinctions, gaining a slippery tongue for the moment while getting further and further from the Way. When will you ever stop? If this matter were in words, are there no words in the twelve-part canons of the three vehicles? Why speak of a separate transmission outside of doctrine? If it came from learned interpretation and intellectual knowledge, the likes of the sages of the tenth stage expound the Dharma like clouds and rain, yet are still criticized for their perception of essence being as if screened by gauze. Hence we know that all thinking is as far off as the sky is from earth. Even so, if you have attained, you may speak of fire but it cannot burn your mouth. You may speak of things all day without it sticking to your lips and teeth—you haven't said a word. You may wear clothes and eat rice all day without ever touching a grain of rice or putting on a single thread. Even so, this is still talk of the doorway; you must really get to be this way before you can attain. According to the school of patchrobed monks, potential is presented in a phrase—it is a waste of effort to stand there thinking. Even if you understand at a single statement, you are still snoozing.

At that time a monk asked, "What is a single statement?"
    Yunmen said, "Brought up."

Dahui said, "Snoozer."

[483]

Duan, "the Lion," lectured in Huading, saying, "The lion of Spiritual Mountain roars in the clouds. There's nothing to discuss in Buddha's teaching; it's better to do a flip." Then he bounded down from the chair.

[484]

Ananda asked Kasyapa, "The World Honored One transmitted the golden-sleeved vestment; other than that, what teaching did he transmit?" Kasyapa called, "Ananda!" Ananda responded. Kasyapa said, "Take down the flagpole in front of the gate."

Fenyang said, "If he didn't ask, how would he know?"

Wuzu Jie said, "Evident."

Cuiyan Zhi said, "The thousand-year shadowless tree, the present-day bottomless shoes."

[485]

Master Zhenjing said to an assembly,

Are there any questions? [Silence.] After thirty years of horse riding, I've been kicked by a mule. [Rubbing his knees.] After all, with the polar mountain steep and high, the ocean waters sending waves leaping, the thirty-three deities withdraw from their position all at once, the eighteen great hells stop their pains. Do you see? If you can see here, Shakyamuni folds his hands, Maitreya furrows his brow, Manjushri and Samantabhadra serve as attendants. If you do not see, watch me free in all ways, and get it within complications. Ha, ha, ha! Exalted worthies, tell me, what am I laughing at? Oh, I'm laughing at the firefly light and mosquito understanding of Yunmen, Linji, Deshan, and Yantou of olden times. One said, "When the great enlightened World Honored One was first born, he pointed to the sky with one hand, pointed to the earth with one hand, and said, 'In the heavens above and on earth below, I alone am honored.' If I had seen him at the outset I would have killed him with one blow and fed him to the dogs." The likes of this bunch of thieving phonies are all just temporarily claiming honor where there is no Buddha. If they were called back now, I would start an inquisition of them at once. As for the rest, it will not do to let them off. Haven't you read how a monk asked Jianfeng, "For the Blessed Ones of the ten directions, there is one road to nirvana—where does that road start?" Jianfeng described a line with his staff and said, "Here." What about this answer of Jianfeng—did he ever see, even in a dream? If it were me, I'd do otherwise. "For the Blessed Ones of the ten directions, there is one road to nirvana—where does the road begin?"—I'd strike the questioner across the back and ask him, "Where is the beginning of the road?" When he's about to open his mouth, I'd shout him out. Then there was this old broken-legged Yunmen, who didn't distinguish the adept from the naive, did not distinguish true from false—holding up his fan, he said, "This leaps up to the Thirty-Third Heaven and bumps into the nose of the emperor of gods; the carp of the eastern sea struck once with a cane, it rains buckets." As for this kind of guy mixing in mud and water, in a pile of crap, what would be wrong with burying five or ten? Ah, ha, ha! Happy? Enough? Now we're fortunate to face the greening of the mountains; over the years this phenomenon is one time. Stop letting body and mind lazily be bound up—everyone better stop snoozing.

[486]

Master Ruiyan Yan asked Yantou, "What is the fundamental constant principle?" Yantou said, "It's in motion." Ruiyan asked, "How is it when in motion?" Yantou said, "It's not a fundamental constant principle." Ruiyan sank into thought. After a long while Yantou said, "If you agree, you haven't yet gotten free of senses and objects. If you don't agree, you're forever sunk in birth and death." Ruiyan finally attained enlightenment. Afterward he visited Jiashan; Jiashan asked, "Where are you coming from?" He said, "From Reclining Dragon." Jiashan said, "When you came, did the reclining dragon get up?" Ruiyan stared at him. Jiashan said, "You put more moxa to burn on a moxibustion scar." Ruiyan said, "Why are you still suffering so?" Jiashan then stopped.

. . .

Dahui said, "If he didn't shoot Shi Hu at Indigo Fields, he might have mistakenly killed General Li."

TRANSLATOR'S NOTE

Shi Hu was the warrior-founder of the short-lived Latter Zhao dynasty established by foreign conquest in part of China during the fourth century CE. General Li was a celebrated Chinese military leader of the Han dynasty, particularly famous for his service in campaigns against the nomadic Xiongnu.

[487]

Nanyuan asked a monk, "What is your name?" The monk said, "Pucan" [meaning "study everywhere."] Nanyuan said, "What if you come upon a piece of crap?" The monk said, "How are you?" Nanyuan hit him.

[488]

Master Lohan Nan said to an assembly,

The Buddhas did not emerge in the world, Bodhidharma didn't come from the West. The mind seal of the founding teachers is like the works of the iron ox. Therefore, if it stamps the sky, sun and moon lose their light; heaven and earth are plunged into darkness. If it stamps water, it compresses the breakers and disturbs the waves; fish and dragons lose their lives. If it stamps mud, the whole earth melts; the roads of the holy and the ordinary are cut off. As for that other seal, who would dare stare at it? Nevertheless everywhere they make descriptions and likenesses; if it comes into my hand, I'll simply make it shatter.

[489]

Master Zhaoqing said to an assembly, "Tonight I've told you all at once; but do you comprehend what it comes down to?" Then a monk came out and said, "If the assembly disperses at once, will it conform to your intent?" He said, "I ought to give a staff." The monk bowed. Zhaoqing said, "Though you have the aim of a blind turtle, you have no way to go under the dawn moon." The monk asked, "What is the way to go under the dawn moon?" He said, "This is the aim of the blind turtle." The monk asked, "What is the conduct of a monk?" He said, "Wrong conduct is not carried out." The monk asked, "What is the meaning of the coming from the West?" He said, "A mosquito gets on an iron ox."

[490]

For a long time Master Deshan made it his task to lecture on the *Diamond Sutra*; later he heard that the Chan school in the South was flourishing greatly, and he couldn't figure out why. Eventually he stopped lecturing, dismissed his students, and took his commentaries to travel south. He first went to Longtan, where as soon as he stepped across the threshold he said, "I have long heard of Longtan [meaning "dragon pond"], but now that I'm here I don't see a pond, and a dragon does not appear." Longtan said, "You have personally arrived at Dragon Pond." Deshan then bowed and withdrew. That night he went into Longtan's quarters and stood in attendance. When it had become late, Longtan said, "Why don't you leave?" Deshan finally bid goodbye, raised the blind, and went out. Seeing it was dark outside, he came back and said, "It's dark outside." Longtan then lit a paper torch and handed it to Deshan. Just as Deshan took it, Longtan blew it out. At this Deshan was suddenly greatly enlightened. He then bowed. Longtan said, "What have you seen, that you bow?" Deshan said, "From now on I won't doubt what the old masters in the land say." The next day Longtan went up in the hall and said, "There is someone here with fangs like sword trees, mouth like a bowl of blood; struck a blow of the cane, he won't turn his head. Someday he'll establish my path on the summit of a solitary peak." Deshan subsequently took his commentaries and held up a torch in front of the teaching hall; he said, "Thorough explanation of the mysteries is like a single hair in cosmic space; exhausting the workings of the world is like a drop in an abyss." He then burned the commentaries, bowed, and departed.

[491]

When Dengyin Feng took leave of Mazu, Mazu said, "Where are you going?" He said, "To Shitou." Mazu said, "The road of Shitou is slippery." He said, "Bringing a pole with me, I'll perform at whatever location I come upon." Then he left. As soon as he reached Shitou, he circled the Chan seat once, planted his staff, and asked, "What doctrine is this?" Shitou said, "Heavens, heavens!" Feng was speechless. He went back and told Mazu about this. Mazu said, "Go again, and when he says, 'Heavens, heavens!' you heave a couple of sighs." Feng went back and asked the same question; Shitou then heaved a couple of sighs. Feng was again speechless. He returned and related this to Mazu. Mazu said, "I told you the road of Shitou is slippery!"

[492]

"Muslin Robe" Zhao one night pointed to the half moon and asked Elder Pu, "Where has the other part gone?" Pu said, "Don't misconceive." Zhao said, "You've lost a piece."

Dahui said, "He gets up by himself and falls down by himself."

[493]

When Guanghui Lian came to Shoushan, Shoushan asked, "Where have you just come from?" He said, "Hanshang." Shoushan raised a fist and said, "Is there this in Hanshang?" He said, "What gurgling is this?" Shoushan said, "Blind!" He said, "As if it were a smack," and immediately left.

[494]

Master "Long Mustache" called on Shitou. Shitou asked, "Where are you coming from?" He said, "From south of the range." Shitou said, "Has the set of virtues of the Dayu Range been completed yet?" He said, "It's been complete for a long time. All that's lacking is the pupils of the eyes." Shitou said, "Do you want the pupils put in?" He said, "Please." Shitou let one leg hang down. "Mustache" thereupon bowed. Shitou said, "What have you seen, that you bow?" He said, "It's like a snowflake on a red-hot furnace."

[495]

Yangshan asked Nanta, "How am I like a donkey?" He said, "Even a Buddha doesn't compare." Yangshan said, "Since even a Buddha doesn't compare, what am I like?" He said, "If you were like anything, how would you differ from a donkey?" Yangshan approved of this.

[496]

Master Yangqi asked a monk, "The colors of autumn are fully developed; where did you leave in the morning?" He said, "Last summer I was in Shanglin." Yangqi said, "How do you say the one expression that doesn't go on a road?" He said, "A double case." Yangqi said, "Thanks for your reply." The monk thereupon shouted. Yangqi said, "Where did you learn this vanity?" He said, "An adept with clear eyes can't be fooled." Yangqi said, "If so, I'll follow you." The monk hesitated. Yangqi said, "Considering that someone from your hometown is here, I forgive you thirty blows."

Yangqi was asked, "What is Buddha?" He said, "The sound of shouting and caning in front of the stairs."

[497]

When Master Muzhou saw a monk coming, he said, "The presently concluded official decision forgives you thirty blows." Yunfeng Yue said, "The thief's heart is cowardly."

Dahui said, "I'll add another." Having said this, he asked Chongmi, "You tell me, am I at fault for having spoken thus?" Chongmi said, "The thief's heart is cowardly." Dahui said, "There are three."

[498]

Master Daowu Zhen said to an assembly,

An ancient said, "If you acknowledge fixedly, as before it's not right." Hard to understand indeed. Under the jaw of a bee there are a lot of whiskers; a Parsi's eyes are deep, and his nose is big. Quite strange! Suddenly they've passed through the realm of Korea.

He also said to an assembly,

Past and present, sun and moon are as ever over the mountains and rivers. If you can understand, it's the one road of nirvana of the Blessed Ones of the ten directions; if you don't understand, you slander this scripture, so you get such a penalty.

[499]

Master Jiashan said to an assembly,

Not cognizant of the dawn in the sky, enlightenment doesn't come from a teacher. The fish leaping at the Dragon Gate do not fall into the hands of fishermen. As long as the intellect doesn't rest on subjective relations, and the tongue doesn't associate with mysterious doctrines, you are a truly good connoisseur. This is called talk that can produce both good and bad. If you focus on mysterious doctrines and go on wondering, they'll cheat you completely. Exhausted fish stay in the shallows;

weakened birds roost in the reeds. Clouds and water are not you; you are not clouds and water. I have gotten freedom amid the clouds and water; what about you?

[500]

Master Muzhou said to an assembly, "Breaking open is in oneself; kneading together is in oneself." A monk asked, "What is breaking open?" He said, "Three times nine is twenty-seven. Bodhi, nirvana, reality as such, and liberation are mind, which is Buddha. I say so for the moment; what about you?" The monk said, "I do not say so." He said, "A cup is knocked to the ground, the number of pieces is seven."

Yunfeng Yue said, "When we're reviling each other, you may go beak to beak; when we're spitting at each other, you may spew slobber."

[501]

Master Cuiyan Zhi said to an assembly,
    There's no oil in sand. Pitiful as it is, I'm chewing food to feed babies. Someday when you know good and bad for sure, only then will you be aware of a previous face full of ash.

[502]

As Angulimalya was begging, he came to the door of a rich man whose wife was having a difficult birth and had not yet delivered. The rich man said, "As a disciple of Gautama you are a supreme sage—what method do you have to avoid birthing difficulty?" Angulimalya said to the rich man, "I have just entered the Path and do not yet know this method. Wait till I go back and ask the World Honored One, and I'll come back and tell you." Then he went back and told the Buddha all about this. The Buddha said, "Go there quickly and announce, 'Ever since I have been following the teaching of saints and sages, I have never killed a living being.'" Angulimalya did as the Buddha said; he went and told this to the rich man. When his wife heard this, she delivered at once.

TRANSLATOR'S NOTE

Before he was converted by Buddha, Angulimalya was a death cultist who believed he could attain spiritual liberation by killing a thousand people. Some see in him evidence of an ancient ancestor of the more recent cult of Thuggee.

[503]

Master Caoshan said to an assembly, "Everywhere they all take up standard examples; why not speak to them so that they don't doubt?" Yunmen was in the assembly; he came forth and said, "Why is the most intimately hidden place not known to exist?" Caoshan said, "Because it is most intimately hidden; that's why it isn't known." Yunmen said, "How can people approach it?" Caoshan said, "Don't approach the most intimately hidden place." Yunmen said, "How is it when one doesn't approach the most intimately hidden place?" Caoshan said, "Only then is one able to approach."

Dahui said, "A wet lamp wick is stuck in contaminated oil."

[504]

Master Deshan Yuanming said to an assembly,
  Coming on thus is a presently complete official decision; coming on not thus is a target arising inviting an arrow. Coming on not so at all is partiality meeting bias. A swift point is already dull. When there are no clouds for ten thousand miles, the blue sky is still there.

A monk asked, "How is it when standing out with no deviation?"
  He said, "A donkey tethering stake."

The monk said, "Where is the fault?"

He said, "One's own shit doesn't seem to stink."

The monk said, "It's all right for you to say so."

He said, "A dung beetle pushes a ball of dung."

He was asked, "No tracks, no traces—whose conduct is this?"

He said, "A thief stealing an ox."

"How is it when attaining the reality body without going through immeasurable eons?"

"This is still standing under a sign."

"How is it before a ram gets hung up by the horns?"

"A dog chasing crap."

"What is the road of the ancient Buddhas?"

"A sacred tree by the wayside."

[505]

Master Fayan of Mount Qingliang said to an assembly,

People who leave home, just go along with the time and season; then when it's cold you're cold, and when it's hot you're hot. "If you want to know the meaning of Buddha-nature, you must observe time and season, causes and conditions." Expedient means past and present have not been lacking. Haven't you seen how when Master Shitou read the treatise of Sengzhao saying, "Those who understand all things as self are only sages, it seems," he then said, "Sages have no self, but there is nothing they do not regard as self." He had a set of sayings he called *Merging of Difference and Sameness*, in which he finally said, "The mind of the great immortal of India"—nothing is beyond these words. In the meantime he just spoke according to the time. Elders, do you want to understand all things as self now? In sum, there is nothing on earth to view. He also charged people, "Don't waste time." A moment ago I told you that it will do to go along with the time and season. If your timing is wrong and you miss the signs of the times, then you are wasting time, understanding the immaterial to be material. If you understand the immaterial to be material, your timing is wrong and you're missing the signs of the times. But tell me, is it then appropriate to understand the material as immaterial? If you understand this way, you're out of touch. Actually this is madly running in two directions; what use is that? Just keep to your lot and go along with the time.

[506]

Master Zhou of Guangde monastery in Rang province was asked by a monk, "I understand that there is a statement in the teachings that Aniruddha didn't cut off afflictions and didn't cultivate meditation concentration, and the Buddha predicted that this man would undoubtedly become a Buddha. What is the principle of this?" He said, "Salt all gone, and no charcoal either." The monk said, "How is it when the salt is all gone and there is no charcoal?" He said, "Sad man, don't tell sad people; if you tell sad people, you'll sadden them to death."

Dahui said, "The ancient answering this way is called washing the feet and boarding the boat."

[507]

The Second Patriarch asked Bodhidharma, "Can I hear about the Dharma seal of the Buddhas?" He said, "The Dharma seal of the Buddha is not gotten from another." The Second Patriarch said, "My mind is not yet at peace; please pacify my mind for me." He said, "Bring me your mind and I will pacify it for you." The Second Patriarch said, "Having looked for my mind, I cannot find it." Bodhidharma said, "I have pacified your mind for you."

Baqiao said, "Diamond scratches a clay man's back."

[508]

Master Xianglin Xiang was asked by a monk, "What is the meaning of hiding one's body in the North Star?"

He said, "The moon is like a drawn bow; little rain, lots of wind."

"What is one lamp in a room?"

"When three people testify it's a turtle, it's a terrapin."

"What is the business under the patch robe?"

"In December fire burns a mountain."

"How is it when a fish swims on dry land?"

"When speaking out, there has to be follow-up reason."

"How is it when descending into an aquamarine pool?"

"The head is heavy, the tail is light."

[509]

When meditation master Hai of Shao province first met the Sixth Patriarch, he asked, "'Mind itself is Buddha'—please provide instruction." The patriarch said, "When the preceding thought is not produced, this is mind itself; the following thought not passing into extinction is Buddha. Formulating all descriptions is mind; detachment from all descriptions is Buddha. If I were to explain in full, it would take eons and still not be finished. Listen to my verse."

> Mind itself is called insight;
> Being Buddha is concentration.
> When insight and concentration are maintained equally,
> In the mind is purity.
> Understanding this teaching
> Depends on the nature you've developed.
> Its function is rooted in no origination;
> Twin cultivation is correct.

Hai believed and accepted, and praised in verse:

Mind itself is basically Buddha;
If you don't understand, you inhibit yourself.
I know the bases of concentration and insight;
Twin cultivation detaches from all things.

[510]

Master Yaoshan didn't lecture for a long time. One day the abbot said to him, "The congregation has been wanting your instruction for a long time." Yaoshan said, "Ring the bell." Then when the congregation had gathered, Yaoshan got down off the chair and returned to his quarters. The abbot followed him and asked, "You agreed to speak to the congregation—why didn't you say a word?" Yaoshan said, "The scriptures have teachers of scriptures, the treatises have teachers of treatises—how can you think me strange?"

Dahui said, "He makes people laugh their heads off."

[511]

Master Ximu went up in the hall; a layman raised his hand and said, "You're an ass." Ximu said, "I'm ridden by you." The layman was speechless. Three days later he came back and said, "Three days ago I ran into a bandit." Ximu took up his staff and drove him out.

[512]

Master Shexian Sheng was asked one day by Master Nian, "If you call it a bamboo knife, you're attached; if you don't call it a bamboo knife, you're turning away. What should it be called?" With this Sheng was greatly enlightened. He then seized the bamboo knife, broke it, tossed it down the stairs, and said, "What is this?" Nian said, "Blind!" Sheng then bowed.

When a monk asked for help with the story of Zhaozhou's cypress tree, Sheng said, "I don't decline to explain to you, but will you believe?"

The monk said, "How dare I not believe weighty words of the teacher?" Sheng said, "Do you hear the sound of rain dripping from the eaves?" The monk's mind was opened; he unconsciously cried, "Yea!" Sheng said, "What principle have you seen?" The monk replied in verse:

> The sound of rain dripping from the eaves
> Is distinctly clear.
> The dripping breaks up heaven and earth;
> Right away the mind stops.

Sheng was delighted.

[513]

Master Fahua Ju said to an assembly,

Speaking of the gradual, it is countering the ordinary to conform to the Path; speaking of the sudden, it doesn't leave any tracks. Even if you discern the sudden, you counter its norm—this is doing it by suppression.

When Ju went to Master Gongan Yuan's place, Yuan asked, "What is a sanctuary?" Ju said, "Deep mountains hide a lone tiger; shallow grass reveals a bunch of snakes." Yuan said, "How about the person in the sanctuary?" Ju said, "Green pines cannot cover him; how can yellow leaves hide him?" Yuan said, "What are you saying?" Ju said, "A youth thoroughly enjoys the moon in the sky; for a dotard, there's no sun in the east." Yuan said, "How is it when the clouds open and the moon appears in one or two statements?" Ju said, "Shining through the Buddhas and patriarchs."

[514]

Master Wuzu Yan said to an assembly,

If there is anyone who can take the waters of the four great oceans for an inkstone and the polar mountain for a brush, and writes in space the words, "The meaning of the founding teacher's coming from the West,"

I will get off my chair, spread my mat, and pay homage to him as my teacher. If you can't write it, then Buddhism has no spiritual effect. Is there anyone? Is there? [Then he got down from the chair; the assembly dispersed. The teacher said loudly,] "Attendant!" [The attendant responded. The teacher told him to put away the mat. He also asked the attendant if he was able to put away the mat. The attendant held up the mat. Yan said,] "I knew you were like this."

He also said to the assembly,

Above is the sky; below is the earth: south, north, east, and west stay in their positions. Old Shakyamuni played with the spirit; Bodhidharma's coming from the West had a lot of taboos. If someone comes forth and tells me to quiet down, I'll just tell him I only want to toss out a brick to draw out a jade.

[515]

Yunmen saw a monk coming to inquire; he held up his vestment and said, "If you can speak, you fall within my vestment loop. If you cannot speak, then you're inside a ghost cave. How about it?" He answered himself on the monk's behalf, "I have no strength."

Dahui said, "In India they cut off heads and sever arms; here you take what's yours and get out."

[516]

Master Xuansha said to an assembly,

The way of Buddhas is vast; it has no standard course. No door is the door of liberation; no thought is the thought of wayfarers. It is not in past, present, or future, so you cannot rise or sink. Definition defies reality; it does not belong to creation. Stir, and you produce the basis of birth and death; stay still, and you get intoxicated in the realm of torpor. If movement and stillness both disappear, you fall into nothingness. If movement and stillness are both taken in, you presume upon Buddha-nature. You simply must be like dead trees or cold ashes in the face of sense data and objects, while acting responsively according to the time, not failing to be appropriate. A mirror reflects all images without that disrupting its shine; birds fly in the sky without mixing up the color of the sky. Therefore there are no reflections in the ten directions, no traces of activity in the triple world. It does not fall into the mechanics of coming and going, nor dwell in thought in between. There is no sound of a drum in a bell, and no sound of a bell in a drum. Bell and drum do not interchange; statements have no before or after. Just as a strong man does not need to borrow another's strength to extend his arm, why would a lion roaming seek companions? There is no blockage in the nine skies—how is it a matter of piercing through? The single light has never been obscured. If you arrive here, your being is at peace; you're always clear. The glowing flames of the sun are boundless, unwavering in the sky of complete awareness, engulfing heaven and earth in light, shining afar. The Buddhas' emergence in the world basically has no out or in; terms and descriptions have no substance. The Way is fundamentally as such, natural reality, not the same as cultivated realization. It only requires being open and free of preoccupation, not befuddling activity, not getting into the mud of sense objects. Herein, if there is the slightest incompleteness of the Way, you become a subject of the king of demons.

Before expression and after expression are points of difficulty for students; hence when one expression is really accurate, eighty thousand doors are forever closed to birth and death. Even if you get to be like the reflection of the moon in an autumn pond, the sound of a bell on a quiet night, ringing unfailingly whenever struck, not scattered on contact with ripples, this is still something on the shore of birth and death. The action of people on the Way is like fire melting ice—it never becomes ice again. Once an arrow has left the bowstring, it does not come back. Therefore they won't be kept trapped, and will not turn their heads when called.

The ancient sages did not make arrangements; even now they have no fixed place. If you arrive here, you ascend into the mystery with every step, not in the province of wrong or right. Perception cannot discern it, intellect cannot know it. Stir, and you lose the source; consciously notice, and you miss the essence. Those on the two vehicles tremble; those in the ten stages are shocked. The road of speech is cut off; the sphere of mental activity disappears. Hence we have Shakyamuni shutting off his room in Magadha, Vimalakirti keeping his mouth closed in Vaisali, Subhuti preaching no explanation to reveal the Way, Indra and Brahma raining flowers without hearing. If it is evident in this way, what would you still doubt? Where there is no abiding is beyond past, future, and present. It cannot be limited; the road of thought is cut off. It does not depend on arrangement or embellishment; it is originally real and pure. Activity, speech, and laughter are everywhere perfectly clear; there is no lack anymore.

People of the present do not understand the principle herein and mistakenly get themselves involved in things and sense objects, getting influenced everywhere, getting bound up everywhere. Even if you awaken, sense data and objects are still profuse; names and descriptions are not real. Then you try to freeze your mind, rein in thoughts, reduce phenomena to emptiness, shut your eyes, break off thoughts as they arise again and again, and suppress subtle thinking as soon as it arises. Views like this are characteristic of outside ways that fall into nihilism, dead people whose ghosts have not yet departed, dark and vague, unaware, unknowing, covering your ears to steal a bell, uselessly fooling yourself. If you discriminate here, it is not so.

This is not standing by the door, at the corner of the gate. Each expression is evident, not open to debate, not literal. To be fundamentally beyond sense data and objects, fundamentally without ranks, is provisionally called a leaver of home, ultimately without tracks or traces. Reality as such, ordinary and holy, hell and heaven, are just prescriptions of obvious lunatics. Even space has no change—how can the Way have rising and sinking? When you are enlightened, you are free in all ways without leaving the fundamental. If you arrive here, ordinary and holy have no place to stand. If you fabricate ideas in expression, this drowns students. If you run seeking outside, you fall into the realm of demons. Real transcendence has nothing to arrange. It is like a blazing furnace does not hide a mosquito. This principle is originally even; what's the need for leveling off? Activity, even raising the brows, is the real path of liberation; it is not forced or calculated. Setups are contrary to reality. If you arrive here, nothing at all is taken on; set your mind and you miss. This is the coming forth of a thousand sages; you cannot label it at all.

You have been standing for a long time; take care.

[517]

When Master Zhaozhou went to Zhuyu, he took his staff into the teaching hall and crossed from east to west and west to east. Zhuyu asked, "What are you doing?" Zhaozhou said, "Testing the depth of the water." Zhuyu said, "Here at my place there isn't even a drop—what will you test the depth of?" Zhaozhou went out leaning on his staff.

Langya Jiao said, "A castrated servant fools the master; a decrepit ghost plays with a human."

Dahui said, "The hook is in an unsuspected place."

[518]

Yangshan was asked by Guishan, "The habit-ridden active consciousness of the people of earth is boundless and unclear, with no basis to rely on. How do you know whether others have this or not?" Yangshan said, "I have a test." At that moment a monk was passing by; Yangshan called to him, "Your Reverence!" The monk turned his head. Yangshan said, "Master, this one's habit-ridden active consciousness is boundless and unclear, with no basis to rely on." Guishan said, "This is one drop of lion milk dispersing ten gallons of donkey milk."

[519]

The hermit of Tongfeng was asked by a monk, "What would you do if a tiger suddenly came while you're here?" The hermit roared like a tiger. The monk made a gesture of fright. The hermit laughed. The monk said, "This bandit!" The hermit said, "What can you do about me?"

Xuedou said, "Right, all right, but both bandits only know how to cover their ears to steal a bell."

[520]

National Teacher Wuye said to some disciples, "The essence of your perception and cognition is the same age as space, unborn and undying. All objects are fundamentally empty and quiescent; there is not a single thing that can be grasped. The deluded do not understand, so they are confused by objects; once they are confused by objects, they go around in circles endlessly. You should know that the essence of mind is originally there of itself, not based on constructs. Like diamond, it cannot be broken down. All phenomena are like reflections, like echoes; none have real substance. Therefore scripture says, 'Only this one thing is true; any other is not real.' If you understand all is empty, there isn't a single thing affecting you. This is where the Buddhas apply their minds; you should practice it diligently."

[521]

Master Guishan said to an assembly,

The mind of people of the Way is simple and direct, without falsehood, without opposition, without inclination, without deceptive mental activity. At all times seeing and hearing are normal. There are no further details. Also one does not shut the eyes or close the ears—as long as feelings do not stick to things, that will do. The sages since time immemorial have just spoken of the problems of impurity; if you don't have so much false consciousness, subjective views, and conceptual habits, you are clear and calm as autumn waters, pure, without contrivance, tranquil, free from obstruction. That is called a "wayfarer," and also called someone with no issues.

At that time a monk asked, "Is there any further cultivation for someone who is suddenly enlightened?"

Guishan said, "If one has truly realized the fundamental, that is when one knows for oneself. Cultivation and no cultivation are a dualism. Now, though a beginner attains total sudden realization of inherent truth from conditions, there is still the habit energy of beginningless ages, which one cannot clear away all at once. It is necessary to teach that person to clean away the currently active streaming consciousness. This is cultivation, but it doesn't mean there is a special doctrine to teach one to practice or aim for. Gaining access to truth from hearing, when the truth heard is profound, the immaculate mind is inherently complete and illumined and does not abide in the realm of delusion. Even if there are a hundred thousand subtle meanings according to the times, this is getting a seat, wearing clothes, and knowing how to live on your own. Essentially speaking, the noumenal ground of reality does not admit a single particle, while the ways of Buddhist service do not abandon a single method. If you enter directly at a single stroke, then the sense of ordinary and holy ends; the substance of being is revealed, real and eternal; noumenon and phenomena are not separate. This is the Buddha of thusness as such.

[522]

When the Fifth Patriarch was in Chang'an lecturing on the *Flower Ornament Scripture*, a monk came and asked, "What is the meaning of the conditional arising of the nature of reality?" The patriarch was silent. Chan master Anguo Ting was standing by in attendance at the time; he said, "Great Worthy, right when you produce a single thought, this is conditional arising in the nature of reality." That monk was greatly enlightened at these words.

Dahui said, "Before a single thought has yet arisen, conditional arising cannot be nonexistent. One might say, when a single thought has not yet arisen, what do you call conditional arising? I just need you to speak thus."

[523]

Master Yueshan first called on Xuefeng and got a taste. Later, when the king of Min invited him to a ceremonial meal up in Clear Breeze Tower, after sitting for a long time he raised his eyes and suddenly saw the sunlight, at which he was at once greatly enlightened. He composed a verse, saying,

> Going to an official meal up in Clear Breeze Tower
> This day my ordinary eye opened wide.
> Now I believe that the remote events of the Putong years
> Did not come handed on from the Onion Range.

He presented this to Xuefeng, and Xuefeng approved of it.

A monk said, "What is the body of Buddha?"
    Yueshan said, "Which Buddha body are you asking about?"
    The monk said, "The body of Shakyamuni Buddha."
    Yueshan said, "His tongue covers a billion worlds."

When he was about to die, he gathered his congregation and told them in verse,

> The light of the eyes, following forms, comes to an end;
> The perception of the ears, pursuing sound, dissolves.
> Returning to the source, there is no separate doctrine
> Today and tomorrow.

TRANSLATOR'S NOTE

The Putong years and the Onion Range both refer to the coming of Bodhidharma, the founder of Chan, from India to China.

[524]

Master Guoqing Feng was asked by a monk, "What is the great meaning of Buddhism?" He said, "Shakyamuni was an ox-headed minion of hell; the founder of Chan was a horse-faced minion of hell."

"What is the meaning of the coming from the West?"

"The east wall hits the west wall."

"What is the unbreakable expression?"

"Without the slightest separation, people of the time receive it from afar."

[525]

Master Luopu said to an assembly,

At the last word you reach the unbreakable barrier; cutting off the essential bridge, you don't let ordinary or holy through. Usually I tell you people that even if the whole world is merry, I alone do not agree. Why? It is like a miraculous turtle with a chart on its back carries the omen of its own destruction; when a phoenix caught in a golden net aims for the sky, how can it hope to succeed? You simply must understand the aim outside doctrine; don't take rules from words. Therefore if the potential of a stone man were like you, it could sing songs of the south; if you are like a stone man, you can chime in to songs of snow.

[526]

Master Jiashan was asked by a monk, "How is it when removing sense data to see Buddha?" He said, "If you want to know this thing, you simply must swing a sword; if you don't swing a sword, a fisherman dwells in a nest." The monk asked the same question of Shishuang. Shishuang said, "He has no country—where will you meet him?" The monk went back and related this to Jiashan. Jiashan said, "For setup of a school, I cannot be denied, but when it comes to profound talk entering into noumenon, I'm still a hundred paces behind Shishuang."

[527]

Master Letan Ying said to an assembly,

An ancestral teacher said, "The nature of all living beings is pure, fundamentally unborn and indestructible. So this body and mind are illusory productions. In illusory projection there is no sin or merit." Such talk of the sage of the past is undeniably extraordinary; nevertheless, in relation to the school of patchrobed monks, when brought up for examination it is still hurting the heart by eating to fullness, pain in the waist from sitting a long time.

He also said to an assembly

Ah, ha, ha! What is this? Last night sitting by myself in the light of the moon, I counted people who've passed. I remember the Oven Breaker back in those times; what is this? Raise your eyebrows and you've already stumbled past.

A monk asked, "How is it when performing on encountering a stage?"

He said, "A red-hot furnace tosses out an iron turtle."

[528]

Master Tianhuang asked Shitou, "Apart from concentration and insight, what doctrine do you teach people?" Shitou said, "Here I have no servants—apart from what?" Tianhuang said, "How can it be understood?" Shitou said, "Can you grasp space?" Tianhuang said, "Then it doesn't depart from Today." Shitou said, "When did you come from the Other Side?" Tianhuang said, "I am not someone on the Other Side." Shitou said, "I already knew where you're coming from." Tianhuang said, "How can you take a bribe to covertly incriminate other people?" Shitou said, "You're physically present." Tianhuang said, "Even so, after all, how do you teach people who come after?" Shitou said, "You tell me—who are people who come after?" Tianhuang had insight from this.

Dahui said, "But tell me, what did he realize?"

[529]

When Elder Taiyuan Fu was at Xiaoxian temple in Yang province lecturing on the *Nirvana Scripture*, there was a Chan practitioner who was staying at the temple; snowed in, he took the opportunity to go listen to the lecture. Coming to the triple-base Buddha-nature and triple-quality reality body, the lecturer spoke extensively about the subtle principle of the reality body. The Chan practitioner inadvertently laughed. When Fu's lecture was finished, he invited the Chan practitioner to tea and said to him, "My basic aspiration is narrow and inferior; I interpret meanings based on the text. Just now I've been laughed at, and I hope to be instructed." The Chan practitioner said, "Actually I laughed at the fact that you don't know the body of reality." Fu said, "What's wrong with explaining this way?" The Chan practitioner said, "Please explain once more." Fu said, "The noumenon of the body of reality is like cosmic space, pervading all times and all places, all-encompassing, containing both yin and yang, coming to the senses in every object, all-pervasive." The Chan practitioner said, "I don't say your explanation isn't right, but you are talking about the scope of the reality body—you still don't actually know the reality body." Fu said, "So explain it for me." He said, "Will you believe?" Fu said, "How dare I not believe?" He said, "If so, stop lecturing for ten days, meditate properly in a room, reining in your mind and controlling your thoughts, letting go of all objects, good and bad, at once." Fu did as he was instructed from the evening until dawn; when he heard the sound of the drum and horn, he suddenly attained enlightenment. He then went to knock on the door of the Chan practitioner. "Who is it?"

the Chan man said. Fu said, "So and so." The Chan practitioner clucked and said, "I'd have you inherit the great teaching and expound the teaching in Buddha's stead; why have you been lying in the street drunk all night?" Fu said, "Ever since I came to lecture on scripture I've been twisting the nose of the father and mother who gave birth to me. From now on I won't dare act like this." The Chan practitioner said, "Go away for now; we'll meet tomorrow." Fu subsequently stopped lecturing and traveled around. He spent a long time with Xuefeng and became very famous. Later he returned to Yang province and was lodged and supported by Ministry President Chen. One day he said to the ministry president, "Tomorrow I'm going to lecture on the *Mahaparinirvana Scripture* to repay you." The ministry president arranged a vegetarian meal, and when tea was finished, Fu finally got up in the chair, brandished a ruler, and said, "'Thus have I heard.'" Then he called to the ministry president. The ministry president responded. Fu said, "'At one time the Buddha was in . . .'" And thereupon he passed away.

[530]

Yantou said to an assembly, "I once studied the *Nirvana Scripture* for seven or eight years; there are two or three principles in it that somewhat resemble the talk of patchrobed monks."

He also said, "Stop, stop."

At that time a monk said, "Please cite them."

Yantou said, "The meaning of my teaching is like three dots. First a dot is set down in the east, opening up the eyes of bodhisattvas. Second, a dot is set down in the west, lighting up the root of life of bodhisattvas. Third, a dot is set down above, opening up the crown of bodhisattvas. This is the first principle."

He also said, "The meaning of my teaching is like the opening up of one eye up on the forehead of the great god Mahesvara. This is the second principle."

He also said, "The meaning of my teaching is like a poisoned drum; at one beat, all who hear it, far and near, die. This is the third principle."

At that time a certain elder Xiaoyan came forth and asked, "What is the poisoned drum?" Yantou put his hands on his knees, straightened up his body, and said, "What Han Xin went to court with."

Dahui, citing this, shouted and said, "Draw in your head."

TRANSLATOR'S NOTE

Han Xin rose from poverty to become a general and a leading figure in the establishment of the Han dynasty. He was ennobled but later demoted and eventually executed on suspicion of treason.

[531]

Master Shoushan Nian went up in the hall; Fenyang Zhao came forth and asked, "What is the meaning of Baizhang rolling up the mat?" Shoushan said, "Imperial sleeves brushed open, the totality is revealed." Zhao said, "What is your meaning?" Shoushan said, "Where a king of elephants goes, there are no fox tracks." Zhao was greatly enlightened at these words. He then held up his seat cloth, looked over the assembly, and said, "In the ancient aquamarine pond, the moon in the sky; you will only know after trying to fish it out two or three times." He bowed and returned to the group. At that time Shexian Sheng was the assembly leader. As soon as they had withdrawn, he asked Zhao, "What principle did you see just now, that you spoke thus?" He said, "This is precisely where I let go of my body and abandon my life." Sheng then stopped.

TRANSLATOR'S NOTE

"Baizhang rolling up the mat"—once when Mazu went up in the hall to lecture, and the community had gathered, after taking the chair Mazu remained silent for a long while. Baizhang then rolled up the prostration mat in front; Mazu then left the hall.

[532]

Master Shexian Sheng said to an assembly,

Chan worthies, patchrobed monks are wayfarers expert in adaptation. If you encounter troubles like boiling water or furnace coals, how do you escape? If you cannot escape, how can you be called wayfarers expert in adaptation? What is an expression of passing through to freedom from all sorts of troubles? Can anybody pass through to freedom? Try to tell the group; I will be your witness. If one cannot pass through to freedom, then even if myriad people constitute one family, no one can substitute for him.

[533]

Master Mingsong of Tang was asked by a monk, "What is the meaning of the ancient's 'the eastern mountains and western ridges are green'?" He said, "A Parsi's nose is big." The monk said, "So then in India there was Kasyapa, in China our teacher." He said, "The thunderbolt bearer's palm is broad."

He was asked, "Of the Great Compassionate One's thousand hands and eyes, which is the true eye?"

He said, "The stone Buddha openly teaching claps and laughs; the maiden of the shrine of Jin is able to sing."

He was asked, "When Linji pushed over Huangbo, why did the duty distributor get beaten?"

He said, "The guard dog didn't steal the oil; a chicken ran off with the lamp saucer."

[534]

Master Xuefeng, seeing some monkeys, said, "Each of these monkeys bears an ancient mirror." Sansheng said, "It has never been named over the ages; how can you characterize it as an ancient mirror?" Xuefeng said,

"A flaw has come about." Sansheng said, "Teacher of fifteen hundred people, and you don't even know a saying?" Xuefeng said, "My tasks as abbot are many."

[535]

Master Huanglong Xin said to an assembly,

Superior people studying the mystery should study the living word; don't study the dead word. Why? If you understand at the living word, you kill all the patchrobed monks in the land; if you understand at the dead word, you enliven all the patchrobed monks in the land. Tell me, how do you say the word that does not fall into dead or living? In the vast expanse of the great lake, the moon is in the heart of the waves—whom can you tell?

A monk asked, "What are the poisonous snakes of the four gross elements?"

He said, "Earth, water, fire, air."

The monk said, "What are earth, water, fire, and air?"

He said, "The poisonous snakes of the four gross elements."

The monk said, "I don't understand—I ask the teacher for an expedient."

He said, "Since a single gross element is thus, the four gross elements are the same."

[536]

Master Qinglin Jian said to an assembly,

In the school of the ancestral teachers, the bird's path is mysterious and subtle; when effort is exhausted, it all turns around. If you don't investigate thoroughly, it's impossible to understand. You simply must seek apart from mind, intellect, and consciousness, study beyond ordinary and holy. Only then can you keep it. Otherwise you are not my children.

. . .

Dahui said, "Even if you seek successfully apart from mind, intellect, and consciousness, and learn successfully beyond ordinary and holy, this is still what Xuefeng said."

[537]

Ministry Vice President Yang asked Guanghui Lian, "I hear you have a saying that all criminal activity comes about on account of wealth, urging people to be indifferent to wealth. But all people live by material goods, countries gather people by material goods, and in the teaching there are two kinds of giving, material and spiritual. How can you urge people to be indifferent to wealth?" Lian said, "On top of a flagpole, an iron dragon head." The vice president said, "A horse of Haidan is the size of a mule." Lian said, "A chicken of Chu is not a phoenix of Cinnabar Mountain." The vice president said, "Two thousand years after the death of the Buddha, few monks have any shame."

[538]

Master Wei of Jian province was asked by a monk, "The essential principle of the canonical teachings is subtle; is it the same as the meaning of Chan, or different?" He said, "You must reflect on it outside the six propositions; don't roll along with the sound and form." The monk said, "What are the six propositions?" He said, "The spoken, the silent, the unspoken, the not silent, all, and none. What should you do?" The monk was nonplussed.

[539]

Master Guishan said to Yangshan, "You should turn attention around and reverse awareness by yourself—other people don't know your understanding. Try to present real understanding to me." Yangshan said, "If you have me see for myself, at this point there is no state of completion, and not a single thing or a single understanding that can be presented to you." Guishan said, "Where there is no state of completion is originally the understanding you formulate—it is still not other than a mental object." Yangshan said, "Since there is no state of completion, where is there a phenomenon? What thing is taken for an object?" Guishan said, "Did you or did you not formulate such an understanding just now?" Yangshan said, "Yes, I did." Guishan said, "If so, this includes mind and object; it is not yet free of the notion of possession. All along you've had an understanding to present to me. I acknowledge that your state of faith is evident, but the stage of person is still concealed."

[540]

Deshan Yuanming said to an assembly,

Whenever Master Judi was asked a question, he just raised a finger. When it's cold, it's cold through sky and earth. Xuedou said, "Where do you see Judi?" When it's hot, it's hot throughout sky and earth. Xuedou said, "Don't make the mistake of acknowledging the zero point of the scale." He also said, "Myriad forms are solitary all the way down; earth, mountains, and rivers are sheer all the way up. Where do you get one-finger Chan?"

Dahui said, "It can be said that this is a case of a noble man forgetting a lot."

[541]

The World Honored One was there when Manjushri came to a gathering place of all Buddhas. When the Buddhas had each returned to their own places, there was just one woman sitting near the Buddha, immersed in absorption. Manjushri then said to the Buddha, "How can this woman sit near the Buddha when I cannot?" Buddha said to Manjushri, "Just rouse this woman from absorption and ask her yourself." Manjushri circled the woman three times, snapped his fingers, then lifted her up to the Brahma heaven; using all his spiritual powers, he could not get her out of absorption. The World Honored One said, "Even a hundred thousand Manjushris could not get this woman out of concentration. Below here, past as many Buddha-lands as grains of sand in forty-two Ganges Rivers, there is a bodhisattva, Netted Light, who can get this woman out of absorption." In a moment the great hero Netted Light sprang up from the ground and bowed to the World Honored One. The World Honored One told Netted Light to get her out. Netted Light went up to the woman and snapped his fingers once; at this the woman emerged from absorption.

Yunju You versified,

> A hundred thousand Manjushris couldn't get her out;
> Netted Light didn't expend the slightest force.
> Descending mist and a lone duck fly together;
> The autumn water and eternal sky are the same color.

Tianyi Huai versified,

> Manjushri lifted her up to Brahma heaven,
> Netted Light lightly snapped his fingers.
> The woman and yellow-faced Gautama—
> Watch them; one falls, one gets up.

[542]

Master Nantai An was asked by a monk, "How is it when still and silent, with no dependence?" He said, "Still and silent!"

Based on this he composed a verse, saying,

> Nantai sits quietly, incense in one burner;
> Still all day long, myriad thoughts are forgotten.
> This is not stopping the mind, removing errant thought;
> It's all because there is nothing to think about.

Dahui shouted one shout.

[543]

When Master Linji came to Sanfeng, Master Ping asked, "Where have you just come from?" He said, "Last night a golden ox encountered water and fire; no trace has been seen ever since." Ping said, "When the autumn wind blows on jade pipes, who recognizes the tune?" He said, "Passing directly through myriad-fold barriers, he does not dwell beyond the blue sky." Ping said, "This question is too lofty." He said, "A dragon gave birth to a golden phoenix, bursting through blue crystal." Ping said, "Sit for a while and have tea." Linji then sat down. Ping again asked, "Where have you just come from?" He said, "Longguang." Ping said, "What is Longguang saying these days?" Linji thereupon left and went to the hall.

[544]

Master Letan Jun said to an assembly,

"Sameness, difference, becoming, disintegration, totality, distinction"—three, four, five, six, seven, eight. If you want to follow the flow into the flow, nothing surpasses understanding this teaching. [Picking up his staff and planting it once.] This teaching cannot be understood by thought and discrimination. If you discriminate, you fall into the realm of sentient beings. But tell me, not thinking, not discriminating, what is this? [Throwing down the staff.] The immovable honored one of subtle and profound mastery; the king of *Heroic Progress*, rare in the world.

He also said to an assembly

It's been raining for a long time without clearing, so that black clouds hang over Five Elders Peak; the white-capped waves on Dongting Lake flood the sky. Great Master Yunmen couldn't help burning incense in the Buddha shrine, joining his palms before the triple gate and praying, wishing that the barren woman of Huangmei would give birth to a child, that child and mother bond completely, that the hornless iron ox of Few Houses always finds the water and herbage sweet. [Shouting:] What connection is there?

Huangmei is a reference to the Fifth Patriarch of Chan. The barren woman represents detachment from the world; giving birth to a child represents return to the world after mystic death. Few Houses is a reference to Bodhidharma, the founder of Chan. The iron ox symbolizes stability, while having no horns here means the immediate reference is to stability alone; hence, finding the water and herbage sweet refers to wisdom as a complement to concentration. Both examples thus symbolize the desired combination of detachment and engagement.

[545]

Master Yuntai Jin said to an assembly,

Can you see as in a mirror? If you can, what worn-out sandal in a village is this? If not, it falls to the ground making a metallic sound.

A monk asked, "What is speaking of the real versus the conventional?"

He said, "You hired laborer, what are you asking?"

The monk asked, "What is following the conventional contrary to the real?"

He said, "Go have tea."

[546]

Master Longtan asked Tianhuang, "Since coming here I've never had you point out the key of mind." Tianhuang said, "Ever since you came I have never not been pointing out the key of mind to you." Longtan said, "Where is it pointed out?" Tianhuang said, "When you bring tea, I take it for you; when you serve food, I receive it for you. When you greet me, I nod my head. Where am I not pointing out the key of mind to you?" As Longtan stood there thinking, Tianhuang said, "When you see, see directly; if you try to think, you'll miss." Longtan was thereupon first enlightened. He then went on to ask how to preserve it. Tianhuang said,

"Go about naturally; be free in all circumstances. Just end the profane mind—there is no holy understanding besides."

[547]

Master Xuefeng was asked by a monk, "How is it when the ancient valley stream's spring is cold?" He said, "Looking straight in, you don't see the bottom." The monk said, "How about one who drinks of it?" He said, "It doesn't enter through the mouth." Zhaozhou heard a monk relating this and said, "It doesn't go in through the mouth; it goes in through the nostrils." The monk asked back, "How is it when the ancient valley stream's spring is cold?" Zhaozhou said, "Painful." The monk said, "How about one who drinks?" Zhaozhou said, "He dies." When Xuefeng heard of this, he said, "Zhaozhou is an ancient Buddha," and he bowed to him from afar and said, "From now on I won't give answers."

[548]

Master Baoen Ze was asked by Fayan, "Whom have you met?" He said, "I've met Master Qingfeng." Fayan said, "What did he have to say?" Ze said, "I once asked what my self is. Qingfeng said, 'The fire god comes looking for fire.'" Fayan said, "How did you understand that?" Ze said, "The fire god is in the province of fire; using fire to seek fire is like seeking the self by the self." Fayan said, "How can you get it by understanding this way?" Ze said, "I am just thus; what do you mean?" Fayan said, "The fire god comes looking for fire." Ze was greatly enlightened at these words.

[549]

Xuansha and Tianlong went into the mountains, where they saw a tiger. Tianlong said, "Master—a tiger!" Xuansha said, "It's your tiger." When they returned to the monastery, Tianlong asked for further instruction: "Master, today when we saw the tiger, what did you mean?" Xuansha said,

"In this world there are four extremely serious things. If someone can pass through, he can undeniably get out of the clusters and elements."

Dahui said on Tianlong's behalf, "I knew you were keen on helping people."

TRANSLATOR'S NOTE

It is not made clear exactly what is meant by the expression "four extremely serious things," but the closest equivalent in standard Buddhist technical terms would be four serious forms of misbehavior prohibited by Buddhist precepts: sexual misconduct, theft, murder, and false claims of sanctity. The clusters and elements refer to mundane existence, as here particularly in the sense of bondage.

[550]

Baoming Yong said in verse,

> A fierce tiger on the road is awesome alone;
> Its claws and fangs are truly sharp as awls.
> Pitiful the one who perishes through carelessness;
> When the shattered bones are gathered up they are indeed
>   pathetic.

[551]

Layman Pang said in verse,

> Mind is thus, objects are thus;
> There is nothing substantial and nothing empty.
> Unconcerned with existence and untrammeled by nonexistence,
> This is not a saint or a sage,
> But an ordinary man done with concerns.
> Easy, again easy, these five clusters have true wisdom;

The worlds of the ten directions are one vehicle,
The same formless body of reality—how could there be two?
If you abandon affliction to enter enlightenment,
Where is the Buddha-land?

[552]

Master Huanglong Nan ascended the seat on the occasion of a missionary's return and said,

There are five kinds of those who are not easy to find. One is a donor; second is a missionary; third is one who transforms the raw into the cooked; fourth is one who sits upright and eats. Now tell me, who is the fifth one who is not easy to find? [After a pause, he said,] A dead ghost. [Then he got down from the seat.]

At the time Cuiyan Zhen was the chief monk; the librarian asked him, "Who is the fifth one not easy to find?" Zhen said, "If you see jowls from behind his head, don't go along."

[553]

Master Shikong used to be a hunter. He passed by Mazu's hut while pursuing deer, and asked Mazu, "Did you see a deer go by?" Mazu said, "Who are you?" He said, "I'm a hunter." Mazu said, "How many can you shoot with one arrow?" He said, "One arrow shoots one." Mazu said, "You don't shoot well." He said, "Do you know how to shoot?" Mazu said, "I can shoot." He said, "How many can you shoot with one arrow?" Mazu said, "One arrow shoots a whole herd." He said, "They are all lives—why shoot the whole herd?" Mazu said, "If you know this much, why don't you shoot yourself?" He said, "If you have me shoot myself, I simply have nowhere to start." Mazu said, "This guy's eons of afflictions of ignorance have suddenly stopped today." Right then and there Shikong threw down his bow and arrows and became Mazu's disciple.

[554]

Master Xuansha went up in the hall; the community gathered. He then took his staff and drove them out at once. Now he turned to an attendant and said, "Today I've created an instance of danger; I'm going to hell like an arrow shot." The attendant said, "I hope you'll return to a human body."

Cuiyan Zhi said, "Even the great Xuansha didn't get to the village before and didn't reach the shop after."

Daowu Zhen said, "Even the great Zhi is biased. I do not concur. Xuansha and the attendant each have one eye."

[555]

Master Luoshan once asked Shishuang, "How is it when arising and passing away don't stop?" Shishuang said, "You simply must be like cold ashes, a dead tree, ten thousand years in one thought, box and lid matching, completely clear, without a spot." Luoshan didn't get it; he then went to Yantou and asked the same question. Yantou shouted and said, "Whose arising and passing away is it?" At this Luoshan had an insight.

[556]

Master Mingzong of Tang asked Shoushan, "What exactly is the main meaning of Buddhism?" Shoushan said, "By the city wall of the king of Chu, the Ru River runs eastward." Mingzong had an insight at this, and suddenly understood what the Buddha meant. Then he composed three mystic verses:

> If you get the function, just use it;
> Don't stir your mind.

When a three-year-old lion roars,
There are no foxes anywhere.

I have the nature of reality as such;
It's as if hidden inside curtains.
Breaking open the barriers of the senses,
It reveals the symbol of Vairocana.

The adamantine body with bones of reality is worthy of pride;
Once sense objects are swept away, there is never any obstruction.
In the world of openness, emptiness is the body;
With no contrivance in the body, one truly arrives home.

When Shoushan heard them, he invited him to tea and asked, "Did you compose these verses?" He said, "Yes." Shoushan said, "What if someone asks you to show the thirty-two marks of a Buddha?" He said, "I'm not a wild fox spirit." Shoushan said, "Be careful of your eyebrows." He said, "How much of yours have been lost?" Shoushan rapped him on the head with a bamboo ruler. He said, "Hereafter this fellow will go on acting at random."

[557]

Yunmen once said, "When the light doesn't penetrate freely, there are two kinds of sickness. When everywhere is not clear, and there is something present, this is one. Also, having penetrated to the emptiness of all things, subtly it seems like there is some thing. This too is the light not passing through freely. Also, the reality body has two kinds of sickness. Having reached the reality body, because clinging to phenomena is not forgotten, the notion of self is still there, sitting in the reality body. This is one. Even if you penetrate the reality body, you cannot let go; examining closely, what breath is there? This too is sickness."

. . .

Dahui said, "Don't interpret as Chan, don't interpret as the Way, don't interpret as transcendent discussion. Old Yunmen is speaking based on reality. In my saying so, there is immeasurable fault. If you can find it out, I'll admit you have the eye to pick out truth. If you cannot find it out, seek in Yunmen's complications."

[558]

Master Deshan was asked by the attendant Huo, "Where have the sages of all times gone?" Deshan said, "What? What?" Huo said, "The command specified the Flying Dragon horse, but a lame tortoise shows up." Deshan then stopped. The next day, when he came out of the hall, the attendant Huo handed Deshan some tea. Deshan patted Huo on the back and said, "What about yesterday's case?" Huo said, "This old fellow has only just gotten a glimpse today." Deshan again stopped.

[559]

Master Yantang Ji was asked by a monk, "At night the moon unfurls its light—why is there no reflection in the aquamarine pond?" He said, "You're an expert at toying with a reflection." The monk crossed from east to west and stood there. Ji said, "Not only do you toy with a reflection, you also fear for your head."

[560]

Master Daning Guan was asked by a monk, "What is the white ox on open ground?" Guan set the fire tongs across the top of the brazier, and said, "Understand?" The monk said, "I don't understand." Guan said, "The head is not lacking; the tail is not too much." He was asked, "When Danxia burned the wooden Buddha, why did the abbot's eyebrows and whiskers fall out?" He said, "A thief does not hit the house of a pauper."

. . .

When a monk passed away while the master was at Tongan [meaning "common security"], another monk asked, "Since this is 'common security,' why does a sick monk pass away?" He said, "Donation is not as good as returning a loan." He was asked, "If the teaching negates grasping and rejecting, why is it transmitted in succession?" He said, "Transmission has no grasping or rejection." He was asked, "Kasyapa saw correctly—why did he then smile when the flower was held up?" He said, "He couldn't restrain himself." He was asked, "Why can't the Chan students everywhere get out of the empty circle?" He said, "From time to time it's like this."

TRANSLATOR'S NOTE

"The white ox on open ground" refers to the Ekayana, or One Vehicle of Buddhist teaching, the aim of which is described as the opening up of the knowledge and vision of Buddhas.

[561]

Master Zifu Yuan asked Jingqing, "What is the place where Buddhas emerge?" Jingqing said, "Everyone should know." Yuan said, "Then the eyes of the masses are hard to fool." Jingqing said, "Reason can overcome a leopard."

[562]

Master Jinniu, when Linji came, sat in front of the abbot's room with his staff sideways. Linji clapped three times and went back to the hall. Jinniu then went down, and after exchanging greetings asked, "When guest and host meet, there are standard manners for each; how can you be so discourteous?" Linji said, "What are you saying?" As Jinniu was about to open his mouth, Linji hit him once with his seat cloth. Jinniu made a gesture of falling down. Linji hit him once more with his seat cloth. Jinniu said, "Today I didn't get the advantage."

. . .

Guishan asked Yangshan, "Of these two venerable adepts, was there a winner and a loser?" Yangshan said, "As far as winning goes, both won; as far as losing goes, both lost."

[563]

When an attendant announced the king's coming to Master Zhaozhou, Zhaozhou said, "Felicitations, great king!" The attendant said, "He hasn't arrived yet." Zhaozhou said, "But you said he came."

[564]

When the lecturer Liangsui first called on Magu, when Magu saw him coming he took a hoe into the garden and hoed the weeds. Liangsui followed him to where he was weeding; Magu paid no attention to him, but went right back to his room and shut the door. Liangsui went again the next day, and Magu shut the door again. Liangsui knocked, and Magu asked, "Who is it?" Liangsui said, "Liangsui." As soon as he'd called out his name, he suddenly attained enlightenment. He then said, "Master, don't treat me like a fool. If I hadn't come to pay respects to you, I'd likely have spent my whole life being cheated by scriptures and treatises." When he returned to the place where he'd lectured, he told the group, "I know everything you know, but you don't know what I know."

[565]

Master Luoshan of Zhang province asked Master Chang of Guannan, "What is the source of the Great Way?" Chang gave him a punch, and he had an insight. Then he composed a verse, saying,

> I began studying the Way in 866;
> Wherever I went I encountered words but didn't know what
> they were saying.
> The mass of doubt in my heart was like a basket;

For three years I stayed by the forest springs unhappy.
Suddenly I met a Dharma king sitting on felt;
Then I set forth my doubts sincerely to the teacher.
The teacher rose from the felt like a dragon;
The patriarch punched me in the chest,
Dispelling my mass of ignorance with a shock.
The giant wolf was felled;
When I raised my head and looked,
I saw the sun was finally round at last.
Since then I've climbed, steeply, right up till now,
Always happy and lively, just feeling my belly full,
No longer going east and west carrying a begging bowl.

Dahui said, "Too bad this punch can't be passed on to others."

[566]

When Master Ciming saw Quan Dadao coming, he said, "A fleck of cloud lies across the mouth of the valley; where does the traveler come from?" Quan looked left and right and said, "Since last night what place did fire burn the graves of people of old?" The master said, "Not yet—say more." Quan roared like a tiger. The master hit him once with a seat cloth. Quan pushed the master onto his seat. The master then roared like a tiger. Quan said, "I've met over seventy teachers, and you're the only one who amounts to anything."

[567]

Yunmen said, "There are three kinds of people. One attains enlightenment through speech. One attains enlightenment by being called. The third goes back as soon as it's brought up. You tell me, what is the meaning of immediately going back?" He also said, "Better give thirty strokes of the cane."

[568]

Chan master Che was a man from Jiangxi; his surname was Zhang, his given name was Xingchang. When he was young he was a soldier of fortune. After the Southern and Northern schools of Chan divided, though the leaders of the two schools had no mutual opposition, their followers competed, producing partiality and antagonism. The members of the Northern School set up Shenxiu as the Sixth Patriarch and resented the fact that Great Master Huineng had inherited the mantle and was famous throughout the land. The patriarch Huineng, knowing beforehand what would happen, placed ten ounces of gold in his room; at that time Xingchang, commissioned by members of the Northern School, went into the patriarch's room armed with a sword. As he went on the attack, the patriarch stretched out his neck to him. Xingchang swung the sword three times, but no harm was done. The patriarch said, "A righteous sword does not do wrong; a wrongful sword does not do right. I only cede you gold; I don't cede you my life." Xingchang collapsed in shock; after a long while he revived and begged for mercy, repenting of his misdeed and vowing to become a mendicant. The patriarch gave him the gold and said, "Go away for now, lest the community of followers do you harm in revenge. Someday you may come in a different guise; I will accept you."

Xingchang did as he was told, fleeing by night and entering into the order of monks. He received the precepts and practiced diligently. One day he recalled what the patriarch had said and came from afar to respectfully visit him. The patriarch said, "I've been thinking about you for a long time; why have you been so late in coming?" He said, "Previously you forgave me; now, though I've become a monk and have been practicing intensely, I can hardly repay your kindness. It seems that would only be transmission of the teaching to liberate people. I've read the *Nirvana Scripture* but still don't understand the meanings of permanence and impermanence; I beg your kindness and compassion to expound them summarily for me." The patriarch said, "The impermanent is Buddha-nature; the permanent is the mind that discriminates all things good and bad." He said, "What you say is very different from the doctrines of the scripture." The patriarch said, "I transmit the seal of the Buddha-mind; how dare I deviate from Buddhist scripture?" He said, "The scripture says Buddha-nature is permanent, while you say it is impermanent. All things good and bad, including the will for enlightenment, are impermanent, yet you say they are permanent. This contradiction confuses me all the more." The patriarch said, "I heard the nun Wujinzang recite the *Nirvana Scripture* a long time ago, and I explained it to her without a single word or single meaning failing to accord with the scripture. Now what I am telling you is no different." He said, "My intellectual capacity is shallow and benighted; please explain in detail."

The patriarch said, "Whether you know it or not, if the Buddha-nature were permanent, what good or bad would still be spoken of? No one would ever awaken the will for enlightenment. Therefore the impermanence I speak of is precisely the way to true permanence expounded by the Buddha. Also, if all phenomena were impermanent, then every thing would have its own nature subject to birth and death, and real permanent nature would not be universal. Therefore the permanence I speak of is precisely the meaning of true impermanence spoken of by the Buddha. Buddha compared the grasping of false permanence by ordinary people and outsiders with the notion of people of two vehicles that the permanent is impermanent to collectively constitute eight inversions. Therefore in the complete teaching of the *Nirvana Scripture* he refuted those biased views and revealed real permanence, real bliss, real self, and real purity. Now you are going by the words but against the meaning, misinterpreting the Buddha's complete sublime final subtle words in terms of nihilistic impermanence and fixed stagnant permanence. Even if you read them a thousand times, what is the use?"

Xingchang was all at once like someone awakening from a stupor; he then spoke a verse, saying,

> Because of keeping to the idea of impermanence,
> Buddha expounded a permanent nature.
> Those who don't recognize expedient means

Are as if picking up pebbles from a springtime pond.
Now Buddha-nature has appeared to me without expending
effort;
It is not given to me by a teacher, and I have not acquired
anything.

The patriarch said, "You have now penetrated; you should be named Zhiche, 'penetration by will.'" Zhiche then bowed in thanks and left.

TRANSLATOR'S NOTE

"Eight inversions"—thinking the impermanent to be permanent, thinking what is not pleasant to be pleasant, thinking what is not self to be self, thinking what is not pure to be pure, thinking what is permanent to be impermanent, thinking what is pleasant to be unpleasant, thinking self to be selfless, thinking what is pure to be impure.

[569]

Master Guizong Hui was asked by a monk, "How is it when cutting off the water to stop the wheel?" He said, "The millstone doesn't turn."

Dahui said, "When a boon is great, it's hard to requite."

[570]

When Dongshan invited head monk Tai to have some fruit, he asked, "There is something that supports the heavens above and supports the earth below; black as lacquer, it is always in the midst of activity, yet activity cannot contain it. You tell me, where is the fault?" Tai said, "The fault is in activity." Dongshan called an attendant to take away the fruit table.

Dagui Zhe said, "Do you know what Dongshan was getting at? If you don't know, time and again you'll understand in terms of right and wrong, gain and loss. Benevolent ones, it is not only head monk Tai who couldn't eat this fruit; even if everyone in the world came, they still couldn't look right at it."

[571]

Master Daliao asked Mazu, "What is the precise meaning of the coming from the West?" Mazu knocked him down with a foot to the chest; he was greatly enlightened. Getting up, he clapped and laughed out loud, saying, "Marvelous, marvelous! The source of a hundred thousand absorptions and countless subtle meanings is perceived all at once on a single hair tip!" Then he bowed and withdrew. Later the master said to a group, "Ever since getting kicked by Master Ma, I haven't stopped laughing even now."

Master Jiangshan Quan said, "Suddenly glimpsing is even more laughable."

[572]

When a monk entered his room, Master Yunfeng Yue cited, "A monk asked Zhaozhou, 'Myriad things return to one; where does the one return?'" Yue then shouted. The monk was at a loss. Yue asked, "What did Zhaozhou say?" The monk hesitated; Yue hit him at once with his whisk.

[573]

Xuefeng said, "I have met with you at Wangzhou Station; I have met with you on Black Rock Ridge; I have met with you in front of the communal hall." Baofu asked Ehu, "Leaving aside 'in front of the communal hall' for the moment, where were the meetings at Wangzhou Station and Black Rock Ridge?" Ehu rushed back to his room; Baofu then went into the communal hall.

[574]

Xuefeng asked a monk, "Where are you going?" The monk said, "If you were perceptive, you'd know where I'm going." Xuefeng said, "You are an accomplished man—why are you running wild?" The monk said, "Better not sully people." Xuefeng said, "I'm not sullying you. How would you explain to me the ancient's blowing on a blanket?" The monk said, "There have already been people who ate leftover soup and rancid rice." Xuefeng stopped. Yunmen gave a different answer for the foregoing saying: "If you bump into it, it stinks like shit." He also gave a substitute for the latter saying: "I thought you were a hawk piercing the skies; after all you're just a frog in stagnant water."

Xuedou produced a saying for Xuefeng: "Once dead, you do not revive."

TRANSLATOR'S NOTE

"Blowing on a blanket"—for this story, see chapter 627 below.

[575]

Master Zhenjing's six verses on three contemplations of the reality realm:

> Matter and emptiness interpenetrate
> At will, freely;
> The dense web of myriad forms
> Appear as reflections, inside and out.
> Emerging and disappearing, going and coming,
> This land and other realms.
> The mind seal is open,
> All pervasive, immensely vast.

> Noumenon and phenomena interpenetrate,
> At will, freely,

Grabbing the polar mountain upside down,
Setting it up in a mustard seed.
The pure body of reality—
A complete clod of earth.
A mirror and lamp at one point—
The oceanic congregation of ten directions.

Phenomena interpenetrate
At will, freely.
The immutable site of enlightenment—
The worlds of the ten directions.
Welling up in the east, sinking in the west;
A thousand differences, myriad oddities.
An insect in a fire
Swallows a crab.

Phenomena interpenetrate
At will, freely;
The hand holds a pig's head,
The mouth recites precepts of purity.
Chased out of a brothel,
Yet to pay the bill for wine,
At a crossroads
One opens a cloth bag.

Phenomena interpenetrate
At will, freely;
Picking up a single hair,
The multiply inter-reflecting realm of reality.
One thought enters everywhere
The infinite ocean of lands;
It is just the immediate present,
Some evident, some obscure.

Phenomena do not know each other;
Who understands emptiness and matter?
Once noumenon and phenomena stop,
An iron boat enters the ocean.
Sparks and lightning flashes—
Tsk!—they're not swift.
The sharpest sword held sideways,
The army of demons loses heart.

[576]

Dongshan was asked by a monk, "Which of the three bodies expounds the teaching?" Dongshan said, "I am always keen on this." The monk later asked Caoshan, "What is the meaning of Dongshan's saying 'I am always keen on this'?" Caoshan said, "If you want my head, go ahead and chop it off and take it away." The monk also asked Xuefeng. Xuefeng immediately hit him with a staff and said, "I've been to Dongshan too." Chengtian Zong said, "With one saying, the sea is calm and the rivers are clear; with one saying, the wind is high and the moon is cold; one saying rides a brigand's horse chasing the brigand. Try to distinguish them. If a patchrobed monk should come forth and say it's all not so, I'll grant that he has one eye."

Dahui said, "With such complications, he hasn't even dreamed of seeing the three old fellows." He also said, "Don't stick an acupuncture needle in the opening of incurable illness."

[577]

Master Yunju You said to an assembly,

The Realized Ones of the past are not tested anymore; the bodhisattvas of the present cannot be let go; the practitioners of the future cannot be treated as fools. Therefore it says in the teachings that if people want to know the Buddhas of all times, they should view the nature of the universe as all mentally constructed. Even so, in my school this is precisely what is meant by gold dust getting in the eyes.

A monk asked, "How is it when a turtle withdraws into its shell?"

He said, "A pattern is already showing."

The monk said, "What about the fact that there are no tracks anywhere?"

He said, "Go ahead and trail mud and water."

The monk said, "How is it when going on thus?"

He said, "So it turns out."

[578]

Master Baiyun Duan said to an assembly,

If you truly manage to break out in a sweat once, you manifest a coral tower and jade palace on a single blade of grass. If you haven't truly broken out in a sweat, even if you have a jade palace and coral tower they're covered by a single blade of grass. Now tell me, how can you break out in a sweat? [Silence.] Ever since having a pair of hands with the characteristics of poverty, I've never easily danced to a party tune.

[579]

Xuansha said, "To discuss this matter, it is like a piece of land which has all been sold by contract to you, except for a tree in the center that still belongs to me."

[580]

Master Dongshan Jie asked a monk his name; the monk said so-and-so. Dongshan said, "Who is your master?" The monk said, "The one presently replying." Dongshan said, "Ouch, ouch! People these days are all like this—they just recognize what's in front of an ass but behind a horse as the self. This is the cause of the disappearance of Buddhism. If you don't even understand the host within the guest, how can you discern the host within the host?" The monk then asked, "What is the host within the host?" Dongshan said, "Say it yourself." The monk said, "Whatever I say is the guest within the host—what is the host within the host?" Dongshan said, "It is easy to speak this way, but continuity is very difficult." Subsequently he composed a verse, saying,

> Followers of the Way these days,
> Thousands and tens of thousands, recognize the threshold,
> As if they've gone to the capital to go to the court of the emperor
> Then stop when they've only gotten as far as an outlying pass.

[581]

Master Jingqing asked Caoshan, "How is it when the pure empty noumenon is ultimately bodiless?" Caoshan said, "Given that the noumenon is like this, what about phenomena?" Jingqing said, "As is noumenon, so are phenomena." Caoshan said, "You may treat me, one man, like a fool, but what about the eyes of the sages?" Jingqing said, "If there are no eyes of the sages, how can they see the reflection of what isn't so?" Caoshan said, "Officially not even a needle is admitted; privately, a horse and carriage can pass."

Dagui Zhe said, "Although Caoshan can polish skillfully, nevertheless Jingqing's jade is originally flawless. Do you want to understand? If it isn't put into clever hands, it turns out to be a useless tool."

[582]

Master Rang said one day, "Daoyi is in Jiangxi expounding the teaching for people; I haven't had any news." So he sent a monk there, telling him to wait till Daoyi went up in the hall, then ask him, "What are you doing?" and report what he said. The monk went and questioned him as instructed. Mazu [Daoyi] said, "Ever since the confusion, for thirty years I haven't lacked salt and vinegar."

[583]

Master Deshan of Lang province was asked by a monk, "'When you meet a master of the Way on the road, you do not respond with speech or silence'—what does one respond with?" He answered, "Just this." The monk remained silent. The master said, "Ask again." The monk asked again. The master shouted him out.

Dahui said, "Undoubtedly a good shout, but he did it too late."

[584]

Master Fengxue said to an assembly,

The eye of participatory study requires great function to appear; don't restrict yourself to small measures. Even if you understand before verbalization, this is still lingering in a shell, lost in limitation. Even if you comprehend precisely at a statement, you do not escape crazy views on the road. Your learned understanding hitherto must be dichotomized into light and dark; now I will sweep it away for you all at once. You must each be like a lion roaring, standing like a mile-high wall. Who would dare look straight at you? If anyone looked, it would blind them.

A monk asked, "'Speech and silence get into detachment and subtlety'— how can one get through without transgressing?"

He said, "I always remember spring in the south, the hundred flowers fragrant where the partridges sing."

"What is Buddha?"

"A bamboo-strand whip at the foot of the mountain in the forest grown from a staff."

. . .

Zhenjing's verse said,

> "A bamboo whip at the foot of the mountain in the forest
>   grown from a staff"—
> Water is in the deep valley stream; the moon is in the sky.
> I don't know where the good horse has gone;
> Ananda, as ever, stands before the World Honored One.

[585]

Guishan asked Yangshan, "Speak quickly, without entering into the body-mind clusters and elements of sense." Yangshan said, "I don't even establish faith." Guishan said, "Do you not establish it after having had faith, or without having had faith?" Yangshan said, "It's just I—who else would I have faith in?" Guishan said, "If so, you are a listener of fixed nature." Yangshan said, "I don't even see Buddha."

[586]

Master Dadian said to an assembly,

People who study the Way need to know their own basic mind. You can only see the Way when it is shown by mind. I often see people of the time who just acknowledge raising the eyebrows and blinking, sometimes speaking, sometimes silent, and right away give approval as the essence of mind. This is really not comprehending. I will now explain for you clearly; each of you should listen. Just get rid of all random operation of conceptual assessment, and then this is your true mind. This mind has nothing at all to do with sense objects or keeping notice of when it is still and silent. Mind itself is Buddha; it doesn't depend on cultivation. Why? Responding to situations according to perception, it functions on its own clearly and coolly; when you search out the seat of its function, it cannot be found. This is called subtle function; this is the basic mind. You really need to preserve it; don't take it lightly.

[587]

Langya Jiao said to an assembly,

My late teacher Fenyang said, "At the school of Fenyang there is a lion of West River sitting at the gate: any who come, it bites and kills. What expedient will you use to enter the gate of Fenyang and get to see the man of Fenyang?" Here at Langya I have a little: Langya has a lion; any who come lose their lives themselves. What expedient will you use to enter the gate of Langya and see the man of Langya? Can you check out these two sayings? If you can, that is called the eye that discerns truth; if not, you have no place to settle yourself and establish your life.

[588]

Xuansha asked Jingqing, "'Not seeing a single thing is considered a big problem'—tell me, not seeing what?" Jingqing pointed to a pillar and said, "Isn't it not seeing this thing?" Xuansha said, "You may partake of the clear water and white rice of Chekiang, but you still don't understand Buddhism."

Dagui Zhe said, "Had it not been Jingqing, he might have forgotten before and missed after. Why? If he didn't meet someone different he'd never open his fist."

[589]

Master Heishui called on Master Huanglong Ji and asked, "How is it when snow covers white flowers?" Huanglong said, "Blazing." Heishui said, "Not blazing." Huanglong again said, "Blazing." Heishui again said, "Not blazing." Huanglong then hit him; Heishui got an insight from this.

[590]

Master Dayang Mingan asked Liangshan, "What is the formless site of enlightenment?" Liangshan pointed to a picture of Guanyin and said, "This was painted by Wu Daozi." As Mingan was about to speak further, Liangshan hurriedly demanded, "This is the one with form; what is the formless one?" Mingan attained enlightenment at these words. He bowed, then stood there. Linagshan said, "Why don't you say something?" Mingan said, "I don't decline to speak, but I'm afraid it will get into paper and ink." Liangshan laughed loudly and said, "These words will wind up on a memorial stone yet."

[591]

When Master Zhaozhou was traveling around, he came to the place of an old adept. The adept asked him, "Where did you just come from?" He said, "Gu province." The adept said, "How many stages did your trip here take?" He said, "I stumbled here in one stumble." The adept said, "Quite a speedy spirit!" Zhaozhou said, "Felicitations, Great King!" The adept said, "Go to the hall." Zhaozhou said, "Yes, yes." A Confucian scholar saw Zhaozhou and said in praise, "You're an ancient Buddha." Zhaozhou said, "You're a new Realized One."

[592]

Master Bima Yan always carried a forked stick; whenever he saw a monk come, he'd hold up the forked stick and say, "What demon made you leave home? What demon made you go traveling? Even if you can say, you'll die at the forked stick; if you can't say, you'll still die at the forked stick. Speak quickly, speak quickly!" Later Master Huoshan heard of this and went to visit him. As soon as he saw him, before he'd bowed he tossed it inside his vest; then Bima patted Huoshan on the back three times. Huoshan clapped his hands and said, "Elder brother, you've cheated me from three thousand miles away! You've cheated me from three thousand miles away!"

[593]

Master Baoen Ming asked two Chan travelers, "Where have you elders just come from?" They said, "From the capital city." He said, "When you left the capital city and came to this mountain, the capital city was missing you, while this mountain had you added. That means there is something outside mind, and the reality of mind is not pervasive. If you can explain the principle, you can stay, but if you don't understand, then go." The two men had no reply.

Dahui said in their place, "You can't fool us, and we can't fool you either." *He also said,* "Now isn't there anyone who can articulate an expression of mutual deception? If you can, I'll grant that you can leap out of an unbreakable cage and can swallow a chestnut thorn ball."

[594]

Master Ciming asked the head monk Xianying, "Where have you just come from?" He said, "Jinluan." Ciming asked, "Where were you during the previous summer?" He said, "Jinluan." Ciming asked, "Where were you the summer before that?" The head monk said, "Master, why don't you get what's being said?" He said, "I can't test you. Have the supply servant come test, and I'll make a cup of tea for you to wet your whistle."

[595]

Master Laian said to an assembly,
    What are you people all coming to me looking for? If you want to become Buddhas, you are inherently Buddhas, yet you run elsewhere in haste, like thirsty deer chasing a mirage. When will you ever succeed?

Oh, if you want to be Buddhas, just don't have an impure mundane mentality with so much perverted clinging to objects, false thought, wrong consciousness, and defiling desire; then you are truly enlightened Buddhas as beginners. Where else would you seek? That is why in the thirty years since I've been on Mount Gui, I've eaten the food of Mount Gui and shat the shit of Mount Gui, but I haven't studied the Chan of Mount Gui. I've just watched over a water buffalo: if it went off the path into the weeds, then I pulled it out; if it invaded people's plantings, then I disciplined it with a whip. Eventually it came to accept human speech nicely. Now it has turned into a white ox on open ground, always present, standing out all day long, not going away even if chased. You people each have an invaluable jewel of your own, radiating light from your eyes shining on mountains, rivers, and land, radiating light from your ears taking in all beautiful and ugly sounds. Always radiating light day and night from your six senses—it is also called radiant concentration. You yourselves don't recognize it, but its reflection is in your physical body, supporting it inside and out, not letting it fall over. It is like someone carrying a heavy load over a single-log bridge; it still doesn't let you lose your footing. Now tell me, what is it that provides such support enabling you this way? If you seek in the slightest you won't see. Therefore Mr. Zhi said, "Pursuing a search inside and out, it is not there at all; applied in action objectively, it's all very much there."

[596]

Zhaozhou asked a monk, "Have you ever been here?" He said, "Yes." Zhaozhou said, "Go have some tea." Another said, "No," and Zhaozhou also said, "Go have some tea." The temple superintendent asked the master why he told them to have tea whether or not they'd been there. Zhaozhou said, "Superintendent!" The superintendent responded. Zhaozhou said, "Go have some tea."

Baofu said, "Zhaozhou is used to getting the advantage."

[597]

Duan, "the Lion," was asked by a monk, "How is it when the ram has not yet grown horns?" He said, "I'm afraid." The monk said, "Since you're a man of knowledge, why are you afraid?" He said, "I've never seen such a strange animal."

He also composed a verse on letting an ox go:

> Ox, ox, ox, stop, stop, stop—
> Don't pull a plow or a reaper anymore.
> Pass winters and summers, springs and autumns, as you will,
> Without a rope, without a halter, without guidelines, without
>   a hook.
> When morning comes, go free in uncultivated land;
> In the dark, trackless, rest, again rest.

[598]

Master Dalong was asked by a monk, "What is Buddha?" He said, "You are." The monk said, "How to understand?" He said, "Do you still object to your bowl having no handle?"

[599]

Jiashan said to an assembly, "Find me on the tips of the hundred grasses; recognize yourself in a busy town." Yunmen said, "A frog drills your nostrils, a viper penetrates your pupils. Now recognize it in the midst of complications."

Dahui said, "Jiashan represents a case of 'when a target arises, it invites an arrow.' Yunmen represents a case of 'taking a thief to be your son.' Even so, the grateful are few while ingrates are many."

[600]

Master Huanglong Nan said to an assembly,

There is someone who reads the *Flower Ornament Scripture* in the morning and reads the *Wisdom Scripture* at night, working diligently day and night, without taking a break. There is someone who doesn't study Chan, doesn't discuss doctrine, but takes a worn-out mat and sleeps in the daytime. Now both come alike to Huanglong; one strives, one has no striving: Which would it be right to lodge?" [Silence.] 'A wise host does not admit either the goddess of fortune or the girl of darkness.'

[601]

In olden times there was an old adept who didn't go to the hall. An attendant came and asked him to go to the hall. The adept said, "Today I've eaten my fill of pastries at the manor." The attendant said, "You haven't gone out." The adept said, "Just go ask the lord of the manor." As soon as the attendant had gone out the gate, he saw the lord of the manor coming back to thank the master for going to the manor to eat pastries.

[602]

Master Baotang was asked by the minister Du, "I've heard that Master Jin preaches a three-phrase teaching—'no recollection, no thought, don't stray.' Is this so?" He said, "Yes." The minister said, "Are these three phrases one or three?" He said, "'No recollection' is called discipline; 'no thought' is called concentration; 'don't stray' is called wisdom. When the whole mind is not aroused, this embodies discipline, concentration, and wisdom—they are not one and not three." The minister said, "Shouldn't the word 'stray' in the last phrase be 'forget'?" He said, "'Stray' is correct." The minister said, "Is there any proof?" He said, "The *Dhammapada* says, 'If you arouse the idea of diligence, this is straying, not diligence; if you are able to keep your mind from straying, diligence is boundless.'" When the minister heard this, his sense of doubt was washed away.

[603]

Meditation master Cheng served meditation master Shenxiu at Jade Spring in Xingnan. Later, because the teaching activity of both schools was flourishing, Shenxiu's followers slandered the Southern School from time to time, saying that the great teacher Huineng was illiterate and questioning his excellence. Shenxiu said, "He has attained the knowledge that has no teacher and profoundly understands the supreme vehicle. I am not as good as he is. Moreover, our Fifth Patriarch personally entrusted him with the robe and the teaching—how could this be for no reason? My regret is that I cannot go away to associate with him. I am vainly receiving the benevolence of the nation. You should not remain here, but go to Caoqi to ask him about what you doubt; come back someday and explain to me."

Cheng then respectfully took leave and went to Shaoyang, where he participated in inquiry along with the community, not saying where he'd come from. At that time the Sixth Patriarch announced to the community, "Now there is someone stealing the teaching hidden in this congregation." Cheng came forth and told the whole story. The patriarch said, "How does your teacher direct the community?" Cheng replied, "He always instructs the community to still the mind and contemplate quiescence, perpetually sitting without lying down." The patriarch said, "Stilling the mind and contemplating quiescence is illness, not Chan. Perpetual sitting binds the body—what use is it in principle? Listen to my verse."

> Living we sit, not lie;
> Dying, we lie, not sit.
> Basically it is stinking bones—
> How can virtue or fault be established for it?

Cheng said, "What do you teach people?" The patriarch said, "To say I have a doctrine to give people would be to deceive you. I just untie bonds by whatever means, provisionally calling this *samadhi.* Listen to my verse."

Not minding at all is inherent discipline;
Having no obstruction at all is inherent wisdom.
Not increasing, not receding, is inherent indestructibility.
A body goes, a body comes—fundamental *samadhi*.

When Cheng heard this verse, he repented, gave thanks, and took refuge. He then composed a verse, saying,

The five clusters are an illusory body;
How can the illusory be ultimate?
Heading back to reality as such,
Doctrine is after all impure.

The patriarch affirmed this, and he subsequently returned to Jade Spring.

[604]

Maser Cuiyan Zhen said to an assembly,

"Not seeing a single thing is a great affliction." Mountains, rivers, earth, sun, moon, stars, planet, form and void, light and dark—those are not a single thing. [Holding up his staff:] Ordinary people, seeing a staff, call it a staff. Listeners, seeing a staff, recognize insensate void and negate the staff. As for bodhisattvas seeing a staff, when have they ever hung it on their teeth? When they get hungry, they eat; when they get tired, they sleep. When it's cold they turn to the fire, when it's hot they try to cool off. Haven't you heard it said that knowledge of all knowledge is pure? Such talk laughs off the nostrils of earth.

A monk asked, "What is Buddha?"

He said, "In the same pit there's no different dirt."

The monk asked, "What is the meaning of the founding teacher's coming from the West?"

He said, "Plowing deep, planting shallow."

"What is the great meaning of Buddhism?"

"Sages and saints with five powers."

"I don't understand."

"The tongue is up against the Brahma heaven."

"What is a student's turning point?"

"With one fence a hundred residences are arranged."

"Where is a student's empowerment?"

"A thousand days of chopping wood, burned in one day."

"Where does a student approach?"

"The whole family sends off a ferry."

[605]

When Huangbo was head monk at Nanquan's, one day he took his bowl and sat in Nanquan's place. Nanquan, entering the hall, saw him and asked, "Elder, what year did you practice the Way?" Huangbo said, "Before the prehistoric Buddha." Nanquan said, "You're still my descendant. Get down." Huangbo then moved to the second place and sat down. Nanquan let the matter rest.

Guishan said, "One who lies to an enemy dies." Yangshan said, "Not so; it should be known that Huangbo had a device to fell a tiger." Guishan said, "Your view is so excellent."

Xuedou said, "Too bad Nanquan only saw the sharpness of the awl. If I had been Nanquan, when he said, 'Before the prehistoric Buddha,' I'd sit in the second seat, so Huangbo could never get up all his life. Even so, it would still be necessary to rescue Nanquan."

Dahui said, "Why wait to ask him what year he practiced the Way? As soon as he entered the hall and saw him in the main seat, I'd take my bowl and sit in the second place. Even if Huangbo had a device to fell a tiger, where would he set it up?"

[606]

Master Fojian said to an assembly,

A monk asked Zhaozhou, "What is the meaning of not moving?" Zhaozhou depicted flowing water with his hands. The monk had an insight. Also, a monk asked Fayan, "When one does not grasp appearances, suchness as is does not move. How does one not grasp appearances and see the unmoving?" Fayan said, "The sun rises in the east, and at night sets in the west." That monk also had an insight. If you can see here, then you will know "the whirlwind flattening mountains is fundamentally always still; the rivers pouring furiously basically do not flow." If you cannot, you will not escape the sky turning to the left and the earth turning to the right by too much talk—since of old, and from now, how many times has it happened? The sun flies, the moon runs—no sooner do they rise over the ocean than they set behind the green mountains. The waves of the rivers go on and on, right into the sea, flowing day and night. [Raising his voice:] Chan worthies, do you see suchness as is?

[607]

Meditation master Huang first called on the Fifth Patriarch; though he sought for certainty, he followed gradual practice. Later he went back to Hebei, built a hut, and sat constantly for twenty years, never evincing any slacking. Later he met a disciple of the Sixth Patriarch, Chan master Ce, who had come to the area on his travels. He heard that Huang had studied with the Fifth Patriarch and had been living in a hut for many years, considering himself correctly attuned. Ce knew that Huang's attainment was not consummate, so he went and asked him, "What are you doing sitting here?" He said, "Entering concentration." Ce said, "You say you are entering concentration—mindful or mindless? If mindful, all creatures would have attained concentration; if mindless, all plants and trees would have attained concentration." Huang said, "When I actually go into concentration, I don't see the existence of any mind that is there or not." Ce said, "If you don't see the existence of any mind present or absent, this is constant concentration—how could there be coming out or going in? If there is exit and entry, this is not great concentration."

Huang was at a loss. After a long while he asked, "To whom did you succeed?" Ce said, "My teacher was the Sixth Patriarch of Caoqi." Huang asked, "What did the Sixth Patriarch consider meditation concentration?" Ce said, "My teacher says subtle and clear mental calm is completely peaceful, essence and function as such; the five clusters are fundamentally empty; the data of the six senses are not existent. Not emerging, not entering, not concentrated, not confused, the essence of meditation has no dwelling—detachment from dwelling is the peace of meditation; the essence of meditation has no production—detachment from production is meditation contemplation. Mind is like space, yet without the idea of space."

When Huang heard the essentials of the teaching, he left his hut and went to call on the Sixth Patriarch. The patriarch was sympathetic to him having come from afar, and gave him instruction at once. Huang was enlightened at his words. The state of mind he'd attained over the previous twenty years had no more influence at all. That night his patrons in Hebei, gentry and peasantry, heard a voice in the sky say, "Meditation master Huang attained the Way today." After that he returned to Hebei and taught monks, nuns, lay men, and lay women.

[608]

When Yantou went to Deshan, as soon as he straddled the threshold he immediately asked, "Is this ordinary or holy?" Deshan immediately shouted. Yantou thereupon bowed. Later a monk cited this to Dongshan. Dongshan said, "If it hadn't been Yantou, it would be very hard to get." When Yantou heard of this, he said, "The old fellow Dongshan doesn't recognize good and bad; he misapplies labels. At that time I was holding up with one hand and pressing down with one hand."

[609]

Master Mingzhao said to an assembly,

Opposing successfully with blade intact—one rarely meets a connoisseur. Dying the same and born the same—there is not one in ten thousand. Those who pursue words and go after sayings are as numerous as sand grains in the Ganges River. Those who cite the old and quote the new are destroying the Buddhists. As for the one road beyond, even breaking in and breaking out is contrary. When Confucians meet, they grip their riding crops and turn their heads; the views of Buddhist ascetics are truly miserable, discarding real gold and picking up dirt along with the crowd. I tell you youngsters, don't be conceited—impulsively interpreting others' mysteries still includes rubble. It is better to leap beyond cosmic space at once—who dares approach this spiritual blade? I'll allow you oncoming arrows—only then is one called a strong man. If you try to swallow your voice, you're not worth a dig.

[610]

Master Sanjiao was asked by a monk, "What are the Three Treasures?" He said, "Rice, wheat, and beans." The monk said, "I don't understand." Sanjiao said, "Everybody gladly serves them."

[611]

Zihu said,

> For over thirty years I've dwelt at Zihu;
> Strength from two meals is rough.
> With nothing to do, I climb the mountain and walk about;
> I ask, do people of the time understand or not?

Dahui said, "You cannot construe this as discussion of Buddhism; you cannot construe this as interpretation of worldly truth. Do you understand?"

[612]

Nanyuan asked a monk, "Where have you just come from?" He said, "Rang province." Nanyuan asked, "What did you come for?" He said, "I came especially to pay respects to you." Nanyuan said, "It so happens I'm not here." The monk thereupon shouted. Nanyuan said, "I told you I'm not here—why do you shout?" The monk shouted again; Nanyuan then hit him. The monk bowed. Nanyuan said, "Originally you should have hit me; I've just hit you to get this story to circulate. Blind fellow, go to the hall."

[613]

Master Huanglong Nan said to an assembly,

Chan master Yongjia said, "Traveling over river and sea, traversing mountains and rivers, seeking a teacher, asking about the Way, is called studying Chan. Ever since I recognized the road of Caoqi, I've realized birth and death are irrelevant." Elders, what are the mountains and rivers traversed? What are the teachers sought? What is the Chan studied? What is the Way asked about? If you seek teachers and ask about the Way in Huainan; the river lands; Mount Lu; Nanyue, Yunmen or Linji; or study Chan with Dongshan or Fayan, this is running in search outside—this is called being an outsider. If you can take the inherent nature of Vairocana for an ocean, and consider the quiescent knowledge of insight to be Chan, this is called inward seeking. If you seek outside, it runs you to death; if you seek inside the five clusters of matter, sensation, perception, conception, and consciousness, this binds you fatally. Therefore Chan is not internal, not external, not existent, not nothing, not actual, not empty. Haven't you read the statement that inner views and outward views are both mistaken; the path of Buddhas and the path of demons are both bad? If you get a glimpse this way, the moon sets on the mountains to the west; if you go on pursuing sound and form, where will you name and describe?"

[614]

When Mazu was staying in Temple for Transmitting the Teaching, he always sat meditating. Master Rang knew he was a vessel of Dharma; he went and asked, "Great worthy, what are you aiming for by sitting meditating?" He said, "I aim to become a Buddha." Rang then picked up a tile and rubbed it on a rock in front of the hermitage. Mazu said, "What are you doing?" He said, "Polishing a tile to make a mirror." Mazu said, "How can you make a mirror by polishing a tile?" He said, "How can you become a Buddha by sitting meditating?" Mazu said, "What would be right?" He said, "It is like someone riding a cart—if the cart doesn't move, should you hit the cart or hit the ox?" Mazu had no reply. Rang also said, "Are you learning sitting meditation or are you learning sitting Buddhahood? If you're learning sitting Buddhahood, Buddha is not a fixed form. You shouldn't grasp or reject things that don't abide. If you keep the Buddha seated, you're killing the Buddha; if you cling to the form of sitting, you do not arrive at the truth."

Hearing this instruction was to Mazu like drinking ambrosia. He bowed and asked, "How should I apply my mind to accord with formless concentration?" Rang said, "Your studying the teaching is like planting seed; my expounding the essence of the teaching is like moisture from the sky. Because conditions are meet for you, you will see the Way." Mazu also asked, "If the Way has no form, how can one see it?" Rang said, "The spiritual eye of the mind ground can see the Way. The same is true of formless concentration." Mazu asked, "Does it have becoming and disintegration?" Rang said, "If you see the Way in terms of becoming and disintegration, assemblage and dispersal, that is wrong. Listen to my verse."

> The mind ground contains seeds;
> When moistened, all sprout.
> The flower of concentration is formless;
> What disintegrates, and what forms?

Having been enlightened, Mazu's state of mind was transcendent. He attended Rang for ten years, daily attaining mystic profundity.

[615]

Master Changsha sent a monk to go ask Master Tongcan Hui, "How was it after you saw Nanquan?" Hui was silent. The monk said, "What about before you'd seen Nanquan?" Hui said, "Couldn't be anything special besides." The monk went back and told Changsha about this. Changsha composed a verse, saying,

> The person who sits atop a hundred-foot pole
> May have gained entry, but it's not yet reality.
> Atop the hundred-foot pole one must step forward;
> The worlds in the ten directions are the whole body.

The monk asked how to step forward at the top of the hundred-foot pole. Changsha said, "The mountains of Lang province, the rivers of Li province." The monk said he didn't understand. Changsha said, "The four seas and five lakes are within the imperial sway."

Dahui said, "If you want to see Changsha, take another step forward. If anyone asks how to take this step forward, I'll wait till you're relaxed to give you complications."

[616]

When Master Furong Xun first called on Guizong, he asked, "What is Buddha?" Guizong said, "I'll tell you, but will you believe?" Xun said, "How dare I not believe your truthful words?" Guizong said, "You are Buddha." Xun asked how to preserve it. Guizong said, "One cataract in the eye, and flowers in the sky shower in a flurry." At this Xun had insight.

. . .

Fayan said, "If not for the latter saying, where would you look for Guizong?"

[617]

Master Zhenjing, opening a hall, said to the assembly,

Questions will be stopped for now; you only know to ask about Buddha, ask about the Teaching, but don't know where Buddha's teaching comes from. Tell me, where does it come from? [Letting down one leg, he said,] In past days Huanglong personally enforced this order; the Buddhas of the ten directions didn't dare violate it; the ancestral teachers through the generations and all sages and saints didn't dare transgress. Countless methods of teaching, all subtle meanings, the sayings of the teachers all over the world, one seal beginning to end, never dared differ. Leaving aside for the moment not differing, where is the seal? Do you see? If you see, you are not monks, not lay people; you have no partiality, no factionalism—everyone is entrusted. If you do not see, I withdraw myself. [Then drawing in his leg, he shouted and said,] The army rolls with the seal, the general goes with the talisman. The Buddha's hand, a donkey's leg, circumstances of birth—ultimately a painful beating is deserved. Now in the present assembly, isn't there anyone who doesn't accept? If there is, he's undeniably exceptional. If not, the new elder goes on fooling you people. So our great enlightened World Honored One in ancient times in the country Magadha on the eighth day of the twelfth month, when the morning star appeared, became enlightened, and all the living beings on earth became Buddha at the same time. Now there is a Buddhist monk, Kewen, in the eastern country of China, in the city of Chunyang; on the thirteenth day of the sixth month, when the blazing sun appeared, he also realized—what? [Drawing one line with his whisk, he said,] I don't dare take you lightly—you will all become Buddhas.

TRANSLATOR'S NOTE

"The Buddha's hand, a donkey's leg, circumstances of birth" refers to a famous device of Huanglong in which the master asks, "How is my hand like Buddha's hand? How is my leg like a donkey's leg? Everyone has circumstances of birth—what are your circumstances of birth?"

[618]

Master Zhaozhou asked Nanquan, "Where does one who knows of existence go?" Nanquan said, "To the house of the patron in front of the mountain, becoming a water buffalo." Zhaozhou said, "Thanks for your direction." Nanquan said, "Last night the moon came to the window in the middle of the night."

Yunfeng Yue said, "Were it not Nanquan, he might have suffered the breakup of Cai province."

TRANSLATOR'S NOTE

"Cai province"—Cai was known for the large turtles whose shells were used for divination.

[619]

National Teacher Wuye asked Mazu, "What is the mind seal secretly transmitted when the founding teacher came from the West?" Mazu said, "Great Worthy, right now you're noisy—go away for now and come another time." As soon as Wuye went off, Mazu called, "Great Worthy!" Wuye turned his head. Mazu said, "What is this?" Wuye suddenly attained enlightenment. He thereupon bowed. Mazu said, "This dullard! Why are you bowing?"

[620]

Master Huaitang said to an assembly,

If one only understands oneself and doesn't understand what's present, this person has eyes but no feet. If one understands what's present but doesn't understand oneself, this person has feet but no eyes. In the case of these two people, there's always something in the chest twenty-four hours a day. Since there's something in the chest, signs of unease are always present. Since there is unease present, they get stuck all along the way—how can they be at peace? Didn't a patriarch say that "if you cling to it you lose balance and inevitably enter a false path; let it go naturally and the being neither goes nor stays"?

[621]

Two monks were arguing about the wind and a flag. One said, "The wind is moving"; one said, "The flag is moving." The Sixth Patriarch said, "It's not the wind moving, not the flag moving—it's your minds moving." The two monks were cowed.

Xuefeng said, "Even the great patriarch had a dragon's head but a snake's tail. He should be given twenty strokes of the cane." Elder Fu, standing by, gnashed his teeth. Xuefeng said, "My speaking this way also deserves twenty strokes of the cane."

Dahui said, "Do you want to know Elder Fu? When a rhinoceros gazes at the moon, a pattern is produced on its horn. Do you want to know Xuefeng? When an elephant is startled by thunder, a pattern gets into its tusks."

[622]

Fayan asked the master of Xiushan, "'The slightest miss is as the distance between sky and earth'—how do you understand?" Xiushan said, "The slightest miss is as the distance between sky and earth." Fayan said, "How can you get it understanding this way?" Xiushan said, "I am just thus; what about you?" Fayan said, "The slightest miss is as the distance between sky and earth." Xiushan had an insight at this.

Baoning Yong versified,

> At Stone City he closely questions a fellow student—
> He doesn't speak of east or west; he points right to the south.
> Light and dark a two-lane road, coming and going,
> Vague, winding, in the smoky haze.

TRANSLATOR'S NOTE

Pointing to the south means giving direction, guiding.

[623]

Master Fayun Quan was asked by a monk, "When Bodhidharma came from the West, what did he transmit?" He said, "Zhou, Qin, Han, Wei."

He was asked, "A monk asked Yunmen, 'What is the expression going beyond the reality body'? Yunmen said, 'Hiding the body in the North Star.' What does this mean?"

He said, "A bit of sincerity."

The monk said, "If it were up to me, I'd disappear."

The master said, "What would you say?"

The monk said, "Last night I looked up and saw the North Star; indistinct, it resembled a sweet rice cake."

The master said, "You just think of water plants, and have no other knowledge."

TRANSLATOR'S NOTE

Zhou, Qin, Han, and Wei were successive dynasties prior to the Chan founder Bodhidharma's coming to China.

[624]

Master Suxi was asked by a monk, "What is the Buddha of Stable Light?" He said, "A duck swallows a snail." The monk asked, "Do you allow me to turn around?" The master said, "Eyes pop out."

[625]

Master Xiangyan Duan said to an assembly, "Speech is slander, silence is deception. There is still something beyond, but my mouth is narrow and I can't explain it to you." Then he got down from the seat.

[626]

Master Tianzhu Hui was asked by a monk, "Before Bodhidharma came to this land, was there any Buddhism?" He said, "Leaving aside before he came, what about now?" The monk said, "I don't understand; I beg the teacher's instruction." He said, "The eternal sky of all time, one morning's wind and moon. [After a long silence:] Understand? What about for your own part? What's it got to do with Bodhidharma's coming or not having come? Someone else's coming is much like someone selling auguries; seeing you don't understand, he pokes through the text of a hexagram just to come up with fortune and misfortune. It's all up to you; see everything for yourself." The monk asked, "What is the person who knows how to augur like?" He said, "As soon as you go out the gate you miss."

[627]

When the Bird's Nest Monk's attendant Huitong wanted to leave one day, he asked, "Where are you going now?" The attendant said, "I left home for the Dharma but you've never given me instruction. Now I am going to other places to study Buddhism." The master said, "If it's Buddhism, I have a little bit here too." The attendant said, "What is your

Buddhism here?" The Bird's Nest Monk held up the blanket on his body and blew on it. The attendant was greatly enlightened by this.

Dagui Xiu said, "Too bad this monk acknowledges sound and form at another's mouth, taking it for a norm, not knowing his own light covers heaven and covers earth."

Dahui said, "Such a critique still has not seen Bird's Nest even in a dream."

[628]

Master Letan Jun, when an attendant announced his departure, took up a brush and wrote a verse saying,

> Bird's Nest blew on his blanket,
> Kindly acting for his attendant.
> Though the path is the same now as ever,
> I do not agree.
> In the season of the second and third months
> A gentle breeze fills the land.
> Everywhere a hundred flowers bloom,
> Mountains far and near are like a picture.
> On byways in spring, animals are noisy;
> On high cliffs spring waters pour.
> Every place is a gateway to *samadhi*;
> Open and clear, throughout the vast countryside.
> A fine bit of true information
> I write to you returning to your abode.
> The last statement of a patchrobed monk—
> Phew! What words are these?

[629]

Master Zhaozhou was asked by a monk, "Does a dog have Buddha-nature or not?" Zhaozhou said, "No."

Wuzu Yan versified,

> Zhaozhou's bare-bladed sword—
> Its cold frosty light blazes.
> If you try to ask about it,
> It splits your body in two.

The monk said, "From the Buddhas above down to ants, all have Buddha-nature; why then has a dog none?" Zhaozhou said, "There is still conditioned consciousness."

Zhenjing versified,

> He says there's still conditioned consciousness;
> Who would say the meaning's not profound?
> When an ocean dries up, ultimately you see the bottom,
> But people's hearts are not known even till they die.

[630]

When Master Nan was dwelling on Huangbo, he said to the assembly, "How is it when reciting hymns up in the bell tower, planting vegetables at the foot of the bed?" Many people made statements, but none was fitting. Finally Master Zhenjiao Sheng said, "A fierce tiger sits in the road." Nan agreed.

[631]

Master Shimen Cong said to an assembly,

> Each individual's a heroic stalwart,
> Magnificent, imposing, what further doubt about things and self?
> Present, evident, clear as the sun,
> Expanding and contracting, when the person concerned shows
>   illness,
> Transcendent, ungraspable, the road of the eternal sky.
> Independently liberated, the light of meditation can be known
>   on one's own;
> The expedient of learning discusses present and past.
> To save people you need to show lightning-like action.

[After a long silence, he said,] "Go, go—the road to India is very far, a hundred thousand and more."

A monk asked, "'If one can turn things around, one is the same as the Realized'—how can the triple gate and Buddha shrine be turned around?"

He said, "I'll tell you—will you believe?"

The monk said, "How dare I not believe the teacher's truthful words?"

The master said, "This lacquer bucket!"

[632]

Master Fenyang said,

Those who expound the teaching need to include ten knowledges of same reality. If it doesn't include ten knowledges of same reality, false and true are not distinguished, black and white are not differentiated, and one cannot be an eye for humans and celestials, determining right and wrong. It would be like a bird trying to fly with broken wings, like trying to shoot an arrow at a target with a broken bowstring. When the bowstring is broken, no shot can hit the target; when its wings are broken, a bird cannot fly. Only when the bowstring is sound and wings are strong is it possible to hit the target and fly in the sky.

What are the ten knowledges of same reality? I will point them out for you. The first is the same one substance. Second is the same great matter. Third is total same study. Fourth is the same true knowledge. Fifth is the same universality. Sixth is the same completeness. Seventh is the same gain and loss. Eighth is the same enlivening and killing. Ninth is the same voice calling. Tenth is the same attainment.

With whom is the same attainment of entry? With whom is the voice calling the same? What is the same life-giving and killing? What thing is gained or lost the same? What is completely fulfilled the same? What same universality is it? Who has the same true knowledge? Who can totally study the same? What is the same great matter? What is the same one substance? Is there anyone who can point them out? Those who can point them out don't begrudge compassion. Those who cannot point them out do not yet have the eye of study. You urgently need to discern; it is necessary to know right and wrong. The face is present. Don't stand long.

Dahui said, "If old Fenyang did not have the final 'the face is present,' he'd have lost. Even so, he still didn't avoid losing his own descendants. Ha!"

[633]

When Master Baoshou opened a hall, Sansheng pushed a monk forward; Baoshou immediately hit him. Sansheng said, "If you do for people this way, you'll blind the eyes of everyone in the city." Baoshou immediately returned to his quarters.

Yunfeng Yue said, "The whole school of Linji has been wiped out—how did it come to this?" Holding up his staff, he said, "Where did it go?"

Zhenjing versified,

Seeking out a steed, he comes flying, pacifying with a staff.
Blind people, on the other hand, fill the city.
Great peace is originally brought about by the general
But it is not permitted for the general to see great peace.

Zhenru versified,

The eye of the teaching, brought forth, to whom is it handed
over?
Sansheng, pushing a monk forward, settles all doubts;
When the general's order is cited, the multitude of men are
shook up,
Resulting in the voices of the blind penetrating all around.

[634]

Master Changqing Yan said to an assembly
Maitreya Buddha entered a monastery in the morning and attained
true enlightenment in the evening. Then he uttered a verse, saying,

The phenomena of the triple world, above and below
I say are all mental.
Apart from mental phenomena
There is nothing that can be grasped.

See how extremely alert he was in speaking thus; compared to my disciples, he was still a dullard. So if you see the Way in an instant, the sense of past, present, and future ends. It is like a seal stamping mud; there is no more before and after. Disciples, the matter of birth and death is important; you need to understand it—don't consider it idle. Conditioned consciousness is boundless—it's all because of losing oneself and pursuing things. When the World Honored One was about to enter nirvana, Manjushri asked the Buddha to turn the wheel of Dharma again. The World Honored One scolded him: "I remained in the world for forty-nine years, but never had a single word to give people. You're asking me to turn the wheel of Dharma again—this implies that I have already turned the wheel of Dharma." So in the present time, setting up guest and host in the community, with questions and answers, is a matter than cannot be helped, just for the sake of beginners.

[635]

Master Baqiao Qing was asked by a monk, "What is the school of Kanadeva?" He said, "The red flag on the left." He was asked, "When a thief comes you should strike; when a guest comes, you should attend. Suppose it happens that a guest and a thief both come—then what?" He said, "There's a worn-out pair of straw sandals in the house." He was asked, "Can worn-out straw sandals still be used?" He said, "If you take them away, it is ominous before and unfortunate after." He was asked, "How is it before the ancient Buddhas appeared?" He said, "A thousand-year eggplant root." He was asked, "How about after emerging?" He said, "A thunderbolt bearer's eyes bulge in anger."

[636]

Master Daan Gan was asked by a monk, "What is the meaning of the founding teacher's coming from the West?" He said, "A goat-head cart pushes the bright moon."

[637]

As Yantou and Luoshan were looking for a location for a memorial tower, on the way Luoshan suddenly called, "Master!" Yantou turned his head and said, "What?" Luoshan pointed and said, "Here's a good spot." Yantou shouted and said, "Melon-seller in melon-land!" They went another mile or so, then as they were resting Luoshan bowed and said, "Weren't you at Dongshan's thirty years ago but didn't agree with Dongshan?" Yantou said, "Yes." Luoshan said, "And weren't you a spiritual successor of Deshan, yet didn't agree with Deshan?" Yantou said, "Yes." Luoshan said, "I don't ask about not agreeing with Deshan; as for Dongshan, what flaw did he have?" After a long silence Yantou said, "Dongshan was a fine Buddha; it's just that he had no light." Luoshan then bowed.

Dahui said, "Yantou and his successor, though skillfully going in darkness and coming in light, when carefully examined do not yet avoid skulls colliding."

[638]

Master Shishuang Xingkong was asked by a monk, "What is the meaning of the founding teacher's coming from the West?" He said, "It's like a man in a thousand-foot well; if you can get this man out without using an inch of rope, then I'll give you an answer to the meaning of the coming from the West." The monk said, "Recently Master Qiang of Hunan has appeared in the world; he also talks to people of one thing and another." Xingkong called a novice, "Haul out this corpse!"

That novice was Yangshan. Later Yangshan cited this and asked Danyuan, "How can one get the man out of the well?" Danyuan, scolding him, said, "Ignoramus! Who's in the well?"

Yangshan also asked Guishan, "How can one order each one of the senses?" Guishan said, "If you realize enlightenment, no senses will be out of order." Yangshan said, "What about Xingkong's saying, 'It is like a man in a thousand-foot well—how can you get him out without using any rope'?" Guishan said, "I have a method of getting him out." Yangshan said, "How do you get him out?" Guishan called Yangshan by name; Yangshan responded. Guishan said, "He's out." At this, Yangshan had an insight. Later, after he was dwelling on Mount Yang, he said to the community, "At Danyuan's I got the name, at Guishan's I got the state."

[639]

Master Yungai Zhi said to an assembly,

Zhaozhou asked a monk, "Where are you going?" He said, "To pick tea." Zhaozhou said, "Idler." Speaking of it does not touch upon it; where can you go look for it? In back are dragon scales; in front, donkey legs. Turning a flip, a lone cloud; the wild crane laughs aloud.

He also said to an assembly,

There is only one solid body appearing in all objects. As far as I am concerned, today a thousand mountains are lush; birds and beasts cry and call. A hundred flowers bloom together; myriad trees bring forth branches. All this is the particularized reality as such of the Buddhas; as you people roam the mountains and enjoy the waters you simply must focus your eyes intently and not be fooled by them.

[640]

Buddha was asked by an outsider, "I don't ask about what has verbal expression or what has no verbal expression." Buddha remained silent. The outsider said in praise, "Your great kindness and great compassion have cleared away the clouds of my confusion, enabling me to gain entry." After the outsider left, Ananda asked Buddha, "What did the outsider realize, that he said he gained entry?" Buddha said, "Like a good horse, as soon as he sees the shadow of the whip he goes."

Tianyi Huai versified,

> Twin swords, covering and protecting, both break:
> Clouds of confusion are henceforth cleared.
> After taking over the bell at the start,
> Lightly shaking it moves clouds and thunder.

[641]

When Great Master Yongjia first arrived at Caoqi, he circled the rope seat three times, shook his ringed staff, and stood there. The patriarch said, "A monk embodies three thousand dignified manners and eight hundred details of conduct. Where have you come from, Great Worthy, to give rise to such conceit?" Yongjia said, "The matter of life and death is important; impermanence is swift." The patriarch said, "Why don't you realize no birth and comprehend no speed?" Yongjia said, "Realization basically has no birth; comprehension basically has no speed." The patriarch said, "That is so. That is so." Yongjia now paid respects with full ceremony, and then bade farewell. The patriarch said, "Isn't that too quick?" Yongjia said, "It's basically inherently not movement; how could there be quickness?" The patriarch said, "Who knows nonmovement?" Yongjia said, "You're creating distinction yourself." The patriarch said, "You've gotten the meaning of no birth." Yongjia said, "Does no birth have meaning?" The patriarch said, "Without meaning, who would discriminate?" Yongjia said, "Discrimination is not meaning either." The patriarch said, "Good, good! Stay overnight."

[642]

Chan master Guoyi of Jingshan was summoned to court and honored by Emperor Daizong of the Tang dynasty. One day the master, in the inner courtyard, saw the emperor and stood up. The emperor said, "Why do you get up?" He said, "Patron, how can you see me within walking, standing, sitting, or lying down?"

Dahui said, "Yet how can you see Guoyi except within walking, standing, sitting, and lying down?"

[643]

Deshan said to a group in an informal gathering, "Tonight I won't give answers—whoever has a question gets thirty strokes of the cane." At that time a monk came forth and bowed. Deshan immediately hit him. The monk said, "I haven't asked a question yet; why do you hit me?" Deshan said, "Where are you from?" The monk said, "Korea." Deshan said, "You should have been given thirty strokes of the cane before you got on the boat."

Dagui Zhe versified,

> Holding high the seal of the patriarchs, he sits in the center of the heartland.
> Who is willing to determine fortune and misfortune at the moment?
> If not for this patchrobed one from Korea,
> How could the pure wind be kept in motion forever?

[644]

Master Yunju Ying was asked by a monk, "Whence do mountains, rivers, and earth come to be?" He said, "They come to be from false imagination." The monk said, "Can I produce a bar of gold by imagination?" Ying stopped. The monk didn't agree. Yunmen said, "This is already a complication he can't reconcile. When he said, 'Can I produce a bar of gold by imagination?' I'd pick up my staff and hit him."

[645]

When Master Gaoding Jian first went to Deshan, he saw Deshan on the other side of a river, sitting on the riverbank. He asked after him from across the river; Deshan beckoned him with his hand, whereupon Jian became enlightened. Then he ran past to the side and didn't cross the river; he returned to Gaoding and became abbot.

[646]

Master Zhenjing said to an assembly,

The doctrinal teacher Yinzong asked the workman Lu, "When you were at Huangmei, what did he teach you to pass on the transmission?" Lu said, "What he taught was just about seeing essential nature to become a Buddha; he didn't talk about meditation concentration, liberation, no thought, or no contrivance." Yinzong said, "Why didn't he talk about meditation concentration, liberation, no thought, or no contrivance?" Lu said, "Because these are dualisms, not Buddhist nondualism." Yinzong said, "What is nondualism?" Lu said, "It's like when you lecture on the *Nirvana Scripture*—clearly seeing Buddha-nature is called Buddhist nondualism. Half the Chan worthies at that time were already on a Chan path of petty cleverness. Most of the monasteries now just talk about meditation concentration, liberation, no thought, and no contrivance."

But tell me, is the Sixth Patriarch right, or are the contemporaries right? Is distinction right, or is not distinguishing right? If you distinguish, there is deviation and there is accord; there is right and there is wrong. But if you don't distinguish, you don't distinguish false from true, burying away our school's vehicle. It is like roads in the world: there are the straight, there are the winding, there are the dangerous, there are the good. Those who travel the road go when it is suitable to go, stop when it is appropriate to stop. Do you know me, after all? [Silence.] "Serving countless lands with this profound mind is called requiting the benevolence of Buddha."

[647]

Caoshan asked Elder De, "'Bodhisattvas in concentration hear a musky elephant crossing a river'—what scripture does this come from?" He said, "From the *Nirvana Scripture*." Caoshan said, "Do they hear it before concentration, or do they hear it after concentration?" De said, "The master is flowing." Caoshan said, "You've said quite a bit, but have only managed to say half." De said, "What about you?" Caoshan said, "Receive it at the riverbank."

Dahui said, "Where do you get involved?"

[648]

Whenever Master Baizhang held meetings, there was an old man who listened to the teaching along with the community. When the group withdrew, the old man withdrew too. Suddenly one day he didn't withdraw; Baizhang asked him, "Who is this person standing before me?" The old man said, "I'm not a human being. In the past, in the time of Kasyapa Buddha, I once dwelt on this mountain; a student asked if greatly cultivated people still fall within cause and effect, and I said they don't fall within cause and effect. After that I fell into the body of a wild fox for five hundred lifetimes. Now I ask you to say something on my behalf." Then he asked, "Do greatly cultivated people still fall within cause and effect, or not?" Baizhang said, "They are not blind to cause and effect." The old man was greatly enlightened at these words. He bowed and said, "I have been liberated from the body of a wild fox. I stay on the other side of the mountain; I ask for the rites customary for a monk that's passed away." Baizhang had the duty distributor announce to the community that they'd send off a dead monk after the meal. After the meal, Baizhang led the group to a crag on the other side of the mountain, where he fished out a dead fox with his staff, then cremated it according to the norm.

That evening Baizhang went up in the hall and related the foregoing events. Huangbo then asked, "An ancient gave a mistaken answer and fell into the body of a wild fox for five hundred lifetimes; what becomes of one who makes no mistake time after time?" Baizhang said, "Come here, and I'll tell you." Huangbo went up and gave Baizhang a slap. Baizhang clapped and laughed; he said, "I thought foreigners' beards were red—there is even a red-bearded foreigner here!"

Guishan was serving as the cook; the ascetic Sima told him the foregoing story and asked Guishan about it. Guishan rattled the door thrice. Sima said, "Too crude." Guishan said, "Buddhism is not this principle." Guishan also quoted this to ask Yangshan. Yangshan said, "Huangbo always uses this device." Guishan said, "Did he have it by nature, or did he get it from someone?" Yangshan said, "This is received from a teacher's transmission, and also his inherent communion with the source." Guishan said, "So it is. So it is."

Zhenjing versified,

> "Not falling"—a concealed point; "not blind" distinguishes.
> He wants him to shed the fox body from this.
> Everyone says they're going to retire from office,
> But when has a single one been seen in the forests?

Zhenru versified,

> The immense furnace of the great smith
> Forges Buddhas and forges patriarchs;
> When the mold is thoroughly melted,
> Those who know are at a loss.

[649]

Mr. Bao said, "As my body is empty, all things are empty. A thousand kinds, myriad categories, are all the same." Yunmen said, "You stand not seeing standing, walk not seeing walking. The four gross elements and five body-mind clusters cannot be grasped—where do you see that there are mountains, rivers, and earth? You take your bowl and eat food every day; what do you called food? Where is there even a single grain of rice?"

[650]

Master Tiansheng Tai went to Master Langya Jiao's place. Jiao asked, "Hiding an army and spoiling for a fight is not yet expert; please meet me with a lone lance on a single horse." Tai pointed to Jiao and said, "If the general is not fierce, this burdens all the armed forces." Jiao hit him once with a seat cloth. Tai also struck out with a seat cloth; Jiao grabbed it and stopped him, saying, "The previous seat cloth was my order going into effect; where does your seat cloth fall?" Tai said, "I humbly hope for your hospitality." Jiao pushed him away and said, "When you get up early in the morning, there's already someone who's been traveling by night." Tai said, "You're drawing a bow after the thief has gone." Jiao said, "For now sit and have tea."

[651]

Master Changsha was asked by Ministry President Zhu, "When a worm is cut in two, both parts move—which one is the Buddha-nature in?" Changsha said, "Don't think falsely." The ministry president said, "What about the movement?" Changsha said, "If you understand, air and fire have not yet dispersed."

The ministry president again called on Changsha. The master called to him, and he responded. Changsha said, "This is not your birth star." The ministry president said, "There cannot be a separate second self apart from this present response." Changsha said, "Can I call you the emperor?" He said, "Then if I don't respond at all, isn't this my inner self?" Changsha said, "It's not just when you respond or don't respond—since beginningless time this is the root of birth and death." Then he produced a verse, saying,

> People studying the Way do not know reality;
> They just recognize the usual conscious spirit.
> The root of birth and death for countless ages,
> The ignorant call the original person.

        . . .

Dahui said, "Given that the one presently responding is not the original person, what do you call the original person?" [After a silence, he said,] "My speaking thus too is making medicine for a dead horse."

[652]

Master Baiyun Duan said to an assembly,

It is like my pressing the oceanic symbol with my finger, radiating light. [Holding up his staff:] Mountains, rivers, earth, birds, forests, animate and inanimate beings today are all on my staff roaring the great lion's roar, expounding great wisdom. But tell me, what teachings do Tiantai and Nanyue expound? Nanyue expounds the Dong progression's cultivation of five positions of ruler and subject, father and son, each finding the proper place. Don't keep to the green of the unusual plants on a cold crag; if you sit persistently in the white clouds, the source is not subtle. Tiantai expounds the Linji succession's three mysteries, three essentials, and four propositions, one shout distinguishing guest and host, observation and action activated at the same time. If you want to understand the meaning here, chime midnight at noon. Mount Lu comes forth and says, "You two are right in a nest of complications. Haven't you heard it said that if you want to avoid bringing on action with immediate consequences, don't slander the Buddha's wheel of true teaching?" If you take views of these three groups and put them on the balance of a patchrobed monk, one weighs eight ounces, one weighs half a pound, one isn't worth half a cent. Now tell me, which one isn't worth half a cent? [Silence.] I only pray the spring wind will exert its force equally, blowing into our gate at the same time.

[653]

One day as Officer Wang was at work, Mi Hu arrived. Wang held up his writing brush and showed it to him. Mi Hu said, "And can you judge space?" Wang then threw down his brush and went into his residence and didn't interact any further with Mi Hu. Mi Hu had doubts.

The next day, when Master Huayan had a gathering for tea, he asked Wang, "What did Mi Hu say yesterday that you didn't interact with him anymore?" Wang said, "A lion bites people; the hound of Han chases a clod." As soon as Mi Hu heard this, he let out a clear laugh and said, "I understand! I understand!" Wang said, "It's not that you have no understanding, but try to say it." Mi Hu said, "Please bring it up." Wang then stood up one chopstick. Mi Hu said, "This wild fox sprite!" Wang said, "This fellow has penetrated."

Dagui Zhe said, "Though Mi Hu was like this, he only got one piece. When Officer Wang said 'This fellow has penetrated,' it was much like seeing a tower and making it out to be a tower. I am otherwise. Though the officer was a layman, he had the authority to give life or kill at his pen. Mi Hu was a teacher of one region, but he couldn't get out of the other's cage. At that time, when he threw down his pen, I'd say to him, 'I'd doubted this fellow hitherto.'"

[654]

When Master Linji was in the community of Huangbo, the head monk urged him to ask Huangbo, "What is the actual great meaning of Buddhism?" Huangbo gave him twenty strokes of the cane. This happened three times; each time he asked, he was caned. Then he announced his departure to the head monk, saying, "I was lucky enough to be kindly and compassionately directed to go question the master. I posed the question three times and was caned three times. I regret to myself that due to obstruction I didn't understand the deep message; now I will leave." The head monk said, "If you are going, you should take leave of the master before you go." Linji then bowed and withdrew. The head monk went to Huangbo first and told him, "The youth who was questioning is very much in accord with the Dharma; later on he will become a great tree sheltering everyone in the land. If he comes to take leave from you, please give him instruction." Linji then took leave of Huangbo; Huangbo said, "Go to Dayu's place by the shoals of Gaoan; he will explain for you."

Linji went to Dayu; Dayu asked, "Where have you come from?" He said, "From Huangbo." Dayu said, "What has Huangbo been saying?" Linji cited the foregoing story and asked, "I don't know where I was wrong." Dayu said, "Huangbo was so kind, he wore himself out for you, yet you still come here asking whether you were wrong or not." Linji was greatly enlightened at these words. He said, "After all there's nothing much to Huangbo's Buddhism." Dayu grabbed and held him and said, "You bed-wetting devil! Just now you spoke of being wrong or not, and now you say there is not much to Huangbo's Buddhism. What principle do you see? Speak quickly, speak quickly!" Linji thumped Dayu in the ribs with his fist three times. Dayu pushed him away and said, "Your teacher is Huangbo—it's none of my business."

Linji returned to Huangbo. Seeing him coming, Huangbo said, "When will there be an end to this fellow's comings and goings?" Linji said, "It's just because of your kindness." Then he recounted the foregoing story. Huangbo said, "That old fellow Dayu—why is he so talkative? Wait till he comes." Linji said, "Why do you want him to come?" Huangbo said, "When he comes I'll give him a sound beating." Linji said, "What 'when he comes' are you talking about? Take it right now!" And then he slapped Huangbo. Huangbo said, "This madman has come back here to grab the tiger's whiskers." Linji then shouted. Huangbo said, "Attendant, bring this madman to the hall."

Guishan asked Yangshan, "Did Linji get Dayu's empowerment, or did he get Huangbo's empowerment?" Yangshan said, "Not only did he mount the tiger's head, he also knew how to control the tiger's tail."

TRANSLATOR'S NOTE

The account in *Zutang ji* says that Linji went back and forth between Huangbo and Dayu for twenty years.

[655]

Master Yanguan asked a lecturer, "What scriptures and treatises have you plumbed?" He said, "The *Flower Ornament Scripture*." Yanguan said, "How many reality realms are in the *Flower Ornament Scripture*?" The lecturer said, "In sum there are four; in extension they are infinitely multiplied." Yanguan stood up his whisk and said, "Which type of reality realm is this contained in?" The lecturer was silent. Yanguan said, "To know by thinking and understand by cogitation is the livelihood of ghosts. A lone lamp under the sun in effect loses its radiance."

Dahui said, "The two steps are not the same; it is contained in the top class."

[656]

Master Dabai said to an assembly

You people each turn your mind around by yourself and get to the root—don't pursue the branches. Just get the root, and the branches will come of themselves. If you want to know the root, just comprehend your own mind. This mind is originally the root of all things, mundane and transcendental. Therefore when the mind is aroused, all sorts of phenomena occur; when the mind is quiescent, all sorts of phenomena pass away. Just don't conceive them sticking to any good or bad at all, and myriad things are inherently as such.

A monk asked, "What is the great meaning of Buddhism?"

He said, "Reed blossoms, willow flowers, bamboo needles, hemp thread."

[657]

Master Wuzu Yan said to an assembly,

Every day we get up and lean on Linji's cane, play Yunmen's tune, respond to Zhaozhou's clapping, carry Yangshan's hoe, drive Guishan's ox, plow Baiyun's field, gradually making a livelihood over the last seven or eight years. I tell you all furthermore to each put forth a hand for mutual assistance and sing the song of returning from the fields, getting along for now this way with simple soup and plain food. What do I mean? Let's just hope the silkworms and wheat mature this year, and the sun gives a dime.

A monk asked, "Before Niutou met the Fourth Patriarch, what was he like?"

The master said, "Wearing a drape on his head."

"What about after meeting?"

"Blue cloth covering in front."

"Before he met the Fourth Patriarch, why did the birds bring him flowers?"

"Wealth and status are what people desire."

"After meeting, why didn't the birds bring him flowers?"

"Poverty and lowliness are disliked by people."

[658]

Master Guling met Baizhang on his travels and became enlightened. Then he returned to Dezhong monastery in Fuzhou. His original tutor asked him, "When you left me and went elsewhere, what practice did you learn?" He said, "No practice at all." So the tutor sent him off to do chores. One day as he was bathing he ordered Guling to wash his back. Guling patted him on the back and said, "A fine Buddha shrine, but the Buddha isn't holy." The tutor looked back at him. Guling said, "Though the Buddha isn't holy, still he can radiate light." Another day, the tutor was reading a scripture by the window; a bee was flying into the paper covering the window, trying to get out. Guling looked at it and said, "The world is so wide, yet it won't go out, but bores into that old paper; it will never get through." The tutor put the scripture aside and asked, "Whom did you meet on your travels? I see you've been making extraordinary statements." Guling said, "I had Master Baizhang point out a place of rest for me. Now I just want to requite the benevolent blessing." The tutor then asked him to expound the teaching. Guling then quoted Baizhang, saying, "Spiritual light shines alone, utterly liberated from senses and objects. The essence reveals true eternity, not contained in writings. The nature of mind is stainless, fundamentally perfect in itself; just detach from delusive relations—this is Buddha as is." That tutor experienced enlightenment at these words.

[659]

At the *Nirvana* assembly, the Buddha rubbed his chest with his hand and said to the crowd, "You should carefully observe my violet burnished golden body, gazing upon it to your satisfaction so you won't have any regrets later. If you say I have passed away, you are not my disciples. If you say I have not passed away, you are not my disciples either." At that time a million billion people all realized enlightenment. Yunfeng Yue said, "But the seat of fatal illness is not susceptible to medication. Today I am temporarily making medicine for a dead horse; do you people have blood under your skin?"

[660]

Yunmen asked Wolong, "Do people who understand self still see that there is self?" Wolong said, "Only when not seeing there is self does one understand self." He also asked, "What order of operation is what is learned on the long bench?" Wolong said, "The second order of operation." Yunmen said, "What is the first order of operation?" Wolong said, "Tying your shoes tightly."

Dahui said, "He rides a brigand's horse to chase a gang of brigands, borrows an old woman's skirt to pay respects to an old woman's age."

[661]

Emperor Wuzong of the Tang dynasty was fond of clams; officers in charge of the seashore went along in succession and worked hard. One day in the imperial kitchen there was a clam they couldn't open. The emperor considered this strange. He burned incense and prayed over it, and it opened; then he saw an image of a bodhisattva, with all the iconic features. The emperor subsequently put it in a golden grain sandalwood incense bag, wrapped it in beautiful brocade, and presented it to the community at the Temple of Promoting Goodness. The monks looked upon it with reverence and asked the officials, "What auspicious sign is this?" The emperor therefore summoned Chan master Zheng of Zhongnanshan and asked him. The master said, "I've heard that there is no meaningless response to beings; this simply opens up Your Majesty's faith. Hence scripture says, 'To those who would be liberated by this body, he manifests this body to expound the teaching.'" The emperor said, "The body of the bodhisattva is manifest, but I haven't heard the exposition of the teaching." The master said, "Do you see this as eternal or not eternal? Do you have faith or not?" The emperor said, "It's a marvel—I have profound faith in it." The master said, "You have heard the exposition of the teaching." The emperor was overjoyed, imbued with a sense of wonder. He ordered all the temples in the land to erect statues of Guanyin.

[662]

Master Fenyang Zhao said to an assembly,

Any statement must include three hidden gates; each hidden gate must include three keys. There is observation; there is action. Sometimes observation precedes action; sometimes action precedes observation. Sometimes observation and action are simultaneous; sometimes observation and action are not simultaneous. When observation precedes action, it is calling for discussion with you. When action precedes observation, you have to be the person to get it. When observation and action are simultaneous, how will you meet it? When observation and action are not simultaneous, how will you stay?

A monk asked, "What is the source of the Great Way?"

He said, "Digging the earth looking for the sky."

"How can it be like this?"

"Not perceiving the hidden mystery."

"What is the guest within the guest?"

"Joining the palms in front of the hermitage and questioning the World Honored One."

"What is the host within the guest?"

"No peer facing."

"What is the guest within the host?"

"Marshalling clouds across the ocean, drawing a sword stirring up and rattling the Dragon Gate."

"What is the host within the host?"

"With three heads and six arms, holding up sky and earth, a raging demon king strikes the imperial bell."

[663]

Chan master Tong read the *Lankavatara Scripture* over a thousand times but did not understand the three bodies and fourfold knowledge. He paid respects to the Sixth Patriarch and sought interpretation of these doctrines. The patriarch said, "As for the three bodies, the pure reality body is your essence; the fulfilled reward body is your knowledge; and the hundred thousand billion projection bodies are your activities. If you speak of the three bodies apart from your own essence, this is called embodiment without knowledge. If you realize the three bodies have no identity of their own, this is called enlightenment with fourfold knowledge. Listen to my verse."

> Inherent essence contains three bodies;
> When you discover them, that forms fourfold knowledge.

Without departing from objects of perception,
You rise transcendent to the state of Buddhahood.

"I have now explained for you; believe assuredly, and you'll never get confused. Don't imitate those who run in search talking about enlightenment all day."

Tong said, "May I hear about the meaning of the fourfold knowledge?"

The patriarch said, "Once you understand the three bodies, you understand the fourfold knowledge—why ask further? If you speak of the fourfold knowledge apart from the three bodies, this is called having knowledge with no embodiment, so this having knowledge turns into having no knowledge. I will again utter a verse."

> The great round mirror knowledge is purity of essence;
> The knowledge of equality is mind without illness.
> Observing knowledge sees, not as a result of effort;
> Knowledge for accomplishing tasks is the same as the round
>   mirror.
> Five and eight, six and seven, effect and cause revolve;
> It's just use of terminology, with no substantive nature.
> If you do not keep feelings on the revolving,
> Flourishing, you'll always be in dragon concentration.

Tong bowed in thanks and expressed praise in a verse:

> The three bodies are originally my being;
> The fourfold knowledge is clarity of the basic mind.
> Body and knowledge merge without hindrance,
> Responding to people, freely adapting.
> Initiating cultivation is all arbitrary action;
> Maintaining stasis is not true refinement.
> The subtle message understood through the teacher,
> Finally I've lost defiling terms.

TRANSLATOR'S NOTE

"Five and eight, six and seven"—five refers to the basic sense consciousnesses, which are the channels of the operation of the knowledge for accomplishing tasks; eight refers to the repository consciousness, which becomes the mirror knowledge. Six refers to the cognitive sense, seven to the intellectual consciousness; these are the channels of the observing knowledge and knowledge of equality. The four-scroll Chinese translation of the *Lankavatara Scripture* originally used in the Chan school is notoriously obscure and went out of fashion in a few generations.

[664]

Master Wuzu Yan said to an assembly,

Talking about Buddha, expounding the teaching, taking up the gavel, standing up the whisk—white clouds for thousands of miles. Deshan would strike as soon as anyone entered the door, Linji would shout as soon as anyone entered the door—white clouds for thousands of miles. After that, "thus" won't do, "not thus" won't do, "thus and not thus" won't do at all—this is also white clouds for thousands of miles. If someone should suddenly come forth and say, "Elder, your speaking this way is also white clouds for thousands of miles," this talk is called a dwarf watching a performance, following people up and down. After thirty years it will be a laugh. But tell me, laughing at what? Laughing at white clouds for thousands of miles.

A monk asked, "I request the teacher to speak directly, without being blind to the present opportunity."

He said, "Kneading together, cutting apart."

He also said to the assembly,

Root and branch must return to the source; noble and base use their language. A sharp sword is hurled into space; a big stick hits a rat.

[665]

As Yunyan was sweeping the ground, Daowu said, "Why so busy?" Yunyan said, "You should know there is one who is not busy." Daowu said, "If so, then there is a second moon." Yunyan stood up the broom and said, "Which moon is this?" Daowu then stopped.

Xuansha said, "If I had seen him at that time, I'd have said to him, 'This is precisely the second moon.'"

Yunmen said, "When the manservant sees the maid, he is polite."

Zhenru said, "He uses diligence to compensate for clumsiness. Of those three sayings—one can settle heaven and earth, one can test patchrobed monks, one can deal with beginners. Can you distinguish? If you can distinguish them, I'll allow that you've personally seen me. If you can't distinguish, don't say this mountain is steep; from across the river gaze afar at the quiet of the blue clouds."

[666]

Master Dongshan Chu said to an assembly,

To bring out the vehicle of the source and express the great teaching, it is necessary to have thorough clarity of vision of truth. Only then can you discern black and white. Because truth and falsehood have the same source, and water and milk are in the same container, when you get here it's hard to distinguish them. I always use the eye within the mind to observe appearances outside the body; observing over and over, then I distinguish true and false. Otherwise, what do you call a teacher? A teacher drives off the plowman's ox, takes away the hungry man's food—only then is one called a teacher. Right now, who in the world is a real teacher? Chan worthies, how many teachers have you called on? This is not an idle matter—you need to investigate thoroughly and see all the way through. When a thousand sages cannot testify, only then is a great person revealed. Have you not seen how old Shakyamuni was greatly enlightened when the morning star appeared, and all the living beings on earth simultaneously attained Buddhahood? Isn't this comprehensive? But even so, if he met a clear-eyed patchrobed monk, he'd still deserve a whack on the back.

A monk asked, "When Vimalakirti held up four worlds, where was he himself?"

The master said, "Behind you."

The monk said, "Why would he be behind me?"

The master said, "Return the statement to me."

"How is it when spotless, with no traces?"

"A pointed measure cannot measure it completely."

"What is a patchrobed monk's proper concern?"

"A camel crosses the Han River."

"What is an expression of hindrance?"

"Bodhidharma has no front teeth."

[667]

When Deshan came to Guishan, he went directly to the teaching hall with his seat cloth under his arm, crossed from west to east and east to west, looked around and said, "Nothing, nothing," then left. When he got to the gate, he said, "Still, it won't do to be crude." Then he went back ceremoniously to meet. As Guishan sat there, Deshan held up his seat cloth and said, "Master . . ." Guishan made to pick up his whisk. Deshan shouted and abruptly left; turning his back on the teaching hall, he put on his sandals and went. That evening Guishan asked the head monk, "Where is the newcomer who arrived earlier?" The head monk said, "At that time he turned his back on the teaching hall, put on his sandals, and left." Guishan said, "Later on this guy will make a reed hut atop a solitary peak and scold Buddhas and revile patriarchs."

Dahui said, "The two venerable adepts, in meeting like this, each lost one eye."

[668]

Dahui said to an assembly,

An ancient said, "Great knowledge has no discrimination; great function has no pattern or preoccupation. It is like the moon reflected in a thousand rivers, like waves going along with a multitude of waters." Now then, which is the great knowledge that has no discrimination? Which is the great function that has no pattern or preoccupation? Is it not that eloquence like a waterfall that gives ten answers to every question is great knowledge? Is it not that things like coarse words and fine sayings all referring to ultimate truth, overturning seats, scattering crowds with shouts, giving a slap across the jaw, abruptly leaving, immediately blocking as soon as there is hesitation thinking are great function? If you make this kind of interpretation, don't say you're a patchrobed monk; you can't even be a menial picking up sandals and lugging a sack of antiques in the school of patchrobed monks.

A teacher is really enlightened, with genuine realization; if the great teaching is unclear, when you try to help people you won't avoid directing them with your own subjective understanding and your own subjective realization, blinding people's eyes. How much the more literalist types without enlightenment or realization blind people—it goes without saying.

This matter is very difficult; when immeasurably great people get here, they have no place to plant their feet. You devils with small faculties and no knowledge, how dare you carelessly open your mouth? Try sitting in quietude assessing minutely—in your heart, have you actually arrived at a state where you do not doubt? If you haven't yet really arrived, on the other hand I would commend your letting go and holding still, not letting yourself be diverted by other people. Those who do this sort of thing are called the dregs of hell. Patrons all over bring a grain of rice, a stalk of vegetable, and offer them to you, just hoping your work on the Way will be completed and you'll head alike to the vehicle of Buddhahood, seeking rewards in another lifetime in another age. If your work on the Way is not clear, how can you digest this?

If you are determined to succeed to the way of this school, it is necessary for mind and environment to be as one before you have a little bit of accord. Hearing me say something like this, don't immediately close your eyes and play dead, forcibly arranging your mind to be at one with the environment. In this, no matter how you try, how can you arrange it? Do you want to attain genuine unity of mind and environment? You just need to make a complete break and resolute cutoff, take away what forms false imagination in your skull, cut off the eighth consciousness in one sword stroke, naturally, not applying arrangement.

Haven't you seen the saying of Master Yantou that whenever you have an object of esteem, it becomes a nest? You people who have spent your whole lives in monasteries investigating this matter without attainment are not worth talking about. A lot of those with white hair and yellow teeth still sit in a nest, unable to get out all their lives, totally unaware of their error. Those who get a taste for the sayings of people of old make extraordinary sayings and wonderful statements into a nest. Those who get a taste for the terminology and interpretation of scriptural teachings make scriptural teachings into a nest. Those who get a taste for the cases of people of old make the ancients' dialogues, substitute sayings, alternative sayings, words of praise, and words of censure into nests. Those who get a taste for the nature of mind make "the triple world is only thought, myriad things are only perceptions" into a nest. Those who get a taste for a state of quiescent silence without words or speech make a nest of closing the eyes and sitting in a ghost cave in a mountain of darkness on the other side of the prehistoric Buddhas. Those who get a taste for the goings-on of daily activities make a nest of raising their eyebrows, blinking their eyes, and alerting attention. Those who get a taste for saying it is not in speech, not in sense or consciousness, not in activity, mistakenly taking conditioned consciousness for Buddha-nature, make the flash of sparks or lightning into a nest.

All the aforementioned have esteem for what they have gotten a taste for. If you do not have a strong will and discipline to step back and realize your error, you will imagine what you esteem to be extraordinary, imagine it to be mysterious and marvelous, imagine it to be peace and security, imagine it to be ultimate, imagine it to be liberation. Those who enter-tain such imaginations could not be helped even if the Buddha appeared in the world. In the teachings this is called the confusion of ignorance and benightedness. Why? Because you are ignorant you cling to error and consider it right. Because you are benighted you remain plunged into what you esteem and cannot budge.

If you do not produce anything in your mind, and are not fixated on anything, then you have no object of esteem. When you have no object of esteem, you naturally have no greed and no dependence on things, inde-pendent in the midst of things, with bare-boned strength.

If you want such accord right now, it is not difficult; just be equani-mous in mind, unaffected by anything. What is affectation? Formulating concepts of sentient beings, concepts of Buddha, concepts of the mun-dane, concepts of the transcendental, concepts of seeking detachment, concepts of seeking enlightened knowledge. These are all called affec-tations. Just concentrate intensely on the brink of arousal, and leap out in one jump—this mind will be clear, independently liberated. Then as soon as you sense this, turn upward, and you will spontaneously be lucid everywhere; it will be evident in everything.

When you manage to reach such a state, don't keep taking note of it. If you keep taking note of it, then you'll have an object of esteem. As soon as you have an object of esteem, this mind leaks. This is just called a leaking mind, not an equanimous mind.

Equanimity means equanimous toward good and bad, equanimous toward turning away and turning to, equanimous toward principle and phenomena, equanimous toward ordinary and holy, equanimous toward the finite and the infinite, equanimous toward substance and function. This principle is only known to those who realize it experientially. If you haven't realized experientially, you simply must get experiential real-ization. Only when you've attained experiential realization can you be called real home-leavers. If your mind does not experience realization and you grasp realization outside of mind, this is called an outsider who has left home; you are not fit to be a monk.

This mind is vast, unlimited, boundless. Countless Buddhas attaining true enlightenment, mountains, rivers, earth, and all forms and all things are not beyond this mind. This mind can name everything, but nothing can name this mind. Therefore the Buddhas and the patriarchs have no choice but to assign names according to your confusion, calling it reality as is, Buddha-nature, enlightenment, nirvana—they impose various different names. Because your views in the world of living beings are biased, there are various distinctions; that is why these different terms are set up, to get you to perceive this undifferentiated mind in the midst of distinctions. It is not that this mind has distinctions.

Therefore when a monk asked Mazu, "What is Buddha?" Mazu said, "Mind itself is Buddha." If you truly realize and truly awaken, what distinctions are there? If you seek extraordinary understanding without enlightenment, you do not truly realize and truly awaken, and do not believe this mind is certainly Buddha—this "mind is Buddha" becomes a causal condition of distinction.

Buddha said, "If you want to use similes for expression, there is ultimately no simile to which this can be likened." This talk of vastness is already limiting it. How much the more so wanting to enter this vast realm with a limited mind. Even if you manage to enter, it is like dipping water from the ocean with a gourd. Even if the gourd is filled, how much can it contain? However, before the water in the gourd goes into the gourd, it is identical to the measureless water. Because your perspective is just so, you imagine this is plenitude; so this infinite realm also fills you according to the measure of your capacity. It is not that there is only so much water in the immense ocean. Therefore the Buddha has said that the immense ocean does not refuse small streams; from insects to titans, those who drink the water all get filled. This water represents the mind, while the insects and titans represent differences of great and small. There are fundamentally no distinctions in the essence of mind. If you perceive this mind without producing any views, you will also be able to perceive all sorts of distinctions on your own.

Sages of yore did not even allow holding to this mind as real; outside of mind, what real things are there to obstruct you? My trailing mud and water now too is unavoidable, doting, presenting something attractive to

410 Treasury of the Eye of True Teaching

pacify beloved children. Therefore I am pulling out branches and drawing out vines; don't memorize what I say and consider it right. Today I speak this way, but tomorrow I won't speak this way. As soon as you are this way, I am not this way. When you are not this way, I am this way. Where will you look for my dwelling place? I myself don't know anywhere to dwell—how will anyone else find me? This is the living door; only when you have the action of views die out can you enter.

Nowadays students take a little bit of diligence, bowing to Buddha, recitation, and discipline of conduct, speech, and thought for fodder to seek realization. What connection is there? They're much like ignoramuses burying their heads running westward to get something in the east. The more they run, the further away they are; the more they hurry, the later they are. This is a great teaching with no contrivance, no affectation, no effort; if you arouse the slightest thought of getting realization, you run away from it. How can you hope to seek it by a little bit of contrived practice?

So it is that people of old, seeing it so close, said, "I sit there watching you find out," and "I stand there watching you find out." That is, they never taught you to produce a model or draw a likeness, accumulating achievement and piling up merit seeking to accomplish the Way. Even if your quest is accomplished, as soon as it is done it deteriorates; you wear yourself out in vain.

When you see this said, don't then dismiss cause and effect and do hellish deeds, calling constant unconcern having no view of Buddhism, eating when hungry and sleeping when tired and taking this to be having no practice and realization, considering this to be effortlessness. Don't misunderstand: to bear this thing you have to be totally strong, cast of raw iron—how could it be taken up carelessly by your small faculties and small capacity? Haven't you read how Linji asked Huangbo the exact great meaning of Buddhism three times and was beaten three times, then afterward got a pointer from Dayu and suddenly was greatly enlightened; unconsciously he uttered, "Ah, basically there's not much to Huangbo's Buddhism!" Dayu said, "You just said you were trying to find out whether or not you were wrong, but now you say there's not much to Huangbo's Buddhism; what have you seen, that you speak this way?" Linji stuck Dayu twice in the ribs. Then Dayu pushed him away and said, "Your teacher is Huangbo; it's none of my business." Has your study of Chan gotten to be like this yet? Master Yunan said in verse,

> No provisions supplied at all
> For years at a crossroads he fears being further and further away.
> Immediately given threescore painful blows,
> When night comes he lodges as ever in the reed flowers.

He also versified Linji's enlightenment:

> Right off he says Huangbo hasn't much teaching;
> How can a strong man turn away from himself?
> Two fists on the ribs—clearly there's a message;
> It wasn't passed on from Huangbo.

Also Master Duan's verse says,

> Knocking down Yellow Crane Pavilion with one punch,
> Kicking over Parrot Island with one kick,
> Where there is spunk, he adds spunk;
> Where he is inelegant, he is still elegant.

Based on the verses of these two old fellows it is possible to succeed to Linji and be a descendant of Linji, truly, without disgracing or usurping.

Since olden times there has fortunately been such a constitution; why not apply some eye and brain to see what principle this is. This matter is like the bright sun in the blue sky—what obscuration is there? In other places there are exceptional distinctions, the Chan of a dipper-full of ocean, with complicated details: "this saying is examining another," "that saying is finding out," "this saying is not getting hooked on another's line, not going into another's cage," "this saying is interchange of relative and absolute," "this saying is avoidance in the sanctuary, not daring to be direct." There is also a type who take for realization the likes of statements in the *Heroic Progress Scripture, Source Mirror*, and verses of Linji that "what the eyes see and ears hear is all mental—there is nothing else," citing "crossing the mystic peak is not the human world—outside mind there are no things; green mountains fill the eyes," calling this the immediately present matter, calling this the basis, calling this close attention. You undeniably understand well, but if you understand this way, aren't you taking things for mind? Since the mind is your mind, how will you recognize that if you want to?

There is also a type who take Linji's three mysteries and Yunmen's three statements and pursue the expressions to interpret, taking the sayings of the ancestral teachers from the *Transmission of the Lamp* and *Expanded Lamp*, individually categorizing methods, taking the likes of "as soon as a mote of dust arises, the whole earth is contained therein," "in the lion on the tip of a hair, lions on the tips of a hundred billion hairs appear," "the whole earth is a door of liberation, the whole earth is one eye of a monk," "if people know the mind, there's not an inch of soil on the whole earth; mountains, rivers, and land, light and dark, form and void, are all things in the wonderfully clear true mind," and categorize them as the mystery within the substance, the expression containing heaven and earth. They take "a three-legged donkey romps," "sawing apart a balance beam," "an insect swallows a tiger in a fire," "Manjushri gave rise to the notion of Buddha and the notion of Dharma and was banished to two iron enclosing mountains," "the eastern mountain walks on water," "hide the body in the North Star," generally anything that can't be explained in words, and say "a mosquito climbs an iron ox; no place for you to get your beak into," calling this type "the mystery within an expression" and "expression that cuts off all streams." They take the likes of "stepping on a balance beam, hard as iron," "mountains are mountains, waters are waters," "when going, just go; when sitting, just sit," "a long month is thirty days, a short one twenty-nine," and call them "the mystery within mystery," and "expression of going along with the waves." Haven't you seen Master Fenyang's verse saying,

The three mysteries and three essentials are hard to distinguish in fact;
When you get the meaning and forget the words, the Way is easy
  to draw near.
One expression very clearly includes myriad forms;
On the ninth day of the ninth month the chrysanthemum flowers are new.

This old master has clearly pointed out the marrow of Linji to you,
but you come back adding line-by-line interpretations, saying "the three
mysteries and three essentials are hard to distinguish in fact" is a comprehensive versification; "when you get the meaning and forget the words,
the Way is easy to draw near" is "the mystery within the substance," "one
expression very clearly includes myriad forms" is "the mystery within
the expression," "on the ninth day of the ninth month the chrysanthemum flowers are new" is the "mystery within the mystery." There were
among our predecessors those who were famous and had genuine enlightenment, but incompetents who don't understand the great teaching and have no teacher's transmission blind people like this. As for the
rest, the hucksters, they are nothing to talk about. I imagine old Fenyang
wouldn't nod. He clearly tells you that the three mysteries and three essentials are in fact hard to distinguish; when you get the meaning and
forget the words, the Way is easily approached. One expression clearly
includes myriad forms; on the ninth day of the ninth month the chrysanthemum blossoms are new. This having been said, if you go on to add a
handle to a bowl, don't say you have a great reputation, great eloquence,
and great knowledge. If even the great teacher Bodhidharma came forth
and acted like this, he should be arrested and buried alive, to avoid letting him spoil the men and women of other people's families.

One blind person leads many blind people. When asked about the
three essentials and they can't explain, then they equate this with Deshan carrying his bowl, Yantou's last word, Nanquan's killing a cat,
Baizhang's wild fox, Guizong's killing a snake, Dasui's burning off a field,

Zhaozhou's checking the woman and checking the hermits, Muzhou's "carrying a board," Ministry President Chen Cao testing monks, Xuansha's "I dare say the old brother isn't through yet," Dongshan's "you've said it all right, but you've only said eighty percent," and Bodhidharma's returning west with one shoe—they call all examples like this "the last word," and cite Luopu's saying, "At the last word you finally arrive at the impenetrable barrier." "Cutting off the essential ford, not letting ordinary or holy pass," "let the whole world delight happily—I alone do not agree" they call, "I am king of Dharma, independent in respect to Dharma." "You students may freely exercise all your spiritual powers and show all your skills; I will just hold you still and not allow you" they call the impenetrable barrier. They just wait to be promoted to set up a community and be abbot of a monastery, giving transmission from mouth to ear in a closed room. Types like this destroy the right basis themselves, and instead carry on bedeviling talk.

There is also a type who say stories like Nanquan killing a cat, Baizhang's wild fox, Guizong's killing a snake, Dasui's burning off a field, or Zhaozhou's testing a woman and testing hermits are setup methods, and there were actually no such events, wishing to entrap students.

There is also a type who take interchange of relative and absolute to be the message of the school. For example, as Dongshan and Yunju were crossing a stream, Dongshan asked, "How deep is the water?" Yunju said, "Not wet." Dongshan said, "Crude man." Yunju asked back, "How deep is the water?" Dongshan said, "Not dry." They say "water" is a euphemism for "wet," and to directly say "wet" and not be able to interchange is called being a crude person; when Yunju instead said, "Not wet," this was violating the taboo and hence inability to interchange; Dongshan's saying "not dry" is the wordless within words: what are words? "Not dry." What is called the wordless? "Not dry." "Not dry" means "wet"—these are living words, because they are able to interchange and not violate the taboo.

They also use black and white circles to make descriptions of the five ranks. They take a totally black circle to be "the other side of the prehistoric Buddhas," "before being born," "before the empty eon," "before chaos is differentiated," calling it the absolute state. They use a circle two parts black and one part white for the relative within the absolute, resorting to the white part to explain the black part, yet not allowing touching upon the word "black," as touching upon the word "black" would be violating a taboo. They go on to cite Dongshan's verse saying, "The relative within the absolute; in the third watch, at the beginning of the night, before the moon is bright," and call it ability to associate, just saying "the third watch" is black, "the beginning of night" is black, "before the moon is bright" is black—it doesn't say black, but only says "the third watch," "the beginning of night," and "before the moon is bright." This is ability to interchange and not violate the taboo name. They take a circle two parts white and one part black to be "the absolute within the relative," resorting to the black part to explain the white, not allowing touching upon the content of the white, saying that "The absolute within the relative; an old woman who's slept late comes upon the antique mirror" is ability to associate the words "bright" and "white" and not violate the taboo name. This is because "slept late" is light within dark, so "antique mirror" is also light within dark. An old woman's head is white—it doesn't say white, but says "old woman," in which "white" is implied; this is because of being able to associate the word "white."

They also explain the verse on coming from within the absolute, which says, "Coming from within the absolute; there is a road within nothingness, apart from the dust," or "leaving the dust," saying that whenever there are spoken expressions they are all pronounced from within nothingness and hence inherently contain the subtle. None do not come from the absolute state; whether light or dark, whether reaching or arriving, all subtly carry communion with the source. Each rank includes these five things, like a hand's five fingers, no less, no more. "Arriving in both" they say includes black and white, relative and absolute, thus arriving. What does arriving mean? It is like someone returning home and arriving at another job before getting there. This refers to helping people on the way. It is also able to associate the subtle before embodiment. "Attainment in both" they say includes the preceding four ranks, all containing subtlety and winding up in the rank of the absolute.

They call this "after all coming back to sit in the ashes," thus also expressing the black in the final analysis, while interchanging the word black, saying "ashes" instead of "black."

Some also say Caoshan had a statement that "the absolute state is the realm of emptiness, where there is nothing at all; the relative state is the realm of form, in which there are myriad forms of all kinds. Arriving in both is leaving phenomena and entering into noumenon. Coming from within the absolute is turning away from noumenon and going to phenomena. Including both is mysteriously responding to all conditions without going along with existents, neither defiled nor pure, with no absolute or relative. So it is called the essential path of open mystery, the true school with no attachments. The worthies of the past since time immemorial have considered this state most subtle, most mysterious; it is necessary to thoroughly discern its actuality." They also say the five ranks all are three-character expressions, relative and absolute, higher and lower, interchanging without violating the center, the center being the absolute state; expounding noumenon, expounding phenomena, there are clear passages in the teachings. Is the path of direct pointing transmitted alone outside doctrine actually like this? If it is actually like this, what good old Caoshan are you looking for?

They also cite Fushan's eulogy on the image of Dayang; where it says, "A black dog flashes silver claws," their own comment is that this says there is the relative state within the absolute, the "black dog" being the absolute and "flashing silver claws" being the relative. "A white elephant ridden by the Kunlun Mountains," their own comment is that this says there is the absolute within the relative. "There is no interference in these two," their own comment says this speaks of not falling into existence or nonexistence, hence Dongshan's saying, "Who presumes to harmonize without falling into being or nonbeing?" "A wooden horse neighs in fire," their own comment says subtlety is held in it, and emptiness and mystery expound the Way; this kind of talk requires you to burn your head and burn your arm and vow not to pass it on at random before it is transmitted. They also call this the last word.

[Snapping his fingers:] Fine "concealing color Chan"—if you are one with blood under your skin, would you be willing to consume this tea and rice? I ask you, on the last day of the last month, when the four gross elements are about to disintegrate, can what you have learned all along by memorization be kept in mind? When you can keep it in mind, do you pay attention? At such a time, consciousness is already dim—how can you keep anything in mind? Since you can't, you'll surely enter the wombs of donkeys, the bellies of horses, experiencing retribution for what you have done. At this time, even if you want to "touch upon the taboo name" or be a "crude person," you can't; how indeed can you fend off birth and death?

There is also discussion of Dongshan's saying to the community, "How is the time of proceeding? How is the time of service? How is the time of achievement? How is the time of collective achievement? How is the time of achievement over achievement?" At the time a monk asked, "What is proceeding?" Dongshan said, "How is it when eating meals?" "What is serving?" Dongshan said, "How is it when turning away?" "What is achievement?" Dongshan said, "How is it when putting down the hoe?" "What is collective achievement?" Dongshan said, "Not apprehending form." "What is achievement over achievement?" Dongshan said, "Not collective." "How is the time of proceeding?" means proceeding to this task. The answer "How is it when eating?" means this task should not be interrupted, without working while eating. "How is the time of service?"—service means taking on service, like someone serving superiors, first expressing respect and then taking on service. Proceeding is established by achievement; as soon as there is proceeding, there is the duty of taking on service. The answer "How is it when turning away?" means this task is uninterrupted; as when serving it is so, when turning away it is also thus. "Turning away" means service, because service and turning away are both accomplishments. "How is the time of achievement?"—achievement is function. As for the answer "How is it when putting down the hoe," taking up the hoe is function, putting down the hoe is absence of function. Dongshan means function and no function are both accomplishments. This also means no interruption. "How is the time of collective achievement?" means Dharma and objects are opposed. The answer "not apprehending form" means Dharma and objects cannot become uniform. The very time of function reveals that which has no function; no function is function. If they are made uniform, this is the dead word of total completeness; Dongshan's teaching avoids completeness, so he says "not apprehending form"—this is the living word. "How is the time of achievement over achievement?" means Dharma and objects are all empty. This is called great effortless liberation. Therefore he said, "Not collective"—nothing can be associated. The meaning of noncollectivity all goes back to accomplishment, like the interpenetration of phenomena in the reality realm. "There is no one before you, no you before me." That is why Jiashan said, "There is no one here, no you there." Such talk is all proceeding and taking up service in daily activities, in walking, standing, sitting, and lying down, fulfilling the mundane and the transcendental, managing everything. This is called the five ranks of accomplishment.

Tell me, was the ancients' meaning actually like this? If so, what is extraordinary about it? These are just complications passed on by word of mouth and handed on by thought. Since it was not like this, what was the ancients' meaning after all? I add a footnote for you, wanting everyone to check. Haven't you seen Fenyang's saying, "The face is there— I leave it to you to discern." Therefore Vimalakirti said, "Just get rid of the disease, don't get rid of the method." Also, the *Heroic Progress Scripture* says, "If you listen to the teaching with an objectifying mind, the teaching is also an object." Although the sayings of the ancients were extending compassion, they were all prior to excretion. Coming to the likes of the three mysteries, three essentials, four choices, ten equal realities of knowledge, this principle also applies. When I talk like this, I'm not tearing down everyone else; I just want people involved to distinguish the initiate and the naive.

There's also another kind—"It's not in words; it's not in the cases of the ancients; it's not in the nature of mind; it's not in mystic subtlety; it's not in being or nonbeing, gain or loss. It's like fire—touch it, and you get burned. It is not standing apart from reality—right where you are is reality. Taking up what comes to hand, you transcend present and past. One statement comes, one statement goes; in the end one statement is left over—this is getting the advantage." People like this are just playing with the mass of ignorance of conditioned consciousness; so they say there is no cause and effect, no consequences, and no person and no Buddha, that drinking alcohol and eating meat do not hinder enlightenment, that theft and lechery do not inhibit wisdom. Followers like this are indeed insects on the body of a lion, consuming the lion's flesh. This is what Yongjia called "opening up to emptiness denying cause and effect, crude and unrestrained, bringing on disaster."

There is also a type who evaluate cases of the ancients and call this the work of needle and thread; they also call this the Chan of scholarly youth. For example, they evaluate the woman coming out of absorption in these terms: "Manjushri was the teacher of seven Buddhas; why couldn't he get the woman out of concentration?" "Manjushri and the woman had no affinity." "Netted Light was a bodhisattva of the first stage; why was he able to get the woman out of concentration?" "He had affinity with the woman." They make the remark, "An enemy has a chief; a debt has a creditor." There is also discussion that says, "Manjushri shouldn't have thought—that's why he couldn't get her out. Netted Light had no ideas, therefore he got her out." They make the remark, "When there is intentional function, there must be error; when there is no willful seeking, then it's clear." There is also discussion saying, "Why couldn't Manjushri get the woman out of concentration? The handle of the ladle was in the woman's hand. Why was Netted Light able to get her out? It was like insects chewing wood." They also say, "He used the wind to fan the fire." They also say, "What can be done about the woman?" Extreme misinterpretations include those such as adopting a posture of entering concentration and acting like emerging from concentration, giving a shove, snapping the fingers and wailing "heavens" several times, "Please accept an offering," and brushing out the sleeves and leaving abruptly. When observed coolly, this is mortifying.

Also, Baqiao said, "If you have a staff, I give you a staff. If you have no staff, I take the staff away." They evaluate this, saying, "If you are this kind of person, I speak this way to you—this is 'giving you a staff.' If you are not this kind of person, I switch your eyes face to face—this is 'taking away your staff.'" They remark, "He measures abilities to assign jobs." They also say, "Seeing a tower, he hit the tower." There are also those who evaluate it in these terms: "Having and not having, giving and taking away, are capturing and releasing students." Opinionated interpretations like this are very common.

The foregoing explanations are all oral tradition, handing on thoughts, slogans, complications, set on printing blocks, produced out of models; not only are they self-repudiating, they also insult the people of old. This is the Chan of a gourd of ocean water, learned in various places. Do you believe completely? Haven't you heard it said, "When extending compassion, then there are teachings; no teaching does not extend compassion." "Recognize the meaning on the hook; don't acknowledge the zero point."

My way of teaching is oyster Chan; when the mouth is opened you see the heart, liver, and guts—unusual valuables and extraordinary gems are all before you. When the mouth is closed, where will you look for a gap in it? It is not forced—the teaching is fundamentally like this.

Time is to be valued; take advantage of robust physical strength to concentrate intensely to understand. Don't take a liking to the exceptional—the exceptional cheats people; mixed poison is in the consciousness. Sometime later on don't say you've gained power; when you die without glimpsing liberation, how can you talk about opposing birth and death?

The ignorance and afflictions of the world have limits; the moment you recognize this, their very being is extinct. Wrong knowledge, wrong views, the afflictions of religion as an object are unlimited; they can obstruct the eye of the Way and make your mind restless day and night, insulting Buddha, Dharma, and Sangha, creating hellish karma. Though it is a good cause, it brings on bad results.

If you are actually strong people with wisdom, only then will you discern thoroughly and not be afflicted by others. Haven't you heard how

Yunmen said, "Take the whole universe all at once and put it on your eye-lids"? When you hear this kind of talk, I dare not hope you'll come forth and hastily give me a clout. For now take your time to look at it closely: Does it exist? Does it not? What principle is this? Even if you can under-stand, here in the school of patchrobed monks you deserve to get your legs broken. If you are an individual, when you hear it said, "Where are there seasoned adepts appearing in the world?" you should directly spit in my ears and eyes. If you don't have this ability, even understanding as soon as you hear someone bring it up you have already fallen into the secondary. And haven't you heard of Master Luoshan having said, "The mystic school has no dogma; it does not set up regulations"? If you want to seek, look before it's voiced.

Buddhists, the true mind has no fixation; true wisdom has no bounda-ries. If I were to flap my lips talking continuously from today throughout all time to come, I still wouldn't borrow someone else's energy. This is something inherent in everyone; it cannot be augmented, cannot be re-duced. When Buddhas and patriarchs realize it, it is called the Dharma door of great liberation; when ordinary people miss it, it is called the af-flictions of troubling over sense objects. However, when gotten it has never been gotten, and when missed has never been lost. Getting and losing are in the person, not in the reality. Therefore an ancestral teacher said, "The ultimate Way has no difficulty; just avoid picking and choos-ing. Just don't hate and love, and it is thoroughly clear. The slightest de-viation is as the distance between sky and earth. If you want it to appear, don't keep following or opposing." You Channists have each memorized this—but have you ever paid attention and understood? The ancestral teacher put a name on it, calling it a poem on faith in mind, just wanting people to believe this vast peaceful subtle mind is certainly not obtained from another. Therefore in it he says, "If the one mind is not aroused, myriad things are blameless. No fault, no dogma, not aroused, not mind-ing—the subject disappears along with objects; objects disappear along with the subject. Objects are objects depending on the subject; the sub-ject is the subject depending on objects."

It also says, "The essence of the Great Way is broad, with no ease, no difficulty." It also says, "When you cling to it you lose measure and will surely enter false paths; let it go naturally and the essence has no going or staying." You just trust this teaching of one mind; don't grasp, don't reject—then you should let body and life go here. If you can't let go, your faculties are slow and dull. On the last day of your life, don't make the mistake of suspecting me.

The season is hot; you've been standing a long time. [Shouting once, he got down from the seat.]

Select Glossary of Names and Terms

[A]

Acceptance of no origin—realization of all phenomena as interconnected, nothing occurring independently.

Accumulation of Fragrance—name of a Buddha-land, or field of awareness, appearing in the popular scripture *Vimalakirti's Advice*; see Cleary, *Vimalakirti's Advice*.

Adamantine sword—also called diamond or precious sword, stands for insight and wisdom, cutting through illusion.

Amitabha—"Infinite Light," name of the meditation Buddha especially invoked by Pure Land Buddhists, said to preside over a Buddha-land called Sukhavati, "Blissful," in the remote west, the direction of the setting sun, which symbolizes the ending of life, either by ordinary death or mystic death, internal quiescence, at which time Amitabha is believed to welcome the devotee into the world of bliss.

Ancient mirror—pristine awareness, simply reflecting being as such without interpretation or conceptual overlay.

Ashes—symbolize detachment, dispassion, equanimity, nirvana; "ashes on my head, dirt on my face" represents inward detachment with outward engagement.

[B]

Beating the grass to scare the snakes—teachers' words or acts intended to elicit reactions to gauge the mentality or state of students.

Bird's path—the practice of detachment; see "The Three Roads of Tung Shan" in Cleary and Cleary, *The Blue Cliff Record*, "Traditional Teaching Devices."

Birth and death—arising and passing away of thoughts, states, and conditions of existence; commonly used as a general term for mundane existence.

Blind baldies—renunciants in form only, monastic careerists without enlightenment.

Blue-eyed foreign monk—refers to Bodhidharma.

Bodhidharma—regarded as the founder of Chan in China.

Bodhisattva—*bodhi* means enlightenment, *sattva* means being or essence; bodhisattvas are typically characterized as working for universal enlightenment. According to the scripture on perfect wisdom *Questions of Suvikrantavikramin*, "This practice of the bodhisattva, that is the practice of perfect insight, is unexcelled, clear, unsurpassed, transcendent.... This practice of the bodhisattva, namely the practice of perfect insight, is the practice of rising above all worlds"; see Cleary, *Zen and the Art of Insight*.

Bow falls into a wine cup—a reflection of a bow in a cup of wine looks to the drinker like a snake in the wine; the drinker gets sick, but then sees the bow hung on the wall, realizes the "snake" was a reflection of the bow, and, relieved of the influence of his false perception, recovers his well-being.

Brahma—in Hindu cosmology, Brahma as a god represents the creative force.

Buddha Victorious by Great Penetrating Knowledge—a figure in a story in the *Lotus Sutra*, said to have sat on the site of enlightenment for ten eons without fulfilling Buddhahood; see example 9 in Cleary, *Unlocking the Zen Koan*.

Buddha-nature—potential for enlightenment, regarded as inherent in all living beings.

Burning Lamp Buddha—symbol of the essential nature of awareness, mythically represented as an ancient Buddha in whose presence the historical Buddha Shakyamuni originally vowed to attain enlightenment.

[C]

Cao Valley—Caoqi, refers to the Sixth Patriarch of Chan; see Cleary, *The Sutra of Hui-neng.*

Celestial devil—conceptual consciousness; said to dwell in the "heaven of free use of others' emanations"—that is, using the data from the organs and consciousnesses of the senses to construct subjective perceptions, conceptions, ideas, and attitudes.

Cessation—stilling the mind, stopping the flow of thought; see Cleary, *Stopping and Seeing,* and *Body, Mind, and Breath: A Meditation Handbook.*

Circle—symbol of completeness, no beginning or end, Buddha-nature; for a detailed treatment of the use of circular figures, see Cleary, *The Five Houses of Zen,* "The House of Kuei-Yang," by Sun-chi.

Clothing sticking to the body—mental baggage, persistent mental habits, fixed ideas, attachments.

Clusters and elements—ordinary existence in the world, living beings and their experiences.

Complete all-at-once teaching—the teaching of the *Flower Ornament* school, based on the all-in-one, one-in-all vision of the *Flower Ornament Scripture.*

Concentration and insight—two complementary essential ingredients of meditation; "stopping and seeing."

Concentration of heroic progress—a state of concentration from which it is possible to enter into all states of concentration.

Counterfeit wisdom—secondhand understanding, imitation.

Crouching lion—power, potential.

Cyprus tree in the yard—being as is, thusness; see case 37 in Cleary, *Unlocking the Zen Koan.*

[D]

Danxia burned the wooden Buddha—while temporarily lodging in a temple on his travels one winter, Master Danxia burned an effigy to keep warm, greatly discomfiting the abbot. This story is used to illustrate the difference between enlightenment as a personal experience and what amounts to idolatry or religiosity as an attribute of ego; for a treatment of this story, see case 25 in Cleary, *The Empty Valley Collection.*

Dayu Range—a reference to the Sixth Patriarch of Chan; instructed by the

Fifth Patriarch to flee jealous monks, he was overtaken by pursuers on the Dayu Range. See Cleary, *The Sutra of Hui-neng*.

Dead tree—detachment, dispassion, nirvana.

Dead word—expressions only understood literally or conceptually, not experientially, or expression that "explains" so much as to induce complacency and fail to stimulate or induce the "doubt" used to break through automatic association. Baizhang said, "Now if you create an idea of Buddha, create an understanding of Buddha, as long as there is anything envisioned, anything sought, it's all called the excrement of fabricated conceptualizations. It's also called crude speech, and it is called dead words."

Degenerate teaching—the final age of a teaching, last of three periods, referred to as true, imitation, and ending. In the period of true teaching there are both practice and realization; in the imitation age, only practice, without realization; in the final age, neither practice nor realization. This typically tracks a process of institutionalization, in which the original spiritual science is turned into a religion, and then into a path of personal prestige and profit.

Demonic activity—delusion, deception.

Dependent understanding—understanding or interpretation that is not direct firsthand perception.

Deshan's staff—reference to a practice of the famous Master Deshan striking a student strategically to cut off thought, bringing attention to the immediate present, used generally to represent the impact of experience or existence.

Donkey-tethering stake—a statement that may be useful for sustained concentration, or a statement that becomes a hindrance due to fixation.

Donkey's womb, horse's belly—mundane existence, life in the world.

Dragon concentration—ability to remain focused and stable while in the midst of the turbulence of the world.

Dragon Gate—the threshold of awakening of enlightenment.

Dragons—used in reference to people, dragons, or dragons and elephants, represent outstanding Chan practitioners. Dragons can also refer to water spirits, especially rain-making celestials.

Dragon's head, snake's tail—starting out well, ending up incompetent. (Snakes turning into dragons, in contrast, refers to wisdom becoming manifest.)

Drawing legs on a snake—unnecessary elaboration, or imposition of imagination.

Dwelling at the peak—attachment to detachment, clinging to nirvana.

[E]

Eight inversions—eight misconceptions: considering the impermanent to be permanent, the unpleasant to be pleasant, what is not self to be self, what is impure to be pure; what is permanent to be impermanent, what is pleasant to be unpleasant, self as not self, and what is pure to be impure.

Emptiness—according to Nagarjuna (considered an ancestor of Chan) in the *Mulamadhyamakarika,* "Emptiness is said by the Victors [Buddhas] to be departure from all views; yet it is said that those who have the view of emptiness are incorrigible." He also wrote, "When something occurs dependently, it is inherently quiescent." And, "Emptiness wrongly understood destroys the slow-witted." The *Treatise on the Great Scripture on Perfect Insight* says, "People who see into true emptiness have previously practiced immeasurable charity, discipline, and concentrated meditation, so their hearts are soft and their bonds and compulsions are slight. After getting to be like this they attain true emptiness. In a false view of emptiness there is no such thing—there is only the desire to grasp emptiness with the mind warped by subjective thought and imagination"; Cleary, *Zen and the Art of Insight.*

Entry—initial awakening, access to enlightenment.

Essence—essence is sometimes used to refer to the essence of awareness, particularly as distinct from function; it is also used to refer to the essence of phenomena as distinct from appearances.

Ethereal being—existence as identical to emptiness.

Expedients—temporary methods to inspire and guide, adjusted to potentials and circumstances.

Eye of reality—direct perception, accurate insight.

[F]

Few Houses—name of a mountain, a reference to Bodhidharma.

First, second, and third statement—(1) direct perception; (2) deduction; and (3) learning.

Five clusters—the mortal body-mind.

Five positions—a teaching device associated with the Cao Dong school of Chan: the relative within the absolute, the absolute within the relative, coming from within the absolute, arrival in the relative, and arrival in both relative and absolute together.

Five powers—extraordinary abilities attributed to advanced yogis and arhats: clairvoyance, clairaudience, mind-reading, knowledge of past lives, and spiritual flight.

Flowers in the sky—illusions.

Forest of thorns—life in the mundane world, with all its difficulties.

Four fruitions—four stages of realization in lesser-vehicle Buddhism, known as entry into the stream, once-returner, non-returner, and arhat (saint).

Four gross elements—earth, water, fire, and air; a general reference to material existence.

Four hundred princes—social structure, the conventional world.

Four infinite attitudes—basic attitudes cultivated by bodhisattvas: infinite friendliness, compassion, joyfulness, and equanimity.

Four kinds of formless state—states of absorption practiced in lesser-vehicle Buddhism: infinite consciousness, infinite space, infinite nothingness, and neither perception nor nonperception.

Four meditations and eight concentrations—a combination of ancient yogic systems learned by Buddha before his enlightenment and incorporated into lesser-vehicle Buddhism as expedients.

Four propositions and hundred negations—all propositions of logic.

Fourfold knowledge—four aspects of awareness: mirrorlike knowledge, knowledge of equality, observing knowledge, and practical knowledge; see "The Four Cognitions," in Cleary, *Kensho, the Heart of Zen.*

Foxy charmers—charlatans, deceivers, false teachers.

Freezing the spirit—keeping the mind still.

Frog in a well—a narrow view.

[G]

Gautama—the historical Buddha.

Ghost cave   attachment to quiescence, mental inertia, or vacuity.

Ghosts—nihilists, false students, and false teachers; also, vain imaginings, insubstantial notions, conceptual icons, dead traditions, traditionalists without inspiration. "Hungry ghosts" represent greed.

Glue—attachment, fixation, clinging.

Gold dust—attachment to holiness, spiritual experiences, or religious doctrines. Also called "golden chains."

Golden fish—an enlightened individual.

"Golden Lion" essay—a famous work on Huayan (*Flower Ornament*) Buddhism by the Tang dynasty master Fazang.

Gourd—as a "dipper," a measure, this symbolizes a small capacity, a limited understanding.

Gourd floating on water—a state of fluidity, said of someone who is not attached or fixated anywhere and cannot be pinned down.

Great death—initial attainment of detachment, cessation; in the description of the famous Japanese Zen master Hakuin, "The rank of the relative absolute refers to the absolute state, where you experience the great death, explode, see the Way, and penetrate the noumenon. . . . Space itself vanishes and iron mountains shatter. Above, there is not a single tile to cover your head; below, there is not an inch of earth to stand upon" (Cleary, *Kensho: the Heart of Zen*).

Great immortal of India—Shakyamuni Buddha.

Great Vehicle—Mahayana Buddhism, dedicated to all-knowledge, complete enlightenment, and universal salvation.

Guanyin—a Chinese name of Avalokitesvara, symbol of universal compassion, said to appear in many forms according to the needs of those to be liberated; for the vows of Avalokitesvara, see Cleary, *The Flower Ornament Scripture*, p. 1273 et passim.

Guest and host—guest can mean object or field of perception, in contrast to the "host" perceiver; or it can mean a party to a dialogue, especially a seeker or inquirer; or a phenomenon in relation to another. Guest can also mean function, in contrast to the "host" essence.

[H]

Habit energies—force of habit, mental habit, conditioning.

Half a person—partial realization.

Hanshan and Fenggan—famous eccentrics, representations of wisdom outside convention.

Hired laborer—an image from an allegory in the *Lotus Sutra*, representing followers of the Lesser Vehicle unaware of inherent Buddha-nature.

Horns on a rabbit—superimposed representations, imagination, subjective notions of what does not exist objectively.

Hundred-foot pole—peak experience, detachment, nirvana; see case 46 of the *Wumenguan*, "Stepping Forward atop a Pole," in Cleary, *Unlocking the Zen Koan*.

Hungry man's food—clinging to a particular spiritual state or realization, or to a sustained focus on an object of meditation.

[I]

Indra—Hindu lord of gods.

Insensate void—fixation on a thoughtless state or blank mind, fixation on nothingness.

Iron hammerhead with no hole—ungraspable, impenetrable; also can mean useless.

Iron ox—impenetrable, inscrutable, immovable, unshakable, unaffected.

It—also referred to as "This," immediate actuality, presence directly perceived.

[K]

Kanadeva—successor of Nagarjuna, regarded as an ancestor or patriarch of Chan; see Cleary, *Transmission of Light*, for traditional stories of Nagarjuna and Kanadeva.

Karma—action (physical, verbal, mental), often used in reference to heritage of habit, or ongoing indulgence in accustomed behaviors and resultant perpetuation of bondage.

Kasyapa—successor to the Buddha, regarded as the first ancestor or patriarch of Chan.

Killing sword—cutting off habitual train of thought, stopping the force of mental habits, realization of emptiness.

[L]

Lacquer bucket—ignorance.

Last word—threshold of understanding, limit of conceptual or theoretical knowledge.

Leakage—impulse, attachment, mental involvement with objects.

Leavers of home—renunciants, monastics; also used to refer specifically to the inward state of detachment from force of habit or acquired views.

Legs on a snake—excess, superimposition, imagination, subjective interpretative elaboration.

Level ground—equanimity, cessation, tranquility.

Life after annihilation—same as life-giving sword.

Life-giving sword—wisdom, transition from focus on emptiness or the absolute to focus on the relative, returning to life after the great death.

Lion's milk—realization of ultimate truth.

Listener—follower of the Lesser Vehicle, seeking nirvana as the ultimate goal.

Living word—experiential understanding.

Looking for mind in seven places—a meditation exercise from the *Heroic Progress Scripture*; looking for mind inside, outside, hidden in sense faculties, in the unseen, in encounter, between sense faculties and data, detachment.

[M]

Maitreya—the future Buddha.

Manjushri—supernal bodhisattva representing wisdom.

Mark the boat—from "marking the side of the boat where a sword fell overboard; the sword is long gone," refers to fixation on a particular point, sticking to a specific statement when it no longer applies, when the circumstances of its relevance have passed.

Matanga—an early translator, represented as having introduced Buddhism into China.

Maudgalyayana—one of the Buddha's ten top disciples.

Mental machinations—manipulation of ideas or states.

Merging of Difference and Sameness—a famous work by the great master Shitou; for a translation, see Cleary, *Timeless Spring*.

Mile-high wall—mental stability, being impervious to influences.

Mind ground—essence of awareness, basic mind.

Mind source—mind as the source of representation or description of the world.

Miraculous turtle—a reference to turtle shells anciently used for prognostication. In the Taoist classic *Chuang-tzu* it says that the miraculous turtle would prefer to be dragging its tail in the mud than eviscerated for an ostensibly elevated role; in Chan the image of the miraculous turtle or sacred tortoise dragging its tail in the mud is used to portray residual attachment to spiritual experience, represented as a track or trace of a sense of holiness, or to an idea or concept of sanctity embodied in a particular formulation, doctrine, or practice.

Mirror—immediate awareness.

Mistaking a thief for a son—taking conditioned mentality or its products for inherent basic mind.

Moon—symbol of truth, reality, or clear awareness.

Mount Bear Ear—place of interment of Bodhidharma, founder of Chan.

Mud and water—life in the ordinary world.

Mud ball—material existence.

[N]

Noncontention—tolerance.

Nonstriving—action or repose without impulsive or selfish motivation.

Noumenon—emptiness.

[O]

Observation—the active ingredient of meditation, contemplation, paired with cessation for preparation and stabilization.

Obstacles of habit—compulsive patterns of thought and behavior.

Oceanic reflection—immediate mirrorlike awareness of the totality of being as is; in terms of entry, the great master Mazu said, "When successive thoughts do not await one another, and each thought dies peacefully away, this is called absorption in the oceanic reflection"; see Cleary, *Zen Essence: The Science of Freedom.*

One drop of ink in two places—refers to the finishing of a painting of a dragon with two points depicting the pupils of the eyes, hence means "completion."

One road upward—ongoing transcendence, ongoing progress.

One vehicle Buddhist teaching premised on universal Buddha-nature or potential for enlightenment, positing this as the ultimate goal of all the provisional vehicles of Buddhism; the classic scriptures representing the One Vehicle (Ekayana) are the *Lotus Sutra* and *Flower Ornament Scripture*.

Opening beyond—ongoing transcendence.

Order of spring—return to life after the great death; return to engagement after detachment.

Other Side—the absolute, or transcendence.

Outsiders—cultists attached to doctrines or practices, or those who conceive of enlightenment as something that is not inherent, as an attainment, acquisition, or acquired state; also used to refer to non-Buddhists.

Ox-herding boy—practice taming and guiding the mind.

[P]

Patchrobed monks—Chan monks, often used in the sense of genuine practitioners, in contrast to "blind baldies."

Picture of a cake—doctrine without practice, conceptual understanding without experiential realization of enlightenment; "a picture of a cake cannot satisfy hunger."

Plowman's ox—a practice or state on which one has come to rely or on which one has become fixated as an object.

Pointing at the moon—teachings as expedients; using words to direct attention to what is beyond words.

Poison drum—shattering illusion, stopping the mind, killing attachment.

Poison in milk—approaching spiritual practice with greed.

Poverty—when used symbolically, poverty stands for experiential realization of emptiness, nonattachment.

[R]

Ram hung up by the horns—trackless, traceless; represents transcendence, freedom from lingering attachment, said of someone who cannot be pegged or pinned down.

Realm of reality—can be used to represent the totality of the universe, reality per se, or the ground of mind as the basis of all experience; also defined as fourfold: (1) noumenon, (2) phenomena, (3) interpenetration of noumenon and phenomena, and (4) interrelation of phenomena.

Religious materialism—religiosity as an attribute of ego; dogma as an object of attachment.

Remembrance of Buddha—generally refers to repetition of the name of Amitabha, Buddha of Infinite Light, practiced in Pure Land Buddhism, later incorporated into Chan; by extension, it means awakening mindfulness or manifestation of enlightenment or truth.

Reverse attention—shifting attention from mental objects or mental functions to the essence of awareness itself; a basic method of Tiantai and Chan meditation, also called "turning the light around."

Right seeing—freedom from subjective bias.

Rubbing the eyes to produce optical illusions—concocting interpretations, subjective representations.

Ruler and subject—absolute and relative.

[S]

Samadhi—a state of absorption.

Samantabhadra—"Universal Good," one of the principal figures of the *Flower Ornament Scripture*, representing the totality of the practices of bodhisattvas.

Seals stamping clay—producing imitations.

Seeing nature—direct experience of the essence of awareness.

Shaolin—the temple where Bodhidharma, founder of Chan, stayed in China; often used as a general reference to Chan or Chan tradition.

Sharpness of the awl—penetrating insight.

Shrine of Many Children—one of the sites traditionally associated with the Buddha's recognition of Kasyapa, hence the roots of Chan tradition.

Six notes—standardized conventions.

Six paths of existence—bondage by various habitual behaviors and states of mind.

Six statements—or six propositions, consisting of existence, nonexistence, both, neither, all the preceding, none of the preceding; used to represent conceptual logic in general.

Six teachers of outside paths—originally referring to six gurus of Buddha's time, used in *Vimalakirti's Advice* and derivative Chan symbolism to stand for the six senses.

Sixteen-foot golden body—an idealized image of Buddha.

Sixth grand master—Huineng, revered in Chan tradition as the paragon of the so-called Southern School, which is represented as maintaining the possibility of sudden enlightenment. For teachings attributed to Huineng, see Cleary, *The Sutra of Hui-neng.*

Sixth Heaven—called the heaven of enjoyment of others' emanations, this stands for the cognitive or conceptual faculty that formulates mental images from the data of the senses; the seat of the "celestial devil," or deceptive potential in subjective representation.

Small Vehicle—or Lesser Vehicle; Hinayana Buddhism, called small or lesser because of its focus on individual liberation and nirvana.

Solitary peak—transcendence, psychological and spiritual independence; can also be used to mean isolation or attachment to detachment.

Special communication outside doctrine—hallmark of Chan, direct communication versus handing on doctrine as dogma.

Spiritual Mountain—site of Buddha's silent communication of the heart of Chan to Kasyapa, traditionally cited as the beginning of Chan tradition.

Spiritual ruler—sovereign mind, independent mind.

Squareness of the chisel—practical knowledge, discernment of differentiation.

Stocks and chains—stereotyped practices or dogma imprisoning the mind.

Stone tiger—detachment plus stability plus powerful capacity.

Subhuti—one of the Buddha's ten top disciples, represented in greater-vehicle Buddhism as being foremost in understanding emptiness.

Suchness—thusness, being as is, direct witness of immediate presence without conceptual overlay or subjective representation.

Sudhana—the iconic pilgrim of the final book of the *Flower Ornament Scripture,* typically used to represent the Chan practice of "going south," meaning travel for study.

[T]

Teaching of inanimate things—"this," "suchness," "thusness," "being as is."

Teachings—generally refers to canonical teachings of Buddhism, often contrasted with the nondogmatic interpersonal and situational method of Chan.

Ten bad actions—killing, stealing, sexual misconduct, lying, divisive talk, abusive talk, flattery, greed, hostility, false views.

Tenth-stage bodhisattvas—"Clouds of Teaching," whose foremost attainment is knowledge; the highest of the stages defined in the book of ten stages in the *Flower Ornament Scripture.*

Thirty-six strategies—a classic text of military strategy; see Cleary, *The Japanese Art of War.*

This—immediate reality, directly experienced.

This matter—birth and death, life and death, the question of how to attain liberation and enlightenment.

This side—ordinary life, the mundane world.

Three dots—stands for relativity, emptiness, and the middle way.

Three embodiments—three bodies of a Buddha: may be referred to as elemental, blissful, and temporal; or as metaphysical, mental, and physical. The Sixth Patriarch of Chan spoke of them as essence, wisdom, and activities.

Three essentials—explained in the translator's note at 216.

Three-family village—naïveté or rustic simplicity.

Three mires—states induced by greed, hostility, and folly.

Three mysteries—explained in the translator's note at 216.

Three poisons—greed, hostility, and folly.

Three statements—can refer to propositions of existence, nonexistence, and neither; or to detachment, not dwelling in detachment, and not making an understanding of nondwelling; also can refer to Yunmen's three statements, levels of meaning described as encompassing the universe, cutting off all streams, and going along with the waves.

Three treasures—the Buddha, the teaching (Dharma), and the community (Sangha).

Three vehicles—listeners, individual illuminates, and bodhisattvas or enlightening beings.

Thunderbolt bearer—protector of the Dharma, commonly represented in temple iconography.

Thusness—immediate experience of actuality without overlay of names and descriptions; "being as is."

Today—direct awareness, complete presence of mind; see case 11 in Cleary and Cleary, *The Blue Cliff Record.*

Tower, the—an image from the last book of the *Flower Ornament Scripture*, in which the pilgrim Sudhana sees the bodhisattvas of the ten stages.

Triplex world or three realms—realms of desire, form, and no form; used generally to refer to mundane existence.

True awareness—awareness not constrained by fixed conceptual structures or subjective representations.

True emptiness—contrasted with insensate emptiness, nihilism, attachment to detachment; compare "emptiness" above.

True human with no status—the essential human being not defined by social convention.

Turn awareness around—also "turn the light around," switching attention from objects or images to the essence of awareness.

Turtle hair—mere imagination, taking interpretation for objective reality.

Twin cultivation—combined development of concentration and insight.

Two vehicles—so-called listeners or disciples, and individual illuminates, who seek nirvana as their ultimate goal; these are referred to as the lesser vehicle or vehicles insofar as they aim for individual liberation, in contrast to the universal outreach of bodhisattvas.

[U]

Ultimate extinction—the death of a Buddha.

[V]

Vairocana—the Adi-Buddha (first, or primal, Buddha), representing the body of reality.

Vimalakirti—representation of a fully enlightened Buddha in lay life, the central figure of *Vimalakirti's Advice,* one of the most popular of all scriptures; see example 84 in Cleary and Cleary, *The Blue Cliff Record.*

Void—can be used to mean emptiness or so-called true emptiness (see Glossary entries), and also can be used to mean vacuity or nothingness.

[W]

Wandering son—from the *Lotus Scripture,* a reference to lesser-vehicle Buddhism, particularly in terms of being unaware of, and estranged from, inherent Buddha-nature.

Waving a stick to hit the moon—trying to realize enlightenment just by conceptual understanding.

Wearing fur and bearing horns—return to mundane life in the world.

Wearing stocks—treating teachings as possessions, ego attributes; pretensions or presumptions, being imprisoned by dogma.

West—When used in reference to Bodhidharma, founder of Chan in China, "West" refers to India. ("West" can also refer to the pure land of Amitabha, Buddha of Infinite Light.)

White and black—relative and absolute.

White clouds—existence.

White ox on open ground or white oxcart—from the *Lotus Sutra*, a symbol of Ekayana, or One-Vehicle Buddhism; also represents universal Buddha-nature, the basic premise of Ekayana.

Wild foxes—indulgence in cleverness.

Wind and flag—a reference to a famous story about the Sixth Patriarch: witnessing an argument about a flapping flag, over whether it is the wind moving or the flag moving, the patriarch said, "It is your minds moving"; see Cleary, *The Sutra of Hui-neng*.

Wintertime—mystic death, shedding illusions, breaking down fixations, transcending the ego.

Withered tree—detachment.

Wooden man—detachment.

World of bliss—the pure land of Amitabha, Buddha of Infinite Light; according to the sutra on visualization of Amitayus, "Infinite Life," another name for Amitabha, "When you see the Buddha, you are seeing your own mind; mind is Buddha, mind makes Buddha."

[Y]

Year of the ass—never; no such thing.

Yellow Crane Pavilion—associated with a famous Taoist immortal.

[Z]

Zero point—dwelling in stillness, cessation.

Index of Names by Chapter

Selected Books on Zen Buddhism by Thomas Cleary

The Blue Cliff Record

This work is a translation of the *Pi Yen Lu*, a collection of one hundred famous Zen koans accompanied by commentaries and verses from the teachings of Chinese Zen masters. Compiled in the twelfth century, it is considered one of the great treasures of Zen literature and an essential study manual for students of Zen.

Book of Serenity: One Hundred Zen Dialogues

This collection of Zen koans with commentaries is a translation of the twelfth-century Chan classic *Shoyo Roku*. Each one of its chapters begins with an introduction, along with a main case, or koan, taken from Zen lore or Buddhist scripture. This is followed by commentary on the main case, verses inspired by it, and, finally, further commentary on all of these.

The Five Houses of Zen

In this collection of writings from some of the great Zen masters of China from the ninth and tenth centuries, Thomas Cleary illuminates the history of the development of Zen in China during the Tang Dynasty. The five houses of Zen that arose at that time were not actually separate schools or branches but instead represented distinctive styles of teaching carried out by certain Chinese Zen masters and perpetuated by their students.

Kensho: The Heart of Zen

Kensho is the transformative glimpse of the true nature of all things. It is an experience so crucial in Zen practice that it is sometimes compared to finding an inexhaustible treasure—because it reveals the potential that exists in each moment for pure awareness, free from the projections of the ego. Thomas Cleary provides extensive introductory notes and detailed commentary on selections from the writings of Chinul, Hakuin, and a collection of Chinese koans to help the reader understand the inner meaning of this essential experience of Zen.

Tao Te Ching: Zen Teachings on the Taoist Classic

True to the teachings of the *Tao Te Ching*, as well as to the tradition of Zen, this version presents the classic Taoist text in a unique light, through the eyes of renowned Rinzai Zen master Takuan Sōhō (1573–1645). Takuan draws from everyday experience and common sense to reveal the basic sanity of nature and the inherent wholeness of life.

The Undying Lamp of Zen

Torei Enji (1721–1792) was best known as one of two "genius assistants" to Hakuin Ekaku, who was himself a towering figure in Zen Buddhism who revitalized the Rinzai school. *The Undying Lamp of Zen* is a complete explanation of Zen practice written by Torei, one of the most eminent masters of premodern Japan. It is an indispensable aid to the practice of Rinzai Zen, and provides an accessible entrée to the Zen experience in general.

Zen Essence: The Science of Freedom

Drawn from the records of Chinese Zen masters of the Tang and Song dynasties, this collection may surprise some readers. In contrast to the popular image of Zen as an authoritarian, monastic tradition deeply rooted in Asian culture, these passages portray Zen as remarkably flexible, adaptive to contemporary and individual needs, and transcending cultural boundaries.

Zen Lessons: The Art of Leadership

This guide to enlightened conduct for people in positions of authority is based on the teachings of several great Chinese Zen masters. It serves as a guide to recognizing the qualities of a genuine Zen teacher; it also serves as a study of the character and conduct necessary for the mastery of any position of power and authority—whether religious, social, political, or organizational.

Zen Letters: Teachings of Yuanwu

These teachings are drawn from letters written by Master Yuanwu (1063–1135). They are direct, person-to-person lessons that intimately reveal the inner workings of the psychology of enlightenment. Yuanwu, a key figure in Zen history, is best known as the author of *The Blue Cliff Record*. His letters, here in English for the first time, are among the treasures of Zen literature.